T0325605

Developing Advanced Web Services through P2P Computing and Autonomous Agents:
Trends and Innovations

Khaled Ragab
King Faisal University, Saudi Arabia

Tarek Helmy
King Fahd University of Petroleum and Minerals (KFUPM), Saudi Arabia

Aboul Ella Hassanien
Cairo University, Egypt

INFORMATION SCIENCE REFERENCE

Hershey • New York

Director of Editorial Content:	Kristin Klinger
Director of Book Publications:	Julia Mosemann
Acquisitions Editor:	Lindsay Johnston
Development Editor:	Joel Gamon
Typesetter:	Gregory Snader
Production Editor:	Jamie Snavely
Cover Design:	Lisa Tosheff
Printed at:	Yurchak Printing Inc.

Published in the United States of America by
Information Science Reference (an imprint of IGI Global)
701 E. Chocolate Avenue
Hershey PA 17033
Tel: 717-533-8845
Fax: 717-533-8661
E-mail: cust@igi-global.com
Web site: http://www.igi-global.com/reference

Library of Congress Cataloging-in-Publication Data

Developing advanced web services through P2P computing and autonomous agents
: trends and innovations / Khaled Ragab, Tarek Helmy, and Aboul Ella Hassanien, editors.
     p. cm.
  Includes bibliographical references and index.
  Summary: "This book covers a comprehensive range of topics in the field of Web Service developments, Multi-Agent Systems, Autonomous Agents and P2P computing"--Provided by publisher.
  ISBN 978-1-61520-973-6 (hardcover) -- ISBN 978-1-61520-974-3 (ebook) 1. Peer-to-peer architecture (Computer networks) 2. Intelligent agents (Computer software) 3. Web site development. I. Ragab, Khaled. II. Helmy, Tarek. III. Hassanien, Aboul Ella.
  TK5105.525.D48 2010
  006.7'6--dc22
                          2009052437

British Cataloguing in Publication Data
A Cataloguing in Publication record for this book is available from the British Library.

All work contributed to this book is new, previously-unpublished material. The views expressed in this book are those of the authors, but not necessarily of the publisher.

List of Reviewers

Khaled Ragab, *KFU, Saudi Arabia*
Tarek Helmy, *KFUPM, Saudi Arabia & Tanta University, Egypt*
Iyad Rahwan, *British University, UAE*
Yuri A Tijerino, *Kwansei Gakuin University, Japan*
Jeffery Bradshaw, *IHMC, USA*
Jianhua Ma, *Hosei University, Japan*
Khaled Shaalan, *British University, UAE*
Laurence Yang, *St. Francis Xavier University, Canada*
Jiming Liu, *University of Windsor, Canada*
Zsolt Németh, *Computer and Automation Research Institute, Hungary*
Abdel-Aziz Farrag, *Dalhousie University, Canada*
Debajyoti Mukhopadhyay, *West Bengal University of Technology, India*
Makoto Amamiya, *Kyushu University, Japan*
Yasser Kotb, *Ain Shams University, Egypt*
Moataz Ahmed, *LEROS, USA*
Mohamed Al-Naser, *KFUPM, Saudi Arabia*
Lu Xiaodong, *Tokyo Inst. of Technology, Japan*
R. Kowalczyk, *Swinburne University, Australia*
Salaheldin Adam, *KFUPM, Saudi Arabia*
Sameh El-Ansary, *Swedish Institute, Sweden*
Satoshi Amamiya, *Kyushu University, Japan*
Asrar U. Haquie, *KFU , Saudi Arabia*
Farag Ezidin, *KFUPM, Saudi Arabia*

Table of Contents

Section 1
Multi-Agent Systems Development

Section 2
Context Searching

Section 3
Framework Design

Section 4
Web Service Applications

Detailed Table of Contents

Section 1
Multi-Agent Systems Development

Chapter 1
Davide Guidi, Imperial College London, UK
Mauro Gaspari, University of Bologna, Italy
Giuseppe Profiti, University of Bologna, Italy

This chapter presents a survey of the current state of the art about Web services integration in open Multi-Agent Systems (MAS). The chapter identifies a set of requirements needed to achieve full integration and presents a communication infrastructure, which satisfies these requirements.

Chapter 2
Agostino Poggi, Università degli Studi di Parma, Italy
Michele Tomaiuolo, Università degli Studi di Parma, Italy

This chapter shows how JADE, one of the most known and used software framework for the development of multi-agent systems, has been extended to become the main means to support legacy systems interoperability and to make the realization of scalable distributed peer-to-peer and service-oriented systems easy.

Chapter 3
Tarek Helmy, King Fahd University of Petroleum and Minerals, Saudi Arabia

This chapter presents ensemble multi-agent-based intrusion detection model that combines anomaly, misuse and host-based detection analysis. The agents in the presented model use rules to check for intrusions, and adopt machine-learning algorithms to recognize unknown actions, and to update rules or create new ones automatically. Each agent in the presented model encapsulates a specific classification technique and gives its belief about any packet event in the network. These agents collaborate to determine the decision about any event, have the ability to generalize, and to detect novel attacks.

Chapter 4

This chapter addresses two challenges in developing a framework that simplifies the workflow creation process within the ARGUGRID project. This chapter focused on the use of agents in enabling automatic service compositions in ARGUGRID. Moreover, it provided the design and implementation of a run-time interaction architecture that comprise of a workflow system, registry and brokering system.

Section 2
Context Searching

Chapter 5

This chapter introduces context-aware computing as a one key technology to enable services and applications in the communication environment to adapt their behaviour based on the knowledge of environmental (contextual) information, thereby enhancing the system's ability to become ever more responsive to the needs of the end-user or application domain. The chapter focus on the question: How can highly distributed context information be located and retrieved regarding small-scale as well as large-scale networks, addressing the topics of inter-domain management and scalability of context architectures.

Chapter 6

This chapter justifies the need of distributed cross media content adaptation and the potential of utilizing Web Services as the adaptation providers. It introduces request-driven context to complement constraint-driven and utility-driven approaches. The chapter describes the request context mapping and propose a novel paths determination scheme for determining the optimal service proxies to facilitate the adaptation tasks.

This chapter presents a Collaborative Autonomous Interface Agent (CAIA) that collaborates with the Internet Meta search engines to support the user in finding exactly the Web services consistent with his/her needs.

Section 3
Framework Design

Chapter 8

This chapter investigates the interaction, architecture and design characteristics of Mobile Web Services (MobWS) for P2P computing. The chapter presents two MobWS interaction strategies followed by the architectural discussion, enfolding server and client side components, of a resource-oriented MobWS framework. It also discussed REST design principles to propose an efficient way of architecting P2P MobWS systems, as an alternative to SOAP, enabling significant payload reduction and performance optimization in mobile servers. The detailed performance evaluation is also presented and compared to SOAP based on real-time measurements.

This chapter presents a clustered Peer-to-Peer system as a resource organization structure for Web-service hosting platforms where service quality such as response time and service availability are provided with assurance.

Jesús De Oliveira, Universidad Simón Bolívar, Venezuela
Yudith Cardinale, Universidad Simón Bolívar, Venezuela
Eduardo Blanco, Universidad Simón Bolívar, Venezuela
Carlos Figueira, Universidad Simón Bolívar, Venezuela

This chapter describes JaDiMa (Java Distributed Machine), a collaborative framework to construct Java applications on grid platforms. JaDiMa services are implemented as Web Services following the SOA approach; library repositories are modeled as a JXTA P2P network; and semantic annotations of libraries assist developers on the tasks of discovering libraries. The chapter describes an implementation of JaDiMa as part of SUMA/G, a Globus-based grid environment.

Khaled Ragab, King Faisal University, Saudi Arabia

This chapter presents a self-organized structured P2P overlay network for efficient video streaming. This overlay network is organized into clusters. Each cluster contains peers where their play points located between lower and upper play point limits. Thus it enables peers in the cluster to enjoy the flexibility of watching same media file with low overhead of seek operations.

Section 4
Web Service Applications

Evelina Pencheva, Technical University of Sofia, Bulgaria
Ivaylo Atanasov, Technical University of Sofia, Bulgaria

This chapter presents Parlay X as a set of Web Service interfaces that are designed to provide open access to telecommunication network functions and thus to hide from application developers underlying network technology and its control protocol complexity. It presents an analysis of the interfaces and particularly the discussion about their applicability to Policy and Charging Control architecture in IMS. The usage of Web Services is exemplified with an application for charging control based on the provided QoS.

Preface

Recently, Peer-to-Peer (P2P), Autonomous Agents and Service Orientation are three paradigms that have been influenced heavily on the development of distributed systems especially the Internet. P2P is a class of applications that takes advantage of resources e.g. storage, cycles, content, human presence, available at the edges of the Internet. In addition, the P2P and Autonomous Agents technologies enable peers to modify the way to achieve their objectives. These technologies address the needs for autonomous agents to support self-organization of highly autonomous peers, load balancing, routing, service discovery, etc. Moreover, Service-Oriented Architectures (SOA) support of loose coupling of software components and consequently provide a high degree of interoperability and reuse. Web Service (WS) is an example of SOA that includes three main entities: Consumers, Providers, and Registers of services. These entities work in concert to provide a loosely coupled computing paradigm. WSs are self-contained, loosely coupled application modules with well described functionality that can be published, located and invoked across the Web. The growing number of WS lunched in the Web raises new challenges, such as discovery of WS. P2P and Autonomous Agents technologies are alternatives to tackle these challenges.

This book is designed to cover a wide range of topics in the field of Web services through P2P computing and Autonomous Agents. It includes four sections that cover various frameworks for developing P2P and Web service applications, development technologies for implementing Multi-Agent systems, Web service applications, context searching and Web discovering technologies. Each chapter is designed to be as a stand-alone as possible; the reader can focus on the interested topics only.

This book is intended for anyone who wants to cover a comprehensive range of topics in the field of Web Service developments, Multi-Agent Systems, Autonomous Agents and P2P computing. It is both for an academic audience (teachers, researchers and students, mainly of post-graduate studies) and professional audience (managers, software developers and IT specialists). Readers of this book are presumed familiar with the concepts and paradigms of P2P, Web Services, Multi-Agent Systems and Autonomous Agents.

This volume comprises of 12 chapters including an overview chapter providing an up-to-date and state-of-the research on the multi agent development and web services applications.

The book is divided into 4 main sections:

- **Section 1: Multi-Agent Systems Development**
- **Section 2: Context Searching**
- **Section 3: Framework Design**
- **Section 4: Web Service Applications**

Section 1 on **Multi-Agent Systems Development** contains four chapters that presents survey about Web services, software framework for the development of multi-agent system and multi-agent in intrusion detection system.

In **Chapter 1** "Web Services Integration in Multi-Agent Systems" by *Davide Guidi, Mauro Gaspari, and Giuseppe Profiti,* presents a survey of the current state of the art about Web services integration in open Multi-Agent Systems (MAS). The chapter identifies a set of requirements needed to achieve full integration and presents a communication infrastructure, which satisfies these requirements.

Chapter 2 "Extending the JADE Framework for Semantic Peer-to-Peer Service Based Applications" by *Agostino Poggi and Michele Tomaiuolo,* show how JADE, one of the most known and used software framework for the deveopment of multi-agent systems, has been extended to become the main means to support legacy systems interoperability and to make the realization of scalable distributed peer-to-peer and service-oriented systems easy.

In **Chapter 3** "Adaptive Ensemble Multi-Agent Based Intrusion Detection Model" by *Tarek Helmy* presents an ensemble multi-agent-based intrusion detection model that combines anomaly, misuse and host-based detection analysis. The agents in the presented model use rules to check for intrusions, and adopt machine-learning algorithms to recognize unknown actions, and to update rules or create new ones automatically. Each agent in the presented model encapsulates a specific classification technique and gives its belief about any packet event in the network. These agents collaborate to determine the decision about any event, have the ability to generalize, and to detect novel attacks.

Chapter 4 "Towards Automatic Service Composition within ARGUGRID" by *Nabeel Azam, Vasa Curcin, Li Guo, and Moustafa Ghanem* address two challenges in developing a framework that simplifies the workflow creation process within the ARGUGRID project. This chapter focused on the use of agents in enabling automatic service compositions in ARGUGRID. Moreover, it provided the design and implementation of a run-time interaction architecture that comprise of a workflow system, registry and brokering system.

Section 2 on **Context Searching** contains three chapters discussing the Context Dissemination in Peer-to-Peer Networks, Request-driven Cross-Media Content Adaptation Technique and Collaborative Autonomous Interface Agent approach.

In **Chapter 5** "Context Dissemination in Peer-to-Peer Networks" by *Antje Barth, Michael Kleis, Andreas Klenk, Benoit Radier, Sanaa Elmoumouhi ,Mikael Salaun, and Georg Carle* introduce context-aware computing as a one key technology to enable services and applications in the communication environment to adapt their behaviour based on the knowledge of environmental (contextual) information, thereby enhancing the system's ability to become ever more responsive to the needs of the end-user or application domain. The chapter focus on the question: How can highly distributed context information be located and retrieved regarding small-scale as well as large-scale networks, addressing the topics of inter-domain management and scalability of context architectures.

Chapter 6 "Request-Driven Cross-Media Content Adaptation Technique" by *Mohd Farhan Md Fudzee and Jemal Abawajy* justify the need of distributed cross media content adaptation and the potential of utilizing Web Services as the adaptation providers. It introduces request-driven context to complement constraint-driven and utility-driven approaches. The chapter describes the request context mapping and propose a novel paths determination scheme for determining the optimal service proxies to facilitate the adaptation tasks.

Chapter 7 "Personalized Web Services Selection" by *Tarek Helmy and Ahmed Al-Nazer* presents a Collaborative Autonomous Interface Agent (CAIA) that collaborates with the Internet Meta search engines to support the user in finding exactly the Web services consistent with his/her needs.

Framework Design is the third section in the book. It contains four chapters discussing various frameworks design for developing P2P and Web service applications including Mobil Web Services, Java Distributed Machine, and Overlay Network for Video Streaming.

Chapter 8 "Mobile Web Services for P2P Computing" by *Fahad Aijaz* investigates the interaction, architecture and design characteristics of Mobile Web Services (MobWS) for P2P computing. The chapter presents two MobWS interaction strategies followed by the architectural discussion, enfolding server and client side components, of a resource-oriented MobWS framework. It also discussed REST design principles to propose an efficient way of architecting P2P MobWS systems, as an alternative to SOAP, enabling significant payload reduction and performance optimization in mobile servers. The detailed performance evaluation is also presented and compared to SOAP based on real-time measurements.

Chapter 9 "Peer-to-Peer Platforms for High-Quality Web Services: The Case for Load-Balanced Clustered Peer-to-Peer Systems" by *Ying Qiao, Shah Asaduzzaman, and Gregor V. Bochmann* present a clustered Peer-to-Peer system as a resource organization structure for Web-service hosting platforms where service quality such as response time and service availability are provided with assurance.

In **Chapter 10** "Distributed Libraries Management for Remote Compilation and Execution on Grid Platforms with JaDiMa," *Jesús De Oliveira, Yudith Cardinale, Eduardo Blanco, and Carlos Figueira* describe JaDiMa (Java Distributed Machine), a collaborative framework to construct Java applications on grid platforms. JaDiMa services are implemented as Web Services following the SOA approach; library repositories are modeled as a JXTA P2P network; and semantic annotations of libraries assist developers on the tasks of discovering libraries. The chapter describes an implementation of JaDiMa as part of SUMA/G, a Globus-based grid environment.

Chapter 11 "A Self-Organized Structured Overlay Network for Video Streaming" by *Khaled Ragab* presents a self-organized structured P2P overlay network for efficient video streaming. This overlay network is organized into clusters. Each cluster contains peers where their play points located between lower and upper play point limits. Thus it enables peers in the cluster to enjoy the flexibility of watching same media file with low overhead of seek operations.

The final Section of the book deals with the **Web Service Applications.** It discusses Web Services for Quality of Service application.

Chapter 12 "Web Services for Quality of Service Based Charging" by *Evelina Pencheva and Ivaylo Atanasov* present Parlay X as a set of Web Service interfaces that are designed to provide open access to telecommunication network functions and thus to hide from application developers underlying network technology and its control protocol complexity. It presents an analysis of the interfaces and particularly the discussion about their applicability to Policy and Charging Control architecture in IMS. The usage of Web Services is exemplified with an application for charging control based on the provided QoS.

Finally, the editors are grateful to the readers for any constructive censure and indication of errors, conceptual, inattentions or in typing. We are very much grateful to the authors of this volume and to the reviewers for their great effort by reviewing and providing useful feedback to the authors.

Khaled Ragab
Tarek Helmy
Aboul Ella Hassanien
Editors

Acknowledgment

Numerous individuals have contributed invaluable help and support in making this book happen. This book could not have been completed without the assistance of the book chapter's authors, who spent countless hours experimenting, and editing their manuscripts to be presented in this book. The Editors acknowledge the contributions of the authors presented their research materials in this book. The Editors also gratefully acknowledge the helpful comments and suggestions of the reviewers, which have improved the presented book chapters. Thanks extended to the editorial team at IGI Global who provided valuable support and encouragement, and also for their expert work in producing the final book.

Section 1
Multi-Agent Systems Development

Chapter 1
Web Services Integration in Multi-Agent Systems

Davide Guidi
Imperial College London, UK

Mauro Gaspari
University of Bologna, Italy

Giuseppe Profiti
University of Bologna, Italy

ABSTRACT

The development of distributed systems is influenced by several paradigms. For example, in the last few years, great emphasis has been placed on Service Orientation. In addition, technologies such as Web services are now considered standard, deployed in common development tools and widely used. However, despite this recent trend, the constantly growing number of powerful personal devices will inevitably revitalize the interest in another paradigm known as Autonomous Agents. Agents are in fact considered one of the main building blocks of the emerging next generation Web infrastructure. Web services are very important resources for agents. Agents should be able to retrieve, execute and compose Web services, providing an intelligent and personalized support to users. On the other hand, agents should also be able to export their functionalities as Web services in order to be fully integrated in the Service Oriented paradigm. In this chapter we present a survey of the current state of the art about Web services integration in open Multi-Agent Systems (MAS). Considering these approaches, we identify a set of requirements needed to achieve full integration and we present a communication infrastructure, which satisfies these requirements.

INTRODUCTION

A Multi-Agent System (MAS) is a system composed of several agents, collectively capable of reaching goals that are difficult to achieve by an individual agent or monolithic system. Agents in MAS may range from hardware robots to software agents realized as processes/threads (softbots) or interacting in distributed systems. This chapter is only focused on software agents, although some of the results and considerations that we present could also apply to a hybrid MAS including both robots

DOI: 10.4018/978-1-61520-973-6.ch001

and softbots. Agents may cooperate or they may compete, or some combination of these, but there is some common infrastructure that results in the collection being a system, as opposed to simply being a set of autonomous disconnected agents.

Multi-Agent System is a widely used paradigm. It can be considered the standard solution for addressing problems that require collective intelligence, negotiation and cooperation. It is also used as a software development paradigm in opposition to big monolithic applications, which can be too much complex and hard to maintain and extend. A MAS is also useful in systems with scarce resources, such as embedded systems. In a MAS, agents are autonomous, they have knowledge of local information and usually there is no central management (Nilsson, 1998). In other words, a MAS intrinsically shares many aspects of peer-to-peer systems despite the fact that it can be realized using centralized components. Some of these systems are composed of a fixed set of interacting agents that are created at the beginning of the application. More interesting systems are open: they are composed by agents that can be dynamically added and removed from a running MAS.

The Internet is one of the major fields of application for an open MAS, where user-agents can automate tasks for users (such as searching for information and buying products), avoiding long Web surfing sessions. Such user-agents can be tailored to specific Web pages following ad hoc approaches, or they can be realized by accessing other agents or available Web services in a more general perspective. For these agents, Web services represent the standard Web API to provide remote services to applications over the Internet.

In this chapter we investigate the principal aspects concerning the integration of an open MAS with Web services, presenting a survey of the current state of the art, as well as a generic approach to seamlessly integrating agents and Web services in a bidirectional way. The rest of the chapter is structured as follows. In the first section we provide some background information about the terminology and some basic concepts. In the section entitled "Integrating agents and Web services", we introduce the technical issues and the open problems related to the integration of Web services in Multi-Agent Systems. In the section entitled "Approaches to Web service Integration" we present the current state of the art, discussing a number of integration techniques. Considering those different solutions, the section "Achieving Full Integration" identifies a set of 4 requirements needed for full integration. These requirements are fully satisfied by NOWHERE, the solution proposed by the authors, which is presented and compared with the other platforms in the section "The NOWHERE Agent Communication Infrastructure". In the section entitled "Future Research Directions" we present an interesting open issue, the Semantic Matching of Web services with respect to agents' request, identifying some promising solutions. Finally, in the last section we present the conclusions of our survey.

BACKGROUND: TERMINOLOGY AND BASIC CONCEPTS

This section defines the key terms and concepts used in the rest of the chapter. An *open Multi-Agent System* is a MAS where new agents can be added dynamically to cooperate with the existing ones. Agents can also dynamically leave the MAS when their tasks terminate. An *open Agent Platform* is a runtime infrastructure that supports a minimal set of basic mechanisms: creating and terminating agents, naming agents (providing a notion of agent identity: a property that distinguishes each agent from all others) and connecting agents (supporting their communication).

Web services are procedure calls done over the Hypertext Transfer Protocol (HTTP), usually on the well-known port 80. Web services are usually implemented using standard libraries and applications such as Axis and Tomcat, which are developed by the Apache Software Foundation. Access to Web services is provided using SOAP, the Simple Object Access Protocol (Mitra & Lafon, 2007), which defines the format of services invocations and responses. Web services are described using Web Services Description Language (WSDL), an XML-based language (Chinnici, Moreau, Ryman, & Weerawarana, 2007). A WSDL description contains all the operations supported by a Web service, their parameters and access points. It is composed of two parts: an abstract description of the service and its related implementation. The abstract section defines the interfaces of the service, which contain a set of operations and their input and output parameters. The implementation section declares a set of access points, together with their transport protocol and addresses, which actually host the service. This information can be retrieved from the service provider or from a registry, like the Universal Description, Discovery and Integration registry (UDDI) (Clement, Hately, von Riegen, & Rogers, 2004). UDDI is a standard developed by the Organization for the Advancement of Structured Information Standards (OASIS) consortium, which also developed a mapping of WSDL to UDDI (Colgrave, Januszewski, Clement, & Rogers, 2004).

INTEGRATING AGENTS AND WEB SERVICES

The main reason to integrate Web services in a MAS is reusability. Web services are a widely used methodology to export functionalities, and agents' developers should access them easily. In a MAS, agents are able to retrieve, execute and compose services provided by other agents. In the same way, in a MAS integrated with Web services, agents could use and compose existing Web services in order to achieve more complex goals.

The same approach used to retrieve capabilities exposed by agents could then be used to discover new Web services. This would be useful in any scenario in which an agent need to use a Web service developed by third parties, such as a Web service that implements functionalities not available in the agents' world. Moreover, gaining access to external Web services can expand the features provided by the MAS, offering more interesting possibilities for users and developers.

To fully integrate agents and Web services many technical issues must be addressed. There are three main differences between the technologies used by agents and by Web services (Shafiq, Ali, Ahmad, & Suguri, 2005):

- Agents and Web services use different communication protocols. Agents adopted Agent Communication Languages (ACL) (Finin, Fritzson, McKay, & McEntire, 1997; O'Brien & Nicol, 1998). These languages provide high-level communication primitives, usually more powerful than the SOAP protocol used by Web services.
- Agents and Web Services use different service description languages. It is common for agents to use ontology-based language, such as in FIPA-ACL, while Web services use Web Services Description Languages (WSDL).
- Agents and Web Services use different service registries. Agents can have Directory Facilitators (DF), based on FIPA specifications, while Web services use Universal Description Discovery and Integration (UDDI) (Clement, Hately, von Riegen, & Rogers, 2004), based on W3C specifications.

The solutions to these technical issues become more complex if we consider the open paradigm that characterizes Web services development. The continuous effort of producing new Web services and improving existing ones brought to an open environment where new functionalities are made available and old services may disappear. To work in this dynamic environment agents need specific support to discover new services at runtime. In fact a previously known service may not be available anymore, or new services with similar functionalities could become available in different places.

To fully exploit the agent paradigm, agents need a uniform invocation mechanism able to deal with the two types of services, possibly using a single set of primitives. These issues have a strong impact on the communication component of an agent platform that aims to integrate Web services. Such a platform should be extended with an adequate discovering mechanism and with transparent invocation primitives.

In summary the most relevant issues that should be addressed to integrate Web services with agents are:

- **Service creation:** how new services are imported, created and published in the agent infrastructure. Simple solutions are limited to facilitate the access to external Web services as in WS2JADE (Nguyen & Kowalczyk, 2005) while more sophisticated solutions provide bidirectional compatibility (Soto, 2007; Greenwood & Calisti, 2004).
- **Service invocation:** how services are invoked from agents. Agents can be extended with support to generate SOAP messages sent to Web services (Mari, Poggi, Tomaiuolo, & Turci, 2008) or service invocation mechanisms can be embedded in the Agent Communication Language (Nguyen & Kowalczyk, 2005; Greenwood & Calisti, 2004), allowing agents to transparently interact with Web services in the same way they interact with other agents.
- **Service discovery:** how agents discover available services. Agents can embed facilities to query an UDDI registry (Palathingal & Chandra, 2004) or discovering functionalities can be integrated in the ACL, for

instance providing content-based requests of knowledge (Dragoni, Gaspari, & Guidi, 2006). The use of semantic based mechanisms for service discovering (Chatel, 2006; Kourtesis & Paraskakis, 2008) constitutes another important dimension to approach this problem.

This chapter presents how different approaches for integrating MAS and Web services deal with these issues, putting the emphasis on communication aspects having the goal of proposing a communication infrastructure able to solve this problem in a transparent fashion.

APPROACHES TO WEB SERVICES INTEGRATION

The integration between agents and Web services is an on-going effort. Almost all the solution published in the past and in current years are implemented using Jade (JADE JADE: Java Agent Development Framework, 2001). Jade is one of the most used open agent platform both in academia and in the industry. It was developed by CSELT (Centro Studi e Laboratori Telecomunicazioni) in conjunction with the Computer Engineering Group of the University of Parma. Jade is a full FIPA complaint platform, written in the Java programming language, which uses the following standard FIPA components:

- **The Agent Platform (AP).** It provides the physical infrastructure in which agents can be deployed. The AP consists of the hosting computer(s), operating system, agent support software, FIPA agent management components (DF, AMS and MTS) and agents.
- **The Directory Facilitator (DF).** It is an optional component of the AP that provides yellow pages services to agents. Agents may register their services with the DF or

query the DF to find out what services are offered by other agents.

- **The Agent Management System (AMS).** It is a mandatory component of the AP. It maintains a directory of agents registered with the AP, providing white pages services to other agents.
- **The Message Transport Service (MTS).** This is the default communication method used by agents running on different APs.

Many proposed Web service integration approaches identify two key properties that make the integration between agents and Web services *bidirectional*:

1. Agents should be able to easily use Web services, ideally in the same way they access services provided by other agents.
2. Agents should expose their services as Web services for potential use by non-agent software.

The integration of already existing Web services exploits their WSDL description. Using these descriptions it is possible to know which operations can be requested from a Web service along with their parameters, the structure of the answer, the transport protocol, the encoding and so on.

In the following, we present a set of different integration efforts, highlighting the main aspects such as service creation, discovery and invocation and specifying if they provide bidirectional integration.

WSDL2JADE and WSAI

One of the first works in the integration between agents and Web services was published in 2003 by the "Agentcities Task Force", which produced a recommendation (Agentcities Task Force, 2003). The document specifies a two-part solution for a bidirectional agent-to-Web service gateway.

The first part of the solution is represented by WSDL2JADE. WSDL2JADE is a wrapper for translating agents' requests in appropriate Web service calls and corresponding responses back into ACL responses. For each existing Web service, WSDL2JADE creates a proxy agent, which integrates the Web service in the agent platform.

Technically, WSDL2JADE is accessible as a Web Application (Computer and Automation Research Institute, 2005), which processes a WSDL description and automatically generates an agent ontology as well as agent deployment code implementing the Web service wrapper agent for Jade platforms.

The second part of the solution is WSAI, an application that allows agents' services to be published as Web services. The implementation of WSAI consists of two main components: the Agent Gateway (WSAG) and the Agent Generator. The Agent Gateway transforms synchronous SOAP calls from external Web services in asynchronous ACL communication for the agent that provides the service and vice versa. The Agent Generator is a supporting tool for generating Gateway Agents, which are entities providing a concrete Web service interface for a particular agent.

This first pioneer solution suffered many drawbacks such as being not transparently integrated with respect to the Jade platform. Moreover, from a technical point of view, this solution requires a certain degree of manual configuration.

WSIG

Considering these problems, the same creators of WSAI (Whitestein Technologies) proposed an improved solution, called WSIG (Web Service Integration Gateway). WSIG (Greenwood & Calisti, 2004; JADE Board, 2008) is composed of a stand-alone module that provides transparent bidirectional transformation between agents and Web Services. This component is an intermediary processor in the communication path between the two entities. It allows both agents and Web services to register with it, publishing their service descriptions. After the registration phase, it will intercept requests to the registered services, allowing agents to invoke Web services and vice versa.

Technically, WSIG is a Web application composed of two main elements: a WSIG Servlet and a WSIG agent. The WSIG Servlet acts as an interface to Web services. It serves incoming HTTP/SOAP requests, extracting the SOAP message and forwarding the translated ACL message to the corresponding agent. It also converts the agent's reply to a SOAP message, sending the HTTP/SOAP response back to the requester. The WSIG agent acts as a gateway between the Web and the agents' worlds. It forwards agents' requests received from the WSIG Servlet to the agents that are able to serve them, managing their responses. It also subscribes to the Jade Directory Facilitator to receive notifications about agents' registrations/deregistrations. Finally, it creates the WSDL description for each service registered with the DF, publishing the services in an external UDDI registry.

WSIG supports the standard Web services stack: WSDL for service descriptions, SOAP for message transport and UDDI repository for publishing Web services. Thanks to these components, WSIG offers an improved integration over WSDL2JADE and WSAI.

WS2JADE

A similar approach has been followed in WS-2JADE (Nguyen & Kowalczyk, 2005), developed in accordance with the same directives proposed by the Agentcities Task Force. As a result, all these solutions use a gateway approach to integrate Web services. In WS2JADE, the gateway is implemented as a static management layer, which is used to control special Web Service Agents (WSAG). Web Service Agents are capable of communicating with Web services and of providing their own services as Web services.

WS2JADE uses two internal modules: the Service Assignment Management and the Service Discovery. The Service Assignment Management component is responsible for cardinal mapping and service deployment. The cardinal mapping manages M:N relationships between Web services and WSAGs. Using WS2JADE, a WSAG can offer more than one Web Service and a Web Service can be offered by more than one WSAG. The Service Assignment Management also provides functionalities for deploying and destroying WSAGs, assigning new Web services to a WSAG and removing Web services which are no longer available. As the name suggests, the Service Discovery component is used to discover Web services, translating information received using Web service discovery protocols to agent service descriptions.

The main difference with the WSIG approach is that WS2JADE has an active behaviour. Using WSIG, agents and Web services must register themselves, while WS2JADE can actively discover Web services and register them automatically. WS2JADE can be also triggered by the Directory Facilitator to look up for available services in the Web service environment. If a relevant Web service is found, an associated WSAG agent is generated, which will in turn register the Web service as its own service on the Directory Facilitator. Another key aspect of WS2JADE is the generation of Jade agent classes from a WSDL description, which provides a greater level of automation. However, WS2JADE does not support bidirectional integration with Web services: agent to Web service integration is not provided.

AgentWeb

The use of a gateway to solve integration issues is a technique applied also by AgentWeb (Shafiq, Ali, Ahmad, & Suguri, 2005). In this solution, the authors rely on transformation converters to bridge the gap between Multi Agent Systems and Web services frameworks. These converters are:

- **A Service Discovery converter,** which enables service discovery among agents and Web services. This component is bi-directional: agents can discover services in UDDI repositories and external Web services can discover agents' services in the Directory Facilitator. The Service Discovery converter is composed of two parts: a UDDI search query to DF search query converter (which enables Web services to perform service discovery in the DF) and the complementary DF search query to UDDI search query converter (which enables agents to perform service discovery in UDDI repositories).

- **A Service Description converter,** which enables the publication of services in the Directory Facilitator as well as in UDDI repositories. The Service Description converter is composed of a WSDL to DF-Agent-Description converter (which enables Web services to publish its services in the DF) and the complementary DF-Agent-Description to WSDL converter (which enables agents to publish its services in a UDDI repository).

- **A Communication Protocol converter,** which enables invocation of both agent services and Web services. The Communication Protocol converter is composed of a SOAP to ACL converter (which enables Web services to invoke agent services) and the complementary ACL to SOAP converter (which enables agents to invoke Web services).

In the case of AgentWeb, the gateway can be considered a middleware layer that integrates the MAS and Web services without requiring alteration to existing specification.

WSMTS

The gateway approach used by the these pioneer solutions has been abandoned in more recent proposals. With WSMTS (Soto, 2007), the authors propose a new Message Transport Service (MTS) implementation for the Jade platform, called Web Service based MTS. WSMTS does not use a centralized gateway. It is a middleware grounded on Web services that replaces Jade's http-based MTS. WSMTS offers a FIPA compliant communication where the grounding of messages uses Web services standards. Its implementation relies on Axis2 (Axis2 SOAP Stack Implementation, 2006) and provides message transportation based on a particular standard from the Web service stack, Web Service Addressing (WS-Addressing). WSMTS uses WS-Addressing to achieve interoperability between Web service-compliant and FIPA-compliant entities. WS-Addressing is a key part of the core Web services architecture, which has been submitted to the World Wide Web Consortium for the standardization process.

Internally, WSMTS is composed of an Axis2 Message Receiver component, which can be registered in Jade as any other MTS. WSMTS provides a special message envelope for SOAP that merges both properties from FIPA and from WS-Addressing standards. Agents can then decide which MTS to use to send messages. Jade will automatically dispatch messaging using WSMTS if a special *aclRepresentation* envelop property is set to a value identifying the SOAP representation. Message transportation is delegated to Axis2 whenever SOAP messages must be delivered outside the agent platform.

The implementation of WSMTS does not provide an integrated support for publication and discovery of services. Instead, WSMTS relies on an XML representation of the FIPA Semantic Language (FIPA, 2002), which is a commonly used representation for messages referring to FIPA ontologies. This XML representation allows external Web services to interact with agents that use FIPA Semantic Language as grounding for their content. Using this XML representation, agents are effectively able to communicate to Web services, which however must be able to somehow process the FIPA messages contained in the XML representation.

WSMTS is developed as a Jade add-on and does not require changes in the agent implementation. However, changes in the Web services are required in order to achieve communication with the MAS.

ACHIEVING FULL INTEGRATION

The aim of this section is to discuss the features that an open agent platform should provide to *fully integrate* Web services. We postulate that an agent platform should satisfy the following 4 requirements to be considered fully integrated:

1. The integration must be bidirectional;
2. Interaction between agents and Web services must be achieved using the primitives of the Agent Communication Language;
3. Support for dynamic discovery and integration of Web services should be provided;
4. The integration should not require modifications to agents' code.

The first requirement is an essential feature to achieve full integration. Agents must be able to invoke Web services and Web services must be able to access services provided by agents. If this requirement is satisfied, then it is possible to build applications that compose functionalities provided by agents and existing Web services avoiding the use of ad hoc integration procedures.

The second requirement specifies that the ACL must be used as common communication, subsuming simple SOAP based request/response protocols for invoking Web services. The use

of the ACL for supporting interaction between agents and Web services allows a programmer to transparently use their functionalities. Moreover, since an ACL provides high-level communication primitives, access to Web services is facilitated. For example, if an ACL supports anonymous requests for knowledge (Dragoni, Gaspari, & Guidi, 2007), then an agent can invoke a Web service, or request information to another agent, using a single communication primitive that will be addressed to both agents and Web services. These requirements also facilitate the development of independent code, which will work independently from low-level implementation issues.

The third requirement states that an open agent platform should integrate dynamic discovering mechanisms usually available for agents with mechanisms that allow adding and discovering of Web services at runtime. Satisfying such a requirement puts Web services and agents on the same flexibility level in the MAS. Dynamic discovery also allows developers of Web services to use their usual tools without worrying if the implemented service will be integrated in an agent platform.

Finally, the last requirement is about modifications to be done in pre-existing agents. Fulfilling this requirement means achieving a true transparent integration between the two technologies. Already written agent will be able to contact Web services and to export functionalities as Web services without the need of changing the source code.

In the next section we present the NOWHERE open agent platform, which satisfies the postulated requirements.

THE NOWHERE AGENT COMMUNICATION INFRASTRUCTURE

The solution that we propose is based on an agent communication infrastructure called NOWHERE. The development of NOWHERE has been motivated by a commonly underestimated issue: the concurrency aspect. Due to the fact that a MAS is composed of a set of agents that act concurrently, a number of problems related to concurrency will arise, such as reliability of agents, synchronisation of competing requests, allocation of resources, physical allocation of agents on the network and so on. NOWHERE introduces the use of "Knowledge Level" agents (Gaspari, 1998). Knowledge Level agents are high-level entities, which are only concerned with the use, request and supply of knowledge. This high-level communication is provided by a Fault Tolerant Agent Communication Language, FT-ACL (Dragoni & Gaspari, 2005). FT-ACL adopts asynchronous non-blocking primitives together with success and failure continuations and automatically handled timeouts to provide fault tolerant communication under certain condition (crashes of faulty agents).

More specifically, using FT-ACL a set of agent's communication properties holds (Dragoni & Gaspari, 2006):

1. The programmer does not have to manage physical addresses of agents explicitly.
2. The programmer does not have to handle communication faults explicitly.
3. Communication is Starvation free. A situation of starvation arises when an agent

communication primitive never gets executed despite being enabled.

4. Communication is Deadlock free. A communication deadlock situation occurs when two agents try to communicate, but they do not succeed; for instance because they mutually wait for each other to answer a query.

NOWHERE supports Knowledge Level agents exploiting two components, as shown in Figure 1:

- A Facilitator, which provides high-level primitives for sending and receiving messages, using a fault tolerant architecture;
- An agent Dispatcher. This component provides the basic functionality to support communication between KL agents and the Facilitator. It can easily be implemented in any language that provides TCP support. Using two separate components has several advantages. First of all the developer is free to choose the preferred language for the agent code, while the whole communication is always handled by the Facilitator. Agents written in different programming languages can then talk each other, using the ACL primitives. Furthermore, the agent and the Facilitator could also run on different machines: for example a mobile

Figure 1. Components of a NOWHERE agent

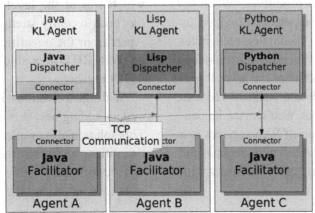

phone, with a limited computational power, could run only the agent code, using the Facilitator hosted on a local computer. The goal is to keep all the communication issues, such as the fault-tolerant behavior, in the Facilitator. The Facilitator component is similar to the Jade's Directory Facilitator, providing yellow pages support in a distributed fashion.

WEB SERVICES INTEGRATION IN NOWHERE

Agents can always use Web services in the standard way, invoking them directly. However, in our vision agents should use Web services in a simpler way. Ideally, the communication from an agent to a Web Server should happen with an ACL primitive, like a communication between two agents. Furthermore, agents should register their competences as Web services, enabling the interaction with conventional programs.

In NOWHERE, Web services can be registered using two approaches:

- Registration of a Web service. NOWHERE provides a functionality that allows agents to register existing Web services locally, in the Facilitator. As soon as a Web service is registered it becomes reachable as a virtual agent and it can be transparently invoked using the FT-ACL primitives. When an agent requires a competence provided by a virtual agent, its Facilitator recognizes that there is a Web service that matches this competence and maps the ask/tell protocol of the ACL into a standard request/ response protocol for Web service invocation. The registration of Web services is a local action: every agent must register the same Web service in order to invoke it with ACL primitives.

- Agentification of a Web service. The agentification of a Web service is a more powerful mechanism that integrates Web services in NOWHERE. It follows the same wrapper-based technique already proposed by other solutions. A special agent, called Worker agent, provides a competence implemented by the Web service. Every time that an agent asks for that competence, the Worker agent simply invokes the associated Web service and replies with the response gathered from the Web service itself. A single Worker agent can handle several Web services. The Worker agent handles the entire communication process with the Web service, converting parameters as needed. As a result, other agents can use the Web service with ACL primitives, for example with a multicast or a one-to-one primitive. Moreover, the Worker agent can extend the Web service to provide additional functionality or to integrate it with other Web services.

In a complementary way, a Worker agent can register a competence as a Web service, so other programs can interact with the agent without sharing the agent architecture. Every time a Worker agent registers a competence as a Web service, a Web service is generated in the Web Agent Server, with the same name of the registered competence.

The integration of Web services in NOWHERE, which was at the level of a proof-of-concept, has been recently strengthened (Profiti, 2008). Apart from the agentification of Web services, NOWHERE is now able to discover them using UDDI register.

With agentification it is possible to expand the system adding new services that may be useful. This solution allows also the replication of functionalities provided by the agents: adding similar services offered by different providers it is possible to work around the lack of availability of a specific service. This integration scheme does not require additional work from the agents in order to invoke Web services. Agent to Web service communication is done using the same messages used for agent-to-agent communication, thanks to the virtual agent. A virtual agent is a special agent whose job is to translate an ACL request into a SOAP message, sending it to the Web service. It also gathers the SOAP answer, translating it back to an ACL message.

Thanks to the NOWHERE's publishing system, with agentification it's possible to expose part of the Web service operations for public use (using multicast requests), leaving other operations accessible on direct request only. In this way a service provider can give public access to some services, while exposing other services only to those who knows its existence (for example to agents that followed a registration phase).

When dealing with a huge number of Web services, agentification may be a limited technique, because it requires agents to actively identify the services to be agentified. A solution to this problem is the discovery/invocation of Web services at runtime, using UDDI.

To enable this feature, a UDDI register should contain extra descriptions for the hosted services, such as operations, semantics, communication protocol. In our solution, the search is done by matching the requested operation name and the operation provided by a Web service. Operation descriptions are not part of the standard WSDL to UDDI mapping (Colgrave, Januszewski, Clement, & Rogers, 2004), but the addition of such information has been proposed in later works (Chatel, 2006; Kourtesis & Paraskakis, 2008). In NOWHERE the discovery is done at Facilitator level, and agents are free to activate this feature. In this way it is also possible to finely tune the system: some agents might need to reach Web services outside the MAS while other agents may want to use only the services already available inside the MAS.

COMPARISON

In this section we present a comparison between some of the analyzed solutions. We identified 4 approaches (WSIG, WS2JADE, WSMTS and NOWHERE), which represent diverse integration attempts developed by researchers in this area.

The main difference between these integrations relies in their different integration approach, as summarized in Table 1. WSIG uses a single agent to perform all the work. It relies on an external gateway component where all the requests must be addressed. WS2JADE follows a decentralized approach, allowing the creation of a wrapper agent for each integrated Web service, called Web Service Agent Gateway (WSAG). These WSAG components are created using an external gateway component, which must be registered in the Directory Facilitator. WSMTS is a more recent proposal, and integrates Web services in a cleaner way. Instead of using an external gateway, WSMTS uses a modified Directory Facilitator extended to handle Web services. However, WSMTS does not directly address publishing or discovery of services. NOWHERE uses its distributed calling mechanism to integrate the agentified Web services in a P2P framework.

The compliance with our requirements is shown in Table 2.

Bidirectional interaction is not achieved by WS2JADE, which does not allow the exposure of agents as Web services. While the bidirectional support in NOWHERE is complete, Web service to agent communication is still implemented as proof-of-concept.

In our opinion, the requirement about ACL integration needs is not fully achieved in the FIPA-ACL based integration. This limitation is not a problem of the agent platform but just a consequence of the FIPA design, which does not include first-class discovering mechanisms. These mechanisms, such as anonymous (multicast) request of knowledge, are instead implemented in NOWHERE. The difference between the two

Table 1. Different approaches for integrating web services in MAS

Solution	Integration approach	Distributed access
WSIG	Centralized, using a gateway	No
WS2JADE	Decentralized, using a gateway and Wrapper Agents	Yes (Using WSAG + DF)
WSMTS	Centralized, using Directory Facilitator	Yes
NOWHERE	Decentralized, using Wrapper Agents	Yes (using Agentification)

architectures is fully described in the next section. Both WS2JADE and WSMTS allow direct communication to Web services. However, while WSMTS allows bidirectional communication, it also requires Web services to process the FIPA content expressed in the XML Web service request.

The approach of WSIG is different, because it requires all the messages for Web services to be sent by the gateway agent. Regarding communication NOWHERE provides the unique feature of reaching Web services via multicast, thanks to the UDDI search at Facilitator level.

Dynamic invocation and discovery is addressed in WS2JADE and NOWHERE. WSIG uses a centralized approach that requires Web services to be registered to the gateway agent, therefore its implementation lacks both dynamic invocation and discovery.

The last requirement specifies if the agents' source code must be modified to handle Web services integration. In WSIG the source code must be modified to handle the registration of

Web services. However, after the registration the communication proceeds in the usual agent-to-agent fashion. WS2JADE allows agents to call Web services without source code modification, but lacks mechanisms to publish agents' capabilities as Web services. Finally, WSMTS and NOWHERE allow integration of Web services in a fully transparent way, even if Web services must be able to process the XML representation of FIPA SL messages when using WSMTS.

THE ROLE OF FACILITATORS IN FIPA AND IN NOWHERE

While the term Facilitator is used in both FIPA and NOWHERE implementations, the components identified by this name are different. In FIPA, a Directory Facilitator is a centralized registry of entries that associates service descriptions to agents IDs. The DF provides primitives to register agent services and to search for a specific

Table 2. Requirement for full integration

Features:	WSIG	WS2JADE	WSMTS	NOWHERE
Bidirectional	Yes	No	Yes	Yes (Proof-of-concept)
ACL integration	Yes (Partial)	Yes (Partial)	Yes (Partial)	Yes
Dynamic discovery of Web services	No (*must be already registered*)	Yes	No	Yes
Agents can contact WS without source code modifications	No (registration of Web services)	No (for exporting functionalities)	Yes	Yes

service. Moreover, it allows searching for services based on their content rather than their name. The same primitives should be used to search for Web services in integrations such as WS2JADE or WSMTS.

The main difference between this approach and NOWHERE's is that in FIPA the interaction between the agent and the DF is made outside the ACL. To better understand this concept, consider the source code of a Jade agent used to search for a service is shown in Figure 2. The agent searches for services using the DFService.search primitive, which is not part of the ACL. After this phase, the requesting agent must interact with the other agents that provide the wanted service, this time using a primitive of the ACL.

Generally speaking, three different phases can be identified using Jade:

1. To retrieve the names of the agents providing the wanted service
2. To request the execution of the service
3. To manage possible failures

These phases are needed in agent-to-agent communication as well as in agent to Web service communication when the Web service is transparently integrated as agent.

In contrast, a NOWHERE agent can ask for a service using an ACL primitive. For example, in order to ask for a service S to every agent that provides it, a NOWHERE agent can use the multicast primitive *askEverybody*. This approach implements a very high-level communication mechanism, where the agent does not explicitly manage the 3 phases described. Instead, these phases are implicitly achieved using the multicast ACL primitive.

FUTURE RESEARCH DIRECTIONS

A key issue in the service discovery process is how to match an agent request with the corresponding Web service. The solution adopted in NOWHERE and many other proposals is to match the name of the requested operation with the names of the operations provided by Web services. While this assumption can simplify the task of developing small ad-hoc applications, it also limits the development of applications in a broader scope.

Agent Communication Languages such as FIPA-ACL already use ontologies to identify a specific vocabulary. According to Gruber (1993), an ontology is a formalization of a shared conceptualization. In Multi-Agent Systems, an ontology can be considered a shared terminology on which different agents must agree in order to associate a term with a specific concept. The same ontology can then be used to define Semantic Web services. The overall approach is that by augmenting Web services with rich formal descriptions of their competence, many aspects of their management (such as Web service discovery, invocation and composition) will become automatic.

Starting from these premises, the idea of expanding the ACL to take into account also the development of Semantic Web, and in particular of Semantic Web services, is one of the most interesting research problems for future integra-

Figure 2. Search the directory facilitator for a service: Jade platform

```
DFAgentDescription dfd = new DFAgentDescription();
DFAgentDescription[] result = DFService.search(this,dfd);
sd = new ServiceDescription();
sd.setType( "buyer" );
dfd.addServices(sd);
result = DFService.search(this, dfd);
```

tions. To provide such support we plan to extend the core ACL with new primitives and with the related infrastructure to handle the Semantic Web extension. The resulting ACL will be available as a "Semantic agent template", which can be extended in order to create KL Semantic Web agents.

The set of new primitives must include support for the following operations:

- Loading external ontologies that specify the dictionaries known by the agents;
- Loading external Semantic Web service definitions.

A semantic infrastructure is then needed to manage the formal description of the Web services, providing features like automatic service discovery. To clarify this with an example, consider an agent Alfa, which requests a service A (defined in the ontology Oa). The semantic infrastructure can use an extra ontology C to determine that service A has the same formal description of service B (defined in ontology Ob), provided by agent Beta. The semantic infrastructure can then reply to agent Alfa with service B.

To realize this vision many open problems need to be solved. In our opinion, the fundamental ones are:

- The need to develop a language for semantically expressing the capabilities of Web services (or service advertisements) and the service requests. Main ongoing works in this direction are OWL-S (OWL-S 1.0 Release), WSMO (WSMO Working Group, 2004) and SAWSDL (Farrel & Lausen, 2007).
- A requirement to realize an infrastructure that supports the creation of Semantic Web services. The infrastructure must clarify who realize Web services and where the semantic descriptions of Web services are stored (in a centralized or distributed repository). Existing prototypes

include WSMF (Fensel, Bussler, Ding, & Omelayenko, 2002) and IRS-III (Domingue, Cabral, Hakimpour, Sell, & Motta, 2004). Semantic annotations, such as SAWSDL, can then be stored in an extended UDDI registry, as in the FUSION project (Kourtesis, Paraskakis, Friesen, Gouvas, & Bouras, 2007).

- To enable automatic discovery and invocation of Web services, that is, to enable agents to discover and invoke Web services on the basis of the capabilities that they provide. The discovery problem is also known as "Semantic Matching problem" (Paolucci, Kawamura, Payne, & Sycara., 2002).

CONCLUSION

We have presented a survey of open agent platforms that integrate Web services. Analysing the main aspects of the architectures, we have postulated a set of well-defined requirements for achieving full integration of the two paradigms. These requirements are: the integration must be bidirectional; agent to Web service interaction must be achieved using the primitives of the ACL; support for dynamic discover and integration of Web services should be provided; the integration should not require modifications to agents' code. According to the postulated requirements, it is emerging that the more promising approaches have been followed from WSMTS and NOWHERE. One of the advantages of NOWHERE with respect to all the approaches based on FIPA is that it is based on FT-ACL, which includes discovering mechanisms in some communication act, for example providing high-level anonymous request of knowledge. These primitives allow a programmer to reach all the agents and Web services that provide the required capabilities using a single programming construct. This approach is particularly useful considering Web services integration in an open scenario, because it allows agents to reach new Web services without adding extra code. Extending the discovering phase using effective and efficient Semantic based mechanisms is one of the main open issues for all the investigated approaches.

REFERENCES

Agentcities Task Force. (2003, November). *Integrating Web Services into Agentcities*. Agentcities Web Services Working Group.

Axis2. (2006). *Axis2 SOAP Stack Implementation*. Retrieved from http://ws.apache.org/axis2

Bellifemine, F., Poggi, A., & Rimassa, G. (1999). JADE - A FIPA-compliant agent framework. In Practical Applications of Intelligent Agents. *Applied Artificial Intelligence*, *11*(5), 3–4.

Chatel, P. (2006). WSDL 2.0 to UDDI mapping, SAWSDL to UDDI mapping (Technical note). Neuilly-sur-Seine, Frace: Thales Group.

Chinnici, R., Moreau, J., Ryman, A., & Weerawarana, S. (2007). *Web Services Description Language (WSDL) Version 2.0 Part 1: Core Language*. W3C Recommendation.

Clement, L., Hately, A., von Riegen, C., & Rogers, T. (2004). *UDDI Version 3.0.2. (UDDI Spec Technical Committee Draft)*. Billerica, MA: Organization for the Advancement of Structured Information Standard.

Colgrave, J., Januszewski, K., Clement, L., & Rogers, T. (2004). *Using WSDL in a UDDI Registry, Version 2.0.2. (Technical Note)*. Billerica, MA: Organization for the Advancement of Structured Information Standards.

Computer and Automation Research Institute. (2005). *WSDL2Agent*. Retrieved from http://sas.ilab.sztaki.hu:8080/wsdl2agent/

Domingue, J., Cabral, L., Hakimpour, F., Sell, D., & Motta, E. (2004). IRS-III: A Platform and Infrastructure for Creating WSMO-based Semantic Web Services. In *Proceedings of the WIW 2004 Workshop on WSMO Implementations*.

Dragoni, N., & Gaspari, M. (2005). An Object Based Algebra for Specifying A Fault Tolerant Software Architecture. *Journal of Logic and Algebraic Programming*, *63*(2), 271–297. doi:10.1016/j.jlap.2004.05.006

Dragoni, N., & Gaspari, M. (2006). Crash failure detection in asynchronous agent communication languages. *Autonomous Agents and Multi-Agent Systems*, *13*(3), 355–390. doi:10.1007/s10458-006-0006-y

Dragoni, N., Gaspari, M., & Guidi, D. (2006). An Infrastructure to Support Cooperation of Knowledge-Level Agents on the Semantic Grid. *International Journal of Applied Intelligence. Special issue on Agent-Based Grid Computing*, *25*(2), 159-180.

Dragoni, N., Gaspari, M., & Guidi, D. (2007). An ACL For Specifying Fault-Tolerant Protocols. *Applied Artificial Intelligence*, *21*(4), 361–381. doi:10.1080/08839510701252643

Farrel, J., & Lausen, H. (2007). *Semantic annotations for WSDL*. W3C Working draft.

Fensel, D., Bussler, C., Ding, Y., & Omelayenko, B. (2002). The Web Service Modeling Framework WSMF. *Electronic Commerce Research and Applications*, *1*(2). doi:10.1016/S1567-4223(02)00015-7

Finin, T., Fritzson, R., McKay, D., & McEntire, R. (1997). KQML as an agent communication language. *Software Agents*, 291-316.

FIPA. (2002). *FIPA SL Content Language Specification*. Retrieved from: http://www.fipa.org/specs/fipa00008/

FIPA. Foundation for Intelligent Physical Agents. (2002). *FIPA Webpage*. Retrieved from http://www.fipa.org

Gaspari, M. (1998). Concurrency and Knowledge-Level Communication in Agent Languages. *Artificial Intelligence*, *105*(1-2), 1–45. doi:10.1016/S0004-3702(98)00080-0

Greenwood, D., & Calisti, M. (2004). An Automatic, Bi-Directional Service Integration Gateway. *IEEE International Conference on Systems, Man and Cybernetics*. Hague, The Netherlands: IEEE.

Greenwood, D., & Calisti, M. (2004). Engineering Web Service - Agent Integration. *IEEE International Conference on Systems, Man and Cybernetics*. Hague, The Netherlands: IEEE.

Gruber, T. (1993). A Translation Approach to Portable Ontologies. *Knowledge Acquisition*, *5*(2), 199–220. doi:10.1006/knac.1993.1008

JADE. Java Agent Development Framework. (2001). *Jade webpage*. Retrieved from http://jade.tilab.com

JADE Board. (2008). *Jade Web Services Integration Gateway (Wsig) Guide*. Retrieved from http://jade.cselt.it/doc/tutorials/WSIG_Guide.pdf

Kourtesis, D., & Paraskakis, I. (2008). Combining SAWSDL, OWL-DL and UDDI for Semantically Enhanced Web Service Discovery. In Heidelberg, S. B. (Ed.), *The Semantic Web: Research and Applications* (*Vol. 5021*). Berlin, Heidelberg: Springer/Verlag. doi:10.1007/978-3-540-68234-9_45

Kourtesis, D., Paraskakis, I., Friesen, A., Gouvas, P., & Bouras, A. (2007). Web Service Discovery In A Semantically Extended Uddi Registry: The Case Of Fusion. In []. Boston]. *Proceedings of Establishing The Foundation Of Collaborative Networks*, *243*, 547–554. doi:10.1007/978-0-387-73798-0_59

McGuinness et al. (2004). *OWL Web Ontology Language Overview*. W3C Recommendation.

Mitra, N., & Lafon, Y. (2007). *SOAP Version 1.2 Part 0: Primer*. W3C Recommendation.

Newell, A. (1982). The knowledge level. *Artificial Intelligence*, *19*, 87–127. doi:10.1016/0004-3702(82)90012-1

Nguyen, T. X., & Kowalczyk, R. (2007). WS-2JADE: Integrating Web service with Jade Agents. In *Service-Oriented Computing: Agents, Semantics, and Engineering* (*Vol. 4504*, pp. 147–159). Berlin, Heidelberg: Springer. doi:10.1007/978-3-540-72619-7_11

Nilsson, N. J. (1998). *Artificial intelligence: a new synthesis*. San Francisco: Morgan Kaufmann.

O'Brien, P., & Nicol, R. (1998). FIPA - Towards a Standard for Software Agents. *BT Technology Journal*, *16*, 51–59. doi:10.1023/A:1009621729979

OWL-S 1.0 Release. (2004). *OWL-S: Semantic Markup for Web Services*. Retrieved from http://www.w3.org/Submission/OWL-S

Palathingal, P., & Chandra, S. (2004). Agent Approach for Service Discovery and Utilization. In *Proceedings of the 37th Annual Hawaii International Conference on System Sciences* (HICSS 2004).

Paolucci, M., Kawamura, T., Payne, T., & Sycara, K. (2002). Semantic Matching of Web Services Capabilities. In *Proceedings of the first International Semantic Web Conference* (ISWC).

Profiti, G. (2008). *Integrazione di servizi Web in una piattaforma multi-agente*. (Unpublished Master's thesis). Italy: University of Bologna, Department of Computer Science.

Shafiq, M. O., Ali, A., Ahmad, H. F., & Suguri, H. (2005). AgentWeb Gateway - a middleware for dynamic integration of Multi Agent System and Web Services Framework. In *Proceedings of the IEEE International Workshops on Enabling Technologies: Infrastructure for Collaborative Enterprise*.

Soto, E. L. (2007). Agent Communication Using Web Services, a New FIPA Message Transport Service for Jade. In P. P. al. (Ed.), MATES 2007 (Vol. LNAI 5687, pp. 73-84). Berlin-Heidlberg: Springer-Verlag.

Springer.Mari, M., Poggi, A., Tomaiuolo, M., & Turci, P. (2008). *Enhancing Multi-Agent Systems with Peer-to-Peer and Service-Oriented Technologies*. (AT2AI-6 Working Notes). From Agent Theory to Agent Implementation Workshop.

WSMO Working Group. (2004). *Web Service Modeling Ontology (WSMO)*, Working Draft D2v1.2. Retrieved from: http://www.wsmo.org/TR/d2/v1.2/D2v1-2_20050414.pdf

Chapter 2
Extending the JADE Framework for Semantic Peer–to–Peer Service Based Applications

Agostino Poggi
Università degli Studi di Parma, Italy

Michele Tomaiuolo
Università degli Studi di Parma, Italy

ABSTRACT

One of the main challenges of multi-agent systems is to become the main means to support legacy systems interoperability and to make the realization of scalable distributed systems easy. In the last years, however, two technologies, peer-to-peer and service-oriented, have made an impressive progress and seem to have good chances of competing with multi-agent systems for the realization of scalable and interoperable systems. Conversely, neither of these two technologies is able to provide by themselves the autonomy and social and proactive capabilities of agents and thus the development of flexible adaptive distributed systems may be difficult. This chapter shows how JADE, one of the most known and used software framework for the development of multi-agent systems, has been extended with these technologies both to support the realization of multi-agent systems and to facilitate the interoperability with peer-to-peer and service-oriented systems.

INTRODUCTION

One of the main reasons of the success of the research on multi-agent system is that they were considered the most suitable means to support legacy systems interoperability and to make easy the realization of scalable distributed systems (Genesereth, 1997; FIPA, 2000). However, in the last years, two technologies, peer-to-peer and service-

oriented technologies, had an impressive progress and seem to have good chances to compete with multi-agent system for the realization of scalable and interoperable systems. The problem of both these two technologies is that they cannot provide by themselves the autonomy, social and proactive capabilities of agents and so the realization of flexible adaptive distributed systems may be difficult.

Therefore, an integration of multi-agent systems with such two technologies seems to be the most suitable solution for the realization of scalable and

DOI: 10.4018/978-1-61520-973-6.ch002

interoperable distributed applications. In fact, in these last years a lot of works have been presented for the integration of multi agent systems with one of or both the two technologies (see, for example, Willmott et al., 2004; Greenwood et al., 2005; Huhns et al., 2005; Buford & Burg, 2006).

This chapter copes with the problem of the integration of multi-agent systems with peer-to-peer and service-oriented technologies and, in particular, presents how JADE, one of the most known and used software framework for the development of multi-agent systems (Bellifemine et al., 2001), has been extended with these two technologies to both support the realization of multi-agent systems and to make easy the interoperability with peer-to-peer and service-oriented systems. The next section describes the main features of the JADE agent development software framework. Sections three and four respectively describe the peer-to-peer and the service-oriented extensions of the JADE software framework. Finally, section five summarizes the contributions of our work and points to future lines of work.

JADE

JADE (Java Agent DEvelopment framework) is a software framework designed to aid the development of agent applications in compliance with the FIPA specifications for interoperable intelligent multi-agent systems (Bellifemine, 2001; Bellifemine, 2008). The purpose of JADE is to simplify development while ensuring standard compliance through a comprehensive set of system services and agents. JADE is an active open source project, and the framework together with documentation and examples can be downloaded from JADE Home Page (JADE, 2009).

JADE is based on a peer-to-peer communication architecture. The intelligence, the initiative, the information, the resources and the control can be fully distributed across mobile terminals as well as computers connected to the fixed network. The environment evolves dynamically together with peers – that in JADE are called agents – that appear and disappear in the system according to the needs and the requirements of the application domain. Communication between the peers, regardless of whether they are running in the wireless or wired network, is completely symmetric with each peer being able to play both initiator and responder roles.

JADE is fully developed in Java and is based on the following driving principles:

- **Interoperability:** JADE is compliant with the FIPA specifications (FIPA, 2000). As a consequence, JADE agents can interoperate with other agents, provided that they comply with the same standard.

- **Uniformity and portability:** JADE provides a homogeneous set of APIs that are independent from the underlying network and Java version (edition, configuration and profile). More in details, the JADE run-time provides the same APIs both for the J2EE, J2SE and J2ME environment. In theory, application developers could decide the Java run-time environment at deploy-time.

- **Ease of use:** the complexity of the middleware is hidden behind a simple and intuitive set of APIs.

- **Pay-as-you-go philosophy:** programmers do not need to use all the features provided by the middleware. Features that are not used do not require programmers to know anything about them, neither they add a computational overhead.

JADE includes: i) the libraries (i.e., the Java classes) required to develop the application specific agents, ii) the implementation of the two management agents that a FIPA compliant agent platform must provide, i.e., the AMS (Agent Management System) agent and the DF (Directory Facilitator) agent, and iii) the run-time environ-

Figure 1. Architecture of a JADE multi-agent system

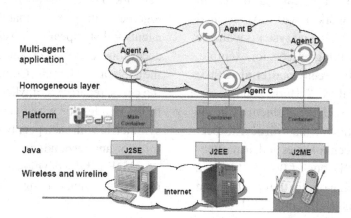

ment that provides the basic services and that must be active on the device before agents can be executed. Each instance of the JADE run-time is called container (since it "contains" agents). The set of all containers is called platform and it provides a homogeneous layer that hides to agents (and to application developers) the complexity and the diversity of the underlying tires (hardware, operating systems, types of network, JVM, etc.). Figure 1 draws the architecture of a JADE multi-agent system deployed on a set of heterogeneous computing nodes.

JADE is extremely versatile and therefore it both fits the constraints of environments with limited resources and has already been integrated into complex architectures such as.NET or J2EE (BlueJade, 2003) where JADE becomes a service to execute multi-party proactive applications. The JADE run-time memory footprint, in a MIDP1.0 environment, is around 100 KB, but can be further reduced until 50 KB using the ROMizing technique (Bergenti et al., 2001), i.e., compiling JADE together with the JVM. The limited memory footprint allows installing JADE on all mobile phones provided that they are Java-enabled. Analyses and a benchmarks of scalability and performance of the JADE Message Transport System are reported by different works (Chmiel et al., 2005; Zimmermann et al., 2006).

As above mentioned, the JADE run-time can be executed on a wide class of devices ranging from servers to cell phones, for the latter the only requirement being the availability of Java MIDP1.0 (or later versions). In order to properly address the memory and processing power limitations of mobile devices and the characteristics of wireless networks (GPRS in particular) in terms of bandwidth, latency, intermittent connectivity and IP addresses variability, and at the same time, in order to be efficient when executed on wired network hosts, JADE can be configured to adapt to the characteristics of the deployment environment. JADE architecture, in fact, is completely modular and, by activating certain modules instead of others, it is possible to meet different requirements in terms of connectivity, memory and processing power.

This is possible thanks to a module called LEAP (Lightweight Extensive Agent Platform) that allows optimizing all communication mechanisms when dealing with devices with limited resources and connected through wireless networks (Bergenti et al., 2001). By activating this module, a JADE container is "split" (as depicted in Figure 2) into a front-end running in the mobile terminal and a back-end running in the wired network. A suitable architectural element, called mediator, is in charge of instantiating and maintaining the

Figure 2. JADE architecture for the mobile environment

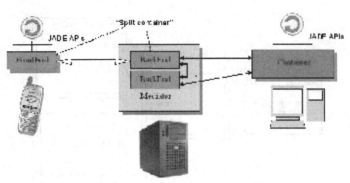

back-end. To better face high workload situations, it is possible to deploy several mediators, each of them managing a set of back-ends. Each front-end is linked to its corresponding back-end through a permanent bi-directional connection. It is important to note that it makes no difference at all, to application developers, whether an agent is deployed on a normal container or on the front-end of a split container, since both the available functionality and the APIs are exactly the same.

This approach has some advantages:

- Part of the functionality of a container is delegated to the back-end and, as a consequence, the front-end becomes extremely lightweight in terms of required memory and processing power.
- The back-end masks to other containers the current IP address dynamically assigned to the wireless device, thereby hiding to the rest of the multi-agent system a possible change of IP address.
- The front-end is able to detect connection losses with the back-end (for instance due to an out of coverage condition) and to re-establish the connection as soon as possible.
- Both the front-end and the back-end implement a store-and-forward mechanism: messages that cannot be transmitted due to a temporary disconnection are buffered

and delivered as soon as the connection is re-established.
- A lot of information that containers exchange (for instance to retrieve the container where an agent is currently running) is handled only by the back-end. This approach, together with a bit-efficient message encoding between the front-end and the back-end, allows the optimization of the usage of the wireless link.

From the functional point of view, JADE provides the basic services necessary to distributed peer-to-peer applications in the fixed and mobile environment. JADE allows agents to dynamically discover other agents and to communicate with them according to the peer-to-peer paradigm. From the application point of view, each agent is identified by a unique name and it provides a set of services; it can register and modify its services and/or search for agents providing some specific services, it can control its life cycle and, finally, it communicates with all other peers.

Agents communicate through the exchange of asynchronous messages, i.e., agents just sends messages to other agents without waiting for an answer, which is a communication model almost universally accepted for distributed and loosely-coupled communications, i.e., between heterogeneous entities that do not know anything about each other. Agents are identified by a name that

Figure 3. Encapsulation of ACL messages

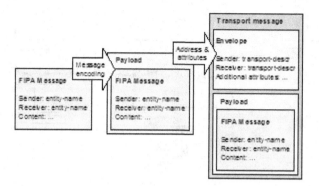

does not statically include the actual distributed object reference of the agent and therefore there is no temporal dependency between communicating agents. The sender and the receiver could not be available at the same time. The receiver may not even exist (or not yet exist) or it could be not directly known by the sender that can specify a property (e.g. "all agents interested in football") as an intentional description of destination agents. Because agents identify each other by their name, hot changes of their object reference are transparent to applications.

Despite this type of communication, security is preserved, because JADE provides, for applications that require it, proper mechanisms to authenticate and verify rights and capabilities assigned to agents. When needed, an application can verify the identity of the sender of a message and prevent any not allowed action. For instance, an agent may be allowed to receive messages from the agent representing its boss, but not to send messages to it. All messages exchanged between agents are transported within an envelope that includes only the information required by the transport layer (see Figure 3). This allows, among other things, to encrypt the content of a message separately from the envelope and to guarantee reachability with no loss of security.

The authentication of agents and the verification of their rights can be done by an optional plug-in of JADE (Poggi et al., 2005). This plug-in leverages on the security means provided by Java and extends them to allow the definition of precise protection domains on the basis of authorization certificates. These certificates, attached to requests and messages, list a set of granted permissions and are signed by trusted authorities according to customizable policies, possibly in completely decentralized way. The authorization certificates owned by the agents can also be used to delegate access rights to other agents, to allow them to complete the requested tasks or to achieve delegated goals.

The structure of a message complies with the ACL (Agent Communication Language) model defined by FIPA (FIPA, 2000) and includes fields, such as variables indicating the context a message refers to and the amount of time that is waited before an answer is received, aimed at supporting complex interactions and multiple parallel conversations.

To further support the implementation of complex conversations, JADE provides a set of skeletons of typical interaction patterns to perform specific tasks, such as negotiations, auctions and task delegation. By using these skeletons (implemented as Java abstract classes), programmers can get rid of the burden of dealing with synchronization issues, timeouts, error conditions and, in general, all those aspects that are not strictly related to the application domain.

To facilitate the creation and handling of message contents, JADE provides support for automatically converting back and forth between formats suitable for content exchange, including XML and RDF, and the formats suitable for content manipulation (i.e., Java objects). This facility is integrated with some well known ontology-creation tools, e.g. Protégé, allowing programmers to graphically create the ontology agents should use to validate and provide semantics to messages.

To increase scalability and to meet the constraints of environments with limited resources, JADE provides the opportunity of executing multiple parallel tasks within the same Java thread. Several elementary tasks, such as communication, can then be combined to form more complex tasks structured as concurrent finite states machines.

JADE supports mobility of code and of execution state. That is, an agent can stop running on a host, migrate on a different remote host (without the need to have the agent code already installed on that host), and restart its execution from the point it was interrupted (actually, JADE implements a form of not-so-weak mobility because the stack and the program counter cannot be saved in Java). This functionality allows, for example, distributing computational load at runtime by moving agents to less loaded machines without any impact on the application.

The platform also includes a naming service (ensuring each agent has a unique name) and a yellow pages service that can be distributed across multiple hosts. Federation graphs can be created in order to define structured domains of agent services. Another very important feature consists in the availability of a rich suite of graphical tools supporting both the debugging and management/monitoring phases of application life cycle. By means of these tools, it is possible to remotely control agents, even if already deployed and running: agent conversations can be emulated, exchanged messages can be sniffed, tasks can be monitored, agent life-cycle can be controlled. Figure 4 presents the GUIs of some JADE software development tools.

EXTENDING JADE WITH PEER-TO-PEER TECHNOLOGIES

The traditional, client-server model describes systems where computational resources and data are centralized in few servers, which respond to requests of clients. On the other hand, clients are supposed to have little capabilities and rely on the resources of servers for most of their tasks. The multi-agent model reverses this paradigm and describes systems organized in a peer-to-peer fashion, where each participant potentially has some resources to share and some services to offer to the community of agents. Thus, according to the context, each agent is able to play either the role of client or server.

JADE implements FIPA specifications for multi-agent systems, and so enables the realization of peer-to-peer distributed systems, constituted by smart and loosely coupled agents communicating by means of asynchronous ACL messages (FIPA. 2000).

Nevertheless, JADE does not exploit some important features of modern peer-to-peer networks, in particular:

- The possibility of building a completely distributed, global index of resources and services, without relying on any centralized entity.
- The possibility of building an "overlay network", hiding differences in lower level technologies and their related communication problems.

Some multi-agent systems, like Agentscape, approached the same issues by developing a dedicated peer-to-peer network layer (Overeinder et al., 2002), our solution is to integrate multi-agent platforms into an already existing and used peer-to-peer environment, i.e., JXTA (JXTA, 2008), thus, benefiting from a well tested system and exposing services to other entities participating in the network.

Figure 4. JADE software development tools

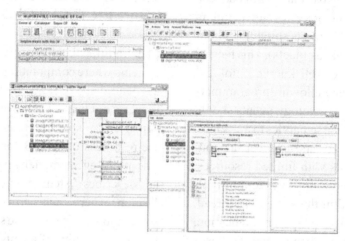

JXTA technology is a set of open, general-purpose protocols that allow any connected device on the network (from cell phones to laptops and servers) to communicate and collaborate in a peer-to-peer fashion. The project was originally started by Sun Microsystems, but its development was kept open from the very beginning. JXTA comprises six protocols allowing the discovery, organization, monitoring and communication between peers. These protocols are all implemented on the basis of an underlying messaging layer, which binds the JXTA protocols to different network transports.

JXTA peers can form peer groups, which are virtual networks where any peer can seamlessly interact with other peers and resources, whether they are connected directly or through intermediate proxies. JXTA defines a communication language which is much more abstract than any other peer-to-peer protocol, allowing to use the network for a great variety of services and devices. A great advantage of JXTA derives from the use of XML language to represent, through structured documents, named advertisements, the resources available in the network. XML adapts without particular problems to any transport mean and it is already an affirmed standard, with good sup-

port in very different environments, to structure generic data in a form easily analyzable by both humans and machines.

JXTA-ADS

What usually happens in a multi-agent platform is the cohabitation of multiple agents interacting in a common and cohesive environment, making use of a formal communication language, defined by its own syntax and semantics, in order to complete tasks demanded by users. For making constructive the communication, it is necessary to provide agents with a system allowing them to reciprocally individuate offered services. This happens thanks to the presence of a yellow pages service, provided by the platform, which can be consulted by agents when needed. However this often limits the search inside a single platform. Solutions are possible, which allow the consultation of other yellow pages services, but they necessitate the a priori knowledge of the address of the remote platform where services are hosted or listed.

An alternative solution is represented by a yellow pages service leaning on a peer-to-peer network like JXTA, thanks to which each network device is able to individuate in a dynamic way services and resources of other network devices.

Technologies inherent to web services are using WSDL as a standard language to publicize all different available resources. In FIPA, a simpler formalism is defined to describe services and resources exposed by agents and linked to their own domain ontology. JXTA does not establish any constraint on the way to describe and invoke services. JXTA protocols simply provide a generic framework, allowing the use of any mechanism, also WSDL or FIPA service descriptions, to exchange information needed to invoke a service.

Particular peers, called rendezvous peers, are in charge of both indexing resources made available in the network and finding them when requested by other peers. Rendezvous peers can also communicate queries to each other, if they do not possess the right information, thus enabling the discovery of advertisements beyond the local network.

In fact, in JXTA, resources are described by advertisements, which are essentially XML documents collecting metadata of available resources. Advertisements are not stored on some single machine, such as a server, or on a hierarchical infrastructure; they are distributed among rendezvous peers, which implement a distributed algorithm, called shared resource distributed index (SRDI), for the creation and management of the index of resources available in the network. On the basis of some indexed attributes, this mechanism can solve queries made anywhere in the rendezvous network. Basically, the global index is a loosely consistent distributed hash table, where the hash of an indexed attribute is mapped to some peer responsible for storing the actual advertisement.

FIPA has acknowledged the growing importance of the JXTA protocols, and it has released some specifications for the interoperability of FIPA platforms with peer-to-peer networks. In particular, in (FIPA, 2003) a set of new components and protocols are described, to allow the implementation of a DF-like service on a JXTA

network (i.e., a yellow pages service that allows to discover on a JXTA network the agents that provide a particular service as is done by a directory facilitator in a traditional JADE multi-agent system). These include:

- **Generic Discovery Service:** a local DF, taking part in the peer-to-peer network and implementing the agent discovery service specifications to discover agents and services deployed on remote FIPA platforms working together in a peer-to-peer network.
- **Agent Peer Group:** a child of the JXTA Net Peer Group that must be joined by each distributed discovery service.
- **Generic Discovery Advertisement:** to handle agent or service descriptions, for example, FIPA df-agent-descriptions.
- **Generic Discovery Protocol:** to enable the interaction of discovery services on different agent platforms. It's a request/response protocol to discover advertisements, based on two simple messages, one for queries and one for responses.

The JADE development environment does not provide any support for the deployment of real peer-to-peer systems because it only provides the possibility of federating different agent platforms through a hierarchical organization of the platform directory facilitators on the basis of a priori knowledge of the agent platforms addresses. Therefore, the JADE directory facilitator has been extended to realize a peer-to-peer network of agent platforms thanks to the JXTA technology (JXTA, 2008) and thanks to two preliminary FIPA specifications for the agent discovery service (FIPA, 2003) and for the JXTA discovery middleware (FIPA, 2004).

This way, JADE integrates a JXTA-based ADS (Agent Discovery Service), which has been developed in the respect of relevant FIPA specifications to implement a GDS (Generic Discovery Service). Each JADE platform connects to the Agent Peer Group, as well as to other system-specific peer

Figure 5. Discovery of agents in a JXTA network

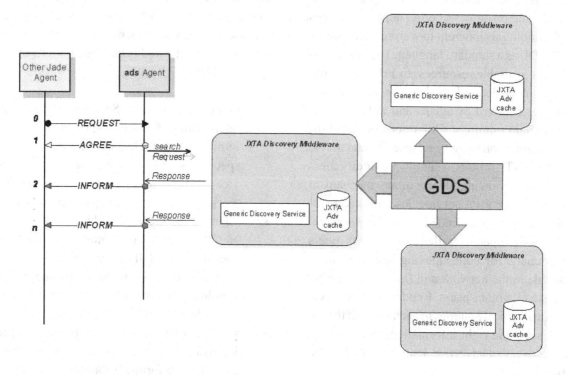

groups. The GDS is finally used to advertise and discover agent descriptions, wrapped in generic discovery advertisements, in order to implement a DF service, which in the background is spanned over a whole peer group. Figure 5 shows how an ADS agent interacts with JXTA discovery service for finding agents of other JADE platform connected through a JXTA network.

JXTA-MTP

In the course of some large projects based on agent technologies like Agentcities and @lis TechNet (Poggi et al., 2004; Willmott et al., 2006), some recurring problems emerged at the level of connection among remote platforms. The importance of these problems invariably grows with the cardinality and geographical extension of the interconnected infrastructure, and has been acknowledged in other similar large scale environments.

Most peer-to-peer networks specifically address this kind of problems allowing the connection of peers located behind firewalls, Network Address Translators (NATs) and Dynamic Host Configuration Protocol (DHCP) servers, or requiring different and particular protocols like HTTP or WAP. To this end, peer-to-peer networks create an overlay infrastructure above underlying diverse and problematic links in order to realize a more abstract and homogeneous ground and simplify the communications among peers.

JXTA is one of the most used technologies to improve connectivity on a global scale. In fact, JXTA does not suppose a direct connection is available between all couple of peers. Peers can use the Peer Endpoint Protocol to discover available routes for sending a message to a destination peer. Particular peers, called routers, are in charge of responding to such queries providing route information, i.e. a list of gateways connecting the sender to the intended receiver. A gateway acts as a communication relay, where messages can be stored and later collected by their intended recipient, overcoming problems related to limited connectivity.

JADE, on the other hand, offers an extensible mechanism for the transport of messages among platforms, in the form of pluggable Message Transport Protocols (MTPs). The default implementations are based on IIOP and HTTP, which are both limited by the requirement of a direct connection between sender and receiver. Therefore, exploiting the extensibility of JADE platforms, a JXTA-MTP implementation has been realized. This MTP allows the exchange of messages between two platforms through JXTA pipes which are dynamically bound to specific endpoints (typically an IP address and a TCP port). JXTA pipes are advertised on the network in the same way as other services offered by peers, and provide a global scope to peer connectivity.

The JXTA-MTP implementation allows using not only plain JXTA pipes, but also secure ones with encryption and signature mechanisms guaranteeing privacy, integrity and authenticity of exchanged messages.

EXTENDING JADE WITH SERVICE ORIENTED TECHNOLOGIES

Industry is increasingly interested in executing business functions that span multiple applications, thus requiring high-levels of interoperability and a more flexible and adaptive business process management. The most appropriate response to this need seems to be having systems assembled from a loosely coupled collection of web services. This technical area appears to be an interesting environment in which the agent technology can be exploited with significant advantages. As a matter of fact, several researches belonging to the agent community have dealt with the issues concerning the interconnection of agent systems with W3C compliant web services, with the aim of allowing each technology to discover and invoke

instances of the other. One evident benefit of this is the central role that agents could play in a service oriented scenario, by efficiently supporting distributed computing and allowing the dynamic composition of web services.

Several works proposed the integration of JADE with service-oriented technologies technologies (see, for example, Martinez & Lespérance, 2004; Nguyen & Kowalczyk, 2005; Soto, 2006). However, there exists a JADE official solution for such an integration that is based on the JADE WSIG add-on (Greenwood & Calisti, 2004) and on an extension of JADE, called WADE (Caire et al., 2008a; Caire et al., 2008b), and supports the use of workflows in the realization of applications integrating agents and web services.

WSIG

JADE supports the invocation of agent services as web services and the capability to realize applications as composition of agents and Web services through a JADE add-on, called WSIG (Web Service Integration Gateway) that is able to automatically expose agent services as web services and to convert SOAP invocations into ACL requests (Greenwood & Calisti, 2004). More in details, JADE agents publish their services through the DF agent of a JADE multi-agent platform. Each registered service is described via a data structure called Service-Description. This structure specifies, among others data, the ontologies, that must be used to access the published service, and defines the actions that the agent is able to perform. WSIG listens to registrations with the DF agent and, for each registered agent service, it automatically exposes a web service described by a WSDL description whose operations correspond to the actions supported by the registering agent. If properly configured, WSIG is also able to publish the exposed web service in a UDDI registry in order to simplify integration of a JADE-based system within a SOA environment. At invocation time, WSIG performs the following tasks: (1) it converts incoming SOAP messages into requests of execution of the corresponding actions, (2) it forwards these messages to the proper agents, (3) it handles action results, (4) and, finally, it sends back the responses to clients encoded as SOAP messages. When an agent needs to invoke a web service, it directly creates the SOAP message and sends it to the provider, e.g., exploited AXIS2 API. In this case, no particular support is provided by WSIG. To date, WSIG supports only simple WSDL descriptions of web services, without taking into account emerging technologies related to the semantic Web.

WADE

In general, the modus operandi to carry out web service compositions is similar to that concerning the definition of workflows, such that existing techniques for workflow pattern generation, composition, and management can be partially reused for this purpose (Henoque & Kleiner, 2007). Therefore, even if workflows can be useful for composing agent tasks they can be also an interesting means to supports the realization of applications merging the execution of agents and web services (Singh & Huhns, 1999; Chen et al., 2000; Savarimuthu et al., 2004; Vidal et al., 2004; Zao et al., 2007; Trappey et al., 2009).

WADE (Workflow and Agent Development Environment) is a software platform, built on top of JADE, for the development of distributed applications based on the agent-oriented paradigm (Caire et al., 2008a). WADE adds to JADE the support to the workflow execution and a few mechanisms to manage the complexity of the distribution, in terms of administration and fault tolerance. WADE adds some additional components to a JADE application:

- A boot daemon on each host on which the application is deployed with the duty of activating the JADE containers of the application on the current host.

- A configuration agent on the main container of the application. This agent is responsible for interacting with the boot daemons and controlling the application life cycle.
- A controller agent for each container in the platform and they are responsible for supervising activities in the local container and for all the fault tolerance mechanisms provided by WADE.
- A set of workflow engine agents able to execute workflows.

In particular, the workflow engine agents embed a workflow engine able to executed workflows encoded by an extended version the XPDL (XPDL, 2008) that adds the possibility of associating the direct execution of pieces of Java code with the activities of a workflow. In fact, the main challenge in WADE is to bring the workflow approach from the business process level to the level of system internal logics, i.e., its main goal is not to support the high level orchestration of services provided by different systems, but the implementation of the internal behavior of each single system. Moreover, the execution of a workflow can be shared by a set workflow engine agents because each workflow engine agent can delegate the execution of some subflows to some other agents. These agents are selected at runtime and can also run on remote computers; of course, the selection criteria depend on the application and are provided to the configuration agent before the execution of the workflow.

The development of the workflows to be executed by the WADE software platform can be easily done thanks to the use the WOLF graphical development environment (Caire et al., 2008b). WOLF is implemented as an Eclipse plugin and allows the management of the whole life cycle of workflows. In particular, WOLF provides support for: i) graphically editing of workflows, ii) controlling a local or remote WADE-based application and iii) deploying and executing workflows in the controlled application. Figure 6 shows the WOLF workflow editor.

Figure 6. WOLF workflow editor

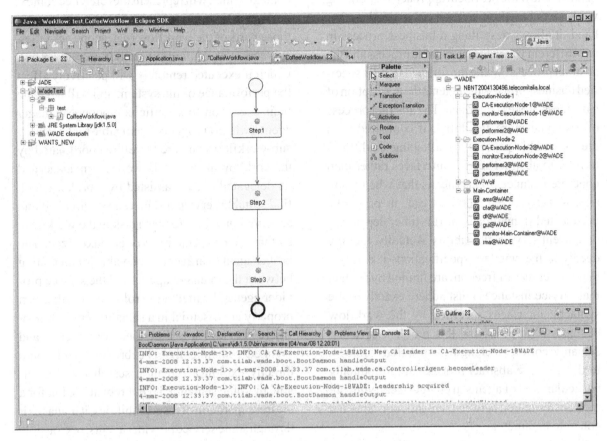

The use of WOLF provide an easy way for realizing workflow whose activities invoke web services. In fact, WOLF allows a developer to browse WSDL files repository and then imports the WSDL files describing the web services to be used in the workflow. The result of the import operation is the generation of a set of classes that will be used during the execution of a workflow for invoking the web services described by the imported WSDL. Unless they have specific customization needs, developers don't need to care about such classes because WOLF and WADE hide all the details of the web service invocation process. In particular, if the imported WSDL declares some complex types, suitable Java bean classes are also generated.

BEJA

A more adequate solution for realizing a more flexible and effective agent-based business process management with JADE is to use BEJA (BPEL Enhanced JADE Agent). BEJA is a software library, built on the basis of the results of the development and experimentation of two previous systems, GAIN (Negri et al., 2006) and MASE (Poggi et al., 2007), that adds the possibility of using into a JADE application some special agents that couple the execution of WS-BPEL (WS-BPEL, 2007) workflows with the semantic retrieval of web services provided by a semantic UDDI.

The reason to choose WS-BPEL as the language to express workflows is twofold. On the one hand, it is now the prevalent approach for defining workflows based on web services. On the other hand, it allows describing a business process in two different ways: the executable process and the abstract process. While the former is a fully specified business process the latter is the description of a business process interface. The abstract process offers some more flexibility, if compared with the executable process, by allowing workflows to refer to abstract service interfaces rather than concrete instances. This means that when using an abstract process, services can, in principle, be selected dynamically at run-time, depending on current service availability. Actually, looking deeply to the standard specifications it emerges that the degrees of freedom are limited by the fact that service instances must adhere exactly to the syntactic interfaces specified by the workflow designers. We get round this problem by using semantic concept, belonging to a shared ontology, to describe the abstract process and introducing particular kind of agents in charge of carrying out the transformation between semantic concepts and concrete parameters.

Two key components of the BEJA software library are: a software tool that transforms a standard WS-BPEL workflow XML representation into a Java object-oriented structure that can be easily decomposed and manipulated during its distributed execution, and a WS-BPEL engine that, while executes a workflow through the use of the most appropriate Web services, can also delegate the execution of some its sub-workflows to other engines.

BEJA comprises four groups of agents: workflow manager agents, component manager agents, broker agents and service provider agents. Once the business process is expressed in terms of a WS-BPEL workflow, it is executed by the workflow manager agent. The workflow manager agent, containing a WS-BPEL engine, is responsible for initiating and coordinating the entire execution process. It generates a process instance and controls its enactment, creating the execution

context, which will represent the reference context during the execution process. Next, it will identify those parts of the workflow (e.g. scope activities, sub-activities of the flow activities, and so on), which if executed remotely will positively affect the performance of the system, and will delegate their execution to specific component manager agents, which are agents responsible for executing sub-workflows and are therefore coordinated by the workflow manager. The workflow manager and its delegated agents, assisted by a broker agent, find suitable service instances to be invoked and set time-out values for each task in the workflow, so that their expected utility is maximized. The broker agent is an agent responsible for mediating between the manager agents and the service provider agents. Its mediation role and coordination property are essential in a semantic environment where services are described, discovered and invoked semantically. The broker agent could directly exploit a semantic search made available by some semantic UDDI registries, but for a clearer separation of responsibilities, it manages it through some service provider agents, responsible for the interaction with semantic UDDI registries.

This solution allows the realization of more fault-tolerant applications. In fact, during the execution of a workflow, a selected web service could be no longer available due to the expiration of a timeout, a failure of a resource or other unpredictable problems. Therefore, the workflow and component managers can rely on the broker agent in order to achieve their goal by replacing such a web service. In the same way as in the engaging phase, the broker agent is responsible for the dynamic provision of web services, which match the business process needs, mediating between the manager agents and one or more service provider agents and enriching the service provision with advanced features. In particular, the broker is responsible for setting the semantic matching constraints and delegating the semantic search to one or more service provider agents, which finally play the role of middle agents during the invocation phase. In their role of mediator the service provider agents perform a two-step translation, i.e., from the business process representation of a service to its ontological internal representation and from there to the concrete Web service representation (vice versa when they forward the result of the Web service invocation).

In case of failure, the workflow manager agent or possibly a component manager agent will ask a broker agent for help. On the basis of its knowledge of a shared ontology and the functionalities required, the broker will send a semantic query to one or more service provider agents, which in turn will send the query to all potentially interested semantic UDDI registries. The UDDI registries, exploiting a matching algorithm, will as a result give a list of suitable services associated with a degree of matching, which gives the information about how much a particular web service and the received query are semantically compatible. They perform service I/O based profile matching, exploiting ontological concepts as values of service input and output parameters. The algorithm used is similar to the one used in the OWLS-MX matchmaker (Klusch et al., 2006), which, at present, is one of the most effective semantic web service matchmakers which have been developed in the last years. At this point, the service provider agent, applying an appropriate strategy (e.g., it selects the first Web service fulfilling the requirements), will decide which web service to use in order to satisfy the broker request. Finally the broker will inform the workflow manager that a web service with the required characteristics is available.

In view of the fact that there may be mismatches between the syntactic description of the selected web service and its real invocation by the workflow manager (i.e., the abstract service, described in the workflow, and the concrete web service can have different syntactic interface even though they provide the same service) the manager agent will refer to the service provider agent for the web service invocation given that it is aware of both the abstract and the concrete description of web

services and it is able to manage the transformation of the data coming from the workflow manager to the web service and vice-versa.

CONCLUSION

This chapter has dealt with the issue of enhancing the multi-agent systems role in the realization of scalable and interoperable systems by exploiting peer-to-peer and service-oriented technologies as key components for their realization. In particular, the chapter has shown how JADE, one of the best known and most used software framework for the development of multi-agent systems, has been extended with these two technologies both to support the realization of multi-agent systems and to facilitate the interoperability with peer-to-peer and service-oriented systems.

This integration shows interesting advantages. On the one hand, the exploitation of the peer-to-peer technology gives a great impulse towards the scalability and interoperability of different agent platforms and agent-based applications. On the other hand, the openness towards the web service standards gives agents the possibility to interoperate with a consolidated industrial reality and one of the most accepted mechanisms used for integration of distributed systems.

Some other works cope with the extension of the JADE software framework with peer-to-peer and service-oriented technologies (see, for example, Yan et al., 2005; Liu et al., 2006). However, the solution presented in this chapter provides a more complete peer-to-peer support and above all provides a sophisticated support for services composition, i.e., BEJA, that uses a standard language for workflow definition and allows the realization of more reliable applications. In fact, it use WS-BPEL as language for expressing workflows and allows a semantic and dynamic discovery of Web services. The use of WS-BPEL as the language to express workflows is important because it is the prevalent approach for defining workflows based on web services. The semantic and dynamic discovery of web services allows a flexible provision of the services and then the realization of more reliable applications.

Of course, further work can done to improve the JADE peer-to-peer and service composition supports described in this chapter. In particular, current work is coping with an important limit of the integration between BEJA and JADE. In fact, BEJA uses a different (and more complex) ontology management support from the one used in a JADE application for supporting the interaction among the agents. It is because in a JADE application, ontologies are used only to define a knowledge model shared by the agents, but not for reasoning about them. Therefore, current work is dedicated to the development of an ontological management support that should replace both the JADE and BEJA ontological supports. It will simplify the realization of JADE / BEJA applications, but also will extend the capabilities of all the JADE agents by providing them the possibility of reasoning about ontologies.

REFERENCES

Bellifemine, F., Caire, G., Poggi, A., & Rimassa, G. (2008). JADE: a Software Framework for Developing Multi-Agent Applications. Lessons Learned. *Information and Software Technology*, *50*, 10–21. doi:10.1016/j.infsof.2007.10.008

Bellifemine, F., Poggi, A., & Rimassa, G. (2001). Developing multi agent systems with a FIPA-compliant agent framework. *Software, Practice & Experience*, *31*, 103–128. doi:10.1002/1097-024X(200102)31:2<103::AID-SPE358>3.0.CO;2-O

Bergenti, F., Poggi, A., Burg, B., & Caire, G. (2001). Deploying FIPA-Compliant Systems on Handheld Devices. *IEEE Internet Computing*, *5*(4), 20–25. doi:10.1109/4236.939446

BlueJade. (2003). *BlueJade software Web site*. Retrieved June 28, 2009, from http://sourceforge.net/projects/bluejade

Buford, J., & Burg, B. (2006). Using FIPA Agents with Service-Oriented Peer-to-Peer Middleware. In *Proceedings from the 7th Int. Conf. on Mobile Data Management*, (pp. 81). Nara, Japan.

Burstein, M. H., Bussler, C., Zaremba, M., Finin, T. W., Huhns, M. N., & Paolucci, M. (2005). A Semantic Web Services Architecture. *IEEE Internet Computing*, *9*(5), 72–81. doi:10.1109/MIC.2005.96

Caire, G., Gotta, D., & Banzi, M. (2008a). WADE: a software platform to develop mission critical applications exploiting agents and workflows. In *Proceedings from the 7th international Joint Conference on Autonomous Agents and Multi Agent Systems: Industrial Track*, (pp. 29-36). Estoril, Portugal.

Caire, G., Quarantotto, E., Porta, M., & Sacchi, G. (2008b). WOLF - An Eclipse Plug-in for WADE. *Proceedings from ACEC: the 6th International Workshop on Agent-based Computing for Enterprise Collaboration*. Rome, Italy. Retrieved June 28, 2009, from http://jade.tilab.com/wade/papers/Wolf_ACEC_2008.pdf

Chen, Q., Hsu, M., Dayal, U., & Griss, M. (2000). Multi-agent cooperation, dynamic workflow and XML for e-commerce automation. In *Proceedings from the 4th international Conference on Autonomous Agents*, (pp. 255-256). Barcelona, Spain.

Chmiel, K., Gawinecki, M., Kaczmarek, P., Szymczak, M., & Paprzycki, M. (2005). Efficiency of JADE agent platform. *Science Progress*, *2*, 159–172.

FIPA. (2000). *FIPA Specifications*. Retrieved June 28, 2009, from http://www.fipa.org.

FIPA. (2003). *Agent Discovery Service Specification*. Retrieved June 28, 2009, from http://www.fipa.org/specs/fipa00095/PC00095.pdf.

FIPA. (2004). *JXTA Discovery Middleware Specification*. Retrieved June 28, 2009, from http://www.fipa.org/specs/fipa00096/PC00096A.pdf

Genesereth, M. R. (1997). An agent-based framework for interoperability. In Bradshaw, J. M. (Ed.), *Software Agents* (pp. 317–345). Cambridge, MA: MIT Press.

Greenwood, D., & Callisti, M. (2004). Engineering Web Service-Agent Integration. In *Proceedings from 2004 IEEE Conference of Systems, Man and Cybernetics*, (pp. 1918-1925). The Hague, Netherlands. Retrieved June 28, 2009, from http://www.whitestein.com/library/WhitesteinTechnologies_Paper_IEEESMC2004.pdf

Greenwood, D., Nagy, J., & Calisti, M. (2005). Semantic Enhancement of a Web Service Integration Gateway. In *Proceedings from SOCABE: the AAMAS 2005 Workshop on Service Oriented Computing and Agent Based Engineering*, Utrecht, Netherlands.

Henocque, L., & Kleiner, M. (2007). Composition - combining web services functionality in composite or-chestrations. In Studer, R., Grimm, S., & Abecker, A. (Eds.), *Semantic Web Services - Concepts, Technologies and Applications* (pp. 245–286). Berlin, Germany: Springer.

Huhns, M. N., Singh, M. P., Mark, H. M. H., Decker, K. S., Durfee, E. H., & Finin, T. W., Gasser, l., Goradia, H. J., Jennings, N. R., Lakkaraju, K., Nakashima, H., Parunak, K., Rosenschein, J. S., Ruvinsky, A., Sukthankar, G., Swarup, S., Sycara, K. P., Tambe, M., Wagner, T., & Zavala Gutierrez, R. L. (2005). Research Directions for Service-Oriented Multiagent Systems. *IEEE Internet Computing*, *9*(6), 65–70. doi:10.1109/MIC.2005.132

JADE. (2009). *JADE software Web site*. Retrieved June 28, 2009, from http://jade.tilab.com

JXTA. (2007). *JXTA Web Site*. Retrieved June 28, 2009, from https://jxta.dev.java.net/

Klusch, M., Fries, B., & Sycara, K. P. (2006). Automated semantic web service discovery with OWLS-MX. In *Proceedings from the 5th international Joint Conference on Autonomous Agents and Multi Agent Systems*, (pp. 915-922). Hakodate, Japan.

Liu, S., Küngas, P., & Matskin, M. (2006). Agent-Based Web Service Composition with JADE and JXTA. In *Proceedings from the 2006 International Conference on Semantic Web and Web Services*, (pp. 110-116). Las Vegas, NV.

Martinez, E., & Lespérance, Y. (2004). IG-JADE-PKSlib: An Agent-Based Framework for Advanced Web Ser-vice Composition and Provisioning. In *Proceedings from the AAMAS 2004 Workshop on Web-services and Agent-based Engineering*, (pp. 2-10). New York.

Negri, A., Poggi, A., Tomaiuolo, M., & Turci, P. (2006). Dynamic Grid tasks composition and distribution through agents. *Concurrency and Computation*, *18*(8), 875–885. doi:10.1002/cpe.982

Nguyen, X. T., & Kowalczyk, R. (2005). Enabling Agent-Based Management of Web Services with WS2JADE. In *Proceedings from ISEAT 2005: the 1st International Workshop on Integration of Software Engineering and Agent Technology*, (pp. 407-412). Melbourne, Australia.

Overeinder, B. J., Posthumus, E., & Brazier, F. M. T. (2002). Integrating Peer-to-Peer Networking and Computing in the AgentScape Framework. In *Proceedings from P2P02: the 2nd IEEE Int. Conf. on Peer-to-Peer Computing*, (pp. 96-103). Linköping, Sweden.

Poggi, A. Tomaiuolo, M., & Vitaglione, G. (2005). A Security Infrastructure for Trust Management in Multi-agent Systems. In. R. Falcone, S. Barber, & M. P. Singh (eds.), Trusting Agents for Trusting Electronic Societies, Theory and Applications in HCI and E-Commerce. Lecture Notes in Computer Science, (Vol. 3577, pp. 162-179). Berlin, Germany: Springer.

Poggi, A. Tomaiuolo, M., & Turci, P. (2007). An Agent-Based Service Oriented Architecture. In *Proceedings of WOA 2007*, (pp. 157-165). Genoa, Italy.

Savarimuthu, B. T., Purvis, M., & Fleurke, M. (2004). Monitoring and controlling of a multi-agent based workflow system. In *Proceedings of the 2nd Workshop on Australasian information Security, Data Mining and Web intelligence, and Software Internationalisation*, (pp. 127-132). Dunedin, New Zealand.

Shafiq, M. O., Ali, A., Ahmad, H. F., & Suguri, H. (2006). AgentWeb Gateway - a middleware for dynamic integration of Multi Agent System and Web Services Framework. In *Proceedings of WETICE 2005: the 14th IEEE International Workshops on Enabling Technologies*, (pp. 267-270). Linköping, Sweden.

Singh, M. P., & Huhns, M. N. (1999). Multiagent systems for workflow. *Intelligent Systems in Accounting. Financial Management, 8*(29), 105–117.

Soto, E. L. (2006). Agent Communication Using Web Services, a New FIPA Message Transport Service for JADE. In P. Petta J.P. Müller, M. Klusch, & M. Georgeff (Eds.). Multiagent System Technologies, Lecture Notes in Computer Science, (Vol. 4687, pp. 73-84). Berlin, Germany: Springer.

Trappey, C. V., Trappey, A. J. C., Huang, C., & Kud, C. C. (2009). The design of a JADE-based autonomous workflow management system for collaborative SoC design. *Expert Systems with Applications, 36*(2), 2659–2669. doi:10.1016/j.eswa.2008.01.064

Vidal, J. M., Buhler, P., & Stahl, C. (2004). Multiagent Systems with Workflows. *IEEE Internet Computing, 8*(1), 76–82. doi:10.1109/MIC.2004.1260707

Willmott, S., Padget, J., Poggi, A., Díaz de León, J. L., Casasola, E., Latorre, H., & de Los Angeles Junco Rey, M. (2006). The case for open source in information and network technology education: experiences from the EuropeAid@lis technology net project. *International Journal of Continuing Engineering Education and Lifelong Learning, 17*(1), 67–83. doi:10.1504/IJCEELL.2007.013231

Willmott, S., Pujol, J. P., & Cortés, U. (2004). On Exploiting Agent Technology in the Design of Peer-to-Peer Applications. In *Proceedings from the 3rd International Workshop on Agents and Peer-to-Peer Computing*, (pp. 98-107). New York.

WS-BPEL. (2007). Web Services Business Process Execution Language Version 2.0, OASIS. Retrieved March 15, 2009, from http://docs.oasis-open.org/wsbpel/2.0/wsbpel-v2.0.pdf

XPDL. (2008). *XPDL support and resources Web site*. Retrieved June 28, 2009, from http://www.wfmc.org/xpdl.html

Yan, J., Yang, Y., Kowalczyk, R., & Nguyen, X. T. (2005). A Service Workflow Management Framework Based on Peer-to-Peer and Agent Technologies. In *Proceedings of the 5th international Conference on Quality Software*, (pp. 373-382). Melbourne, Australia.

Zhao, Z., Belloum, A., De Laat, C., Adriaans, P., & Hertzberger, B. (2007). Using Jade agent framework to prototype an e-Science workflow bus. In *Proceedings of the 7th IEEE international Symposium on Cluster Computing and the Grid*, (pp. 655-660). Rio de Janeiro, Brazil.

Zimmermann, R., Winkler, S., & Bodendorf, F. (2006). Supply Chain Event Management with Software Agents. In Kirn, S., Herzog, O., Lockemann, P., & Spaniol, O. (Eds.), *Multiagent Engineering - Theory and Applications in Enterprises* (pp. 157–175). Berlin, Germany: Springer.

Chapter 3
Adaptive Ensemble Multi-Agent Based Intrusion Detection Model

Tarek Helmy*
King Fahd University of Petroleum and Minerals, Saudi Arabia

ABSTRACT

The system that monitors the events occurring in a computer system or a network and analyzes the events for sign of intrusions is known as intrusion detection system. The performance of the intrusion detection system can be improved by combing anomaly and misuse analysis. This chapter proposes an ensemble multi-agent-based intrusion detection model. The proposed model combines anomaly, misuse, and host-based detection analysis. The agents in the proposed model use rules to check for intrusions, and adopt machine learning algorithms to recognize unknown actions, to update or create new rules automatically. Each agent in the proposed model encapsulates a specific classification technique, and gives its belief about any packet event in the network. These agents collaborate to determine the decision about any event, have the ability to generalize, and to detect novel attacks. Empirical results indicate that the proposed model is efficient, and outperforms other intrusion detection models.

INTRODUCTION

Heavy reliance on the Internet has greatly increased the potential damage that can be inflicted by remote attacks launched over the Internet. It is difficult to prevent such attacks by security policies, firewalls, or other mechanisms. The computer system and the applications always contain unknown weak-nesses or bugs attackers continually exploit them. Intrusion Detection Systems (IDS) are designed to detect attacks, which inevitably occur despite security precautions. A powerful IDS is flexible enough to detect novel attacks (i.e. it has the ability to generalize). The accuracy of the IDS depends on the false positive rate and the false negative rate measuring criteria. False positive rate calculates the rate of events that are considered to be intrusions where they are in fact normal events. However,

DOI: 10.4018/978-1-61520-973-6.ch003

false negative rate measures the rate of intrusions that are considered to be normal where they are in fact intrusion events.

Signature based Intrusion Detection (SID) uses specific known patterns of suspicious behavior to detect subsequent similar patterns, such patterns are called signatures. A good example for SID is a signature that can be as simple as a specific pattern that matches a portion of a network packet. For instance, packet header content signatures can indicate unauthorized actions. Once an intrusion action is detected, it triggers an alert or takes the initiative to do the proper action against the source of the attack (i.e. forward the traffic back to its source). The main disadvantage of this type of detection is that it cannot detect new signature attacks. It suffers also from the problem of signature updating. Snort is a well known example of SID (Roesch, 1999) on the other hand, Anomaly based Intrusion Detection (AID) identifies the normal usage behavior in advance and anything that does not match such behavior will be considered as suspicious actions. AID has the ability to generalize and to detect novel anomalies but cannot determine if the anomaly is caused by intrusive behavior or not. Hence, it generates higher false rate. USAID is an example of AID (Zhuowei et. al., 2005).

Several machine learning paradigms including Neural Networks (NN) (Mukkamala et. al., 2003), Linear Genetic Programming (LGP) (Mukkamala et. al., 2004), Support Vector Machines (SVM) (Mukkamala et. al., 2004), Bayesian Networks (BN) (Feng et. al., 2009), Multivariate Adaptive Regression Splines (MARS) (Mukkamala et. al., 2004), Decision Tree (DT) (Sandhya et. al., 2007), and Fuzzy Inference Systems (FISs) (Shah et. al., 2004) have been investigated for the design of the IDS.

The adaptivety of the IDS is a powerful feature that can lead the system to generalize and to detect novel attacks. By doing so, detection rate will increase, and the user's intension will be minimized. In this chapter, we propose an adaptive ensemble multi-agent-based intrusion detection model. In the proposed model, several agents are used in which each will encapsulate a classification algorithm. Based on the combined results generated from those agents, it is going to be decided whether a specific event in a network is an intrusion or not. The agent will also decide when to make a progress towards the adaptation. The rest of this chapter is organized as follows: Section 2 gives a brief overview of the related work. Section 3 elucidates the overview of the proposed framework architecture and specification. Section 4 describes the experimental dataset. The details of the implementation, the experimental results, and the performance comparison with other models are presented in Section 5. Finally, the conclusion and future work directions are outlined in Section 6.

RELATED WORK

A review of many alternative approaches to Intrusion Detection (ID) is available in (Bishop et. al., 1997). The most common approach to ID, often called "signature verification," detects previously seen, known, attacks by looking for an invariant signature left by these attacks. This signature may be found either in host-based audit records on a victim machine or in the stream of the network packets sent to a victim and captured by a "sniffer" which stores all important packets for on-line or future examination. The Network Security Monitor (NSM) was an early SID system that found attacks by searching for keywords in network traffic captured using a sniffer. Early versions of the NSM (Heberlein, 1995) were the foundation for many commercial IDS including NetRanger (Cisco, 1998) and NID (Lawrence Laboratory, 1998). These types of systems are popular because one sniffer can monitor traffic to many workstations and the computation required to reconstruct network sessions and search for keywords is not excessive. In practice, these systems can have high false-alarm rates because it is often difficult to select keywords by hand, which successfully detect real attacks while not creating false alarms for normal traffic. In addition, these SIDs must be updated frequently to detect new attacks as they are discovered.

In (Sandhya et. al., 2007), different approaches for ID techniques are presented. Statistical approaches compare the recent behavior of a user of a computer system with the observed behavior and any significant deviation is considered as an intrusion. This approach requires construction of a model for normal user's behavior. Any user's behavior that deviates significantly from this normal behavior is flagged as an intrusion. Intrusion Detection Expert System (IDES) (Lunt et. al., 1992) exploited the statistical approach for the detection of intruders. IDES maintains profiles, which are the description of a subject's normal behavior with respect to a set of ID measures. Profiles are updated periodically, thus allowing the system to learn new behavior as the users alter their behavior. These profiles are used to compare the user's behavior and informing significant deviation from them as intrusions. IDES also uses the expert system concept to detect misuse intrusions. The advantage of this approach is that, it adaptively learns the behavior of the users, which is thus potentially more sensitive than human experts. This system has several disadvantages, i.e. the system can be trained for certain behavior gradually making the abnormal behavior as normal, which may make the intruders undetected (Lunt et. al., 1993).

The model-based approach attempts to model intrusions at a higher level of abstraction than audit trail records. The objective is to build scenario models that represent the characteristic behavior of intrusions. This allows administrators to generate their representation of the penetration abstractly, which shifts the burden of determining what audit records are part of a suspect sequence to the expert system. This technique differs from the current rule-based expert system techniques, which simply attempt to pattern match audit re-

cords to expert rules. The model-based approach of (Garvey, Lunt, 1991) consists of three parts, namely, anticipator, planner and interpreter. The anticipator generates the next set of behaviors to be verified in the audit trail based on the current active models and passes these sets to the planner. The planner determines how the hypothesized behavior is reflected in the audit data and translates it into a system-dependent audit trail match. The interpreter then searches for this data in the audit trail. The system collects the information in this manner until a threshold is reached, and then it signals an intrusion attempt. Some of the drawbacks are that the intrusion patterns must always occur in the behavior it is looking for and patterns for intrusion must always be distinguishable from normal behavior and also easily recognizable.

SVM are learning machines that plot the training vectors in high-dimensional feature space, labeling each vector by its class. SVMs classify data by determining a set of support vectors, which are members of the set of training inputs that outline a hyper plane in the feature space. SVM have proven to be a good candidate for ID because of their speed. SVM are scalable as they are relatively insensitive to the number of data points. Therefore the classification complexity does not depend on the dimensionality of the feature space; hence, they can potentially learn a larger set of patterns and scale better than NN (Salameh, 2004).

Neuro-Fuzzy (NF) computing combines fuzzy inference with NN (Abraham et. al., 2001), (Salameh, 2004). Knowledge expressed in the form of linguistic rules can be used to build a FIS. For building a FIS, the user has to specify the fuzzy sets, fuzzy operators and the knowledge base. Similarly for constructing an ANN for an application, the user needs to specify the architecture and the learning algorithm. An analysis reveals that the drawbacks pertaining to these approaches are complementary and therefore it is natural to consider building an integrated system combining these two concepts. While the learning capability is an advantage from the viewpoint of FIS, the formation of linguistic rule base is an advantage from the viewpoint of ANN.

MARS is an innovative approach that automates the building of accurate predictive models for continuous and binary-dependent variables. It excels at finding optimal variable transformations and interactions, and the complex data structure that often hide in high-dimensional data. An IDS based on MARS technology is proposed in (Mukkamala et. al., 2004).

LGP is a variant of the conventional Genetic Programming (GP) technique that acts on linear genomes. Its main characteristics in comparison to tree-based GP lies in the fact that computer programs are evolved at the machine code level, using lower level representations for the individuals. This can tremendously hasten up the evolution process as, no matter how an individual is initially represented. It always has to be represented as a piece of machine code finally, as fitness evaluation requires physical execution of the individuals. An LGP-based IDS is presented in (Mukkamala et. al., 2004).

In (Chebrolu et. al., 2005) different important features of building IDS are examined where they are computationally efficient and effective. Then, they used Bayesian networks and regression tree for classification process. In addition, they used the ensemble of both of three classifiers to obtain the overall higher performance. The authors in (Zhi-Song et. al., 2003) investigated the problem using the NN and C4.5 decision trees to model the intrusive behavior. As reported in (Zhi-Song et. al., 2003), NN cannot detect both User to Root (U2R) and Remote to User (R2U) types of attacks. Thus, they used also C4.5 decision tree together with the NN as hybrid model to model misuse detection.

In (Xiang, Lim, 2005), the authors proposed a multi-level hybrid classifier in which IDS uses a combination of tree classifier and clustering algorithms. In (Vaibhav et. al., 2007), a Probabilistic Agent-based Intrusion Detection (PAID) system is used. It consists of collaborating agents in which each can perform a specific ID task. The agents in this model are also able to share believes.

In (Sandhya et. al., 2007), two hybrid approaches for modeling IDS are used. DT and SVM are combined as a hierarchical hybrid intelligent system model and an ensemble approach combining the base classifiers. In our work, we are proposing an adaptive multi-agent approach with ensemble classifier. Agents provide an automated response, have the ability to continuously learn and adapt over time, which make them very attractive to be implemented in system where a lot of user's intension is required.

THE PROPOSED ENSEMBLE FRAMEWORK

Empirical observations show that different classifiers provide complementary information about the patterns to be classified. The idea is not to rely on a single classifier for decision on an intrusion; instead information from different individual classifiers is combined to take the final decision, which is popularly known as the ensemble approach. The effectiveness of the ensemble approach depends on the accuracy and diversity of the base classifiers.

The proposed model consists of four predictor agents and a classifier agent. The data sniffer sniffs packets from the network. Then it sends a summery about each packet to the predictor agents. Each predictor agent generates a belief about that packet and sends its belief to the classifier agent. The classifier agent receives the beliefs about the specific event. If the event is an intrusion, then it logs the event and sends its feedback to the sender agents to update their knowledge. The architecture of the proposed ensemble approach is depicted in Figure 1. We used the highest scored class as the final output among the base classifier outputs. In the model, Bayes agent has the highest trust factor. According to the performance on the training data, each classifier is assigned different weights. Using these weights and the outputs of the classifiers, scores were calculated. For different classes each classifier has different weights depending on their performance on the training data. So for particular data records if all of them have different opinions, their scores are considered and the highest score is declared as the actual output of the ensemble approach.

Kumar in [19] lists shortcomings of IDS and provides a list of the desirable features in the optimal IDS. We tried to embed most of the following features in the proposed framework.

- **Generic Architecture:** It specifies a generic architecture for the IDS and classifies its components.
- **Efficiency:** A distributed multi-agent system obtains audit data at the appropriate levels and distributes intrusion detection effort.
- **Portability:** IDSs have tended to be developed with an orientation to an organization's security policy. In a different sense, portability of the IDS with respect to operating systems and computer architecture is also an important issue. JADE and Java, two portable languages, have been used to provide portability for the proposed IDS model.
- **Upgradeability:** Any IDS based on a component-based architecture such as that available in the agent-based system satisfies the upgradeability and enhancement concern. New features can easily be added to such system.
- **Maintenance:** Maintaining and updating the learned knowledge used by components of the IDS would depend on the architecture of the components.

Decision Tree C4.5 Agent

A Decision Tree (DT) consists of nodes, leaves and edges. A node of a DT specifies an attribute by which the data is to be partitioned. Each node has a number of edges, which are labeled according to a possible value of edges and a possible value of the attribute in the parent node. An edge connects either two nodes or a node and a leaf. Leaves are labeled with a decision value for categorization of the data. To classify an unknown object, one starts at the root of the DT and follows the branch

Figure 1. Architecture of the proposed intrusion detection model

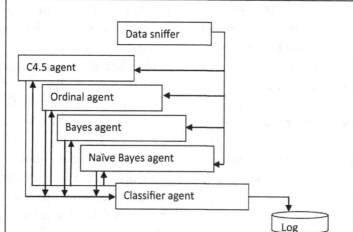

indicated by the outcome of each test until a leaf node is reached. The name of the class at the leaf node is the resulting classification.

Induction of the DT (ID3) (Quinlan, 1986) is one of the classification algorithms in data mining. The classification algorithm is inductively learned to construct a model from the pre-classified dataset. Inductive learning means making general assumptions from the specific examples in order to use those assumptions to classify unseen data. The inductively learned model of classification algorithm is known as classifier. Classifier may be viewed as mapping from a set of attributes to a particular class. Data items are defined by the values of their attributes and X is the vector of their values $\{x_1, x_2, ..., x_n\}$, where the value is either numeric or nominal. Attribute space is defined as the set containing all possible attribute vectors. The main issue is to select the attributes which best divides the data items into their classes. According to the values of these attributes, the data items are partitioned. This process is recursively applied to each partitioned subset of the data items. The process terminates when all the data items in the current subset belong to the same class. ID3 uses the training data, which is described in terms of the attributes. The main problem here is deciding the attribute, which will best partition the data into various classes. The ID3 algorithm uses the information theory approach to solve this problem. Information theory uses the entropy Formula (1), which measures the impurity of data items. Entropy specifies the number of bits required to encode the classification of a data item. The value of entropy is small when the class distribution is uneven, that is when all the data items belong to one class. The entropy value is higher when the class distribution is more even, that is when the data items have more classes. Information gain is a measure on the utility of each attribute in classifying the data items. It is measured using the entropy value. Information gain measures the decrease of the weighted average impurity (entropy) of the attributes compared with the impurity of the complete set of data items.

$$\text{entropy } (T) = - \sum_{i=1}^{n} p_i \log_2 (p_i) \qquad (1)$$

- T represents the set of attributes available in the dataset.
- p_i is just the probability distribution of class *i*.

Now consider what happens if we partition the set on the basis of an input attribute X into subsets T_1, T_2, ..., T_n. The information needed to identify the class of an element of T is the weighted average of the information needed to identify the class of an element of each subset. In the context of building a decision tree, we are interested in how much information about the output attribute can be gained by knowing the value of an input attribute X. This is just the difference between the information needed to classify an element of T before knowing the value of X, H (T), and the information needed after partitioning the dataset T on the basis of knowing the value of X, H(X, T). The information gain due to attribute X for set T calculated using Formula 2. Therefore, the attributes with the largest information gain are considered as the most useful for classifying the data items.

$$\text{Gain } (X, T) = \text{entropy } (T) - \text{entropy } (X, T) \qquad (2)$$

The ID3 algorithm works by recursively applying the procedure above. We generate a decision tree using ID3 as follows (David S. 2004):

```
Algorithm ID3 (I, 0, T) {
/* I is the set of input attributes
* O is the output attribute
* T is a set of training data
*/
If (T is empty) {
Return a single node with the value
"Failure";
}
If (all records in T have the same value
for O) {
```

```
Return a single node with that value;
}
If (I is empty) {
Return a single node with the value of
the most frequent value of O in T;
}
Compute the information gain for each at-
tribute in I relative to T;
Let X be the attribute with largest
Gain(X, T) of the attributes in I;
Let {x_j| j=1, 2,.., m} be the values of
X;
Let {T_j| j=1, 2,.., m} be the subsets of
T when T is partitioned according the
value of X;
Return a tree with the root node labeled
X and edges labeled x_1, x_2,.., x_m, where
the edge go to the trees ID3 (I-{X}, O,
T_1), ID3 (I-{X}, O, T_2),.., ID3 (I-{X}, O,
T_m);
}
```

C4.5 (Quinlan, 1993) is an extension of the basic ID3 algorithm. C4.5 handles continuous attributes and is able to choose an appropriate attribute selection measure. It also deals with missing attribute values and improves computation efficiency. C4.5 builds the tree from a set of data items using the best attribute to test in order to divide the data items into subsets and then it uses the same procedure on each subset recursively. The best attribute to divide the subset at each stage is selected using the concept of information gain. For nominal valued attributes, a branch for each value of the attribute is formed, whereas for numeric valued attributes, a threshold is found, thus forming two branches.

Ordinal Class Agent

Classical classifiers cannot detect class order among different values in the data. Thus, ordinal class classifier agent takes ordering values into account while building the classifier. In this model, the ordinal class agent has been implemented based on the decision tree C4.5. By applying that in conjunction with a decision tree learner, the ordinal class agent outperforms the classical approach, which treats the class values as an unordered set.

Bayes Agent

A Bayesian Network (BN) is a graphic representation of the joint probability distribution function over a set of variables. The network structure is represented as a Directed Acyclic Graph (DAG) in which each node corresponds to a random variable and each edge indicates a dependent relationship between connected variables. Each variable (node) in a BN is associated with a Conditional Probability Table (CPT), which enumerates the conditional probabilities for this variable given all the combinations of its parents' values (F. Jesen 2001). Therefore, for a BN, the DAG captures causal relationships among random variables, and CPTs quantify these relationships. Since individual events in an attack can be represented as nodes and the causal relations between events can be modeled as edges in Bayesian networks, we use a BN as our inference model. A BN model is capable of learning causal relationships from an existing dataset and predicting the consequences of an intervention in the problem domain. A BN is an ideal model for combining prior knowledge with new data and inferring posterior knowledge. In the presented model the Bayes agent uses BN for detecting the intrusion, and K2 algorithm for learning. The K2 algorithm defines a set of variables of interest to build DAG based on the calculation of a local score (Barber D. 2007). K2 is initialized with a single node, and it continues to incrementally add connections with other nodes as long as they increase the whole probability of the network structure. For the inference, the Junction Tree Algorithm has been used (Jemili F., et. al. 2007). Fing in (Fing et. al., 2009) shows how to model an intrusion goal prediction system by using BN.

Naive Bayes Agent

Naïve Bayes is a probabilistic model and can be considered as a special form of BN that is widely used for classification. The name Naive comes from the assumption that all variable are mutually independent of each other. Thus, only the variances of the variables for each class need to be determined and not the whole covariance matrix. Abstractly, the probability model for a classifier is a conditional model $p(C|F_1,\ldots,F_n)$ over a dependent class variable C with a small number of outcomes or *classes*, conditional on several feature variables F_1 through F_n. The problem is that if the number of features n is large or when a feature can take on a large number of values, then basing such a model on probability tables is infeasible. Now the "naive" conditional independence assumptions come into play: assume that each feature F_i is conditionally independent of every other feature F_j for j≠i. This means that $p(F_i|C,F_j)=p(F_i|C)$ and so the joint model can be expressed as Following.

$$p(C\,|\,F_{1,\ldots,}F_n) = p(C)\prod_{i=1}^{n} p(Fi|C)$$

Where, C is a class variable and F is a set of features. The inference time is linear order in the number of components, and the number of query variables. This means that under the above independence assumptions, the conditional distribution over the class variable C can be expressed as following:

$$p(C\,|\,F_{1,\ldots,}F_n) = \frac{1}{Z}\,p(C)\prod_{i=1}^{n} p(F_i\,|\,C)$$

Where Z (the evidence) is a scaling factor dependent only on $F_1,\ldots,F_n$. Models of this form are much more manageable, since they factor into a so-called *class prior $p(C)$* and independent probability distributions $p(F_i|C)$. In the presented model the Naïve Bayes agent uses Naïve assumption for detecting the intrusion.

EXPERIMENTAL DATASET

The famous KDD Cup 1999 intrusion dataset has been used in the experiments. This dataset has 41 features as shown in Table 1. The set of features can be grouped into 3 sets. The first set is numbered form 1 to 9 in Table 1 and is concerned about the basic features of an individual TCP connection. The second set, which is represented by the features numbered from 10 to 22, is content features within a connection suggested by domain knowledge. The rest of the features are those that are concerned with the traffic within a window of two seconds. The dataset contains 24 attack types. These attacks fall into four main categories:

1. **Denial of service (DOS):** In this type of attack, an attacker makes some computing or memory resources too busy or too full to handle legitimate requests, or denies legitimate users access to a machine. *Examples are Apache2, Mail bomb, Process table, Smurf.*

2. **Remote to user (R2L):** In this type of attack, an attacker who does not have an account on a remote machine sends packets to that machine over a network and exploits some vulnerability to gain local access as a user of that machine. *Examples are Dictionary, Ftp write, Guest, Send mail.*

3. **User to root (U2R):** In this type of attacks, an attacker starts out with access to a normal user account on the system, and is able to exploit system vulnerabilities to gain root access to the system. *Examples are Eject, Load module, Perl, Fdformat.*

4. **Probing:** In this type of attacks, an attacker scans a network of computers to gather

Table 1. Data attributes

Num	attribute name
1	duration
2	protocol_type
3	service
4	flag
5	src_bytes
6	dst_bytes
7	land
8	wrong_fragment
9	urgent
10	hot
11	num_failed_logins
12	logged_in
13	num_compromised
14	root_shell
15	su_attempted
16	num_root
17	num_file_creations
18	num_shells
19	num_access_files
20	num_outbound_cmds
21	is_host_login
22	is_guest_login
23	count
24	srv_count
25	serror_rate
26	srv_serror_rate
27	rerror_rate
28	srv_rerror_rate
29	same_srv_rate
30	diff_srv_rate
31	srv_diff_host_rate
32	dst_host_count
33	dst_host_srv_count
34	dst_host_same_srv_rate
35	dst_host_diff_srv_rate
36	dst_host_same_src_port_rate
37	dst_host_srv_diff_host_rate
38	dst_host_serror_rate
39	dst_host_srv_serror_rate
40	dst_host_rerror_rate
41	dst_host_srv_rerror_rate

information or find known vulnerabilities. An attacker with a map of machines and services that are available on a network can use this information to look for exploits. *Examples are Ipsweep, Mscan, Saint, Satan.*

Besides the four different types of attacks mentioned above, we also have to detect the normal class. The experiments have two phases, namely, training and testing phases. Thus, the dataset is divided into training dataset with 10178 records as shown in Table 2 and testing dataset with 18967 records as shown in Table 3. The testing dataset contains new attacks that are not used in the training dataset. In the training phase the system constructs a model using the training dataset to give maximum generalization accuracy (accuracy on unseen data). The testing dataset is passed through the constructed model to detect the intrusion in the testing phase. The experiments were carried out on AMD workstation with CPU speed 2 GHz and 2.5 GB of RAM running Windows XP.

IMPLEMENTATION AND EXPERIMENTAL RESULTS

Implementation

The aim is to design and develop an intelligent intrusion detection model that is accurate, low in false alarms, not easily cheated by small variations in patterns, adaptive, and be of real time performance. The proposed intrusion detection model has been implemented using Sun's Java Development Kit version 1.6 and JADE [10] (Java Agent DEvelopment Framework). JADE is an open source software framework fully implemented in Java language. JADE is a FIPA (the Foundation for Intelligent Physical Agents) complaint specifications. JADE platform supports peer-to-peer communication and distribution. Java was chosen as the development language because of its platform independence, security, and speed of development. Java's plat-

Table 2. Distribution of the training dataset

Class label	Attack type	Number of instances
A	Normal	3000
B	DOS	3000
C	Probe	3000
D	U2R	52
E	R2L	1126
Total		10178

Table 3. Distribution of the testing dataset with novel attacks

Class label	Attack type	Number of instances
A	Normal	5000
B	DOS	5000
C	Probe	4166
D	U2R	70
E	R2L	4731
Total		18967

Table 4. Performance of each classifier alone

	Bayes Net	Naïve Bayes	Ordinal class	C4.5
A	98.5	94.5	98.88	99.2
B	95.6	79.14	96.96	97.2
C	81.56	89.58	83.32	83.29
D	72.86	62.86	34.29	37.14
E	36.55	3.44	23.84	20.78

form independence has allowed us to compile and execute completely shared code on any one of several platforms including commercial operating systems and free operating systems.

Experiential Results

In order to have a good prediction performance, the IDS should be able to correctly differentiate between intrusions and legitimate actions in a system environment. Several experiments have been conducted to make a consistent evaluation of the system's performance. Four experiments have been conducted. In the first experiment, we evaluated the performance of each classifier agent individually. Table 4 shows the performance of using each classifier alone.

In the second experiment, we tested the proposed model without adaptation and the performance results are shown in Table 5.

In the third experiment, the adaptation feature is enabled. We obtained the performance results that are shown in Table 6. The classifier agent uses majority voting classification method. The order of attacks sniffed has an effect on the accuracy of detection. In this experiment, we randomly shuffled the order of attacks.

Clearly, the overall performance of the proposed model with adaptation feature is better than it is without the adaptation feature. Finally, we conducted an experiment to compare the performance of the proposed model with other IDSs. Table 7 shows the result of comparison.

Table 5. Performance of the proposed model without adaptation

	A	B	C	D	E	%
A	4930	8	23	10	29	98.6
B	136	4781	66	13	4	95.62
C	577	40	3418	43	88	82.04
D	8	0	0	50	12	71.43
E	2792	0	138	155	1646	34.79

Table 6. Performance of the proposed model with adaptation

	A	B	C	D	E	%
A	4930	14	22	8	26	98.6
B	132	4758	89	18	3	95.16
C	549	16	3416	66	74	83.08
D	8	0	0	50	12	71.43
E	2593	0	138	88	1912	40.41

Table 7. Comparison of the proposed model with other models

Category	MADAM ID	3-Level Tree Classifier	Multiple Level Hybrid Classifier	Hybrid Intelligent System	Proposed Model
DOS	24.3	37.44	83.59	100	95.16
Probe	96.7	88.54	70.6	99.9	83.08
U2R	81.8	41.94	58.06	68	71.43
R2L	5.9	0.1	28.53	97.2	40.41

CONCLUSION AND FUTURE WORK

In the proposed model, we investigated modeling the IDS using different classifiers and different feature sets. We were being able to obtain an excellent result especially for the U2R type of attacks compared to the result of other models. We explored the effect of adaptation feature. Results show higher accuracy detection rate for adaptive model than the normal one. We were being able to minimize the false negative rate from 18.5% to 17.3%. Although, the false negative rate is high due to the dataset selection. If an excellent dataset is chosen, the false negative rate will be decreased. As a future work, an extension of the proposed model is possible by using more agents in the ensemble approach that will result in better detection rate. The next direction also is to test the model with new type of attacks and to analyze its behavior in such conditions.

ACKNOWLEDGMENT

I would like to thank King Fahd University of Petroleum and Minerals for providing the computing facilities. Special thanks to anonymous reviewers for their insightful comments and feedback. Thanks extended to Mr. David Birkett for his help in proofreading the chapter and to Mr. El-Naser for his help in running the experiments.

REFERENCES

Abraham, A. (2001). Neuro-fuzzy systems: state-of-the-art modeling techniques, connectionist models of neurons, learning processes, and artificial intelligence. In Jose, M., & Alberto, P. (Eds.), *Lecture Notes in Computer Science* (*Vol. 2084*, pp. 269–276). Springer.

Barber, D. (2007). Machine Learning: A Probabilistic Approach, pg.107, 2007.

Bishop, M., Cheung, S., Wee, C., Frank, J., Hoagland, J., & Samorodin, S. (1997). The Threat from the Net. *IEEE Spectrum*, *34*(8), 56–63. doi:10.1109/6.609475

Chebrolu, S., Abraham, A., & Thomas, J. P. (2005). Feature deduction and ensemble design of intrusion detection systems. *Elsevier Computers & Security*, *24*(4), 295–307.

Cisco Systems Inc. (1998). *NetRanger Intrusion Detection System Technical Overview*. Retrieved from David S. (2004). *The ID3 Decision Tree Algorithm*. MONASH UNIVERSITY http://www.csse.monash.edu.au/courseware/cse5230/2004/assets/decisiontreesTute.pdf

Cup, K. D. D. (1999). *Datasets*. Retrieved from http://www.acm.org/sigs/sigkdd/kddcup/index.php?section=1999&method=data

Eibe, F., & Mark, H. (2001). A Simple Approach to Ordinal Classification (Lecture Notes in Computer Science). In *Proceedings of the 12th European Conference on Machine Learning* (Vol. 2167, pp. 145-156).

Feng, L., Wang, W., Zhu, L., & Zhang, Y. (2009). Predicting intrusion goal using dynamic Bayesian network with transfer probability estimation. *Journal of Network and Computer Applications, 32*(3), 721–732. doi:10.1016/j.jnca.2008.06.002

Garvey, T. D., & Lunt, T. F. (1991). *Model based intrusion detection.* In *Proceedings of the 14th national computer security conference* (pp. 372-385).

Heberlein, T. (1995, February). *Network Security Monitor (NSM) Final Report.* U.C. Davis. Retrieved from http://seclab.cs.ucdavis.edu/papers/NSM-final.pdf

JADE. (n.d.). *JADE.* Retrieved from http://jade.tilab.com/

Jemili, F., Zaghdoud, M., & Ahmed, M. (2007). *A Framework for an Adaptive Intrusion Detection System using Bayesian Network.* ISI IEEE.

Jesen, F. (2001). *Bayesian Networks and Decision Graphs.* New York, USA: Springer.

Kumar, S., & Spafford, E. H. (1995). Software architecture to support misuse intrusion detection. In *Proceedings of the 18th national information security conference* (pp. 194-204).

Lawrence Livermore National Laboratory. (1998). *Network Intrusion Detector (NID) Overview.* Retrieved from http://ciac.llnl.gov/cstc/nid/intro.html.

Lunt, T. (1993). Detecting intruders in computer systems. In *Proceedings of the conference on auditing and computer technology.*

Lunt, T., Tamaru, A., Gilham, F., Jagannath, R., Neumann, P., & Javitz, H. (1992). *A real-time intrusion detection expert system (IDES), (Final Technical Report). Computer Science Laboratory.* Menlo Park, CA: SRI International.

Mukkamala, S., Sung, A. H., & Abraham, A. (2003). Intrusion detection using ensemble of soft computing paradigms. In *Proceedings of the 3rd international conference on intelligent systems design and applications,* (pp. 239-248).

Mukkamala, S., Sung, A. H., & Abraham, A. (2004). Modeling intrusion detection systems using linear genetic programming approach. *Lecture Notes in Computer Science, 3029,* 633–642.

Mukkamala, S., Sung, A. H., Abraham, A., & Ramos, V. (2004). Intrusion detection systems using adaptive regression splines. In Seruca, I., Filipe, J., Hammoudi, S., Cordeiro, J. (eds.), *Proceedings of the 6th International Conference on Enterprise Information Systems,* (ICEIS'04), (vol. 3, pp. 26-33).

Peddabachigari, S., Abraham, A., Grosan, C., & Thomas, T. (2007). Modeling intrusion detection system using hybrid intelligent systems. *Journal of Network and Computer Applications, 20,* 114–132. doi:10.1016/j.jnca.2005.06.003

Quinlan, J. R. (1986). Induction of Decision Trees. *Machine Learning, 1,* 81–106. doi:10.1007/BF00116251

Quinlan, J. R. (1993). *C4.5: Programs for Machine Learning.* San Francisco: Morgan Kaufmann.

Roesch, M. (1999). Snort: lightweight intrusion detection for networks. In Proceedings of LISA99 (USENIX), (pp. 229-238).

Salameh, W. A. (2004). Detection of Intrusion Using Neural Networks. *Studies in Informatics and Control, 13*(2).

Sandhya, P., Ajith, A., Crina, G., & Johnson, T. (2007). Modeling intrusion detection system using hybrid intelligent system. *Elsevier Journal of Network and Computer Application, 30,* 114–132.

Shah, K., Dave, N., Chavan, S., Mukherjee, S., Abraham, A., & Sanyal, S. (2004). Adaptive neuro-fuzzy intrusion detection system. In *Proceedings of the IEEE International Conference on Information Technology: Coding and Computing* (ITCC'04), (vol. 1. pp 70-74).

Vaibhav, G., Csilla, F., & Marco, V. (2005). PAID: A Probabilistic Agent-Based Intrusion Detection System. *Elsevier Journal of Computers & Security*, *24*, 529–545.

Xiang, C., & Lim, S. M. (2005). Design of Multi-Level Hybrid Classifier for Intrusion Detection System. In IEEE proceedings of Machine Learning for Signal Processing Workshop (pp. 117-122).

Zhi-Song, P., Song-can, C., Gen-bao, H., & Dao-qiang, Z. (2003). Hybrid Neural Network and C4.5 for Misuse Detection. In *IEEE Proceedings of the second international Conference on Machine Learning and Cybernetics* (pp. 2463-2467).

Zhuowei, L., Amitabha, D., & Jianying, Z. (2005). Unifying Signature-Based and Anomaly-Based Intrusion Detection. In *Proceedings of Springer PAKDD LNAI # 3518* (pp. 702–712). USAID.

ENDNOTE

*   On leave from the College of Engineering, Department of Computers Engineering and Automatic Control, Tanta University, Egypt.

Chapter 4
Towards Automatic Service Composition within ARGUGRID

Nabeel Azam
InforSense Ltd., UK

Vasa Curcin
Imperial College London, UK

Li Guo
Imperial College London, UK

Moustafa Ghanem
InforSense Ltd., UK & Imperial College London, UK

ABSTRACT

Workflow systems play an important role in service-oriented computing as they provide an intuitive mechanism for orchestrating the execution of remote services. Constructing new workflows from raw services however, is not always a straight-forward task. It requires resolving many decisions including locating available services, determining which of them match the user requirements and also deciding how to compose them together into valid applications. Workflow construction activities can be simplified, or possibly even automated, by using a combination of semantic annotations and delegation of the decision making tasks to intelligent agents. Two key challenges arise when developing a practical system that attempts to address this vision. The first is elaborating the key properties of service workflows and the decisions that agents are required to assist in. This information is needed for designing and implementing the internals of the agent mind. The second is designing and implementing the run-time interfaces between the workflow system and the agent system to enable the exchange of information between them. This chapter describes our experience in addressing these two challenges and in developing a framework that simplifies the workflow creation process within the ARGUGRID project.

DOI: 10.4018/978-1-61520-973-6.ch004

INTRODUCTION

Motivation

Over the last decade the service-oriented computing paradigm has been advocated as a new model for developing Grid-based applications (Atkinson, 2005; Foster, 2002; Surridge, 2005; Talia, 2002). The concept builds on the notion of a "service" (e.g. Web Service or Grid Service) that provides a uniform and standardized interface to remote resources. These services are advertised by service providers and can be discovered and used by service requestors. Workflow systems play an important role within the paradigm. They provide the languages and execution mechanisms that enable users to orchestrate the execution of available services, compose them together to build applications and develop new aggregated services that can be used in further applications. Multi-agent systems can play an important role in assisting the users of such systems by providing them with decision making support.

In a service oriented world service providers host remote services and publish their location and properties in a service registry. By querying the registry, service requestors can discover and access these services. In addition to the description of the service functionality and its access methods, published service properties can also include information such as its execution costs (e.g. number of CPUs required), the price of accessing the service and so forth. In a traditional workflow system it is the human users (service requestors) who make the decisions about which services to use and in what sequence. In doing so they need to ensure that the costs and properties of the composed services meet their application requirements.

The process of orchestrating remote services is not a simple task, especially for those users who are not technical experts. Ideally, for such users many of the service selection and workflow construction decisions should be automated. The two key challenges that arise when designing an agent-based system to assist in this process are:

- Elaborating the properties of service workflows and associated decision making processes to the agent designer in order to assist in implementing the internals of the agent mind.
- Designing the middleware that interfaces between a workflow system and an agent system to support the exchange of information between them at run-time.

Addressing the above issues is typically tied to the characteristics of both the workflow system and agent system used. The work presented in this chapter is based on our experience in the ARGUGRID project (Curcin, 2006; Toni, 2008) which investigated the use of an argumentation-based multi-agent system to support service discovery and composition. Since many of the key principles are generic and could be applied easily to other systems, we focus on describing them in a system-independent fashion first before presenting the details of their implementation.

It should be noted that within the full ARGUGRID vision, agents can represent both service providers and requestors and are allowed to enter into negotiation on different service parameters. The discussion on agent negotiation is beyond the scope of this chapter and we focus primarily on exploring the issues relating to interfacing a workflow system to an intelligent agent representing a service requestor. The reader interested in the negotiation aspects of the ARGUGRID system is referred to the following publications: Bromuri (2009), Morge (2008) and Urovi (2008).

Chapter Layout

The remainder of this chapter is organized as follows: In the next section we introduce the necessary background on service oriented workflows with an emphasis on the role of semantic web technologies in simplifying their development. The aim is to highlight the key decisions that need to be addressed during the workflow authoring phase including service discovery, selection and composition. This is followed by a discussion on the key issues in service composition and workflow analysis. The aim is to identify some of the details that need to be addressed by an intelligent agent assisting in automatic workflow creation. We then provide a description of a generic architecture for run-time integration between workflow systems and multi-agent systems and describe how it has been implemented in the ARGUGRID project. A key focus is on the ArguBroker component that supports run-time translation between the representations used in the service-oriented computing and agent worlds. We also present a simple case study showing the functionality of the integrated system and provide a discussion on our experience in using it.

BACKGROUND

Service-Oriented Workflows

Informally, a workflow is a description of the steps required for executing particular real-world processes and the flow of information between them. Each step is defined by a set of activities that need to be conducted. Within a workflow, work (e.g. data or jobs) passes through the different steps in the specified order from start to finish, and the activities at each step are executed either by people or by system functions (e.g. computer programs). In the service oriented computing context, the individual steps in a workflow generally represent invocations of remote services.

A large number of workflow systems for coordinating remote services have been developed in the past decade. Examples include Taverna (Hull, 2006), Triana (Taylor, 2005), Kepler (Ludäscher, 2006), OMII-BPEL (Bradley, 2006) and Discovery Net (Ghanem, 2008), the academic predecessor

of the InforSense tool used in this paper. For a recent review and comparison of such systems the interested reader can consult Curcin (2008).

The generic concepts are similar across most workflow systems. In such systems a workflow is commonly represented as a directed graph where each node represents a task and arcs between nodes define the information flow and dependencies between these tasks. The workflows themselves are represented in an underlying workflow language. However, the workflows are typically developed using a visual front-end for graphically constructing the workflow graph. Once authored, the workflow is submitted by the user to a workflow engine that handles its execution including automatically invoking the remote services as well as coordinating the flow of data between them.

Within the InforSense system workflows are represented and stored using DPML - Discovery Process Markup Language - (Syed, 2002), an XML-based representation language for workflow graphs. It supports two types of information flow; Control Flow and Data Flow. *Control Flow* provides constructs for coordinating the control flow logic of a workflow and includes a range of control flow elements such as branching, synchronisation, conditional branching and looping. *Data Flow* provides a data flow model of computation where the output of one service is passed as input to another. The advantage of separating the two types of flow is that it provides a clean distinction between the focus of each set of operators or constructs. Figure 1 shows an example of a data flow coordinated by a loop control flow construct. A list of images is passed to the loop. The first image from the list is taken and the pollution co-ordinates are mapped onto the image. The pollution hotspots are identified and recorded. The processing loop then takes the next image from the list and repeats the process until the end of the list is reached. The results are combined and passed to the next node which generates a report.

As shown in Figure 2, each node in a DPML workflow has a number of input and output ports for receiving and transmitting data and also a number of run-time parameters. When services are composed, each arc in the graph represents a connection from an output port, namely the tail of the arc, to an input port, namely the head of the arc. A port is connected if there are one or more arcs from/to that port. Metadata of the node describes the input and output ports, including the type of data that can be passed to the component, and parameters of the service that a user might control. The metadata is also used for the verification of workflows to ensure a meaningful chaining of components. A connection between an output port of one node and the input port of another is valid only if the data types are compatible, which is strictly enforced by the system, i.e. if the types are incompatible the system prevents a connection being made between the two nodes.

Semantic Workflows

In a broad sense, workflow authoring may be considered as a form of simple programming; one where calls to remote services from within a workflow are similar to remote procedure calls from within a traditional program. As with traditional program development, when developing more complex workflows become possible further programming abstractions are typically needed to simplify the user's role in developing them.

Figure 1. An example of a generic workflow consisting of control and data flow constructs

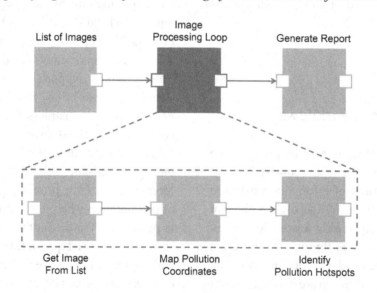

Figure 2. The anatomy of a service node in the data flow layer in the InforSense system

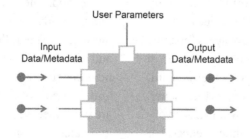

One approach for providing such program-ming abstractions builds on the notion of seman-tically-described workflow nodes, which are not associated with any particular existing service. Semantic annotations describe the node's desired functionality (what computation it should per-form and the properties of its input/output ports) and also any other desired non-functional prop-erties (e.g. execution time performance or price limitations) on its implementation. A semantic workflow is then developed as a composition of a number of semantically-described nodes, thereby enabling the construction and refinement of the overall workflow logic in a top-down manner. An example of a workflow system that provided early support for semantic workflow authoring is the Kepler workflow system (Berkley, 2005).

Typically, semantic workflow descriptions can be defined at different levels of abstraction:

- At the highest level, the semantic work-flow level, the user defines what the over-all workflow is to achieve.
- Moving top-down, the next level is the semantic node level which is used to de-fine the sub tasks or intermediate steps re-quired to achieve the overall task and the order in which they must occur.
- The lowest semantic level requires de-scribing the properties, inputs and outputs for each of the semantic nodes.

Before a semantic workflow can be executed, each semantically described node must be re-placed by, or bound to, an existing remote service. This process typically requires consulting, or searching through, a service registry. Using only higher levels of abstraction will typically provide a wider search space when selecting services to implement the workflow. Using more detailed descriptions will typically restrict the number of matching services. Note that priorities or rank-ings can also be added to service descriptions to guide the search for specific results, i.e. finding the solution that is the cheapest, or the solution that will provide the quickest results. Also note that selected services must respect other con-straints defined by the workflow structure itself. For example, for each workflow node, the input and output types of the real service implementing it must be matched to the node description to ensure that a viable executable workflow graph can be produced.

Semantic Service Discovery and Matchmaking

In order to simplify matchmaking between semantic service descriptions and services pub-lished in registries, a range of existing Semantic Web Service technologies can be used. The term Semantic Web Services is used to denote services that are self-described and amenable to automatic discovery, composition and invocation. Two ma-jor projects are currently tackling this challenge. The first is OWL-S, a joint consortium that is defining ontology for semantic markup of web services. The second is WSMO consortium. Both are based on Ontology Web Language (OWL), an RDF-based representation of ontologies. Both efforts provide the basic mechanisms and controlled vocabularies for formalizing service descriptions including:

- **Service functionality:** essentially what the service does or its capability, i.e. providing a description of the high-level functionality of the service itself.
- **Service inputs and outputs:** a descrip-tion of the input and output data types, their names and any metadata associated with them.
- **Service invocation mechanisms:** details of the access/invocation interface and the service bindings.
- **Quality-of-Service properties:** e.g. de-tails of the properties for each service such as performance and price.

To support the selection between multiple services that match the user requirements, a wide range of metrics can generally be defined for evaluating how close a match is. For example, in addition to non-functional properties such as time and price metrics, fidelity metrics can also be defined to score how well the functional properties of a service match the user's requirements.

It should be noted that non-functional properties can generally be negotiated between service providers and service requestors. For example, a user may be willing to pay a higher price so that the service can be executed in less time. Similarly, the user may also be willing to trade-off one of the functional properties (e.g. quality of results returned by a service) with other functional or non-functional properties.

A final important concept governing the life cycle of service selection and usage is that of SLAs (Service Level Agreements). SLAs (Boniface, 2007) typically state important non-functional properties of a service regarding the terms and conditions that surround the execution. SLAs are typically agreed between the service provider and service requestor before the service is used. In some cases they can be tailored by the service provider for each user independently.

Towards Automatic Service Composition

Figure 3 provides a high-level view of the process of translating a semantic workflow into a concrete workflow consisting of known services. In this simplified example the end user's aim is to retrieve a satellite image of London with a pollution map applied over it. This is represented as two steps, retrieving a satellite image and applying a pollution map. Each of these steps is represented by a semantic node with an arc showing the ordering and flow of information.

For the first step, the property is that the location must be London. There are no inputs and the user would like the results in JPG format. The second step has a property that states the pollution map must show the average pollution densities for last month. The resulting image must be in JPG format and the input must also be in JPG format to meet the type matching restrictions for producing a viable workflow.

Based on these descriptions, services can be searched for in semantic registries. In the example shown, the closest matching and most suitable Get Image and Pollution Map services are returned. The matching services are chained together with the output from Get Image connected to the input

Figure 3. Example showing translation of a semantic workflow into a concrete workflow

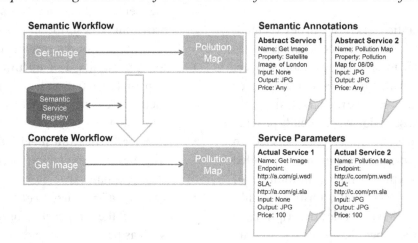

for Pollution Map to create a simple concrete workflow, and their SLAs are also returned to the user.

SERVICE COMPOSITION MODELS

Key Challenges

A number of challenges arise when refining and mapping semantically annotated workflows into concrete implementations. Many of these challenges relate to the properties of service composition constraints and models. An intelligent agent, or any other automatic system, assisting in workflow authoring must be able to address these challenges. Two of the challenges we focus on in this chapter are:

1. **Reasoning about the composition of services through metrics:** ensuring that the metrics for the complete workflow (e.g. overall execution time, price or fidelity) meet the user requirements. Moreover, the agent should ideally be able to suggest and use optimizations that would meet these requirements (e.g. minimizing cost or execution time).
2. **Reasoning about service compatibility:** ensuring that composed services have matching outputs and inputs. In cases where the data types for available services do not match, the agent would ideally be required to locate and add automatically any existing data type conversion operators that could resolve the incompatibility.

Further challenges also exist, for example the agent must ensure that an automatically generated implementation is safe with respect to execution, avoiding illegal conditions such as deadlocks and live locks. Similarly, the security policies that exist on data may impose further restrictions on the validity of the workflows. These issues are not addressed in this chapter. The interested reader can refer to examples of relevant analysis methods and tools supporting them in Curcin (2009).

Service Composition Metrics

The decision making process on service composition must include guidance on how service selection metrics can be calculated for workflows or workflow fragments. In many cases such guidance can be provided as formulae together with rules on how they can be used. In general, this is based on modelling the metric for each service based on its parameters and then aggregating the metrics based on the structure of the workflow pattern used.

For example, the overall execution time for a workflow fragment, *ws*, comprising a sequence of *n* services can be given as:

$$T_{ws} = \sum_{i=1}^{n} (I(s_i) + E(s_i) + O(s_i))$$

Where $E(s_i)$, $I(s_i)$ and $O(s_i)$ are functions representing the execution time for executing the services, passing inputs to the service, and collecting data from its outputs respectively. These models can be further developed to capture the dependency on the service parameters, e.g. input data sizes, number of processors used, etc. Note that the above formula models a general case where each service executes on a different server; therefore data is uploaded and downloaded from each server during workflow execution. When two consecutive services execute on the same server the respective output and input execution costs may be dramatically reduced since data resides on the same server. Inclusion of such information in the agent's reasoning mechanism would enable it to make more informed and practical choices.

Similar formulae and rules can also be provided for common workflow fragment templates, e.g. parallel workflow branches. For example, the execution time for a workflow fragment comprising of two branches executing in parallel depends on where the services are executed. If the services are executed on different servers, the overall execution time is the maximum execution time for each branch; however, if the execution of the services is forced to occur sequentially on the same server, e.g. due to lack of resources, then the overall execution time would more appropriately follow the formula for a sequential execution model.

Composite fidelity and price metrics can also be computed in a similar manner first by modelling them for each service invocation based on its parameters, and then aggregated for all services in a workflow. Examples of how these can be calculated are provided by Cardoso (2002).

Type Matching Models

In many cases when a user attempts to sequentially compose a number of services together, one service may not necessarily directly connect to the next service. This mismatch can occur due to a number of reasons such as input and output data type mismatch between the best available services, or missing information in the user specification. A possible solution to these problems is through the use of auxiliary services, or *shims* (Hull, 2004), that perform operations such as data type conversions. Although conceptually simple, a number of issues need to be considered when using shimming services. The first is being able to select the correct sequence of shims that provide the desired effect. The second is that the shimming services themselves may incur additional computational costs to the overall workflow or affect the fidelity of the overall results.

One possible approach to resolving the shimming problem can be based on using an AI planning technique. At the start of the automatic composition process, the planner is presented with a set of service nodes N_0, their ports, P, a relation on ports, $<$, indicating data dependency and set of shims, H. The algorithm iterates through every relation on ports and checks the type compatibility of ports. If the ports are compatible, the link is added to the relation, L, if not they are added to the list of unresolved links. For each unresolved link, a set of shim operators is searched to find a chain of shims leading from the output of one service to the input of the next. In searching for this chain, the costs of individual shims and their performance are added to the costs of the services. The full workflow is then triple N, P, L, where N is the union of N_0 and N_H where N_H is the set of all the shims added.

```
procedure resolveLinks (<)
    forEach (P₁, P₂ in <)
        if compatible (P₁, P₂)
            add l = (P₁, P₂) to L
        else
            selectShim (P₁, P₂)
    end
end
procedure selectShim(P₁, P₂) returns l[]
    while (all H is not checked)
        pick sequence h∈H
        calculate
```

$$F(h) = \sum_{H}^{|h|} E(h_i) + I(h_i) + O(h_i) \quad \text{if } F(h) \text{ ac-}$$

ceptable

```
        add chain nodes and links to N_H and L
        return
    else
        return failure# no suitable shim
    end
    end
end
```

Example

An example of applying service composition techniques to resolve a semantic workflow is shown in Figure 4. As with the previous example (shown in Figure 3), a semantic workflow consisting of two nodes for retrieving a satellite image and applying a pollution map overlay is defined. In this example, however, the best matching services meet the functional and non-functional properties, but do not satisfy the data type constraints. The output from the first service is in TIFF format and the second service requires a JPG file. To resolve the type mismatch, a shimming service or set of shimming services would need to be introduced to resolve the type mismatch. The shimming service needs to satisfy the type constraints but could increase the costs (both monetary and computational for executing the service) and the overall execution time of the concrete workflow and these effects need to be taken into account.

A number of systems have been developed recently that address similar service composition issues, for a surveys of some of these methods the reader is referred to Rao (2004) and Cordoso (2003). For example, the work of Medjahed (2003) uses a four phase approach based on AI planning techniques to determine whether two services are composable. A specification language CSSL (Composite Service Specification Language) is used to describe the desired composition. A matchmaking phase uses composability rules to generate composition plans that conform to service requestor's specifications. If more than one plan is generated, the service requester is allowed to select one based on quality of composition (QoC) parameters (e.g. rank and cost). The work of Ponnekanti (2002) describes a toolkit called

SWORD for building composite Web services using a rule-based expert system. In SWORD a Web service is represented in the form of a Horn rule that denotes the post conditions are achieved if the preconditions are true.

FRAMEWORK FOR SUPPORTING SEMANTIC WORKFLOWS AND SERVICE ORCHESTRATION USING AGENTS

Having identified the key issues that need to be resolved by an intelligent agent for service selection and composition, the second challenge to address is defining the run-time interfaces between the workflow system and the agent. Such interfaces would be used in exchanging the required information to the agent from the workflow system and semantic registries, and back.

Conceptual View

In order to identify the required interfaces we first list the key components of an integrated service-based workflow system and agent system:

- **Workflow System:** to be used in specifying semantic workflows and for co-ordinating

Figure 4. Example showing translation of a semantic workflow into a concrete workflow based on using shimming operators

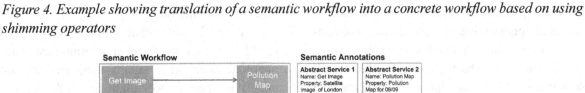
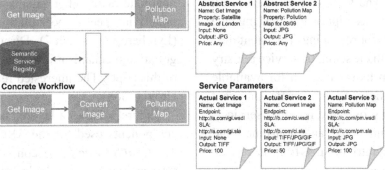

the execution of workflows composed of remote services. This system has to be extended to support semantic descriptions and for enabling submission of semantic workflows to the agents for resolution and the retrieval of concrete workflows.

- **Intelligent Agent:** for performing the service selection and composition tasks automatically on behalf of the user. The internals of the agent mind need be designed to support these tasks and also for supporting potential negotiations with the service provider around SLA terms.

- **Remote Services:** are the applications available through a traditional service interface and that can be accessed and invoked by the workflow tool. Each service is published in a registry and can also provide an SLA describing the non-functional properties associated with its execution for a particular user.

- **Semantic Services Registry:** to hold semantic descriptions and properties of available services that allow for service discovery, reasoning and selection.

- **Translation Tools:** for bridging the information exchange gap between the components of the framework as each typically uses its own internal representation.

Figure 5 shows a conceptual overview of how these components fit together form a workflow end user's perspective. The user creates a semantic workflow and submits it to the agent via the translation tools. The tools convert the overall semantic workflow description into the language used by the agents for reasoning. The agent then communicates with the semantic service registry via the translation tools to search for available services based on the user requirements. The agent performs reasoning over the returned services, including their functional and non-functional properties, and may retrieve SLAs from the service provider. This process may require several itera-

tions of querying the registry and services until a viable workflow description has been successfully composed by the agent. This workflow description is translated back into the native language of the workflow system and returned to the user for execution. If the agent fails to construct a viable workflow description it may seek further information from the user.

Applying the Framework to the ARUGRID Project

In order to support the conceptual view described above, the details of the particular workflow system and agent system must be identified. For example, within the ARGUGRID project the workflow system used is based on the InforSense workflow system described earlier in Section 2. This is a commercial workflow system based on the research outputs of the Discovery Net workflow system (Ghanem, 2008; Rowe, 2003).

The multi-agent system used consists of two key components, GOLEM and MARGO. GOLEM (Bromuri & Stathis, 2008) is a cognitive agent environment middleware which is an evolution of the PROSOCS system (Endris, 2006). MARGO (Morge & Mancarella, 2007) which provides the agent mind and is written in Prolog, implements a reasoning engine based on the argumentation framework of the CaSAPI system (Gaertner & Toni, 2007), a general purpose tool for assumption-based argumentation.

It should be noted that within ARGUGRID, GOLEM agents can discover, communicate and negotiate with other agents supported by an underlying peer-to-peer platform, PLATON ++ (Lymberopoulos, 2007). Discussion of the negotiation mechanism is beyond the presentation of this paper. The interested reader may refer to Urovi (2008).

Figure 6 shows a layered architecture of the components used for the ARGUGRID system. The *Grid Service Layer* consists of remote Grid services which were deployed using the GRIA middleware (Surridge, 2005). GRIA is based on existing Web Service protocols and also adopts parts of the WS-I Basic Profile, WS-I Basic Security Profile, WS-Addressing, WSRF, WS-Notification and WS-Federation specifications. GRIA is built up of a number of different packages. A basic Applications Services package is used for deploying services, providing an interface to the service and provides two web service endpoints to manage applications and their execution, and manage the data on the GRIA server. A Service Provider Management package allows for billing and also provides SLA support. These features make it more suitable for use within this frame-

work. Interfacing the InforSense workflow system to GRIA is described in Ghanem (2006).

The *Discovery Support and Orchestration Layer* is made up of components which aid users and agents in the service discovery process, as well as the orchestration and execution of remote services. The InforSense workflow engine is responsible for submitting the semantic workflow to the agents and also for coordinating the execution of the known services in the concrete workflow returned by the agents. ArguBroker is a brokering system that contains the language translation tools and an executable workflow planner, which converts the Prolog agent workflow into a DPML

Figure 5. An overview of using an intelligent agent based framework to resolve a semantic workflow

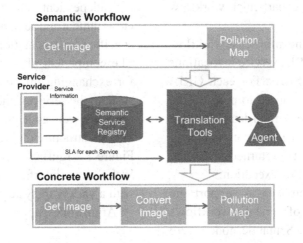

Figure 6. ARGUGRID layered architecture

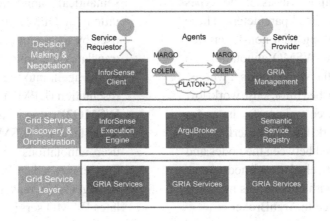

workflow. The semantic service registry houses information about the services available for discovery by the agents.

Users and agents sit at the *Decision Making Layer*. The workflow author uses the InforSense workflow client to construct semantic workflows with annotations written in WSMO. The service provider uses the GRIA management interface to manage his services. The agents use the service registry to identify available services and compose them together to make viable workflows, and negotiate service parameters, to address the user's requirements.

Workflow System Extensions

In order to support the conceptual view described above, the details of the particular workflow system and

The first extension to the InforSense workflow system was to support GRIA service invocations and also to manage its SLAs. For each GRIA service three nodes are required to perform the data upload, service execution and data download operations (Ghanem 2006). Extensions to the client were made to display the returned SLAs and submit them upon workflow execution.

The second extension was to support the creation and submission of semantic workflows in the workflow system. Semantic nodes were developed that are not linked to existing services but that allow the user to add annotations, identify the number of inputs/outputs with associated types and metadata, and associated parameters. These functional properties along with non-functional properties are added as WSMO annotations to each of the nodes and the workflow as a whole.

A semantically described InforSense workflow therefore consists of three main parts: the nodes that comprising the workflow, the ordering with the dependencies defined between the nodes and semantic descriptions attached to each node. Once a semantic workflow with annotations has been completed it is submitted to ArguBroker.

In addition to the workflow system extensions, a Semantic Registry implementation was also prototyped based on adaptation of the Grimoires Service Registry (Wong, 2005). This registry hosts descriptions of the service endpoints, information about properties and ports, metadata and management information and (entry authoring, data added, etc). A visual front end to the registry is provided allowing users to publish and manage their service descriptions.

ArguBroker

The implementation of the ArguBroker component is based on a modular design and the use of its own internal representation of workflows and service descriptions. These features enable it to be flexible and independent from the workflow system, agent environment and semantic registry, thus allowing specific implementations to be interchangeable. The component also implements the interfaces for exchanging information with the workflow system, the services, the service registry and the agent as well as a number of translators. The internal structure of ArguBroker is shown in the Figure 7. ArguBroker itself is accessible through Web Service interfaces to simplify its interaction with a variety of systems.

ArguBroker supports the following translators:

- **DPML2Prolog and Prolog2DPML Translators:** DPML2Prolog translates the semantically annotated workflow representation (in DPML) into the representation used by the agent (Prolog). Prolog2DPML translates the concrete workflow returned by the agent into the workflow system representation (DPML).
- **WSMO2Prolog and WSMO2Prolog Translators:** WSMO2Prolog translates user annotations in the semantic workflow expressed in WSMO into Prolog for the agents to reason over. It also translates WSMO service descriptions from the

Figure 7. ARGUGRID layered architecture

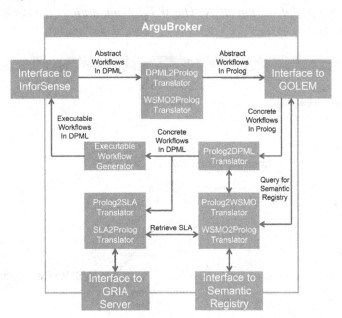

registry into Prolog. Prolog2WSMO translates the Prolog representation of service properties to WSMO primarily for querying the semantic registry.

- **SLA2Prolog and Prolog2SLA Translators:** Converts between the SLA representation used by the service provider (the GRIA SLAs in this case) and the representation used by the agents (Prolog).
- **Executable Workflow Generator:** used for adding InforSense workflow engine specific information, and responsible for first taking a partial DPML representation of a workflow representation to create a complete, executable DPML workflow that can be executed in the InforSense workflow system.

Note that the structure allows for further workflow and semantic description translators to be added or changed in accordance with the implementations chosen.

Example

Figure 8 shows the InforSense workflow authoring environment that has been extended to enable semantic annotations of workflows. The underlying DPML workflow is submitted via a web service call to ArguBroker. ArguBroker extracts the graph information and WSMO descriptions from the DPML and converts them into an internal representation which is then translated into Prolog and submitted to the agent. The internal ArguBroker representation of the workflow is shown in Figure 9.

W_1 and W_2 in this representation of the semantic WSMO descriptions reflect the high level user requirements for both functional properties, such as location and size, and non-functional properties, such as price and resolution.

Once the agent receives the workflow it connects to the registry (via ArguBroker) to retrieve a list of available services for satellite image retrieval and pollution mapping that match the user requirements. It chooses services based on the end user criteria as

Figure 8. Screenshot of the extended InforSense workflow system showing a semantic workflow that consists of getImage and pollutionMap steps. The WSMO annotations for each node are shown in a panel in the InforSense GUI

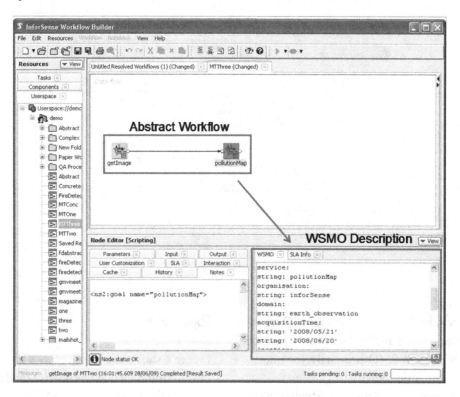

well as the selection, composition and type mapping algorithms described previously. The cheapest services available for image retrieval and pollution mapping do not satisfy the type constraints, image retrieval returns a TIFF file while pollution mapping requires a JPG file. An image retrieval and pollution mapping service are available with matching types, however it may possible to provide a cheaper solution using shimming, i.e. type conversion. Based on the type information, the requestor agent can search for type conversion tools that overcome this type mismatch. A matching shim service is located and the agent must start calculating the total cost of the services including the shimming service. This is compared with the no shims solution and is found to be cheaper.

After the services have been determined, the agent confirms the services with, and retrieves

the SLA for each service from, the GRIA service provider. ArguBroker receives the Prolog concrete workflow from the agent and converts this into its internal representation shown in Figure 10.

In the representation above, each node N has an id A and a description W. An EPR is returned which is the endpoint reference which provides the access point for the service. An SLA is also returned for each service. The connections C between each node are also defined.

ArguBroker then translates this internal representation into DPML adding GRIA specific nodes into the workflow and changes the details for each node to mirror their respective service call. The DPML is returned to the workflow system and displayed in the client as shown in Figure 11. The SLA information for each service returned can be reviewed in a panel in the client interface

Figure 9. ArguBroker1

$$abstractWorkflow\Big(nodes\big(\big[N_1, N_2\big]\big), connections\big(\big[C_1, C_2\big]\big)\Big)$$

$$N_1 = node\Big(id\big("A_1"\big), name\big("get\,Im\,age"\big), notes\big(W_1\big)\Big)$$

$$W_1 = goal\left(\begin{array}{l} name\big("get\,Im\,age"\big), \\ nfp\left(\begin{array}{l} price\big(\big[100,150\big]\big), \\ time\big(\big[200,300\big]\big) \end{array}\right), \\ fp\left(\begin{array}{l} precondition\big(location\big("London"\big)\big), \\ precondition\big(date\big("07/08/09"\big)\big), \\ precondition\big(size\big("1000*1000"\big)\big), \\ precondition\big(location\big(\big["low","medium","high"\big]\big)\big), \\ postcondtion\big(imageFormat\big("JPG"\big)\big) \end{array}\right) \end{array}\right)$$

$$N_2 = node\Big(id\big("A_2"\big), name\big("pollutionMap"\big), notes\big(W_2\big)\Big)$$

$$W_2 = goal\left(\begin{array}{l} name\big("pollutionMap"\big), \\ nfp\left(\begin{array}{l} price\big(\big[100,150\big]\big), \\ time\big(\big[200,300\big]\big) \end{array}\right), \\ fp\left(\begin{array}{l} precondition\big(date\big("07/08/09"\big)\big), \\ precondition\big(time\big("12:00"\big)\big), \\ precondtion\big(imageFormat\big("JPG"\big)\big), \\ postcondtion\big(imageFormat\big("JPG"\big)\big), \end{array}\right) \end{array}\right)$$

$$C_1 = connection\Big(from\big("start"\big), to\big("A_1"\big)\Big)$$

$$C_2 = connection\Big(from\big("A_1"\big), to\big("A_2"\big)\Big)$$

and must be accepted before the workflow can be executed.

FUTURE RESEARCH DIRECTIONS

The design and the fundamental concepts presented in this chapter are applicable beyond the scope of the ARGUGRID project. One of our next tasks is to investigate their use with other popular workflow and agent systems to verify the re-usability of the approach. A key limitation of our approach at present is that users still need to specify their requirements in a relatively formal way, which requires some technical knowledge, e.g. the WSMO notation. Our future work also

aims to address this limitation by investigating the development of more intuitive user interfaces.

CONCLUSION

In this paper, we have presented an overview of the key issues relating to the use of intelligent agents assisting the user in the process of service selection and workflow composition in a service-oriented computing framework. We have developed and evaluated these concepts within the ARGUGRID project where the multi-agent system comprises multiple GOLEM-MARGO agents using assumption-based argumentation implemented in Prolog. The key features of the

Figure 10. ArguBroker2

$$concreteWorkflow\Big(nodes\big(\big[N_1,N_2,N_3\big]\big),connections\big(\big[C_1,C_2,C_3\big]\big)\Big)$$

$$N_1=node\big(id\big(\text{"}A_1\text{"}\big),name\big(\text{"}get\,\mathrm{Im}\,age\text{"}\big),notes\big(W_1\big)\big)$$

$$W_1=service\left(nfp\left(\begin{matrix}name\big(\text{"}get\,\mathrm{Im}\,age\text{"}\big),\\price\big(\big[100\big]\big),\\time\big(\big[300\big]\big)\end{matrix}\right),fp\left(\begin{matrix}name\big(\text{"}get\,\mathrm{Im}\,age\text{"}\big),\\input\big(\text{"}Location\text{"},\text{"}String\text{"}\big),\\input\big(\text{"}Date\text{"},\text{"}Date\text{"}\big),\\input\big(\text{"}Size\text{"},\text{"}Integer[2]\text{"}\big),\\input\big(\text{"}Re\,solution\text{"},\text{"}String\text{"}\big),\\output\big(\text{"}ImageFormat\text{"},\text{"}TIFF\text{"}\big)\end{matrix}\right)\right)$$

$$EPR_1=\text{"}http:\,/\,/\,\arg ugrid.gmv.es\,/\,axis2\,/\,services\,/\,gI2?\,wsdl\text{"}$$
$$SLA_1=\text{"}http:\,/\,/\,\arg ugrid.gmv.es\,/\,axis2\,/\,services\,/\,gI2.sla\text{"}$$
$$N_2=node\big(id\big(\text{"}A_2\text{"}\big),name\big(\text{"}convert\,\mathrm{Im}\,age\text{"}\big),notes\big(W_2\big)\big)$$

$$W_2=service\left(nfp\left(\begin{matrix}name\big(\text{"}convert\,\mathrm{Im}\,age\text{"}\big),\\price\big(\big[50\big]\big),\\time\big(\big[180\big]\big)\end{matrix}\right),fp\left(\begin{matrix}name\big(\text{"}convert\,\mathrm{Im}\,age\text{"}\big),\\input\big(\text{"}Quality\text{"},\text{"}String\text{"}\big),\\input\big(\text{"}Speed\text{"},\text{"}Integer\text{"}\big),\\input\big(\text{"}\mathrm{Im}\,ageFormat\text{"},\text{"}TIFF\text{"}\big),\\output\big(\text{"}ImageFormat\text{"},\text{"}.JPG\text{"}\big)\end{matrix}\right)\right)$$

$$EPR_2=\text{"}http:\,/\,/\,\arg ugrid.gmv.es\,/\,axis2\,/\,services\,/\,cI4?\,wsdl\text{"}$$
$$SLA_2=\text{"}http:\,/\,/\,\arg ugrid.gmv.es\,/\,axis2\,/\,services\,/\,cI4.sla\text{"}$$

$$N_3=node\big(id\big(\text{"}A_3\text{"}\big),name\big(\text{"}pollutionMap\text{"}\big),notes\big(W_3\big)\big)$$

$$W_3=service\left(nfp\left(\begin{matrix}name\big(\text{"}pollutionMap\text{"}\big),\\price\big(\big[100\big]\big),\\time\big(\big[250\big]\big)\end{matrix}\right),fp\left(\begin{matrix}name\big(\text{"}pollutionMap\text{"}\big),\\input\big(\text{"}Date\text{"},\text{"}Date\text{"}\big),\\input\big(\text{"}Time\text{"},\text{"}Date\text{"}\big),\\input\big(\text{"}\mathrm{Im}\,ageFormat\text{"},\text{"}JPG\text{"}\big),\\output\big(\text{"}ImageFormat\text{"},\text{"}JPG\text{"}\big)\end{matrix}\right)\right)$$

$$EPR_3=\text{"}http:\,/\,/\,\arg ugrid.gmv.es\,/\,axis2\,/\,services\,/\,pM2?\,wsdl\text{"}$$
$$SLA_3=\text{"}http:\,/\,/\,\arg ugrid.gmv.es\,/\,axis2\,/\,services\,/\,pM2.sla\text{"}$$
$$C_1=connection\big(from\big(\text{"}start\text{"}\big),to\big(\text{"}A_1\text{"}\big)\big)$$
$$C_2=connection\big(from\big(\text{"}A_1\text{"}\big),to\big(\text{"}A_2\text{"}\big)\big)$$
$$C_3=connection\big(from\big(\text{"}A_2\text{"}\big),to\big(\text{"}A_3\text{"}\big)\big)$$

Figure 11. Screenshot of the extended InforSense workflow system, showing the concrete workflow returned by ArguBroker. Each set of three GRIA nodes corresponds to each node in the original semantic workflow. They correspond to upload data, execute job and download data steps respectively. For each GRIA service execution a SLA is returned and shown in the tab in the lower right hand corner. This SLA must be accepted by the user for the workflow to be executable

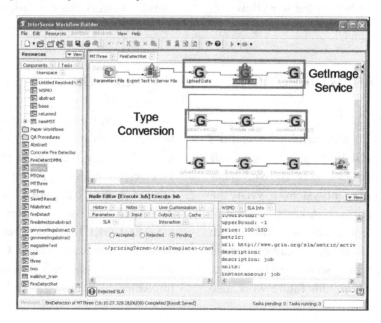

ARGUGRID multi-agent system are the ability of agents to reason about user preferences, their ability to discover and communicate with other agents using a peer-to-peer network paradigm, and their ability to negotiate service parameters. These issues were not directly addressed in this chapter where we have focused on the use of agents in enabling automatic service compositions.

Our contribution in this paper is twofold. Firstly, to clearly describe the key issues relating to service composition and the associated decisions so that supporting them can be implemented by the designers of MARGO. Secondly, to provide the design and implementation of a run-time interaction architecture that comprise of a workflow system, registry and brokering system to enable interaction with GOLEM. We are currently working with the GOLEM and MARGO teams on evaluating the quality of the decisions made by the agents. The initial results are encouraging; however we have not presented them in this chapter since they constitute an evaluation of the agents themselves rather than that of the generic approach we are promoting.

Although our presentation in this chapter has focused on the service requestor side, our architecture and implementation of the ArguBroker has been used also to support the interactions between the service provider agent and the service registry with no extra implementation. This is enabled by the modular design of the translation mechanism of ArguBroker.

REFERENCES

Atkinson, M., Roure, D. D., Dunlop, A., Fox, G., Henderson, P., & Hey, T. (2005). Web Service Grids: An Evolutionary Approach. *Concurrency and Computation, 17*(2-4), 377–380. doi:10.1002/cpe.936

Boniface, M. J., Phillips, S., & Perez, S.-M. A., & Surridge, M. (2007, September). *Dynamic Service Provisioning using GRIA SLAs*. Paper presented at NFPSLA-SOC '07. Vienna, Austria.

Bradley, J., Brown, C., Carpenter, B., Chang, V., Crisp, J., Crouch, S., et al. (2006, September). *The OMII Software Distribution.* Paper presented at the All Hands Meeting. Nottingham, UK.

Bromuri, S., & Stathis, K. (2008). Situating Cognitive Agents in GOLEM. In Weyns, D., Brueckner, S. A., & Demazeau, Y. (Eds.), *Engineering Environment-Mediated Multi-Agent Systems* (pp. 115–134). Berlin/Heidelberg, Germany: Springer Verlag. doi:10.1007/978-3-540-85029-8_9

Bromuri, S., Urovi, V., Morge, M., Stathis, K., & Toni, F. (2009). A Multi-Agent System for Service Discovery, Selection and Negotiation. In *Proceedings of the 8th International Joint Conference on Autonomous Agents and Multiagent Systems (AAMAS),* (Vol 2., pp. 1395-1396). Budapest, Hungary.

Cardoso, J., Miller, J., Sheth, A., & Arnold, J. (2002). Modeling Quality of Service for Workflows and Web Service Processes. *Journal of Web Semantics.*

Cardoso, J., & Sheth, A. (2003). Semantic E-Workflow Composition. *Journal of Intelligent Information Systems, 21*(3), 191–225. doi:10.1023/A:1025542915514

Curcin, V., Ghanem, M., & Guo, Y. (2009) Analysing scientific workflows with Computational Tree Logic. Journal of Cluster Computing: Special issue on Recent Advances in e-Science.

Curcin, V., Ghanem, M., Guo, Y., Stathis, K., & Toni, F. (2006). Building Next Generation Service-Oriented Architectures using argumentation agents. In *Proceedings of the 3rd International Conference on Grid Services Engineering and Management (GSEM 2006).* Berlin, Germany: Springer Verlag.

Endriss, U., Kakas, A., Lu, W., Bracciali, A., Demetriou, N., & Stathis, K. (2006). Crafting the Mind of a PROSOCS Agent. *Applied Artificial Intelligence, 20*(2-4), 105–131. doi:10.1080/08839510500479496

Foster, I., Kesselman, C., Nick, J., & Tuecke, S. (2002). *The Physiology of the Grid: An Open Grid Services Architecture for Distributed Systems Integration*. Open Grid Service Infrastructure WG, Global Grid Forum.

Gaertner, D., & Toni, F. (2007). CaSAPI – A System for Credulous and Sceptical Argumentation. In *Proceedings of the First International Workshop on Argumentation and Nonmonotonic Reasoning*. (p.p. 80-95). Arizona, USA.

Ghanem, M., Azam, N., Boniface, M., & Ferris, J. (2006). Grid-Enabled Workflows for Industrial Product Design. In *Proceedings of the Second IEEE International Conference on e-Science and Grid Computing (e-Science'06)* (p.p. 96). Amsterdam, The Netherlands.

Ghanem, M., Curcin, V., Wendel, P., & Guo, Y. (2008). Building and Using Analytical Workflows in Discover Net. In Dubitzky, W. (Ed.), *Data Mining Techniques in Grid Computing Environments* (pp. 119–140). London: Wiley-Blackwell. doi:10.1002/9780470699904.ch8

Hull, D., Wolstencroft, K., Stevens, R., Goble, C., Pocock, M. R., Li, P., & Oinn, T. (2006). Taverna: A Tool for Building and Running Workflows of Services. *Nucleic Acids Research, 34*(Web Services Issue), W729-W732.

Krauter, K., Buyya, R., & Maheswaran, M. (2002). A taxonomy and survey of grid resource management systems for distributed computing. *Software, Practice & Experience, 32*(2), 135–164. doi:10.1002/spe.432

Ludäscher, B., Altintas, I., Berkley, C., Higgins, D., Jaeger, E., & Jones, M. (2006). Scientific Workflow Management and the Kepler System: Research Articles. In *Concurrency and Computation: Practice & Experience* (pp. 1039–1065). Chichester, UK: John Wiley and Sons Ltd.

Lymberopoulos, L., Bromuri, S., Stathis, K., Kafetzoglou, S., Grammatikou, M., & Papavassiliou, S. (2007). Towards a P2P Discovery Framework for an Argumentative Agent Technology assist GRID. In *Proceedings of CoreGRID Workshop on Grid Programming Model, Grid and P2P Systems Architectures, Grid Systems, Tools, Environments*. Crete, Greece.

Medjahed, B., Bouguettaya, A., & Elmagarmid, A. K. (2003). Composing Web services on the Semantic Web. *The VLDB – The International Journal on Very Large Databases, 12*(4), 333-351.

Morge, M., & Mancarella, P. (2007). The Hedgehog and the Fox: An argumentation-based decision support system. In *Proceedings of the Fourth International Workshop on Argumentation in Multi-Agent Systems*, (p.p. 55-68).

Morge, M., McGinnis, J., Bromuri, S., Mancarella, P., & Stathis, K. (2008). An Argumentative Model for Service-Oriented Agents. In *Proceedings of the International Symposium on Architectures for Intelligent Theory-Based Agents, AAAI Spring Symposium Series*. Stanford University, CA.

Ponnekanti, S. R., & Fox, A. (2002). SWORD: A developer toolkit for Web service composition. In *Proceedings of the 11th World Wide Web Conference*, Honolulu, HI.

Rao, J., & Su, X. (2004). A Survey of Automated Web Service Composition Methods. In *Proceedings of the First International Workshop on Semantic Web Services and Web Process Composition, SWSWPC 2004*. California, USA.

Rowe, A., Kalaitzopolous, D., Osmond, M., Ghanem, M., & Guo, Y. (2003). The Discovery Net System for High Throughput Bioinformatics. *Bioinformatics (Oxford, England)*, *19*, 225–231. doi:10.1093/bioinformatics/btg1031

Surridge, M., Taylor, S., De Roure, D., & Zaluska, E. (2005). Experiences with GRIA – Industrial Applications on a Web Service Grid. In H. Stockinger, R. Buyya & R. Perrett (Eds.), *First International Conference on e-Science and Grid Computing,* (Vol. 1, Issue 1, pp98-105). Melbourne, Australia.

Talia, D. (2002). The Open Grid Services Architecture: Where the Grid Meets the Web. *IEEE Internet Computing*, *6*(6), 67–71. doi:10.1109/MIC.2002.1067739

Taylor, I., Shields, M., Wang, I., & Harrison, A. (2005). VisualGrid Workflow in Triana. *Journal of Grid Computing*, *3*(3-4), 153–169. doi:10.1007/s10723-005-9007-3

Toni, F., Grammatikou, M., Kafetzoglou, S., Lymberopoulos, L. S., Papavassileiou, S., Gaertner, D., et al. (2008). The ARGUGRID Platform: An Overview. In *Proceedings of the 5th International Workshop on Grid Economics and Business Models. Lecture Notes in Computer Science,* (Vol. 5206, pp. 217-225).

Urovi, V., Bromuri, S., McGinnis, J., Stathis, K., & Omicini, A. (2008). Automating Workflows Using Dialectical Argumentation. *IADIS International Journal on Computer Science and Information System*, *3*(2), 110–125.

Wong, S. C., Tan, V., Fang, W., Miles, S., & Moreau, L. (2005). Grimoires: grid registry with metadata oriented interface: robustness, efficiency, security. In Cluster Computing and Grid (CCGrid), Cardiff, UK.

Section 2
Context Searching

Chapter 5
Context Dissemination in Peer-to-Peer Networks

Antje Barth
University of Tübingen, Germany

Michael Kleis
Fraunhofer FOKUS, Germany

Andreas Klenk
Technische Universität München, Germany

Benoit Radier
France Télécom R&D, France

Sanaa Elmoumouhi
France Télécom R&D, France

Mikael Salaun
France Télécom R&D, France

Georg Carle
Technische Universität München, Germany

ABSTRACT

In recent years, peer-to-peer overlay networks have become a popular communication paradigm with the potential to further change communication fundamentally in the future. Overlays allow communication abstraction but suffer from one inherent problem: The overlay is unaware of the context of a service or the context of a service consumer. The concept of context-awareness emerged out of the research done within the area of ubiquitous computing. Context-aware computing is one key technology to enable services and applications in the communication environment to adapt their behaviour based on the knowledge of environmental (contextual) information, thereby enhancing the system's ability to become ever more responsive to the needs of the end-user or application domain. In this chapter we

DOI: 10.4018/978-1-61520-973-6.ch005

first introduce context and context architectures in general. In the remainder of the chapter we focus on the question: How can highly distributed context information be located and retrieved regarding small-scale as well as large-scale networks, addressing the topics of inter-domain management and scalability of context architectures?

INTRODUCTION

The concept of context-awareness emerged out of the research done within the area of ubiquitous computing. Context-aware computing is one key technology to enable services and applications in the communication environment to adapt their behavior based on the knowledge of environmental (contextual) information thereby enhancing the system's ability to become ever more responsive to the needs of the end-user or application domain. Prior research on context-awareness has lead to a number of context-aware applications and middleware implementations. This chapter first gives a brief introduction to context and context-awareness. It explains typical architectures of context frameworks that are suitable for the use in peer-to-peer overlay networks. Next it presents different strategies for the distribution of context applications and the retrieval of context information.

The distribution of context services and context information calls for efficient deployment and communication patterns to ensure that available context information can be located and retrieved across the overlay network in an efficient manner. The scalability of context architectures is an important requirement for supporting implementations in large-scale networks that perfectly reflect the characteristic of overlay networks. In many cases such overlay networks have an expansion across several countries or even continents. A prominent example therefore is Skype, the popular peer-to-peer voice over IP (VoIP) system, providing global communication and built upon an unstructured overlay. The peering of context services is not only a matter of connecting distributed context information but also imposes specific characteristics that must be investigated regarding the impact of failures and the search performance. Hence a careful decision must be made according to which topology should be used for peering context services.

The results from a comparative performance study show the tradeoffs between different possible peering approaches. In the following, different concepts of peering distributed context services will be investigated and search patterns are evaluated regarding overlay-related as well as underlay-related metrics.

CONTEXT

This section will introduce the fundamentals and basic concepts of *context* and *context-aware* computing by giving definitions and by briefly outlining the history of this computing paradigm. Afterwards, the main concepts of *context modeling*, *context sensing* and *context monitoring* will be explained. In recent history, much attention has been devoted to the terms *context* and *context-awareness* in the area of ubiquitous computing, leading to a great variety of definitions and interpretations depending on the respective application scenario.

What is Context?

An early definition of the term context in scientific work emerged in (Schilit, Adams and Want (1994)). The authors refer to context as „*loca-*

tion, identities of nearby people and objects, and changes to those objects." This definition is not generic as it defines the term only by providing a set of examples. The authors in (Abowd, Dey, Brown, Davies, Smith and Steggles, P. (1999)) define context as *„any information that can be used to characterize the situation of an entity. An entity is a person, place, or object that is considered relevant to the interaction between a user and an application, including the user and applications themselves."* This definition is widely used within the area of ubiquitous computing at present.

In this chapter, however, context will be defined more generally as: *"Any information that can be used to characterize the situation of an entity".* Entity refers to something that has a separate and distinct existence and objective, and situation is defined as a combination of circumstances and interactions at a given moment.

What is Context-Awareness?

Context-awareness defines a computing paradigm in which applications can discover and take advantage of context information. This concept was introduced originally as *"software that adapts according to its location of use, the collection of nearby people and objects, as well as changes to those objects over time."* Other sources (Hull, Neaves, and Bedford-Roberts (1997)) (Schilit, Adams and Want (1994)) define context-awareness as *„the ability of computing devices to detect and sense, interpret and respond to aspects of a user's local environment and the computing devices themselves"* and context-aware applications as *„applications that dynamically change or adapt their behavior based on the context of the application and the user."*

A more general definition, and the one used in this chapter, is given by (Dey (2000)): *"A system is context-aware if it uses context to provide relevant information and/or services to the user, where relevancy depends on the user's task."*

Context Information

Context information can come from many sources. According to (Korkea-aho (2000)) available context information can be grouped into these categories.

- **Spatial information:** e.g., location, orientation, speed and acceleration
- **Temporal information:** e.g., time of the day, date, and season of the year
- **Environmental information:** e.g., temperature, air quality, and light or noise level
- **Social situation:** e.g., who are you with, and people that are nearby
- **Resources that are nearby:** e.g., accessible devices, and hosts
- **Availability of resources:** e.g., battery, display, network, and bandwidth
- **Physiological measurements:** e.g., blood pressure, heart rate, respiration rate, muscle activity, and tone of voice
- **Activity:** e.g., talking, walking, and running

Context Modeling

After defining context one has to decide how to model and represent context information. Several approaches have evolved in the past, ranging from assigning key-value pairs to more sophisticated solutions like markup scheme models, logic- or ontology-based models, and object-oriented models. It depends on the usage scenario which model is most appropriate. A short description of each model will be given. Refer to (Baldauf, Dustdar and Rosenberg (2006)) and (Strang and Linnho–Popien (2004)) for a detailed survey and evaluation of the modeling approaches.

- **Key-Value Pairs:** The model of key-value pairs is a simple data structure for accessing context information. Unique keys allow the retrieval of the assigned context data values. The keys refer to different information describing the context. It can be realized, for instance, by providing context information to an application through a set of environment variable. The simplicity of this representation makes it easy to implement, but can be problematic for hierarchical data. The screen resolution of a display could be expressed as follows:

ScreenHeightPixel:200
ScreenWidthPixel:320

- **Markup Scheme Models:** Markup Scheme Models are hierarchical data structures that consist of markup tags with attributes and content. The content of the markup tags is usually recursively defined by other markup tags. Typical representatives of this kind of modeling approach are so-called *profiles*. They are usually based upon a serialization of a derivative of SGML (Standard Generic Markup Language), the superclass of all markup languages such as XML (eXtensible Markup Language). Some of them are defined as extensions to the CC/PP (Composite Capabilities/ Preferences Profile) standard, defined by the W3C (World Wide Web Consortium). A CC/PP profile is a description of device capabilities and user preferences that can be used to guide the adaptation of content presented to that device. CC/PP is based on RDF (Resource Description Framework), which was designed by the W3C as a general purpose meta-data description language. A CC/PP profile contains a number of CC/PP attribute names and associated values. Below is an example for a CC/PP policy that defines a default resolution for a hardware device:

```
<?xml version="1.0"?>
<rdf:RDF xmlns:rdf="http://www.
w3.org/1999/02/22-rdf-syntax-ns#"
    xmlns:ex="http://www.example.
com/schema#">
  <rdf:Description rdf:about="http://www.
example.com/hardwareProfile#HWDefault">
    <rdf:type rdf:resource="http://www.
example.com/schema#HardwarePlatform" />
    <ex:displayWidth>320</
ex:displayWidth>
    <ex:displayHeight>200</
ex:displayHeight>
  </rdf:Description>
</rdf:RDF>
```

- **Graphical Models:** The graphical modeling approach tries to represent context information in a diagram style. One modeling instrument that is applied for this purpose is, for example, the Unified Modeling Language (UML), a popular general purpose modeling language that comprises graphical notations (UML diagrams) and is sufficiently generic to represent context information.

  ○ **Logic-Based Models:** Common to all logic-based models is a high degree of formality. The *logic* defines the conditions under which a concluding expression or fact may be derived from a set of other expressions or facts (a process known as *reasoning* or *inferencing*). A formal system is applied to describe these conditions in a set of rules. In a logic-based context model, context information is consequently defined as facts, expressions, and rules. The information is usually added, updated and deleted in terms of facts or inferred from the rules in the system respectively.

McCarthy (1993) formalized context as first class objects. The basic relation is *ist(c,p)* to assert that the proposition *p* is true in the context *c*.

Take the following assertion as an example which expresses that in the context of Sherlock Holmes stories Holmes is a detective.

ist(context-of("Sherlock Holmes stories"), "Holmes is a detective")

- **Object-Oriented Models:** Object-oriented models profit from the general OO paradigm which fosters concepts like encapsulation, reusability, and inheritance. A specific type of context information can be modeled as a generic object class, whereas a specific piece of context information would be represented as an object instance derived from a generic class. The details of context processing are encapsulated on an object level and hence hidden to other components. Access to context information is only possible through well-defined interfaces.

Imagine a context object that encapsulates the screen size and the physical size of the display. It can have different accessor functions to query not only the encapsulated information, but also derived data such as dots per inch.

- **Ontology-Based Models:** Ontology is a term borrowed from philosophy that refers to the study of describing the kinds of entities in the world and how they are related. The OWL (Web Ontology Language) is one important technology for the emerging semantic web in which web content can be expressed not only in natural language, but also in a form that can be understood, interpreted, and used by software agents, thus permitting them to find, share, and integrate information more easily. An OWL ontology may include descriptions of classes, properties, and their instances. The OWL formal semantics define how to derive logical consequences from a given ontology, i.e. how to derive facts not explicitly present in the ontology but entailed by the semantics. Chen et al present their COBRA-ONT model in (Chen, Finin and Joshi (2003)). Here is an excerpt from these ontologies to express the location of a person:

```
<loc:LocationContext>
    <rdf:type rdf:resource="&tme;Instant
Thing"/>
    <loc:locationContextOf>
      <per:Person>
      <per:name rdf:datatype="&xsd;string">
Harry Chen</per:name>
      </per:Person>
    </loc:locationContextOf>
    <loc:boundedWithin
rdf:resource="&ebgeo;Japan"/>
    <tme:at rdf:datatype="&xsd;dateTi
me">2004-02-23T11:23:00</tme:at>
</loc:LocationContext>
```

Context Sensing

The context information has to be gathered from the environment. This process is called *context sensing*. Due to its highly dynamic character, the sensing of context information is a continuous process. Depending on the way the information is captured, sensors can be categorized into three classes according to (Indulska and Sutton (2003)): physical sensors, virtual sensors, and logical sensors. The term *sensor* refers to any kind of data source which may provide usable context information.

- **Physical Sensors:** The most common type of sensors are physical ones. Such hardware sensors, like tracking systems for determining a person's location, are readily available and capable of capturing almost any physical data. Take a GPS device as an example that provides updates on the user's location.

- **Virtual Sensors:** In contrast, virtual sensors gather context information from software application or services. In the case of location information, for example, the position could be determined by browsing an electronic calendar.
- **Logical Sensors:** Logical sensors combine various information sources, involving physical and virtual sensors, database systems, or other available data sources. For instance, location information could be gathered by observing logins at desktop PCs and performing a database mapping of PCs to location information.

Context Monitoring

Most context information is highly volatile and changes unpredictably. Depending on the application scenario, the context information may deviate from the current sensor data. There are two monitoring concepts for updating context information: performing *synchronous monitoring* or *asynchronous monitoring*.

- Synchronous Monitoring: In the synchronous mode, context information is retrieved upon request. For example, to gather data about a user's current activities, a monitor could be requested to look up the activity in the calendar at the time of the request.
- **Asynchronous Monitoring:** In the asynchronous mode, context information is constantly delivered to a respective information requesting instance (e.g. a context architecture or a context-aware application), which can then process the information further. A location sensor, for instance, could only transmit location

updates if there is a significant change of the location.

CONTEXT ARCHITECTURES FOR OVERLAY SERVICES

There exist a number of context architectures which are suitable for the intended use in peer-to-peer overlay scenarios. This section first explains a generic architecture for highly distributed acquisition and use of context before it introduces three popular context frameworks.

Design Principles

In context architectures, there are three layers that can be commonly found in many context frameworks (see Figure below): The Context Acquisition Layer obtains context information from sensors. The Context Management Layer is in control of the context acquisition and processes context information. The entities at the Client Application Layer implement the interfaces of the context framework and support the context model.

Context Acquisition Layer

The context acquisition layer is involved in the gathering of raw context information from context sources available within the surrounding environment. It consists of two system components of which a number of instances can be installed, depending on the individual application setting:

- Context Sensors
- Context Monitors

The context sensors can be any type of physical, virtual, or logical sensors as discussed previously. For instance, the sensors can be used for gathering device-related, network-related, or application/service-related context information. These con-

Figure 1. Three layers of a distributed context architecture

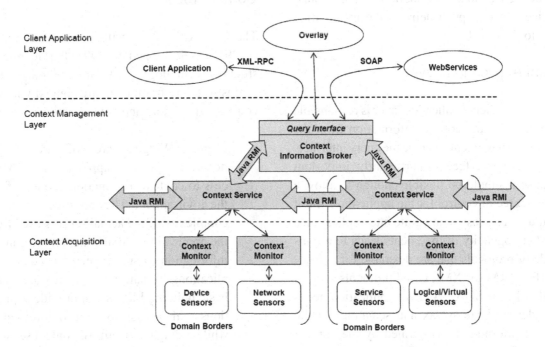

text sensors are connected to so-called context monitors that are responsible for monitoring and distribution of the context information provided by the corresponding context sensor to the context management layer.

Depending on the monitoring mode (synchronous or asynchronous), the context sensors either detect the current state of the context information and report it to the context management layer, or they constantly deliver the currently detected context information to the context management layer.

Context Management Layer

The context management layer is responsible for the coordination and processing of all available context information and for providing communication interfaces to the Client Application Layer (see below). It consists of two system components of which a number of instances can be installed, depending on the individual application setting:

- Context Services
- Context Information Broker

The context service receives, manages, stores, and distributes context information. It is hence the system component that actually performs the core task of context management, making it one of the most important system components. Several context services (each responsible for handling context information in a specific environment/ domain) can cooperate in a peer-to-peer fashion. In this way, dedicated context services can be designed and deployed.

The context information broker acts as a mediator between clients requesting context information and the other context architecture's system components. It therefore provides a query interface and also ensures the interoperability between different communication protocols used by the clients. Subsequent to potential conversions of data types and protocol information, it decomposes the queries and sends a request for the desired context information to the context service. On receipt, it delivers the information back to the client.

Client Application Layer

Finally, the client application layer is responsible for retrieving the context information from the context management layer via the query interface. The query interface is particularly important because it should be flexible enough to allow a large degree of control for the application, but it should still be easy to integrate into applications. The heterogeneity of the clients leads to a multitude of protocols that are desirable for a query interface: RMI or XML based protocols such as XML-RPC or SOAP. A client application needs to understand the syntax and semantics of the context information, as defined by the context model of the framework. The client should be able to obtain an overview of available context information and it should be able to define which information should be monitored by the context framework. The application should also be aware of the varying accuracy of context information and take the uncertainty of this information into account.

Context Frameworks

We present here three popular software frameworks currently available as open source software that allow the development of context-aware applications: the Context Toolkit, introduced in (Salber, Dey and Abowd (1999)), the Context Broker Architecture from (Chen, Finin and Joshi (2003)), and the Java Context Awareness Framework (JCAF) presented in (Bardram (2005)). Refer to (Baldauf, Dustdar and Rosenberg (2006)) for a detailed survey on other related context frameworks.

Context Toolkit

The Context Toolkit (Salber, Dey and Abowd (1999)) was developed in 1999 at the Georgia Institute of Technology, USA. The core components of this software framework are context widgets, context aggregators and context interpretators.

- Context Widgets: are software components that provide applications with access to context information gathered from the environment. They are used to hide the complexity of the actual sensors used from the application and abstract on the context information to suit expected needs of applications. To sum up, context widgets are basic building blocks that provide applications with access to context information while hiding the details of context sensing.
- **Context Aggregators:** Context widgets can be composed to provide richer context information while reusing existing widgets. These composite widgets are then called *context aggregators*.
- **Context Interpreters** can be used to translate between different representation formats of context information or to gain high-level context information out of low-level context information.

The Context Toolkit features two techniques for receiving context information: polling "and subscriptions". Just like GUI widgets, context widgets can be polled to determine their current state. There are two types of polls supported: a request for the last collected state and a request to update and return the current state. Along with polling, context widgets support subscriptions to changes in the context that they are monitoring. Context Widgets have callbacks that other components can subscribe to. When the monitored context changes the callback is fired and the subscribing components are notified of the callback.

Context Broker Architecture (CoBrA)

The Context Broker Architecture developed by Chen et al. (Chen, Finin and Joshi (2003)) is an agent based context architecture for pervasive environments. At the heart of CoBrA is a central *context broker* that has a shared model of context on behalf of agents, services and devices. The context broker is responsible for the acquisition of and reasoning about context information. The framework uses OWL for defining context of people, agents, devices, events, time, and space. Privacy policies allow the user to control the dissemination and sharing of context information. The *context broker* relies on four components:

- **Context knowledge base** for the storage of ontologies describing types of knowledge and for the storage of acquired context information.

- **Context reasoning engine** for logical inference and reasoning about acquired knowledge. This function is responsible for the interpretation and aggregation of sensing data. It detects and resolves inconsistent data.

- **Context acquisition module** receives context information from context sensors and agents. It encapsulates these sensors to provide the other components with a high level interface.

- **Privacy management module** takes access control policies from the user to control the sharing of information.

Java Context Awareness Framework (JCAF)

JCAF was developed by Bardram (2005) with the goal to have a simple, robust and extensible framework. It provides a Java-based lightweight framework with an expressive, compact, and small set of interfaces. Basically, JCAF is divided into two parts: a runtime infrastructure and an Application Programmer Interface (API).

- **Runtime Infrastructure:** The JCAF runtime infrastructure consists of a range of *context services* which are connected in a peer-to-peer setup. A network of services can cooperate by querying each other for context information. Each context service is a long-lived process. An *entity* with its context information is managed by the service's *entity container*. An entity is a small Java program that runs within the context service and responds to changes in its context. The life cycle of an entity is controlled by the container in which the entity has been added. The entity container handles subscribers to context events and notifies relevant clients about changes to entities. An *entity environment* provides methods for accessing key-value attributes and *context transformers*. Context transformers are small application-specific Java programs that a developer can write and add to a *transformer repository*. The transformer repository can be queried for appropriate transformers on runtime. Access to a context service can be controlled through the access control component which ensures authentication of client requests. *Context clients* can access entities and their context information in two ways: Either following a request-response schema, requesting entities and their context data, or by subscribing as an *entity listener*, listening for changes to specific entities.

- **Application Programmer Interface (API):** The JCAF API enables the programmer to create context-aware applications that are deployable in the JCAF infrastructure. It consists of the context service (managing entity objects), entity listeners, and context clients. Two examples of context clients are the context monitors and context actuators. Each context service has an entity environment where entities can access and store application-specific attributes using a key-value data structure.

In JCAF, entities residing in a context service are notified about context events, can access each other locally, and look up remotely located entities without involving any client. Hence, the JCAF event structure is not only used for client notifications, but also for triggering actions in the entities residing in the context services entity container.

JCAF also provides basic support to judge the quality of context. First, context information receives a timestamp at each update. Then, implementations of context items comprise a measure of the accuracy: a value between zero and one. In the case of location information, this value is automatically decreased as the time passes, reflecting the uncertainty that the information is still accurate.

PEERING OF DISTRIBUTED CONTEXT SOURCES

Context information is normally distributed over a multitude of (administrative) domains and thus, needs to be managed efficiently. One key issue of context management is the retrieval of context information. In this sections, possible concepts of peering distributed context services will be investigated and search patterns are evaluated regarding overlay-related as well as underlay-related metrics. Whereby overlay refers to a virtual network of nodes and logical links that are built on top of an existing network (called underlay in the following) with the purpose of implementing a network service that is not available in the existing network. The term network information services is used to denote services that provide network-specific information as result of a net-

work measurement, monitoring or management process. The provisioning of QoS measurements between nodes in a network can be given as one example. In particular, QoS-information such as latency between two network nodes or available bandwidth are highly volatile and require constant measuring and information updating. In the course of this chapter, an overlay network of a respective number of nodes performing measurements of QoS-parameters will serve as the demonstration case for investigation. During the chapter QoS-parameters are selected based on the *S3 Scalable Sensing Service* for monitoring large networked systems (Yalagandula, Sharma, Banerjee, Basu and Lee (2006)), developed by HP Labs in Palo Alto, California. This network service performs such measurements of QoS-parameters on the PlanetLab (http://www.planet-lab.org) testbed between all pairs of PlanetLab nodes providing the network metrics latency, bottleneck bandwidth capacity, available bandwidth, and loss rate. These measurement results are treated in the following as example input of installed context monitors.

Comparative Study of Peering Approaches

The peering of context services is not only a matter of connecting distributed context sources but also imposing specific characteristics regarding safeguarding against failure and search performance. Hence, a careful decision must be made according to which topology to peer the context services. One main goal is to dispose a peering topology that allows to contact the peers within the least possible number of hops to speed-up system-internal query times. In the remainder of this chapter three main peering approaches are analyzed which are: star topology, fully meshed graph and random graphs. In addition, the obtained results are compared with a Distributed Hash Table based approach.

Figure 2. Peering approaches

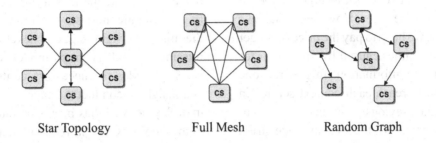

Star Topology   Full Mesh   Random Graph

Star Topology

Peering context services as a star as shown in Figure 2 reveals several advantages. First of all, the topology can be set up relatively fast: One context service has to be assigned to be the *star master* (i.e. the context service that has all other context services as its peers) and has to add all other context services to its peering table. Next, any context information the context service is queried for can be retrieved in a maximum of one hop, i.e., by querying its peers (which are explicitly *all* other available context services) in a directed query. Finally, any client (or context information broker as mediator between context architecture and client) only has to know the address of the star master as the single contact point to send its queries to. However, this single contact point represents a significant disadvantage since it corresponds to a single point of failure. Furthermore, an extraordinary overlay *node stress* is imposed upon one node, namely the star master, as it has to duplicate and forward search queries to all of its peers in the case that it does not dispose of the requested context information itself, constituting a highly unfair burden-sharing.

Fully Meshed Graph

The consideration to avoid any single point of failure leads to the next possible peering topology, a fully meshed graph also shown in Figure 2. Each context service is connected to the other context services. The obvious advantage of this peering approach is that each context service can reach any of the other context services in one hop. One large drawback of this peering topology, however, is the fact that its network setup is very expensive. Each context service has to add all other context services to its peering table and has to maintain the connections. This may be applicable in smaller overlay networks, but exceeds its limits in large-scale scenarios with e.g. millions of nodes. Another disadvantage is the high overlay node stress and unfair burden-sharing, already mentioned with regard to the disadvantages of a star topology. Although within a fully meshed graph, initial queries can be sent to any of the context services, it is still up to this context service to duplicate and forward search queries to all other context services in the case that it does not dispose of the desired context information itself.

Random Graph

To cope with the large-scale scenarios mentioned before, a peering approach is needed that is highly scalable and easy to maintain and manage. That is exactly where random graphs come into play (Figure 2). In a random-graph-based topology, each context service only has to manage a fraction of peers. Thus, it is easier to maintain and manage each context service's peering table and to re-build the topology in the case that one context service fails. Thus, one advantage of this peering topology is its ability to scale in a flexible manner, even in networks with a high number of nodes and context services. However, to achieve this scalability, we have to pay the price of longer system response times caused by the search for requested context information. In general, one cannot assume to reach each context service in one hop as in the previously outlined peering approaches. Nevertheless, the overlay node stress is dealt with in a more fair manner, as each node queried for specific context information only has to duplicate and forward the search query to the fraction of context services it comprises as peers, resulting in a noticeable burden-sharing.

Test Environment

The scenario realised as test environment for the investigation and evaluation of the peering approaches illustrated above consists of a number of overlay nodes performing measurements of QoS-parameters. We adapted the JCAF framework to serve our purpose. We divided the overlay network into a number of **k** domains and limited the measurements of each node to nodes inside the same domain and between domain border gateways. Next, one node in each domain is declared a context service stores and manages the results of corresponding QoS-measurements. For simplicity, the focus will be on one network metric namely the pair wise communication delay between the overlay nodes. In order to make the context information stored in each domain's context service traceable and retrievable overlay-wide, the context services have to be connected. This will be implemented based on the three peering approaches described above and individually evaluated against a set of metrics to rate performance and system/network overhead. For the investigation and evaluation of the peering approaches presented, a generated network topology has been selected. This is traced back to the fact that in order to conduct the theoretical comparative study, a real network testbed with concurrent experiments such as the

PlanetLab would interfere with the results of our experiments due its varying network status (e.g. available nodes), potential cross-traffic, the missing insight (e.g. on packet routing), and missing control. A graph-model, on the other hand, provides the necessary control, stability, and insight to conduct the experiments. Thus, an underlay network has been simulated by means of the Georgia Georgia Tech Internetwork Topology Model Generator (GT-ITM) developed by the Georgia Institute of Technology, USA. Any of those generated underlay nodes can be part of the overlay network, assuming that it is provided with some special kind of equipment.

To summarize, the resulting topology consists of:

- a total number of 1740 underlay nodes,
- connected via 2292 edges (bi-directional),
- each edge is assigned an individual weight (interpreted as delay value),
- distributed over 430 domains,
- contributing 430 overlay nodes (one per domain).

Experiments

The above described topology provides the basis for implementation, testing, and evaluation of the peering approaches. Therefore, the 430 overlay nodes representing context services are implemented and peered in a first experiment according to a star topology, in a second experiment according to fully meshed graph, and in a third experiment according to random graph. For the implementation of the random graph, an Erdös-Renyi random graph $G(n, p)$ has been selected (Batagelj and Brandes (2005)), i.e. a graph with n vertices where each possible edge appears with probability p. p=0.2 has been chosen as parameter, resulting in a connected graph with an average vertex clustering coefficient of 0.19979373 and an average vertex degree of 85.976746. Each peering implementation is subsequently analyzed by

Figure 3. Directed search

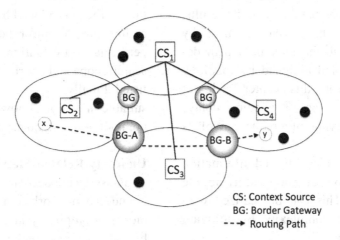

CS: Context Source
BG: Border Gateway
- - → Routing Path

means of a set of overlay and underlay specific metrics as we describe in the next section. We evaluate (where appropriate) two search patterns: broadcasted search and directed search:

- **Broadcasted Search:** A context service that is requested for context information it does not possess copies the request and forwards it to all its peering context services in order to retrieve the desired context information by-and-by.

- **Directed Search:** Each context is enhanced with the knowledge of where to find specific context information. Consequently a query received can be forwarded to the context service that possesses the desired context information, decreasing system overhead dramatically. However, in order to maintain such global knowledge, additional costs are imposed by keeping the information of where to find what up-to-date at each node.

For an illustration of the implemented directed search approach in case of a star topology and four domains we refer to Figure 3. In case a client in the domain of the star master CS_1 requires information about the delay between nodes x and y it queries the star master first. Based on the

knowledge where to find specific context information as well as information about routing between domains, CS_1 can infer the delay between x and y by requesting information about:

1. the delay between x and BG-A from CS_2
2. the delay between BG-A and BG-B from CS_3
3. the delay between BG-B and y from CS_4

Metrics

The three peering approaches are evaluated from an overlay-related as well as underlay-related perspective. 1000 nodes were randomly selected to initiate a query for context information, namely the link delay between two network nodes, selected in a uniformly random fashion. Afterwards, the queries are evaluated by means of the following metrics:

Overlay-Related Metrics
From the overlay's point of view, the metrics request response time, search scope, overlay node stress, and peering table size are of interest.

- **Request Response Time:** Request response time is defined as the time a client has to wait after sending a request to get an answer from the context architecture. To ensure the comparability of the results, measured values have been normalized by dividing through the maximum path delay generated and assigned by topology generation. During this chapter we do not consider processing or queuing delays since the processing of a request involves only two steps:

○ Verification if requested information is available at node receiving the request. This can be realized with low time complexity by utilizing hash-tables

○ Eventually duplication and forwarding of a request based on a static neighbor table which does not involve complex or time intensive routing operations.

- **Search Scope:** Search scope is defined as the number of overlay nodes that are involved in the search for requested context information. The set of services involved is calculated duplicate-free, i.e. each service is only counted one time by its first usage.
- **Overlay Node Stress:** Overlay node stress is defined as the number of copies of a search request that have to be generated and sent by an overlay node. Overlay Node Stress is a "per node" metric only taking copies of search requests into account, not the nodes' consequent responses.
- **Peering Table Size:** Peering table size is defined as the number of peers (neighbors) an overlay node comprises. In most cases, this is a fixed value, constituted by the characteristics of the individual peering approaches.

Request response time has been chosen as a metric because it represents the metric of most interest to any client querying the context archi-

tecture for information. On the system's side, the overhead produced by querying the context architecture for information is significant for performance evaluation, therefore the metrics search scope and overlay node stress have been listed. Finally, the metric peering table size is a suitable indicator of how expensive it is to set-up, maintain, and manage the topology.

Underlay-Related Metrics

To assess the impact of the used peering topology to underlay network communication, metrics as message complexity and underlay link stress can be considered as crucial.

- **Message Complexity:** Message complexity is defined as the number of messages (e.g. IP-packets) that have to be sent through the underlay network during the search for requested context information. To express the overall overhead of the search, the nodes' response messages are also taken into account by this metric.
- **Underlay Link Stress:** Underlay link stress is defined as the number of copies of a search request (network packets) that have to be sent over a single link in the underlay network. This "per link" metric only takes copies of search requests into account, not the nodes' consequent responses, analog to the overlay node stress.

Message complexity serves as a measure for the overhead introduced by the context architecture and the different peering approaches in the underlay network. The metric underlay link stress expresses the overhead per (underlay) network link.

Discussion of Results

The obtained results are illustrated and summarized in tables and histograms, grouped by metric. In case of the histograms, the x-axis is

Figure 4. RTT results

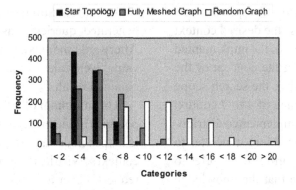

	Star	Fully Meshed	Random Graph
MIN	0.5	0.4	1
MAX	10.4	14.3	25.3
AVERAGE	4.0	5.2	10.2

used to divide the range of measurement results into intervals we denote also as categories. The frequency value on the y-axis corresponds to the number of results falling into a concrete category.

Request Response Time (RRT)

To analyze the RRT of the context architecture, each of the 1000 randomly generated queries was analyzed respectively. Afterwards, the maximum, minimum, and average value of the 1000 RRTs were calculated. The results in form of a table and a histogram showing the distribution of the RRT values are illustrated in Figure 4.

As one can see, the star topology guarantees the smallest RRT. This is due to the fact that the context service that is assigned to act as the star master is ideally chosen in such a way that it is "centered" within the network, i.e. that it provides the smallest possible link delay to each of the other context services. Combined with the fact that by this peering approach each other context service can be reached within 1 hop, it is obviously a highly optimized peering concept with respect to RRT. The fully meshed graph ranks second. Although it also guarantees to reach each of the other context services within 1 hop, the link delays

to the other context services can vary enormously as there is no single contact point for queries. Any of the context services can be contacted by a client requesting context information. Nevertheless, regarding the improvement in safeguarding against failure, the slightly worse RRT is still acceptable, if not actually preferable.

More significant differences in RRT are present in the random graph implementation. Here, generally higher RRTs have to be expected. This can be traced back to the fact that the constraint of reaching each of the other context services in 1 hop is not valid here. In any event, the histogram in Figure 4 shows that the distribution of RRT in the case of the random graph implementation is approximately uniform, reaching its peak in the mid-categories of 10-12.

Search Scope (SScp)

To measure the SScp of a query for context information, each of the 1000 randomly generated queries was analyzed respectively. Afterwards, the maximum, minimum, and average values were calculated. The obtained results are again provided in form of a table and two histograms in Figure 5.

The results indicate that in the case of a broadcasted search (Figure 5 (a)), all other context services have to be contacted if the queried context service does not possess the desired context information itself, regardless of the implemented peering topology. Following the concept of the directed search (Figure 5 (b)), the search scope vastly decreases to an average of 4 to 7 context services, depending on the implemented distribution of context information. More concrete, to explain the values of the fourth raw we refer to Figure 3. Since we assume that the knowledge about context information is distributed among several domains even in case of a star of full mesh topology we can have a SScp in average higher than one. However, as one sees, the peering approaches differ slightly, but maintain the order observed: the star topology leads the score by presenting the smallest SScp values, closely followed by the fully meshed graph, presenting almost the same results. The random graph ranks last, again due to the fact that even a directed search might have to be performed across several hops.

Overlay Node Stress (ONS)

To measure the ONS produced by a query for context information, each of the 1000 randomly generated queries, was analyzed respectively. Afterwards, the maximum, minimum, and average values were calculated. Figure 6 is illustrating the obtained results.

The minimum of 0 throughout all peering topologies is due to the fact that overlay node stress is a "per node" metric; and as only the queried context service has to copy and forward the search request, never are all overlay nodes engaged in this task. The high maximum value, in contrast to the relatively low average value concerning the broadcasted search (Figure 6 (a)), can be explained accordingly: Because the task of copying and forwarding the search request only comes up to mainly one context service, it produces one high value, and the large number of remaining context services are only forced to copy a fraction of requests, if at all. The same argument holds in case of the average values for the directed search. Looking at the directed search (Figure 6 (b)), the

Figure 5. SScp results: (a) broadcast (b) directed

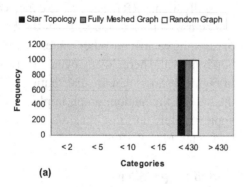

(a)

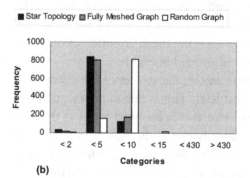

(b)

	Star	Fully Meshed	Random Graph
MIN (broadcasted)	1	430	430
MIN (directed)	1	2	2
MAX (broadcasted)	430	430	430
MAX (directed)	7	8	14
AVERAGE (broadcasted)	430	430	430
AVERAGE (directed)	4	5	7

(c)

peering approaches behave in an equivalent manner. All requests for context information can be resolved within a nearly constant (low) number of copy and forward processes. Zero values in the case of average values can also be caused by the fact that the calculated number has been significantly smaller than 1.

Peering Table Size (PTS)

The maximum, minimum, and average number of peers that comprises each overlay node are mainly defined by the topology itself. Except for the random graph, the topology has been analyzed here accordingly. The results are shown in Figure 7.

The Peering Table Size (PTS) is a crucial metric for rating the costs of establishing and managing the peering topologies. As within the star topology, only one context service has the duty to add all other context services as peers. The topology is set up least cost-intensively. This is followed by the random graph, where each context service

has to add and maintain a list of 85 peers on average. The most cost-intensive topology is the fully meshed graph, as it requires each context service to manage explicitly all other available context services as its peers, resulting in a set-up cost of **n.(n-1)**, where **n** corresponds to the total number of context services.

Since the average of peers that an overlay node comprises is meaningless for star topology and fully meshed graph, as here by definition only one node comprises peers at all (star topology), or each overlay node comprises all other overlay nodes as peers (fully meshed graph). Therefore, these values are not indicated in the Table.

Message Complexity (MC)

To determine the Message Complexity (MC), the underlay network is burdened by a query for context information, each of the 1000 randomly generated queries was analyzed respectively. Afterwards, the maximum, minimum, and average

Figure 6. Results ONS: (a) broadcast (b) directed

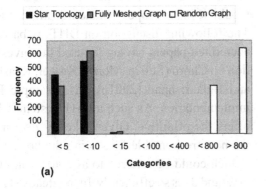

(a)

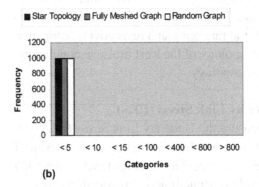

(b)

	Star	Fully Meshed	Random Graph
MIN (broadcasted)	0	0	0
MIN (directed)	0	0	0
MAX (broadcasted)	5577	5577	10153
MAX (directed)	13	13	14
AVERAGE (broadcasted)	6	6	855
AVERAGE (directed)	0	0	0

(c)

Figure 7. Results PTS

	Star	Fully Meshed	Random Graph
MIN	0	429	55
MAX	429	429	112
AVERAGE	–	–	85

values were calculated. The results are shown in Figure 8.

The results show the significant gap between the first two peering approaches, star topology and fully meshed graph, and the random graph implementation, concerning the broadcasted search (Figure 8 (a)). Although the fully meshed graph presents a significant increase in message complexity compared to the star topology, which ranks first as usual, the random graph tops the numbers dramatically. On average, the random graph burdens the underlay network by a 26-fold number of messages compared to the star topology, whereas the fully meshed graph is responsible for only a 1.5-fold increase. Applying directed search (Figure 8 (b)), the message complexity can be decreased to a tolerable level, resulting in a 1.4-fold and 2.8-fold increase for the fully meshed graph and random graph respectively, compared to the topology of the least message complexity, the star topology.

Underlay Link Stress (ULS)

To measure the Underlay Link Stress (ULS) the underlay network has to cope with (as a result of a query for context information) each of the 1000 randomly generated queries, was analyzed respectively. Afterwards, the maximum, minimum, and average values were calculated. The results are shown in Figure 9.

The ULS primarily carries authority regarding broadcasted search (Figure 9 (a)). Here, the maximum reaches a peak of over 10,000 message copies that have to pass one link in the random graph peering topology. The fully meshed graph halves

the value, as does the star topology in comparison to the fully meshed graph. Fortunately, these peaks can be seen as outliers by studying the histogram shown in Figure 9 (a). The average ranges between 6 and 115. Concerning the directed search (Figure 9 (b)), the peering topologies again act in a nearly identical fashion, limiting the message scope to an almost constant low number, on average.

Distributed Hash Tables: A Fourth Peering Approach

Of interest is further the comparison of the three peering approaches, star topology, fully meshed graph, and random graph, with Distributed Hash Tables (DHTs). The use of a DHT implies possessing a globally unique naming and addressing scheme for context information, whose definition would be in the scope of Standardization Bodies. The following discussion on DHTs is based on accredited papers having focused the investigation on Chord (Stoica, Morris, Karger, Kaashoek and Balakrishnan (2001b)), as a sample DHT implementation. As such a DHT system, Chord offers the primitive: Given a key, it determines the node responsible for storing the key's value (which could be referred to as context information) and does so efficiently. In the steady state, in an N-node network, each node maintains routing information for only about $O(\log N)$ other nodes and resolves all lookups via $O(\log N)$ messages to other nodes. Updates to the routing information for nodes leaving and joining require only $O(\log^2 N)$ messages. Attractive features of such a DHT system include simplicity, provable correctness, and provable performance, even in the

Figure 8. Results MC: (a) broadcast (b) directed

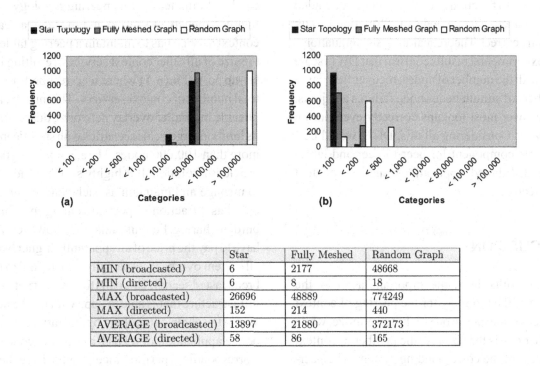

(a)   (b)

	Star	Fully Meshed	Random Graph
MIN (broadcasted)	6	2177	48668
MIN (directed)	6	8	18
MAX (broadcasted)	26696	48889	774249
MAX (directed)	152	214	440
AVERAGE (broadcasted)	13897	21880	372173
AVERAGE (directed)	58	86	165

(c)

Figure 9. Results ULS: (a) broadcast (b) directed

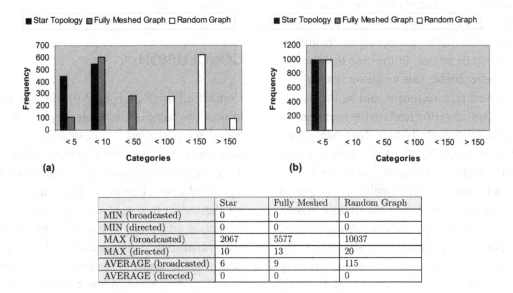

(a)   (b)

	Star	Fully Meshed	Random Graph
MIN (broadcasted)	0	0	0
MIN (directed)	0	0	0
MAX (broadcasted)	2067	5577	10037
MAX (directed)	10	13	20
AVERAGE (broadcasted)	6	9	115
AVERAGE (directed)	0	0	0

(c)

face of concurrent node arrivals and departures. It continues to function correctly, albeit at degraded performance, when a node's information is only partially correct. Theoretical analysis, simulations, and experimental results confirm that DHTs scale well with the number of nodes, recover from large numbers of simultaneous node failures and joins, and answer most lookups correctly even during recovery. Considering all this, DHTs would be a valuable component for peer-to-peer and large-scale distributed applications such as context architectures.

DISCUSSION

As the results show, one important factor for the choice of the topology for the peering of context services is the metric one seeks to optimize, while another one is the size (i.e. the number of context sources) of the corresponding system. The peering of context services as a star provides the best values with regard to request response time. It guarantees the shortest RRT, assuming that the star master is "ideally" located within the network. Furthermore, the peering topology can easy be set up and managed, and only one node has to maintain the peering table. Though, this implies a large drawback of the star topology: it manifests a single point of failure. In the case that the star master is unreachable (for whatever reason), the whole context architecture would be out of service. This consideration leads to the next peering concept, the fully meshed graph. It provides nearly equal results regarding the test metrics, traced back to the fact that the constraint to reach each of the other context services within 1 hop applies here too, although the RRTs are slightly higher. Looking at search scope and overlay node stress, the two peering approaches rank almost equally. The underlay link stress and message complexity turn out higher for the fully meshed graph, as it is connected to each of the other context services via 1 hop, but does not ensure the shortest underlay

path to it. Even though a single point of failure can be eliminated by this peering topology, it is highly expensive to set up and manage, as each context service has to maintain a peering table of the size of all other context services, resulting in a set-up cost of **n.(n-1)** where **n** corresponds to the total number of context services. This may be applicable in smaller overlay networks, but exceeds its limits in large-scale scenarios with significantly more than 100,000 nodes. Here, a random graph provides a solution. It is highly scalable and easy to manage and maintain as each context service only has a fraction of peers, resulting in a fairer burden-sharing. For this scalability, however, you have to pay the price of an apparently higher overall system overhead, especially with regard to the broadcasted search. This calls for a robust network infrastructure that is able to cope with it. The next step in the chain of topology optimizations would be the application of a DHT as peering concept. Corresponding performance results have been adopted from accredited papers. Furthermore, the use of a DHT requires a globally unique naming and addressing scheme for context information, whose design, implementation, and evaluation within a DHT peering approach provide material for future work.

CONCLUSION

Context information is hard to come by in peer-to-peer overlay networks. Hence the integration of context frameworks is a desirable enhancement to acquire and distribute context information. This chapter introduced context in general and described context architectures that are suitable for the use in peer-to-peer scenarios. The main focus was on a study of the performance for the retrieval of context information, particularly in the case of large-scale environments with a distribution of context services and context information over a multitude of (administrative) domains. An overlay network with 430 context services has been set up above a simulated underlay consisting of 1740 nodes in total and distributed over 430 domains. By means of this test environment, possible concepts to peer distributed context services and consequent search characteristics have been implemented, investigated, and evaluated with regard to efficiency and network overhead, both underlay-related and overlay-related. Three typical peering approaches for context services were introduced and analyzed: star topology, fully meshed graph and random graph. After implementation, request response time, message scope, overlay node stress, peering table size, message complexity and underlay link stress were measured for each peering topology, with respect to the two search patterns broadcasted search and directed search. For the directed search we have assumed additional information about network routing and location of context information. While in a classical peer-to-peer scenario such information may not be available, for a network provider it is possible to exploit those values as well for a provider based context architecture. Based on the results shown in Figure 5, Figure 6, Figure 8 and Figure 9 we can clearly indentify a ranking of peering approaches with regard to the corresponding evaluation metrics. Best performance values have been shown by the star topology, followed by the full mesh and the random graph. However, in case of the peering table size the situation changes in a way that the random graph based peering shows the smallest maximum value. In addition there is no single point of failure problem as in the case of a star. Therefore we can recommend in case of small to midrange scale systems containing at least one powerful and reliable node, a star like topology is the most promising approach. In case such a node is not available, the full mesh is more reliable with regard to failures while still showing good performance. If we increase the size of the addressed scenarios towards peer-to-peer networks, the size of a neighbor table to maintain becomes an important issue. In case of millions of context sources a small and constant, or loga-

rithmic growing neighbor table is a key issue. For those systems a random-graph or DHT based peering corresponds to a good tradeoff between performance as well as scalability and reliability.

REFERENCES

W3C. (n.d.). *Composite Capabilities/Preferance Profile (CC/PP)*.

W3C. (n.d.). *OWL - Web Ontology Language*.

Abowd, G. D., Dey, A. K., Brown, P. J., Davies, N., Smith, M., & Steggles, P. (1999). Towards a better understanding of context and context-awareness. In *Proceedings of the 1st international symposium on handheld and ubiquitous computing* (p. 304-307). Karlsruhe, Germany.

Baldauf, M., Dustdar, S., & Rosenberg, F. (2006). A survey on context-aware systems. *International Journal of Ad Hoc and Ubiquitous Computing*.

Bardram, J. E. (2005). The Java Context Awareness Framework (JCAF) A service infrastructure and programming framework for context-aware applications. In Pervasive Computing (p. 98-115). Springer.

Batagelj, V., & Brandes, U. (2005). Efficient generation of large random networks. *Physical Review, 71*(036113).

Chen, H., Finin, T., & Joshi, A. (2003). An ontology for context aware pervasive computing environments. *The Knowledge Engineering Review, 18*(3), 197–207. doi:10.1017/S0269888904000025

Dey, A. K. (2000). *Providing architectural support for building context-aware applications.* (PhD thesis), College of Computing, Georgia Institute of Technology, USA.

Hull, R., Neaves, P., & Bedford-Roberts, J. (1997). Towards situated computing. In *Proceedings of the First international symposium on wearable computers* (ISWC '97) (p. 146-153).

Indulska, J., & Sutton, P. (2003). *Location management in pervasive systems*. In *Proceedings Workshop on wearable, invisible, context-aware, ambient, pervasive and ubiquitous computing* (Vol. 21, p. 143-152).

Korkea-aho, M. (2000). *Context-Aware Application Survey. (Technical Report Tik-110.551)*. Finland: Helsinki University of Technology.

McCarthy, J. (1993) Notes on Formalizing Context. *IJCAI*, 555-562.

Salber, D., Dey, A. K., & Abowd, G. D. (1999). Aiding the development of context-enabled applications. In *Proceedings of chi '99* (pp. 434–441). The Context Toolkit.

Schilit, B., Adams, N., & Want, R. (1994). *Context-aware computing applications*. In *Proceedings of the IEEE workshop on mobile computing systems and applications*. Santa Cruz, CA.

Stoica, I., Morris, R., Karger, D., Kaashoek, F., & Balakrishnan, H. (2001a). *Chord: A scalable peer-to-peer lookup service for internet applications (Rapport technique)*. Cambridge, MA: MIT Press.

Stoica, I., Morris, R., Karger, D., Kaashoek, F., & Balakrishnan, H. (2001b). Chord: A scalable peer-to-peer lookup service for internet applications. In *Proceedings of the 2001 ACM Sigcomm conference* (p. 149-160).

Strang, T., & Linnho-Popien, C. (2004). A context modeling survey. In Proceedings of Ubicomp, The 1st international workshop on advanced context modelling, reasoning and management (p. 34-41).

Yalagandula, P., Sharma, P., Banerjee, S., Basu, S., & Lee, S.-J. (2006). *S3: A scalable sensing service for monitoring large networked systems*. In Proceedings of INM '06: The 2006 sigcomm workshop on internet network management (p. 71-76). Boca Raton, FL: ACM Press.

Zegura, E. W., Calvert, K. L., & Bhattacharjee, S. (1996). How to model an internetwork. In Proceedings of IEEE infocom (Vol. 2, p. 594-602). San Francisco.

Chapter 6
Request–Driven Cross–Media Content Adaptation Technique

Mohd Farhan Md Fudzee
Deakin University, Australia

Jemal Abawajy
Deakin University, Australia

ABSTRACT

Devices, standards and software develop rapidly, but still often independently of each other. This creates problems in terms of content suitability on various devices. Also, in mobile environment, user and system-level applications must execute subject to a variety of resource constraints. In order to deal with these constraints, content adaptation is required. In this chapter, we justify the need of distributed cross media content adaptation and the potential of utilizing Web Services as the adaptation providers. We introduce request-driven context to complement constraint-driven and utility-driven approaches. We describe the request context mapping and propose a novel path's determination scheme for determining the optimal service proxies to facilitate the adaptation tasks. To better illustrate the disjoint portions in content passing between service proxies, two communication models were associated. Then, within Web Services, we explain the related protocols and socket connection between adaptation's services. We conclude with discussion regarding the strengths of the proposed architecture.

INTRODUCTION

With advances in mobile devices (e.g., mobile phones and PDAs) capabilities and wide range of networks, the use of Web on mobile devices is fast becoming widespread and popular. Although, a wide range of devices can now access the Web, it is common that devices and software develop

rapidly and often independently of each other. Also, in mobile environment, user and system-level applications must execute subject to a variety of resource constraints such as network bandwidth, battery power and available screen resolution. All these pose significant challenges in terms of Web content suitability for heterogeneous devices. In order to deal with these challenges, content adaptation is an attractive solution to increase the usability and suitability of Web content in heterogeneous

DOI: 10.4018/978-1-61520-973-6.ch006

devices. As a result, content adaptation has been receiving significant amount of attention within research community.

In this chapter, we address the problem of cross media content adaptation. In cross media content adaptation, a media needs to be converted from one form into another (e.g., text to speech, audio to text, video to audio, video to images, video to text); translated (e.g., one text language into others, one audio language into others); summarized (e.g., video abstraction, video key frame extraction, content filtering); or even integrated (e.g., integrating video into animation, emerging technologies). To achieve this, a flexible platform for passing and delivering the content (e.g., original, partially adapted or fully adapted) across the distributed proxies and servers location is crucial. The platform should be reliable, scalable and consistence in performing adaptation. Moreover, cross media content adaptation must be able to facilitate resources' constraints (especially for mobile devices), media utility and user's accessibility (i.e., user perceived utility).

Over the past years, a considerable amount of researches on content adaptation using methods such as content selection, transcoding, or distillation have been discussed. Transcoding is a technique of converting one encoding to another, in digital to digital conversion. Distillation-based adaptation extracts the most important aspects of a Web page (e.g., page title, main text column). These methods can be performed at a particularly designated proxy or at an origin server or at the client device itself (Fawaz et al., 2008; Md Fudzee & Abawajy, 2008). The common thread among all these methods is that they perform well in browsing (e.g., adapting layout, text column) and single element content adaptation (e.g., converting format within a content media). However, cross media adaptation requires more than various adaptations such as fidelity adaptation (i.e., convert two bits image into black and white image), modality adaptation (i.e., change

one column text into two column), layout adaptation (i.e., change the orientation of the Web) and structure rearrangement (i.e., organize long text into read more option) (Lei & Georganas, 2001; Berhe et al., 2004, 2005; Md Fudzee & Abawajy, 2008; Shahidi, 2008). To this end, most of existing studies focus on device resource constraints' (Mohan et al., 1999; Lum & Lau, 2002, 2003; Hsiao et al., 2008; He et al,. 2007; Zhang, 2007) and do not consider the end-user perceived utility. Thus, how to support transparent delivery and convenient use of Web content across a wide range of networks and devices while providing the best user perceived utility is still an open problem.

In this chapter, we focus on the problem of content adaptation that is tailored to user preferences and to device capabilities. For instance, one may request to have Spanish news to be translated into English audio and this user need can be captured through query-based or other interactive techniques. As such adaptation services are computationally expensive; they should be deployed on distributed infrastructures. To this end, we propose a distributed request-driven cross-media content adaptation technique to address user-driven cross-media adaptation. To the best of our knowledge, this is the first attempt to introduce desire/request-driven content adaptation.

The rest of the chapter is organized as follows. Section 2 presents the background in content adaptation. In Section 3, the service oriented architectural design of the distributed multimedia content adaptation is presented. The content adaptation conceptual framework and the interaction protocol are also discussed. We also describe the semantic representation, discuss the request context mapping using rule-based technique and adaptation task scheduling approach used to achieve the stated aim of the content adaptation. A score tree scheme for the path determination is also discussed. In Section 4, the requirements of distributed adaptation via Web Services are elaborated on the connection conceptuality. This includes explanation on Web Services interaction model, related protocols (UDDI and SOAP) and definition of services using Web Services description Language (WSDL). Section 5 presents the discussion on the reliability, scalability, extensibility, simplicity, generality and portability of the design. In section 6, related work is presented. Section 7 discusses the future research direction.

BACKGROUND

In this section, we motivate the need for cross-media adaptation and explain cross media adaptation as well as various requirements for cross-media adaptations.

Motivational Example

To motivate the need for cross-media adaptation, consider this scenario: Suppose Mohammad went to visit his relative at Royal Women's hospital in Melbourne. Mohammed learns that his relative has been diagnosed with a heart complication. To get more information on the heart complication that his relative diagnosed with, Mohammed decided to browse, using his web-enabled mobile phone, the e-health server at the hospital. Confronted with medical jargons received from the e-health server and to make sense of it all, Mohammed decided to browses an e-learning server. Mohammed prefers graphic-based explanation of the heart condition in Spanish. However, the content on the e-learning server is a video and it is in English. To achieve the desired content form (i.e., summarized Spanish audio corresponded to the related image sequences), at least four adaptation tasks (later referred as tasks) are required: (1) video type conversion to a series of images, (2) text translation, (3) summarization of the information in Spanish; and (4) text to speech conversion.

Several techniques such as client-side adaptation, server-side adaptation and proxy-based adaptation have been proposed to enable content adaptation. In client side approach, the client (e.g., PDA, smart phone) is responsible to perform the adaptation. In server-side approach, adaptation is performed at the server. For example, when the user request for Web content, the server automatically collects the client context (e.g., device's profile, user preferences and network profile) and using this information, performs the necessary adaptation of the content before sending it to the user. In proxy-based approach, the proxy intercepts the Web content and performs the necessary adaptation based on the client context (e.g., device's profile, user preferences) and forwards it to the client. A hybrid approach that distributes adaptation process between servers and clients is also possible. For example, transcoding of image requires intensive resources and can be delegated to a server while adapting the Web page-based dimension (i.e., resizing icon size, resizing heading font size) can be done at the client side. None of these approaches are suitable for the motivational example given above. To show this, assume that the content server supports text to speech conversion but not the remaining 3 needed adaptation. Also, assume that the client device is not capable of performing any adaptation (e.g., due to unavailability of converting software). Suppose via Web Services, a specific proxy supports text related adaptation such as text translation and text summarization and another proxy supports video type conversion. In this sense, neither the user's device nor the origin content server nor the specific proxy alone is capable to perform entire tasks. Also, to find a specific proxy (out of a sudden) to support the ever-growing adaptation strategies seems to be a difficult (this is where the service profile is essential). Besides, building one centralized system to facilitate various cross media adaptation is almost impossible, inefficient and costly.

Hence, there is an urgent need to perform and manage the entire tasks in distributed location where it can be possibly done. Moreover, the emergence of Web Services has made it possible to support distributed approach to a new level; where the tasks are facilitated by service proxies via the Web Services (Berhe et al., 2004; Fudzee & Abawajy, 2008). Many distributed content adaptation techniques have exploited Web services (El-Khatib et al., 2004; Berhe et al., 2005; Shahidi et al., 2008; Fawaz et al., 2008). A flexible platform for passing and delivering the content (e.g., original, partially adapted or fully adapted) across the distributed proxies and servers location is crucial. The platform should be reliable, scalable and consistence in performing adaptation. With these criteria satisfied, best effort and performance can be guaranteed.

DISTRIBUTED CONTENT ADAPTATION ARCHITECTURE

In this section, we describe a service oriented framework for distributed content adaptation.

We also describe the path determiner algorithm using path's score tree and the association of messages (content) passing with communication model.

Conceptual Framework

Figure 1 illustrates the logical concepts of the proposed distributed content adaptation system architecture. The system is based on service oriented architecture (SOA), which is a form of distributed system architecture that is typically characterized by logical view of actual entity; message oriented with service description; and platform neutral (Booth et al., 2004). In SOA, software applications are built on the basic components called services, processes, types, etc., and defined in terms of what it does (Hashimi, 2003).

The framework consists of five main components: client devices (e.g., multimedia desktop, PDA and mobile phones), content server, local proxies, service proxies, and registry (service profile and client profile).

Content server is the origin server where the Web content resides. It is distributed across the Internet. Web content is mostly designed for desktop environment with rich media contents. A service proxy registers and periodically updates their services at the service profile database. Also, based on the local proxy instruction, the service proxy adapts content on behalf of the user. The

Figure 1. Distributed content adaptation framework

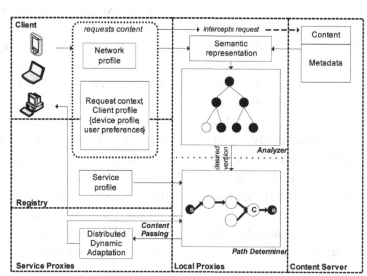

local proxy is mainly responsible for collecting necessary information (e.g., network profile, client profile) for adaptation and mapping them into the semantic representation. To accomplish this task, the local proxy uses the analyzer and path determiner. The analyzer is mainly concerned with information gathering and processing while the path determiner acts as a broker and plans for optimal adaptation strategy and matches adaptation request with available adaptation services from service profile database. The path determiner plans for the tasks allocation to the related service proxies. The network profile (e.g., UMTS/GPRS/ GSM Data) is gathered on-demand as it is hard to determine the user network environment in advance. The local proxy gathers this information using a particular network monitor for each client. This information is stored in the local proxy's virtual or volatile memory.

Client profile stores information on user preferences (e.g., display preference, cost, and tolerable response time) and client device profiles (e.g., display size, bandwidth, memory, user display preference, software and energy). This registry can be maintained at client profile server and is updated by the local proxies on a regular basis. Client profile is represented according to the composite capabilities/preference profile (CC/ PP) specification introduced by World Wide Web Consortium (W3C). This profile can be detected through Bluetooth or ZigBee configuration, if activated. As a device is identical based on the model, it can be represented by a model code. When a model code is detected, the model attri-

butes are quickly achieved from the registry. In contrast, service profile registry stores information or list of adaptation service proxies on the Internet. This list is maintained at a particular service registry server (e.g., Universal Description Discovery Integration (UDDI) server). Examples of information that are maintained in service profile include adaptation service proxies, adaptation service types with supported formats, available bandwidth, availability status, cost, adaptation time, location and configuration (refer Table 1). A new adaptation service proxy must publish their services. Existing adaptation service proxies update their service listings periodically and a reputation bootstrapping for trust establishment among Web Services (Malik & Bouguettaya, 2009) can be used to enhance trustworthiness of the service proxies.

Interaction Protocol

We now describe how the system components described in Figure 1 interact with each other to accomplish the desired cross-media content adaptation. Figure 2 shows the interaction sequence diagram. When a user issues a request for the content, the nearest local proxy intercepts the request and sends it to the corresponding content server. The local proxy then fetches user preferences from the client profile database. Also, it asks the service profile to check with the service proxies for the available adaptation services.

In response to the local proxy request for the Web content, the content server sends to the local

Table 1. Example of service registry in service profile

	Service Listing	Input (format)	Output (format)	Loc	Cost	Time	Status	Rating
Service 1	Translate()	word (doc)	Word (txt, rtf)	http://...	free	10 sec	idle	good
Service 2	Convert()	Video (avi)	Images (tif)	http://...	50cents	15 sec	busy	...
Service n	...	...	...	...	...	...	...	...

Figure 2. Content adaptation sequence diagram

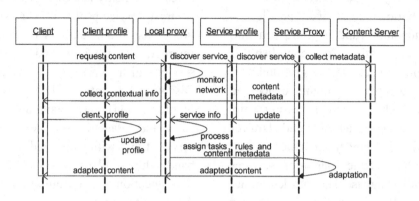

proxy metadata for the requested content. At the same time, the local proxy gets the client profile from client host. The local proxy also gathers the network profile. It then matches the collected client profile with the client profile that exists in the client profile database. If there is no entry for the client, the collected client information is added to the client profile database. The service proxy updates its information to the service profile, which then sends these updates to the local proxy. Using these profiles, parameters and metadata, semantic representation is constructed. Then, the local proxy via the analyzer analyzes and maps the tasks using the constructed representation. The output from the analyzer is the required tasks. Using the output from the analyzer, the path determiner computes an optimal adaptation path. The local proxy assigns tasks to the selected service proxies for adaptation and monitors the overall content adaptation, including the content passing/delivery. Finally, the local proxy retrieves the entire adapted content and sends it to the user.

Semantic Representation Model

The information collected by the local proxy is mapped into the semantic representation. Semantic representation is used to convey the collected data into linguistic term in order to relate their form together. These representation is then processed by the analyzer which computes the required tasks (to produce desired version) using rule-based technique. Generally, we can describe the entire context semantic using the Equations 1-3. There are n adaptation factors (Equation 1). Each adaptation factor, $factor_i \in adaptation_{factors}$, has m attributes (Equation 2) and each attribute, $attribute_j \in factor_i$, has k quantization steps (where each quantization can be represented in a certain value) (Equation 3):

$$adaptation_{factors} = \{factor_1, factor_2, request_{context}, \dots factor_n\} \qquad (1)$$

$$factor_i = \{attribute_1, attribute_2, attribute_3, \dots atrribute_m\} \qquad (2)$$

$$attribute_j = \{qstep_1, qstep_2, qstep_3, \dots qstep_k\} \qquad (3)$$

The following is an example of adaptive context representation:

$$adaptation_{factors} = \{user_{preferences}, user_{situation}, device_{profile}, netword_{parameters}\}$$

$$request_{context} = \{preffered\_language, readability, visual\}$$

$$user_{preferences} = \{scrolling\}$$

$user_{situation} = \{meeting, driving\}$

$network_{parameters} = \{bandwidth\}$

$device_{profile} = \{screensize, color, supported\ format\}$

$color_{properties} = \{blackwhite, 2bits, 16bits\}$

For more detail regarding semantic representation for the constraints/resources based context, and media utility context, interested readers can refer to (Lum & Lau, 2002, 2003; Hsiao et al., 2008; He et al., 2007; Virgilio et al., 2007; Yang & Shao, 2007; Yang et al., 2008), and (Prang et al., 2006, 2007) work, respectively.

We assume that the Web authors provide the Web page and content with the metadata during authoring process. This will make unnecessary real time content decomposition and information loss. The authors will have some control over the final presentation. We use the universal content structure model (Yang & Shao, 2007) to represent the content metadata as follow:

$web\_content_{properties} = \{property_1, property_2, property_3, ... property_n\}$

$property_n = \{object1_{metadata}, object2_{metadata}, ... objectN_{metadata}\}$

$object1_{metadata} = \{qstep_1, qstep_2, qstep_3, ... qstep_n\}$

The following is an example of the web content metadata representation:

$web\_content_{properties} = \{content, navigation, presentation\}$

$content_n = \{video_{metadata}, audio_{metadata}, image_{metadata}, language_{metadata}\}$

$navigation_n = \{hypertext_{metadata}, link_{metadata}, hypermedia_{metadata}\}$

$presentation_n = \{modality_{metadata}, column_{metadata}\}$

$column_{metadata} = \{single, double, triple\}$

Request context is important to facilitate user immediate desire. For example, a person visiting France could state "I want to hear the news in English". We can describe the request context as follows:

$request_{context} = \{language_{media}, readability_{media}, browsing_{media}\}$

where the conditions can be assumed as below:

condition 1: $language_{audio} = \{English\}$

condition 2: $readability_{text} = \{summarize\}$

condition 3: $browsing_{text} = \{change\_audtio\}$

These request contexts can be captured using mechanisms such as the query-based approach (Chakravarthy et al., 1990) or interactive approaches (Yang & Shao, 2007).

Mapping Representation to Tasks

We use rule-based technique for mapping requests to tasks. The rule takes a form as shown below:
    Condition n:

```
If situation == x
      then y;
```

where "condition" is the particular request to be fulfilled, "x" is the default media state/format to be analyzed and "y" is the required tasks.

For example, suppose we have a user requesting for a sport news video highlight in English while driving using his PDA. In this case, we have to express rules for "driving situation", "audio_length", "video_length", and "audio_original". Based Equation 5, these rules can be stated as follows:

Condition 1:

```
If video_length > 1 minute
      keyframe extraction ( );
```

Condition 2:

```
If situation == driving
      convert video to audio ( );
```

Condition 3:

```
If highlight_audio == long
    summarize audio( );
```

Condition 4:

```
If audio_original =! audio preferred_
language
      translate audio ( );
```

Then, the analyzer gathers all the required tasks and lists it as below:

```
keyframe extraction(), convert video to
audio(), summarize audio(),and translate
audio().
```

We can rearrange the sequence of the tasks (based on logical dependency) as in Figure 3:

Next, the path determiner plans for the tasks allocation to the related service proxies by taking into account the information from service profile registry. The original content or partial adapted content will be passed within service proxies to be adapted.

For the service proxy to adapt content on behalf of the user, it uses the offered services. In contrast, an adaptation task can be performed by one or more service proxies. There is many to many relationships between tasks and service proxies. As such, a complete adaptation request may consist of several tasks that require services from several adaptation service proxies. This requires a mechanism to schedule the tasks to the service proxies. In the following subsection, we will elaborate on how this is achieved.

Adaptation Task Scheduling

Tasks can be performed serially, in parallel or both. Therefore, a proper task scheduling is required to increase overall adaptation performance. The outputs of the path determiner are the assignment of tasks to the related service proxies.

We have n tasks: $t = \{t_1, t_2 \dots t_n\}$ a and m service proxies: $p = \{p_1, p_2 \dots p_m\}$. A task may depend onto another task $\{t_2 \rightarrow t_1\}$ or independent of one another $\{t_2 \leftrightarrow t_1\}$. A service proxy $p_i \in p$ may provide adaptation to one or more tasks.

$$Pt = \{p_1: t_1, t_2; p_2: t_3, t_4; p_3: t_5, t_6\} \qquad (4)$$

The problem of determining the best path for the tasks $t = \{t_1, t_2 \dots t_n\}$ by service proxies $p = \{p_1, p_2 \dots p_n\}$ can be generally viewed as decision making problem. El-Khatib et al. (2004) and $p - \{p_1, p_2, \dots p_n\}$ Berhe et al. (2005) consider the solution using directed acyclic graph (DAG) where the path start with a start node and finish with an end node. The transformation prescript graph is organized in serial manner.

Figure 3. Required tasks precedence graph

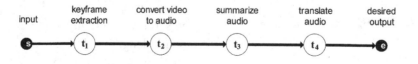

We apply a horizontal (from left to right rather than up to down, in order to clearly show the possible connection between start and end node) path's tree, where the desired path will be selected based on score node and availability status. In addition, adaptation tasks can be executed in parallel without being bounded by the media data format. The aggregate score can be calculated using summative or multiplicative approach. Using multiplicative approach is good in the sense that we can easily incorporate availability criterion. However, it will increase complexity of the calculation. Therefore, we apply summative formula as in Berhe et al. (2005). However, the approach used in Berhe et al. (2005) and Fawaz et al. (2008) increases the chances to generate identical aggregate score (especially before assigning weight to each criterion) and include availability criterion into the score computation. For instance, if we have 2 identical score for top two options, then we need to have another decision making condition/rules. This will complicate the overall path determination process, which should be avoided. Therefore, unlike the method used in Berhe et al. (2005) and Fawaz et al. (2008) for calculating score at each path node, we use the comparative method (e.g., compare the value at the ith node with the maximum or minimum node value at the same level). The comparative method is simple and the score is fine-grained as well as reduces the potential to generate identical final score. Moreover, we consider availability criterion into a different decision category.

To illustrate the proposed technique, suppose we have tasks $t = \{t_1, t_2, t_3\}$, where t_1 is conversion of video to animation, t_2 is translation of Spanish to English audio (of the video) and t_3 is media summarization of the animation. Tasks t_1 and t_2 are independent of each other, but both are the predecessors of t_3. Suppose the three tasks t_1, t_2 and t_3 can be performed by any of the following service providers: $\{p_1 p_2\}$, $\{p_3 p_4\}$ and $\{p_5 p_6\}$. The assignment of the tasks to the service proxies can be represented as critical path analysis as shown in Figure 4. We represent this as a decision problem to find the optimal score in a path tree. The maximum number of available paths to be generated is bounded by Equation 5, where n is a number of service proxies available for a particular task, and m is a number of tasks for a particular n.

$$1^{m_1} \times \ldots \times (n-1)^{m_{n-1}} \times n^{m_n} \qquad (5)$$

Decision criteria are divided into two categories (based on their pertinent functionality), namely score-based category and deterministic category. The former category associates path with an aggregate score. The latter category determines the availability of the path. Table 2 depicted some examples of criteria categorization. New criterion can be simply included according to the relevant category.

In Figure 5, each path (1 to 8) is associated with an aggregate score. Together, a path also associated with bitwise AND operation table. Score for each criterion in a node is represented by a normalized score. Note that t_1 and t_2 are independent, so, their sequence is flexible.

Score-Based Category

Path's Aggregate Score

The Aggregate Score *AgS (P)*, for each path is based on the sum of weighted criteria score S_l *(ccw)*, where k is the maximum number of weighted score in a particular path, is defined as Equation 6:

$$AgS(P) = \sum_{l=1}^{k} S_l(ccw) \qquad (6)$$

Figure 4. Possible adaptation paths

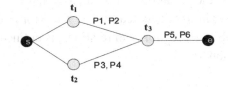

Table 2. Examples of criteria categorization

Score-based function		Deterministic function
Positive relation	Negative relation	Bit-wise
Rating	Service cost	Availability
Reliability	Adaptation time	
Trustworthy	Transport time	

Figure 5. Horizontal tree for selecting the best candidate's path based on associated node score

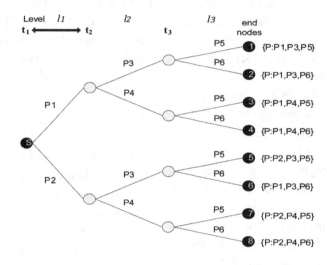

Highest aggregate score is represented as the best adaptation path.

Generic Node Score

If a node is associated with more than one criterion, score for the combine criteria $S_l(cc)$ for that node is defined as Equation 7, where n is the maximum number of criterion c_m:

$$S_l(cc) = \sum_{m=1}^{n} S_l(c_m) \qquad (7)$$

Also, each criterion can be associated with a weight, $w_m \in [0, 1]$ subject to the total weight $\sum w = 1$ and $w_m > 0$. For example, one may concern more about the cost rather than time. So, the cost criterion has a higher weight (value) compared to time criterion (for instance, 0.75 for cost and 0.25 for time). Note that only the score-based cat-

egory can be associated with weight. To associate weight for each criterion and compute the score, we define Equation 8:

$$S_l(ccw) = \sum_{m=1}^{n} (S_l(c_m) \times w_m) \qquad (8)$$

Positive and Negative Score Behavior

Each score belongs to either positive or negative behavior. In general, the behavior is modeled using the first order modeling in order to monitor the change of S_l against the criteria value v_i. This modeling is used to captures the variation of S_l against the variation of v_i in a particular criteria c_m domain. It is denoted by $S_l = f_j(v_j)$ for j^{th} criteria. Score $S_l c_m$ for both relations, is defined as equation 9:

Figure 6. (a) First order model for group a (positive relation) (b) group b (negative relation)

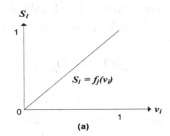
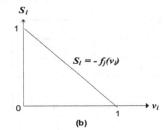

$$S_l(c_m) = \begin{cases} a \text{ for } & f_j(v_l) \\ b \text{ for } & -f_j(v_l) \end{cases} \qquad (9)$$

where v_i is the value for criteria c_m, for each service path p_x, and j the maximum number of v_i.

In the positive behavior a, S_l increases linearly when v_i increases, vice versa as in Figure 6a ($S_l = f_j(v_l)$). For instance, consider the reliability criterion. Higher reliability should be represented by a higher score. The corresponding score at each node for criteria c_m is defined as Equation 10, where $v_i max$ is the maximum value of the row:

$$a = \frac{v_i}{v_i \max} \qquad (10)$$

In the negative behavior b, S_l decreases linearly when v_i increases, vice versa as in Figure 6b ($S_l = -f_j(v_l)$). As such, higher criterion value doesn't represent that they are better. For instance, consider the adaptation time criterion. On the user point of view, higher adaptation time should be represented by a lower score, while lower time should have a higher score. Score for the second group is defined as Equation 11, where $v_i min$ is the minimum value of the row:

$$b = \begin{cases} \dfrac{v_i \min}{v_i} & if\, v_i \min > 0 \\ 1 - a & if\, v_i \min = 0 \end{cases} \qquad (11)$$

Note that in Equation 11, the case $v_i min = 0$ can only occurs in the cost criterion because, it is possible to have free adaptation cost for the time being. However, when adaptation services become commercial, service providers will definitely charge at least a minimum cost. As such, the probability of using the second formula in this equation is very low.

Deterministic Category

The second category is the deterministic criteria such as availability criterion, where the value is either 0 or 1. This criterion is represented using separated bitwise AND operation table (see Table 3). The result of the *AND* operation determines whether a path do exist (result = 1) at a given moment or not (result = 0). Note that, the change of the value in this table will not affect the score in the score-based.

After the optimal adaptation path is chosen based on the proposed strategy, the original content or partial adapted content is passed within service proxies. This requires a mechanism to deliver the content (including the adaptation instruction) to the service proxies. In the following subsection, we will elaborate on how this is achieved.

Content Passing / Delivery

In content passing and delivery, we demonstrate the process using communication models (Aggarwal et al., 2008; Huang et al., 2006; Jayram et

Table 3. Basic bitwise AND operation table for availability criterion

1st node	2nd node	Result
0	0	0
0	1	0
1	0	0
1	1	1

al., 2008) because it is straightforward and clearly show the disjoint portions. It is applied either using one-way communication model (OCM), or simultaneous communication model (SCM), or both. For instance, content (message) is treated as input output in a symmetric function $f(t)$ given with two disjoint portions of the adaptation task input t, as in equation 12.

$$t = t_a t_b \qquad (12)$$

In OCM, is the predecessor of. Assume, is translation of Spanish to English text and is summarization of English text. Service proxy 1, performs portion, and sends the output) to service proxy 2, who performs portion based on input (refer Figure 7a). Service proxy 2 then combines both inputs (as in Equation 9) and sends the output (fully adapted content) to the local proxy.

$$E(D(t_a), t_b) = f(t_a t_b) \qquad (13)$$

SCM is applied in the case where both task is independent. Assume, is conversion of video to images and is conversion of Spanish to English audio. As shows in Figure 7b, both service proxies

1 and 2 send an adapted input) and) respectively, simultaneously to local proxy who combines the end result, as in equation 14.

$$C(D(t_a), D(t_b)) = f(t_a, t_b) \qquad (14)$$

Now, let us consider a scenario with three disjoint portions. Assume, is conversion of video to animation, is translation of Spanish to English audio (of the video) and is media summarization of the animation. Let say and are the predecessor of. Service proxies 1 and 2, performs portion and respectively and send the output) and) to service proxy 3. Then, service proxy 3, performs portion based on) and) and sends the output to the local proxy (refer Equation 15). Finally, the local proxy forwards the final output to the user (Figure 8a).

$$E(C(D(t_a), D(t_b)), t_c) = f(f(t_a, t_b), t_c) \qquad (15)$$

Consider another scenario with three tasks. Assume, is conversion of video to images, is translation of Spanish to English text and is summarization of English text. Let say is an independent task, while is the predecessor of. So, service proxy 1, performs portion and sends the output) to the local proxy. Alongside, service proxy 2, performs portion and sends the output) to service proxy 3, with which performs based on) input and sends the output to the local proxy (refer Figure 8b). As a final point, the local proxy computes both inputs (as in equation 16) and sends the output (fully adapted content) to the user.

Figure 7. (a) OCM (b) SCM

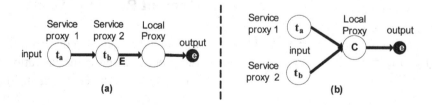

(a)

(b)

$$C(E(D(t_a),t_b),D(t_c)) = f(f(t_a,t_b),t_c) \qquad (16)$$

To ensure consistency of choosing the best adaptation services between similar service proxies, especially when handling similar requests, a selective strategy such as empirical-based, popularity-based, object-based or cluster-based can be applied (Buyya et al., 2008). This selective strategy is applicable after the local proxy determines the suitable candidates (based on the service registry information).

In order to pass and adapt the content between service proxies, a mechanism to connect and manage the proxies (both local and service) is required. In the following section, we will elaborate on how this is achieved.

WEB SERVICES AS THE ADAPTATION SERVICE PROXIES

The local proxy determines the adaptation path and bonds together the selected service proxies. These service proxies are responsible to complete their assigned adaptation task/s. To steer the content delivery, each proxy is provided with the address of previous and next destination proxy. Based on the determined path, the current proxy is required to deliver/pass their partially adapted content to the consecutive assigned proxy. This passing procedure is continual until a complete version is produced and sent back to the local proxy before reaching the user. Next, the basic

requirement of using Web Services as the service proxies is elaborated.

REQUIREMENTS

Web Services is an application accessible through a uniform resource locator (URL), that is accessed by clients using extensible markup language (XML) based protocols such as simple object access protocol (SOAP) (Rajesh et al., 2006). It is designed to support machine to machine interaction over the hypertext transfer protocol (HTTP) used on the Internet. Web Services are defined using Web Services definition language (WSDL) file. WDSL provides the XML grammar for describing network services as collections of communication endpoints capable of exchanging messages (Christensen et al., 2001).

As depicted in Figure 9, the local proxy performs interaction with service proxies via SOAP. First, the local proxy seeks for suitable adaptation service from service registry. Service proxies register and update their state at the service registry using WSDL. Service registry discovers the available services using universal description discovery and integration (UDDI) on behalf of the local proxies. The local proxy specific program connecting to a Web Service can read the WSDL and choose the available adaptation services. Then, through SOAP, the local proxy calls the related adaptation services to perform adaptation tasks. While using the services, the service proxy's

Figure 8. (a) Combining SCM tasks with OCM (b) Combining OCM tasks with SCM

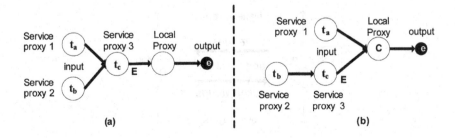

resources should be locked to avoid possible interruption and corruption by using any relevant locking mechanism (Jorstad et al., 2005).

Related Protocols

SOAP: It is a protocol for messages exchange using HTTP/HTTPS or even (parallel) PHHTP (Brock & Goscinki, 2008) in a distributed environment. It consists of three parts: an envelope that defines a framework for describing what is in a message and how to process it, a set of encoding rules for expressing instances of application-defined data types, and a convention for representing remote procedure calls (RPC) and responses (Rajesh et al., 2006).

UDDI: It is a XML-based registry for service providers to list their services and discover each other on the Internet. It is designed to be interrogated by SOAP messages and to provide access to WSDL documents describing the protocol bindings and message formats required to interact with the Web Services listed in its directory. For more information about setting and configuration of UDDI and service discovery, interested readers can refer to (Newcomer, 2002; Zhang et al., 2003; Tsai et al., 2003) and (Schmidt & Parashar, 2004; Ran, 2003; Zhu et al., 2005) respectively.

Figure 10 depicts the typical port binding using socket number via the TCP layer between two machines. Socket number is a unique port number with machine IP address. To establish binding operation, the sending machine sends request together with the socket number, while the receiving machine acknowledges the binding and replies with the related socket number. Together, they need to maintain a port table consisting the active port numbers in a process called binding. Both machines will have reversed entries for each session between them, with which is referred as binding (Comer, 2006). Note that the socket numbers of both machines is still unique as both IP addresses are not the same.

Figure 9. Local proxies-web services interaction model

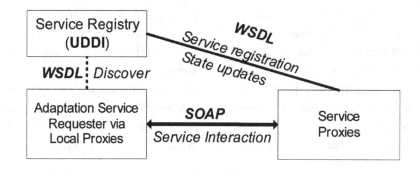

Figure 10. A typical port binding

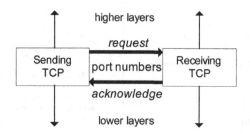

Figure 11 depicts the simultaneous service proxies' interaction with the local proxy for content passing or delivery. For example, the local proxy sends adaptation tasks to the service proxies through agreed destination port. Then, after performing the assigned tasks, both service proxies 1 and 2 send output to the same destination socket (same destination IP address and port) in a process called multiplexing.

Figure 12 shows the example of defining a translation adaptation service using WSDL. The document is provided in an XML format defining the ports and messages. Together with reusable

binding, a port is associates with a network address. A message comprises of an abstract description of exchanged data (Comer, 2006). Port types represent the collections of supported operation (in our work, it is called adaptation services). Altogether, WSDL describes the Web service public interface.

DISCUSSION

In this section, we justify the strength of our proposed design in terms of reliability, scalability, extensibility, simplicity, generality and portability.

Figure 11. Simultaneous service's proxies' interaction for content passing

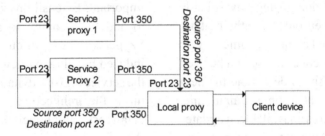

Figure 12. An example of a translation adaptation service's definition using WSDL

```
<binding name="TranslationBinding"
 type="tns:Translation">
  <soap:binding style="rpc"
    transport="http"/>
  <operation name="Translate">
   <soap:operation soapAction="translate"/>
    <input>
     <soap:body use="encoded"
       Namespace="Translate"
      encodingStyle="soap encoding"/>
    </input>
   </operation>
</binding>
<service name="TranslationService">
 <port name="Translation"
   Binding="tns:TranslationBinding">
<soap:address location="http://Translation"/>
       <state>
        <DescriptionName="......">
        </Description>
       </state>
  </port>
</service>
.........
<nextDestination>
 <soap:targetAddressLocation="..."/>
</nextDestination> ...... passing partially adapted content
```

In the application architecture perspective, reliability is viewed as the degree to which the architecture is susceptible to failure at the system level in the presence of partial failures within components, connectors, or data (Fielding, 2006). As such, distributed approach improves reliability by avoiding single points of failure (that occur in centralized system), enabling replication between similar service proxies, allowing monitoring by the local proxy, or even reducing the scope of failure to a recoverable action. Moreover, using different category for path determination criteria, benefit in two ways. First, if we have similar (if not identical) requests for content adaptation, the current generated solution path tree can be used. The similarity mapping (applicable when requests are dissimilar) can be done using any suitable clustering technique. Then, only the paths' ranking needs to be revised based on the real time service proxies' availability. Second, it also can be used as a recovery mechanism to determine the next optimal path. Suppose that at some point in time, when a service proxy turns unavailable, it updates the availability table. Automatically, the system re-computes the status (based on the *AND* logic), and any path concerning that service proxy will also becomes unavailable. The updated top path is then chosen to be the new adaptation path.

In term of score-based mechanism, our work differs from previous studies, where we consider the comparative approach to compute score, results in fairer score, rather than the ranking approach (Lum & Lau, 2003). In addition, we concentrate on more reliable model (here, we refer the reliability as the ability to reduce the chances to produce identical paths' ranking). Unlike (Berhe et al., 2005; Fawaz et al., 2008), in which this issue is neglected, we assume that having a reliable model is essential to increase the path determination performance (for instance, if we have 2 identical score for top two path options, then we need to have another decision making condition/rules, with which increases the decision complexity).

Next, we discuss the scalability of the architec-

ture. We refer scalability as the ability of content adaptation architecture to support large numbers of components including interaction among them, within an active configuration (Fielding, 2006). As such, by simplifying components; by controlling interactions; and by distributing/decentralizing services across many components, scalability can be improved. In our design, these factors are influenced by determining available adaptation services and its state; the extent of adaptation tasks distribution and monitoring interactions; allowing new updates on service listing; and even a good balance on performing adaptation tasks between service proxies. This guarantees content adaptation on a best effort basis.

In addition to scalability, extensibility is also important. Extensibility is defined as the ability to add functionality to a system (Pountain & Szyperski, 1994). In our design, extensibility is induced by allowing new services to be listed in the service registry dynamically, without restructuring the architecture. New adaptation tasks or data types can be facilitated as long as the new Web Services is introduced. Furthermore, our generic rule-based for context mapping can be easily extended with new rules.

In our design, simplicity of the architecture is also considered. We refer simplicity as simplifying the functionality of each component in the architectural design. We induce simplicity by applying principle of separation of concerns to the allocation of functionality within components (Fielding, 2006). As such, each main process is separated into independent module (e.g., the analyser, the path determiner and content passing). Moreover, each adaptation service provider can specifically facilitate a particular adaptation task, thus reducing adaptation complexity and eases the implementation process. Web Services provide specific services, offer better adaptation services and becoming intelligent (Kassoff et al., 2009; Malik & Bouguettaya, 2009).

In term of generality, the path construction technique is compared. The usage of basic directed acyclic graph (DAG) to facilitate the path construction problem has been considered in El-Khatib et al. (2004) and Berhe et al. (2005). The transformation prescript graph for DAG is organized in serial manner and bounded by the media format. Although this method reduces the selection complexity, however, it also reduces the number of options for the possible adaptation paths (especially for more general applications). Alternatively, we believe, by illustrating the adaptation path selection problem as a horizontal score tree graph representation (this is the extension of DAG), it will provide us with generality.

Finally, we discuss the strength of the architecture in term of portability. Software is portable if it can run in different environments (Ghezzi et al., 1991). As such, we induce portability by the mean of platform neutral and providing message oriented interface for public interaction.

RELATED WORK

Several techniques such as client-side adaptation, server-side adaptation and proxy-based adaptation have been proposed to enable content adaptation. In client side approach, the client (e.g., PDA, smart phone) is responsible to perform the adaptation. The advantage of this approach is that it is suitable for static adaptation (multiple versions of the Web page's content is pre-processed and stored, at the authoring time. When the user request for the page, the appropriate version will be matched based on the user and device context. In contrast, dynamic adaptation supports adaptation on-the-fly). Furthermore, the device capabilities can be determined directly. However, content adaptation is a computationally intensive task that places a significant overhead on CPU and/ or disk if compared to the delivery of traditional Web resources. Also, as some resources such as bandwidth, memory, and encoder may not be available, cross-media adaptation poses challenges to the client-side adaptation.

In server-side approach, adaptation is performed at the server. For example, when the user request for Web content, the server automatically collects the client context (e.g., device's profile, user preferences and network profile) and using this information, performs the necessary adaptation of the content before sending it to the user. InfoPyramid (Mohan et al., 1999) is an example of a system that uses server-side adaptation. Server-side approach leads to several drawbacks including single point failure and scalability problems. For relatively small number of users, server-side approach performs very well. As the number of users' increases, the server may be overload causing delays. Some of the problems with server-side approach can be ameliorated by using multiple servers. Canali et al. (2005a, 2005b) found that distributed content adaptation is relatively better when content is adapted in different servers.

In proxy-based approach, the proxy intercepts the Web content and performs the necessary adaptation based on the client context ((e.g., device's profile, user preferences) and forward it to the client. PDCAS (Lum & Lau, 2003), Xadaptor (He et al., 2007) and VTP (Hsiao et al., 2008) are some of the personal systems that implement proxy-based adaptation. Although the proxy-based approach eliminates the burden to adapt at the client or server, but only successful when it's based on both context and author provided metadata. Moreover, a proxy is bounded by its own capability (i.e., document converter proxy only deal with document adaptation) and available applications (i.e., document converter proxy only own related software libraries). Moreover, it leads to several drawbacks including single point failure and scalability problems.

A hybrid approach that distributes adaptation process between servers and clients is also possible. For example, transcoding of image requires intensive resources and can be delegated to a server while adapting the Web page-based dimension (i.e., resizing icon size, resizing heading font size) can be done at the client side. It is also possible to integrate server-based and proxy-based approaches. For example, Internet content adaptation protocol (ICAP), distributes content from the servers, via proxy caches (ICAP clients), to dedicated ICAP servers (Elson & Cerpa, 2003). The ICAP server performs tasks such as language translation, advertisement insertion, content filtering and virus scanning. It also deals with method for forwarding HTTP messages. ICAP servers are limited to simple content adaptation, thus not suitable for cross media content adaptation.

FUTURE RESEARCH DIRECTIONS

Content adaptation research in the emerging area of mobile and pervasive computing is crucial for many years to come (Adelstein et al., 2005), as adaptation is becoming an attracting solution. Many ongoing projects are tailored along this direction, yet still more productive ideas are expected to be presented. The main challenge is now to perform content adaptation from multitude of distributed resources while maintaining computing efficiency. Method for dynamically sharing resources between wired and wireless computer within the neighborhoods is also crucial to offer better content adaptation. In our next step, we plan to investigate in detail on how to automatically map from high-level to low level mapping in the efficient way. Then, we want to explore an automatic mean to generate a flexible rule-based. We also want to observe on method to determine the arrangement of tasks (in serial, parallel or both) automatically.

CONCLUSION

There is a widespread use of wireless and mobile devices - mobile phones, PDAs, Pocket PCs, handheld PCs, car navigation systems, and notebook PCs - with sufficient computing and networking capabilities to browse the Web. These devices have different capabilities due to varying processors, physical memory, network protocols, screen sizes, input methods, software libraries, and more. And with this variety of devices, certain inconveniences arise for users who want to browse the Web. This chapter builds on and contributes to the work in distributed content adaptation, focusing on supporting variety of ever growing cross-media adaptation. First, we provided some insights on the approach taken in most of the existing content adaptation systems based on the locality perspective. Then, we discussed in detail the service oriented architectural as it provide platform neutral message oriented interaction to the public on the Internet. A flexible platform for exchanging of the original content, partially adapted, or fully adapted content across the distributed proxies and server location using straightforward communication model (OCM and SCM) is proposed. These included the explanation on the content adaptation framework and interaction protocol. Then, we explained in depth the request context mapping, analysis using rule-based technique and adaptation task scheduling. We proposed score tree scheme for optimal path determination. Next, we elaborated the Web Services, as the requirement of distributed content adaptation via service providers. Web Services interaction model; related protocols (UDDI and SOAP); and definition of services using WSDL, are discussed based on the theoretical and practical perspectives. We also provide an example of defining a Web service as an adaptation service. Future direction is also discussed. Finally, we concluded with discussion regarding the scalability, reliability, simplicity, extensibility and portability of the designed architecture. Our next step is to investigate in detail the tasks allocation within the suitable proxy's candidates. This includes handling and optimizing the content exchange and delivery between local proxies and service proxies.

REFERENCES

Adelstein, F., Gupta, S. K. S., Richard, G. S., III, & Schwiebert, L. (2005). Fundamentals of mobile and pervasive computing. In Chapman, S. S. (Ed.), 1st edition Communication Engineering. New York: McGraw-Hill Press.

Aggarwal, G. (2008). Theory research at Google. *ACM SIGACT News, 39*(2), 10–28. doi:10.1145/1388240.1388242

Ardon, S. (2003). MARCH: A distributed content adaptation architecture. *International Journal of Communication Systems, 16*, 97–115. doi:10.1002/dac.582

Berhe, G., Brunie, L., & Pierson, J.-M. (2004). Modeling service-based multimedia content adaptation in pervasive computing. In *Proceedings of the 1st Conference on Computing Frontiers* (pp. 60-69). New York: ACM Press.

Berhe, G., Brunie, L., & Pierson, J.-M. (2005). Content adaptation in distributed multimedia systems. *Journal of Digital Information Management: Special Issue on Distributed Data Management, 3*(2), 96–100.

Booth, D., et al. (Eds.). (2004). W3C working group note 11: Web Services architecture. *World Wide Web Consortium*. Retrieved Nov 6, 2008, from http://www.w3.org/TR/ws-arch/#stakeholder

Brock, M., & Goscinki, A. (2008). Publishing dynamic state changes of grid resources through state aware WSDL. In *Proceedings of the 8th IEEE Int. Symposium on Cluster Computing and the Grid*. New York.

Buyya, R., Pathan, M., & Vakali, A. (Eds.). (2008). *Content delivery network*. Berlin, Heidelberg: Springer-Verlag Press. doi:10.1007/978-3-540-77887-5

Canali, C., Cardellini, V., Colajanni, M., & Lancellotti, R. (2005). Performance comparison of distributed architectures for content adaptation and delivery of Web resources. *In Proceedings of the 25th IEEE International Conference on Distributed Computing Workshops* (pp. 331-337). New York: IEEE Press.

Canali, C., Cardellini, V., Colajanni, M., Lancellotti, R., & Yu, P. S. (2005). A two-level distributed architecture for efficient Web content adaptation and delivery. In *Proceedings of the 2005 Symposium on Applications and the Internet* (pp. 132-139). New York: IEEE Press.

Chakravarthy, U., Grant, J., & Minker, J. (1990). Logic-based approach to semantic query optimization. *ACM Transactions on Database Systems, 15*(2), 162–207. doi:10.1145/78922.78924

Christensen, E., Curbera, F., Meredith, G., & Weerawarana, S. (2001). Web Services description language (WSDL) 1.1. *W3C Note 20010315*. Retrieved Nov 6, 2008, from http://www.w3.org/TR/wsdl

Comer, D. E. (2006). *Internetworking with TCP/IP: Principles, protocols and architecture* (5th ed.). Upper Saddle River, NJ: Prentice Hall Press.

Definition (n.d.). *Universal Description Discovery and Integration*. Retrieved Oct 29, 2008, from http://en.wikipedia.org/wiki/UDDI

El-Khatib, K., Bochmann, G., & El-Saddik, A. (2004). A QoS-based framework for distributed content adaptation. In *Proceedings of the 1st International Conference on Quality of Services in Heterogeneous Wired/Wireless Networks* (pp. 308-312). New York: IEEE Press.

Elson, J., & Cerpa, A. (2003). Internet content adaptation protocol (ICAP). *Network Working Group*. Retrieved Nov 6, 2008, from http://www.icap-forum.org/documents/specification/rfc3507.txt

Fawaz, Y., Berhe, G., Brunie, L., Scuturici, V.-M., & Coquil, D. (2008). Efficient Execution of Service Composition for Content adaptation in Pervasive Computing. *International Journal of Digital Multimedia Broadcasting*, 1-10.

Fielding, R. (2006). *Architectural styles and the design of network-based software architectures.* (Unpublished doctoral thesis). Irvine, CA: University of California, Irvine.

Ghezzi, C., Jazayeri, M., & Mandrioli, D. (1991). *Fundamentals of software engineering.* New York: Prentice-Hall.

Hashimi, S. (2001). Service-oriented architecture explained. *O'Reily ONDotnet.com.* Retrieved Nov 6, 2008, from http://www.ondonet.com/pub/a/dotnet/2003/08/18/soa_explained.html

He, J., Gao, T., Hao, W., Yen, I.-L., & Bastani, F. (2007). A flexible content adaptation system using a rule-Based approach. *IEEE Transactions on Knowledge and Data Engineering*, *19*(1), 127–140. doi:10.1109/TKDE.2007.250590

Hsiao, J.-L., Hung, H.-P., & Chen, M.-S. (2008). Versatile transcoding proxy for Internet content Adaptation. *IEEE Transactions on Multimedia*, *10*(4), 646–658. doi:10.1109/TMM.2008.921852

Huang, W., Shi, Y., Zhang, S., & Zhu, Y. (2006). The communication complexity of the hamming distance problem. *Journal of Information Processing Letters*, *99*, 149–153. doi:10.1016/j.ipl.2006.01.014

Jayram, T. S., Kumar, R., & Sivakumar, D. (2008). The one way communication complexity of hamming distance. *Journal of Theory and Computing*, *4*, 129–135. doi:10.4086/toc.2008.v004a006

Jorstad, I., Dustdar, S., & Thanh, D. (2005). A service oriented architecture framework for collaborative services. In *Proceedings of the 14th IEEE Int. Workshops on Enabling Technologies: Infrastructure for Collaborative Enterprise* (121-125). New York: IEEE Press.

Kassoff, M., Petrie, C., Zen, L.-M., & Genesereth, M. (2009). Semantic email addressing. *IEEE Internet Computing*, *13*(1), 48–55. doi:10.1109/MIC.2009.20

Lei, Z., & Georganas, N. D. (2001). Context-based media adaptation in pervasive computing. In *Proceedings of IEEE Canadian Conf. on Electrical and Computer* (pp. 913-918). New York: IEEE Press.

Lum, W., & Lau, F. (2002). A context-aware decision engine for content adaptation. *IEEE Pervasive Computing / IEEE Computer Society [and] IEEE Communications Society*, *29*(3), 41–49.

Lum, W., & Lau, F. (2003). User-centric content negotiation for effective Adaptation service in mobile computing. *IEEE Transactions on Software Engineering*, *29*(12), 1100–1111. doi:10.1109/TSE.2003.1265524

Malik, Z., & Bouguettaya, A. (2009). Reputation bootstrapping for trust establishment among Web Services. *IEEE Internet Computing*, *13*(1), 40–47. doi:10.1109/MIC.2009.17

Md Fudzee, M. F., & Abawajy, J. H. (2008). Classification of content adaptation system. In *Proceedings of the 10th International Conference on Information Integration and Web-based Application and Services* (pp. 426-429). New York: ACM Press.

Mohan, R., John, S., & Li, C.-S. (1999). Adapting multimedia Internet content for universal access. *IEEE Transactions on Multimedia*, *1*(1), 104–114. doi:10.1109/6046.748175

Newcomer, E. (2002). *Understanding Web Services: XML, WSDL, SOAP and UDDI.* Boston: Addison-Wesley.

Pountain, D., & Szyperski, C. (1994). Extensible software systems. *Byte Magazine*, 57-62.

Prangl, M., Hellwagner, H., & Szkalicki, T. (2006). Fast adaptation decision taking for cross-modal multimedia content adaptation. In *Proceedings of the International Conference on Multimedia Expo* (pp. 137-140). New York: IEEE Press.

Prangl, M., Szkalicki, T., & Hellwagner, H. (2007). A framework for utility-based multimedia adaptation. *IEEE Transactions on Circuits and Systems for Video Technology, 17*(6), 719–728. doi:10.1109/TCSVT.2007.896650

Rajesh, P., Ranjiith, S., Soumya, P. R., Karthik, V., & Datthathreya, S. (2006). Network management system using Web Services and service oriented architecture – A Case Study. In *10th IEEE/IFIP Network Operations and Management Symposium* (pp. 1-4). New York: IEEE Press.

Ran, S. (2003). A model for Web Services discovery with QoS. *ACM SIGcom Exchanges, 4*(1), 1–10. doi:10.1145/844357.844360

Schmidt, C., & Parashar, M. (2004). A peer-to-peer approach to Web service discovery. *Journal of World Wide Web, 7*(2), 211–229. doi:10.1023/B:WWWJ.0000017210.55153.3d

Shahidi, M., Attou, A., & Aghvami, H. (2008). Content adaptation: requirements and architecture. In *Proceedings of ERPAS: The 10th International Conference on Information Integration and Web-based Application and Services* (pp. 626-429). New York: ACM Press.

Tsai, W. T., Paul, R., Cao, Z., Yu, L., & Saimi, A. (2003). Verification of Web Services using an enhanced UDDI server. In *Object Oriented Real-Time Dependable System* (pp. 131–138). New York: IEEE Press.

Virgilio De, R., Torlane, R., & Houben, G.-J. (2007). Rule-based adaptation of Web information systems. *Journal of World Wide Web, 10*, 443–470. doi:10.1007/s11280-007-0020-2

Yang, S., & Shao, N. (2007). Enhancing pervasive Web accessibility with rule-based adaptation strategy. *Journal of Expert Systems with Applications, 32*, 1154–1167. doi:10.1016/j.eswa.2006.02.008

Yang, S. J., Zhang, J., Huang, A. F., Tsai, J. J., & Yu, P. S. (2008). A context-driven content adaptation planer for improving mobile Internet accessibility. In *IEEE International Conference on Web Services* (pp. 88-95). New York: IEEE Press.

Zhang, D. (2007). Web content adaptation for mobile handheld devices. *Communications of the ACM, 50*(2), 75–79. doi:10.1145/1216016.1216024

Zhang, L.-J., Chao, T., Chang, H., & Chung, J.-Y. (2003). XML-based advanced UDDI search mechanism for B2B integration. *Electronic Commerce Research, 3*(1), 25–42. doi:10.1023/A:1021573226353

Zhu, F., Mutka, M., & Ni, L. (2005). Service discovery in pervasive environments. *IEEE Pervasive, 4*(4), 81–90. doi:10.1109/MPRV.2005.87

ADDITIONAL READING

Abawajy, J. (2009). Adaptive hierarchical scheduling policy for enterprise grid computing systems. *Journal of Network and Computer Applications, 32*(3), 770–779. doi:10.1016/j.jnca.2008.04.009

Billsus, D. (2002). Adaptive interface for ubiquitous web access. *Communications of the ACM, 45*(5), 34–38. doi:10.1145/506218.506240

Brewer, E. A. (1998). A network architecture for heterogeneous mobile computing. *IEEE Personal Communications, 5*(5), 8–24. doi:10.1109/98.729719

Brian, D. N. (2000). System support for mobile, adaptive applications. *Personal Comm. IEEE, 7*(1), 44–49. doi:10.1109/98.824577

Brian, D. N. (1997). Agile application-aware adaptation for mobility. *SIGOPS Oper. Syst. Rev., 31*(5), 276–287. doi:10.1145/269005.266708

Buyukkokten, O. (2002). Efficient Web browsing on handheld devices using page and form summarization. *ACM Transactions on Information Systems, 20*(1), 82–115. doi:10.1145/503104.503109

Chen, G., & Kotz, D. (2000). *A survey of context-aware mobile computing research* (Computer Science Tech. Rep. TR2000-381). Hanover, NH: Darthmouth College.

Chen, L. Q., et al. (2002). *DRESS: A slicing tree based Web representation for various display size.* (Tech. Rep. MSR-TR_2002-126). Beijing, China: Microsoft Research Asia.

Chen, L.-Q., et al. (2003). Image adaptation based on attention model for small-form-factor device. In *Proceedings of The 9th International Conference on Multi-Media Modelling* (pp.483-490).

Chua, H. N., et al. (2005). Web-page adaptation framework for PC & mobile device collaboration. In *Proceedings of the 19th International Conference on Advanced Information Networking and Applications* (pp.727-732). New York: IEEE Press.

Fawaz, Y., Bognanni, C., Scuturici, V.-M., & Brunie, L. (2008b). Fault Tolerant Content Adaptation for a Dynamic Pervasive Computing Environment. In *Proceedings of the 3rd International Conference on Information and Communication Technologies: From Theory to Applications, 2008,* (pp.1-6). New York: IEEE Press.

Gleb, B., Ana, P., & Tomasa, C. (2007). *Aggregation functions: a guide for practitioners.* Berlin, Heidelberg: Springer Publisher.

Irving, V. W., John, J. R., & Jack, L. N. (Eds.). (2003). *Handbook of psychology.* New York: John Wiley and Sons.

Laakko, T., & Hiltumen, T. (2005). Adapting Web Content to Mobile User Agents. *IEEE Internet Computing, 9*(2), 46–53. doi:10.1109/MIC.2005.29

Laakko, T., & Hiltumen, T. Adapting Web content to mobile user agents. *IEEE Internet Computing, 9*(2), 46–53. doi:10.1109/MIC.2005.29

Lee, S., & Chung, K. (2008). Buffer-driven adaptive video streaming with TCP-friendliness. *Computer Communications, 31*(10), 2621–2630. doi:10.1016/j.comcom.2008.02.011

Mark, B. (2002). Device independent and the Web. *IEEE Internet Computing, 6*(5), 81–86. doi:10.1109/MIC.2002.1036042

Md Fudzee, M. F., & Abawajy, J. H. (2009). *Modeling request-driven cross-media content adaptation using service oriented architecture (Tech. Rep. TR C09).* Geelong, Australia: Deakin University, School of Info. Tech.

Md Fudzee, M. F., & Abawajy, J. H. (2009). *On the design and evaluation of a novel path determination technique for content adaptation systems (Tech. Rep. TR C09).* Geelong, Australia: Deakin University, School of Info. Tech.

Meyers, L. S., Guarino, A., & Gamst, G. (2005). *Applied multivariate research: design and interpretation.* Thousand Oaks, California: Sage Publications Inc.

Muntean, C. H., & McManis, J. (2004). A QoS-aware adaptive Web-based system. *IEEE International Conference on Communications* (pp.2204-2208), New York: IEEE Communications Society.

Ramaswamy, L. (2005). Automatic fragment detection in dynamic Web pages and its impact on caching. *IEEE Transactions on Knowledge and Data Engineering, 17*(6), 859–874. doi:10.1109/TKDE.2005.89

Roses, K. (2007). *Discrete mathematics and its applications, 6 editions*. New York: McGraw Hill.

Thompson, B. (2002). *Score reliability: contemporary thinking on reliability issues*. Thousand Oaks, California: Sage Publications Inc.

Chapter 7
Personalized Web Services Selection

Tarek Helmy*
King Fahd University of Petroleum and Minerals, Saudi Arabia

Ahmed Al-Nazer
King Fahd University of Petroleum and Minerals, Saudi Arabia

ABSTRACT

Web services have gained an increasing popularity over the Internet. Because of today's wide variety of services offered to perform a specific task. The task of finding selected Web services to perform a specific task becomes very hard, and it is essential that users are supported in the eventual selection of appropriate services. Web services are a great application area for agent techniques and a great substrate for developing serious autonomous agent-based systems to support a personalized Web services selection. In this chapter, we present a Collaborative Autonomous Interface Agent (CAIA) that collaborates with the Internet search engines and supports the user in finding exactly the Web services consistent with his/her needs. CAIA system has been designed, fully implemented and tested. As a case study, the testing results show a big improvement in the relevancy of the retrieved results and of the user's satisfaction by using CAIA+Google compared to using Google only.

INTRODUCTION

With so much information available on the Web portals, finding what is exactly needed is a big problem. Intelligent agents can take "instructions" about the types of things a person is interested in, report immediate findings, remember search parameters over time, repeat the search at intervals to adapt the results, and create customized research lists. Tools that make it easier to find, retrieve, and organize information will be in demand more and more as the amount of available information continues to increase. In this chapter, we present a Collaborative Autonomous Interface Agent (CAIA) that will collaborate with the Internet search engines (i.e. Google) and support communities of people in finding exactly the information consistent with the their interest. The CAIA uses data mining and machine learning techniques in order to learn and discover user's preferences. The rest of this chapter

DOI: 10.4018/978-1-61520-973-6.ch007

is organized as follows: Section 2 gives a brief overview of the related work. In Section 3, we present an overview of the CAIA framework architecture for the personalized discovery and selection of Web services. Section 4 presents the methodology of capturing the user's preferences by CAIA. Section 5 presents the details of the implementation. The performance evaluation is presented in Section 6. Finally, conclusion and future work directions are outlined in Section 7.

RELATED WORK

Personalization; carry out retrieval for each user incorporating his/her interests; of Web searching process has long been a topic of study, (Eirinaki, Vazirgiannis, 2003), (Lee, Tsai, 2003), (Sugiyama et. al., 2004), (Tijerino et. al., 2007), (Somlo, Howe, 2003), (Joana, Gauch, 2004). Customized intelligent search agents (Helmy, 2006), (Helmy et. al., 2003), (Helmy, Al-Nazer, 2007) may allow institutions to offer tools focused internally on their own collections. Offered perhaps through a web portal, these search tools will return reliable, accessible results for the campus community. As the tools become more sophisticated they will be able to search different collections of a variety of materials, regardless of format or of where the materials may be housed. The following examples show how intelligent searching is being applied in various settings.

- **Arts & Design.** Using new search tools like IBM's Query by Image Content (QBIC), users sift through the online databases of thousands of images, specifying content-based parameters like texture, shape and color that search the visual properties of images without using text descriptors.
- **Medicine.** Medicine students use a special search tool with integrated thesaurus to locate references tagged with a variety of related keywords, producing an extensive list of resources around a single topic.
- **Science.** Using intelligent search agents and a technology like RSS, a biologist creates a custom Web page that automatically finds and posts new research abstracts in his/her field as they are published.
- **Theater.** A costume designer collects images and descriptions of period clothing, easily locating source documents related to a particular period with a single search, whether the documents reside on his/her own system, the university's digital archives, or elsewhere on the Internet.

Regarding our approach to personalized Web service discovery and selection, we briefly survey ongoing Web service standardization activities and relate them to other work concerned with interface agents for personalization of Web portals search as follows:

- **ACM Digital Library** (portal.acm.org/dl.cfm): The ACM digital library offers a service to its subscribers called my binders, in which users can save found articles. Articles can be added manually, by means of a saved search, or by an Agent which can periodically run the search and add any new findings.
- **DSpace** (dspace.mit.edu/): The Massachusetts Institute of Technology's (MIT) enables advanced searching of research in digital form held by MIT. Users can create their own collections within DSpace to bookmark articles of interest.
- **Dashboard** (www.nat.org/dashboard/): As you go about your work, dashboard proactively finds documents, links, bookmarks, and other files related to whatever you happen to be doing, and displays these in a friendly way, keeping relevant files at your fingertips.

- **Letizia** (http://web.media.mit.edu/~lieber/ Lieberary/Letizia/Letizia-Intro.html): An autonomous interface agent that utilizes observed user's browsing patterns to recommend pages to view. It analyses pages in the neighborhood of the page the user is currently browsing, using limited breadth-first search. This analysis is based on page keywords and what links a user has previously followed. The agent then recommends related pages. Letizia doesn't require the user to provide an explicit feedback. It uses only implicit feedback and some examples are:
- Saving a page as a bookmark is taking as strong positive evidence,
- Links skipped are taken as negative support,
- Selected links can indicate positive or negative evidence, depending on how much time the user spends on the page,

The main shortcomings in Letizia are firstly the depending on only implicit feedback. Secondly, it maintains persistent and slowly-changing user models. Finally, Letizia does not take care of the fact that different browsing sessions by the same user or even a single session may involve different user's interests.

- **WebWatcher**   (http://www.cs.cmu.edu/ ~webwatcher/): A goal-oriented browsing assistant that makes link suggestions by highlighting links that may lead to the pre-defined goal. WebWatcher requests an initial explicit goal from the user, and the e-mail address to keep track of the user's interests. The agent tracks user's behaviour and constructs new training examples from the encountered hyperlinks. Each hyperlink is evaluated using a utility function based on the Page, the Goal, the User and the Link. Web Watcher has the same disadvantages of Letizia except the first one where WebWatcher is using only explicit feedback (Joachims, et. al., 1997).

- **UDDI** (Universal Description, Discovery and Integration; http://www.uddi.org): It is an initiative proposed by Microsoft, IBM and Ariba to develop a standard for an on-line registry of Web services. UDDI enables the publishing and dynamic discovery of networked services and allows developers to locate services for direct invocation or integration into new complex services. A Web service provider registers its advertisements along with keywords for categorization. A potential service's user will retrieve advertisements out of the registry based on keyword search. It is assumed that user and provider use the same set of keywords for service characterization. The search mechanism relies on pre-defined keyword categorization and does not refer to the semantic content of the advertisements.

- **WSDL** (Web Services Description Language; http://www.w3.org/TR/wsdl): It is an XML vocabulary, closely associated with UDDI as the format for specifying interfaces to Web services registered with a UDDI repository. WSDL attempts to separate services - defined in abstract terms - from the concrete data formats and protocols used for implementation. It therefore describes a binding scheme between the abstract service description and its specific implementation. Note that the abstraction of services is at a comparatively low level in terms of abstraction from message protocols, service bindings and communication ports. WSDL has a concept of input and output types but, like UDDI, does not support semantic description of services.

- **E-Speak** (http://www.e-speak.hp.com/): It is an initiative driven by Hewlett-Packard to enable enhanced service discovery. E-speak and UDDI have similar goals in that they both facilitate the advertisement and discovery of services. E-speak is comparable to WSDL in that it supports the description of service and data types and features a matching service that compares service requests with service descriptions. E-speak describes services as a set of attributes within several different vocabularies which are sets of attributes common to a logical group of services. Lookup requests are matched against service descriptions with respect to these attributes.

- **DAML-S** (http://www.ai.sri.com/daml/services/): It is an ontology-based approach to the description of Web services developed as part of the DARPA Agent Markup Language (DAML) program. DAML-S aims at providing a common ontology of services and is inspired by other research in the area of the so-called semantic Web that encompasses efforts to populate the Web with content and services having formal semantics. The design of DAML-S follows the layered approach to semantic Web markup languages. The ultimate goal of DAML-S is to provide an ontology that allows agents and users to discover, invoke and compose Web services.

- **WSMF** (Web Service Modeling Framework; http://www.swsi.org/resources/wsmf-paper.pdf): It provides another concept based on semantic Web technology for developing and describing Web services and their composition. WSMF describes the pre-condition and post-condition of services together with a service model. WSMF aims at strongly de-coupling the various components that implement a Web service application while at the same time providing a maximal degree of mediation between the different components. WSFM builds on comprehensive ontologies such as DAML-S and provides the concepts of goal repositories and mediators to solve complex service requests.

CAIA ARCHITECTURE OVERVIEW

A Collaborative Autonomous Interface Agent (CAIA) collaborates with the Internet search engines (i.e. Google) and supports communities of people in finding exactly the information consistent with their interest. CAIA uses data mining and machine learning techniques in order to learn and discover user's preferences. CAIA is developed to reside in the user's machine not in the Internet to make all private information on the user's machine. CAIA learns the user's preferences either explicitly or implicitly from his/her browsing behavior. CAIA stores user's preferences along with the Websites' information in a User's Profile (UP). The UP contains all visited Websites' information and their relevant keywords. We mean by "relevant keywords" the keywords the user entered when s/he searches of a specific Web service and the Websites' keywords automatically collected from the Web services Webpage's titles and summary. CAIA has three main processes illustrated in Figure 1. In general, the goals of CAIA system are:

- To improve the Web service discovery process by the Internet search engines based on specified, measurable attributes.
- To develop an autonomous agent that depends on Meta search engines and monitors the user's actions to prioritize the search results based on the context.
- To implement a method for the agent to learn the user's preferences during his/her behavior while browsing the search results.
- To build a UP based on his/her preferences and tune it over time to reflect the current user's interest.
- To filter and refine the query entered by the user.
- To filter the retrieved information based on the current user's preferences/context.
- To collaborate with other CAIA agents for exchanging the search results.

Figure 1. Overview of CAIA

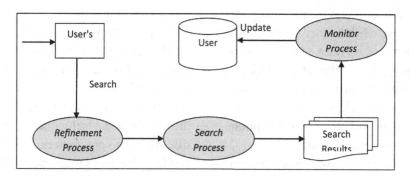

When the user enters new keywords to search for a specific Web service, three main processes will be done by CAIA as follows:

1. **Refinement Process:** CAIA starts the refinement process immediately after the user enters a new query. There are three main steps in the refinement process as follows:
   - Filter the query by removing any noise words. Noise words are defined in a table in the database and can be grown based on the user's preferences. Noise words are like suffix, prefix, (in, the, etc.), and ....
   - Spell-check the query's word by word and suggests the nearest words. We utilize Google spell checker through some APIs.
   - Refine the query by checking the UP, if there are any relevant keywords to any keyword in the query, then CAIA will suggest new keywords to the user and give him/her the flexibility to either take or ignore them.
2. **Search Process:** CAIA starts the search process after finishing the refinement process. There are three main steps in the search process as follows:
   - CAIA will first check for relevant Websites in the UP, and will be ordered & displayed if any were found.
   - If CAIA does not find any relevant Web site in the UP, then it forwards the refined query to the Google search engine through special APIs.
   - CAIA collaborates with other live agents in the community by forwarding the user's query to them. These agents will deal with any coming request with reserving the user's privacy so it will provide only the shared Websites.
   - CAIA receives from Google and/or other agents the relevant Websites, reorders and displays them to the user.
3. **Monitor User's Behaviors Process:** CAIA represents the UP as a set of categories; each category is a set of URLs and keywords have similarity over a predefined threshold value; which reflects a specific user's category of interest. CAIA looks over the shoulder of the user and records every action into the UP. CAIA receives the results returned by the search engine; the results consist of a set of URLs and their similarity value to the refined query. The user either explicitly marks the relevant URLs using CAIA's feedback icons or CAIA implicitly catches the user's responses through his/her actions, i.e. period of visiting, bookmarking, saving, printing, copying/pasting, scrolling,

or following a link. The responses are used to adapt the contents of the UP.

There are five main components in the CAIA system and two outside the system. They are explained as follows.

1. **Search Engine Component:** It is responsible for searching the search engine portal for any search request comes from the *Brain Component*. The *Search Engine Component* deals with the portal and gives the portal the filtered search keywords in order to get the search results. After getting the search results, the *Search Engine Component* forwards them back to the *Brain component* where they will be filtered and re-ordered.

2. **Brain Component:** It is the core component of the system and is responsible for:
   ○ Refining the user's query (which entered in the *GUI Component*) to get better search results.
   ○ Filtering the search results; received from the *Search Engine component*; according the UP.
   ○ Capturing the user's activities through *Sensor Component* which senses all users' activities and reactions with search results.
   ○ Initiating collaboration request to *Collaboration Component* to enhance

the search results for the user's query. Also, it looks for appropriate agents to the user which can help him/her.
   ○ Controlling the UP (i.e. the database) and the preferences.

The design of *Brain Component* follows MVC paradigm (Model, View, and Control) since it is reliable, easy to understand and it is the standard nowadays. There will be a view for each component talks with the *Brain Component*. We have the following views:

- **Search Engine View:** This class interfaces with the *Search Engine Component* and is responsible for providing a refined query to the search engine and handling the search results got from the *Search Engine Component*.
- **GUI View:** This class interfaces with *GUI Component* and is responsible for getting the search query from the user, refining it and returns the search results.
- **Sensor View:** This class interfaces with *Sensor Component* and is responsible for handling any event done by the user after displaying the search results.
- **Collaboration View:** This class interfaces with *Collaboration Component* and is responsible for delivering the search results for a certain query got from different

Figure 2. CAIA components

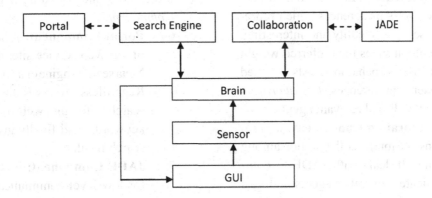

agent. Also, it is responsible for determining the user's preferences for other agents through the *Collaboration Component*. Also, the *singleton controller* is responsible for interfacing with the controllers of the views. There are two controllers and two data models as follows:

- **Search & Query Processing:** This class interfaces with the *Search Engine View*, the *GUI View* and the *Collaboration View*. It is responsible for filtering and refining the user's query. Filtering will remove the noise words from the query while refining will add more keywords from the database. This class is also responsible for issuing the search from different sources, database, portal and external agents that have similar preferences to the user's agent. Then, it filters the search results based on the UP and re-orders them based on the keywords weights.

- **Monitor Processing:** This class interfaces with the *Sensor View*. It is responsible for handling all events done by the user after displaying the search results. It updates the UP, to reflect his/her actions to the search results.

- **The User's Profile:** This data model stores the user's preferences for any visited Websites and any entered keywords. It also represents the weight of different keywords whether they were entered by the user or got from the visited Websites.

- **User's Preferences File:** This data model stores the user's preferences which represent the user's personality and interesting. For example, it saves the preferred weight for each user's behaviors. Also, based on the user's preferences, *Collaboration Component* will find relevant agents.

3. **Collaboration Component:** it is responsible for the collaboration among agents. It deals with JADE to communicate with other agents and gets

information to help in the search. It will be responsible for the protocol that each agent understands.

4. **Sensor Component:** it is responsible for sensing user's activities and reporting them to the *Brain Component* which will process them and reflect them in the UP. It deals with *GUI Component* to retrieve any action done by the user.

5. **GUI Component:** it is the end user interface. It provides the user with a mechanism to enter query, and to display the search results, then it gives him/her a floor to explicitly give his/her feedback. It will have the following functionalities:

- Gets user's search keywords, and feeds them to the *Brain Component*.

- Displays search results taken from the *Brain Component*.

- Browses any Web page of the search results and forwards any user's action to the *Sensor Component*.

- Gets user's explicit feedback for any Web page and forwards it to the *Brain Component*.

- Gives the user's options to save, print, add to favorite and forwards any user's action to the *Sensor Component*.

- Gives the user's options to search for another agent using *Collaboration Component*.

- Gives the user's options to set his/her preferences and forwards it to the *Brain Component*.

6. **Portal Component:** it has the index of the Web service site; it might be a Meta search engine or a portal database. Regardless, it takes the keywords, searches for the Websites match the keywords, and finally gives back the search results.

7. **JADE Component:** it is responsible for low level communication among

agents. It deals with the *Collaboration Component*, looks for live agents and gives back the list of available agents. If there is a request to get information from other agents, it will get it from them. We use JADE as the middleware in the communication between agents because it is reliable and globally used in all agents.

CAIA system has a relational database which represents the User's Profile. It holds all historical data for the user such as the visited Websites and the search queries. The database design schema [Figure 4] contains five tables named: *Keywords*, *URL*, *URLKeywords*, *Events* and *NoiseWords*. The first four tables are related with relationships and the last, *NoiseWords*, is not related to all other tables. The *Keywords* table holds the keywords which are the words that help CAIA to identify the Websites. The *URL* table holds the Web service provider' URL (i.e. http://www.kfupm.edu.sa which is the URL for KFUPM Website). The *Keywords* and *URL* tables are related with a many-to-many relationship. I.e. a URL can have more than one keyword and a keyword can have more than one URL. For example, KFUPM Website has the keywords: King, Fahd, University, Petroleum,

Minerals and KFUPM while CCSE in KFUPM has keywords same as KFUPM keywords and more CCSSE, Computer, Engineering, etc. We observe that a URL has more than one keywords and a keyword has more than on URLs. So, we created a table, *URLKeywords*, to holds their primary keys, *keywordID* and *URLID*, and the weight for each keyword that related to a certain URL. The *Events* table holds all events that were done to the URL, such as printing, saving, bookmarking, etc. The *URL* table is related to the *Events* table with a one-to-many relationship as one URL obtains many events. That is why we keep the *URL* table's primary key as reference key in *Events* table. Finally, the *NoiseWords* table holds all noise words that are used in the query refinement process. Figure 4 gives a complete design schema of the database followed by an explanation for each table individually.

The *URL* table [Table 1] holds the *title* and *summary* attributes which are related to the URL. In addition, it has some attributes related to the properties of the URL. For example, it has *private* and *rank* attributes which are attributes of the URL. Finally, the *URL* table holds some attributes related to the events obtained on the URL. For example, it holds *noOfVisites* and *lastVisit* attributes which help us in getting that

Figure 3. Brain component design

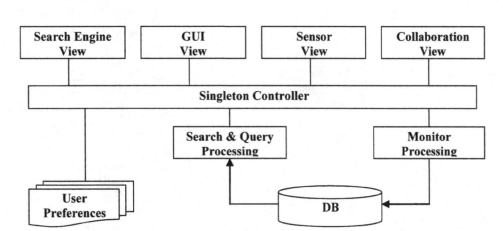

information quickly rather than accessing *Events* table and search for last record and count all related records.

The *Keywords* table [Table 2] holds the keywords which are the words that help us to identify Websites. It has an identifier which is *keywordID* and the keyword itself as a string of characters.

The *URLKeywords* table [Table 3] holds the *URL* and *Keywords* tables' primary keys, *keywordID* and *URLID*. It also holds the weight for each keyword that related to a certain URL.

The *Events* table [Table 4] holds all events that were done to the URL, such as printing, saving etc. It holds the *URL* table's primary key as reference key. It also holds the event's attributes such as the event's name and the event's time.

The *NoiseWords* table [Table 5] holds all noise words that are used in query refinement process. It has an identifier, *noiseWordID*, and the *noiseWord* filed as string of characters.

CAPTURING THE USER'S PREFERENCES

The main goal of CAIA is to personalize the Web service discovery/selection for the user. In order to personalize, we need to learn the user's behaviors. Leaning those behaviors is not an easy task. Therefore, we thought to conduct a survey to help in learning those behaviors and also in sorting those behaviors in a way so that each behavior has some weight [5, 6]. I.e. Assume a user is visiting a Website, there are many possible behaviors can be done. For example, s/he can print, save, or/and add the Website to the favorite list etc. So, we aim to have default values of the weights for each factor, although CAIA gives the ability to the user to change them. The survey was conducted by following some steps. First, a form contains the survey questions was developed and published on the Internet. Then, the form's link was distributed among certain professional people. During three months, we have collected the responses from most of them. Finally, the results of the survey were analyzed in order to get

Figure 4. Database design schema

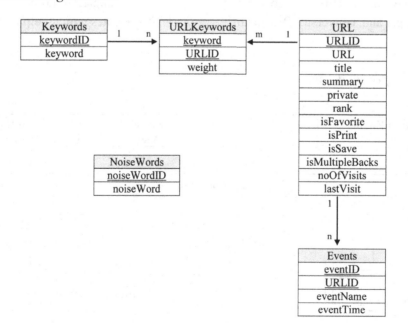

Table 1. URL table

Attribute	Data Type
URLID	Number(integer)
URL	Text
title	Text
summary	Memo (Text)
private	Number (0/1)
rank	Number(1...5)
isFavoirte	Number (0/1)
isPrint	Number (0/1)
isSave	Number (0/1)
isMultipleBacks	Number (0/1)
noOfVisits	Number (0/1)
lastVisit	Date/Time

Table 2. Keywords table

Attribute	Data Type
keywordID	Number(integer)
keyword	Text

Table 3. URL keywords table

Attribute	Data Type
keywordID	Number(integer)
URLID	Number(integer)
Weight	Number (double)

a conclusion and come up with weights assigned to different factors that reflect the user's interest in a Website. We used Internet to post the survey form and to collect the survey responses because it is available all the time for the respondents of the survey. The survey was distributed among 78 persons who are high-education professionals. They all belong to Middle East culture and specifically they live in Saudi Arabia. Their ages were in the range between 20 and 50 years. They are characterized as frequently Internet users and more specifically Google search engine users. They use Google to search for any term in daily basis. The native language of them is not English but they speak English as second language. Their responses were collected within three months and they answered all inquiries in the survey. Furthermore, they highlighted additional factors

to be considered that reflect their interest. The survey contains two inquiries: the first one gets an evaluation of the different factors that reflect the user's interest in a Website and the second one gets further factors if any. Respondents were asked to give their feedback about the following inquiries:

Inquiry 1: "Suppose you are searching Google and you got some results. Your behavior with the results will differ and we are interested in that. Please rank the following factors which determine more your interest in a Website."

The respondents were asked to refer to the following factors and evaluate each of them:

* Print the Website
* Add the Website to favorite (bookmark)
* Save the Website
* Time of Visit (the duration of visiting the Website)
* Multiple Visits to the same Website

Table 4. Events table

Attribute	Data Type
Eventide	Number(integer)
URLID	Number(integer)
eventName	Text
eventTime	Date/Time

Table 5. noiseWords table

Attribute	Data Type
noiseWordID	Number(integer)
noiseWord	Text

- Explicit feedback (if it the Website asks for your feedback e.g. interested...)
- Multiple backs to a Website (going to internal links and then coming back)

Following is the scale used by subjects to compile the survey for each individual factor listed within our Web form.

- *Very important:* means that this factor is very important and significant in determining the user's interest when s/he visits a web-site.
- *Important:* means that this factor is just important in determining the user's interest when s/he visits a web-site.
- *Normal:* means that this factor is neither important nor neglected, so it is a factor that does not help much in determining the user's interest when s/he visits a web-site.
- *Not important:* means that this factor is not important in determining the user's interest when s/he visits a web-site.
- *Not applicable:* means that this factor is neglected and it does not mean anything in determining the user's interest when s/he visits a web-site.

Inquiry 2: "Please determine any other factors that reflect your interest in a Website."

This inquiry permitted respondents to write-in any additional factor that helps in determining

their preferences in visiting a Web-site. In order to get the results of the survey, we need to calculate a weight for each factor. There were five scale choices for each factor in the survey. A weight was assigned for each scale and the analysis is based on those assumed weights. Table 6 shows the weight for each scale.

Then, we calculate the average weight for each factor using Formula 1:

$$\text{Average weight} = \frac{\sum_{i=1}^{5} a_i \times x_i}{\sum_{i=1}^{5} x_i} \qquad (1)$$

Where a_i is the weight for each scale i, and x_i is the number of responses of the scale i. For example, for "*print*" factor we observed that 12 responses "Very Important", 18 responses "Important", 22 responses "Normal", 18 responses "Not Important" and 8 responses "Not Applicable". Table 7 shows the average weight for "*print*" factor.

Average weight for "print" factor = 15/78 = $0.1923 \approx 0.2$. It is observed that the "*add to favorite*" factor has a weight of 0.5 which is considered to be the highest weigh in the survey. That gives us a great hint on the user's interest when s/he just adds the Website to his/her favorite Websites. Adding a Website to the user's favorite list has no cost and requires a short time. Since the survey got responses from professional people who have limited time, they find this way of reflecting their interest in a Website is more effective than other ways like printing or saving the Web site. Also,

Table 6. Weights of each scale in the survey

Scale	Weight
Very Important	1.0
Important	0.7
Normal	0.5
Not Important	-0.7
Not Applicable	-1.0

Table 7. The average weight for the print factor

Scale	i	ai	xi	ai × xi
Very Important	1	1	12	12.0
Important	2	0.7	18	12.6
Normal	3	0.5	22	1
Not Important	4	-0.7	18	-12.6
Not Applicable	5	-1	8	-8
Total			78	15

"*multiple visits*" factor has a weight of 0.5 which is considered to be the highest weigh in the survey. It means that the user is very interested in a Website if s/he has many visits to it. In addition, "*multiple backs*" factor has a weight of 0.5 too. Multiple visits to the same Website, i.e. going to internal links inside the website then coming back to the same website, tells us how the user is interested in this Website. On the other hand, "*Time of visit*" factor have less 0.4 which means it reflects the users' interest but with less weight. It means that the time of visit is great implicit factor that determines the user's interest but sometimes it is misleading. For example, the user visits a Website and looks inside it and tries to figure some good information but s/he did not find enough information although s/he spent good time in the Website. "*Save*" factor is 0.3 which means less also. That may be because of the need of space and time to save a Website and the people who did the survey are always busy. Moreover, "*print*" factor got 0.2 which means that it is not weighted much in reflecting the user's interest. It is clear that it has the same reason which is the need of extra resources like ink and papers while there are more economical ways to mark a Website as interested for the user. Finally, "*explicit feedback*" factor has the lease 0.1 which means the users are not interested in making explicit feedback in normal search. They see this factor is not important to them since it asks to do some action explicitly. As conclusion, users don't want to do extra activity to reflect their inertest. They would like to deal with implicit factors rather than explicit factors.

IMPLEMENTATION DETAILS

The CAIA system fully implemented using Java programming language and has the following features. Figures 5 and 6 shows some screen snapshots of running CAIA.

- *Three tier architecture*: GUI Component,

Sensor Component and Brain Component. Each component is considered as a stand alone sub-system.
- *Extendibility*: the system is designed very well in such away adding a new major functionality is just matter of plug-in.
- *Portability*: the system is implemented using JAVA language which is platform-independent.

We have utilized some third party packages and enhanced some of their functionality in CAIA system. The following third party packages were used:

- JADE (Java Agent DEvelopment Framework) [12]: it is a software framework fully implemented in Java language. It simplifies the implementation of multi-agent systems through a middle-ware that claims to comply with the FIPA (The Foundation for Intelligent Physical Agents) [13] specifications. We use JADE for easily communicate between agents.
- Google Web APIs (beta) [14]: The Google Web APIs service gives us query access to Google's web search, enabling us to develop software that accesses billions of web documents that are constantly refreshed. We use these APIs to get optimal search results for the user's query. Also, we use the Google's spell-checker API to spell-check the user's query.
- The Wintertree Thesaurus Engine class library [15]: The Wintertree Thesaurus Engine Java SDK contains a Java class library that can be used to add a general-purpose thesaurus capability to your Java applications. We use this class library to get thesaurus for the words to make the search more practical.
- EZ JCom [16]: EZ JCom provides a bridge between Java programs and COM (ActiveX) objects. Using EZ JCom, Java

Figure 5. Snapshots of CAIA

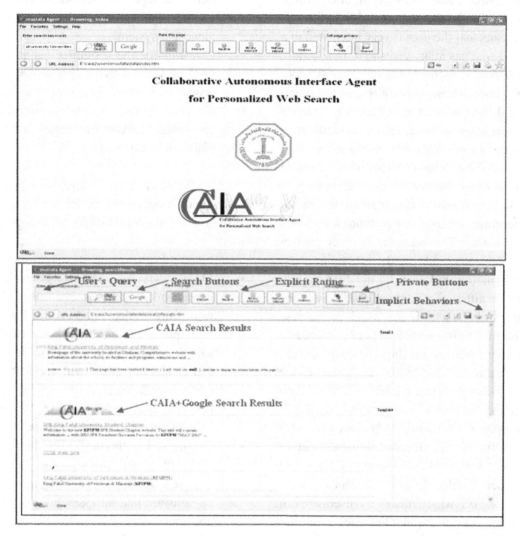

programs can call COM objects, can receive events from COM objects, and can even embed the COM objects inside Java user interface elements. We use EZ JCom to embed Internet Explorer in our system and to listen to the events the user do in the Explorer.

EXPERIMENTAL RESULTS

We have conducted experiments to make a consistent evaluation of the CAIA's performance for selecting the Web services. We found that Precision is a good indicator to the user's satisfaction of the retrieved results; *Precision* is how much the retrieved results are consistent with the user's needs and calculated by dividing the number of relevant URLs retrieved on the total number of URLs retrieved. Improving the Precision can tell us of how much the query expansion and filtration of the retrieved result is useful. *In the first experiment*, we submit twenty queries to Google and then submit the same queries to CAIA with its features of enhancing the queries and filtering the retrieved results. We assume the number of

Figure 6. Snapshots of CAIA

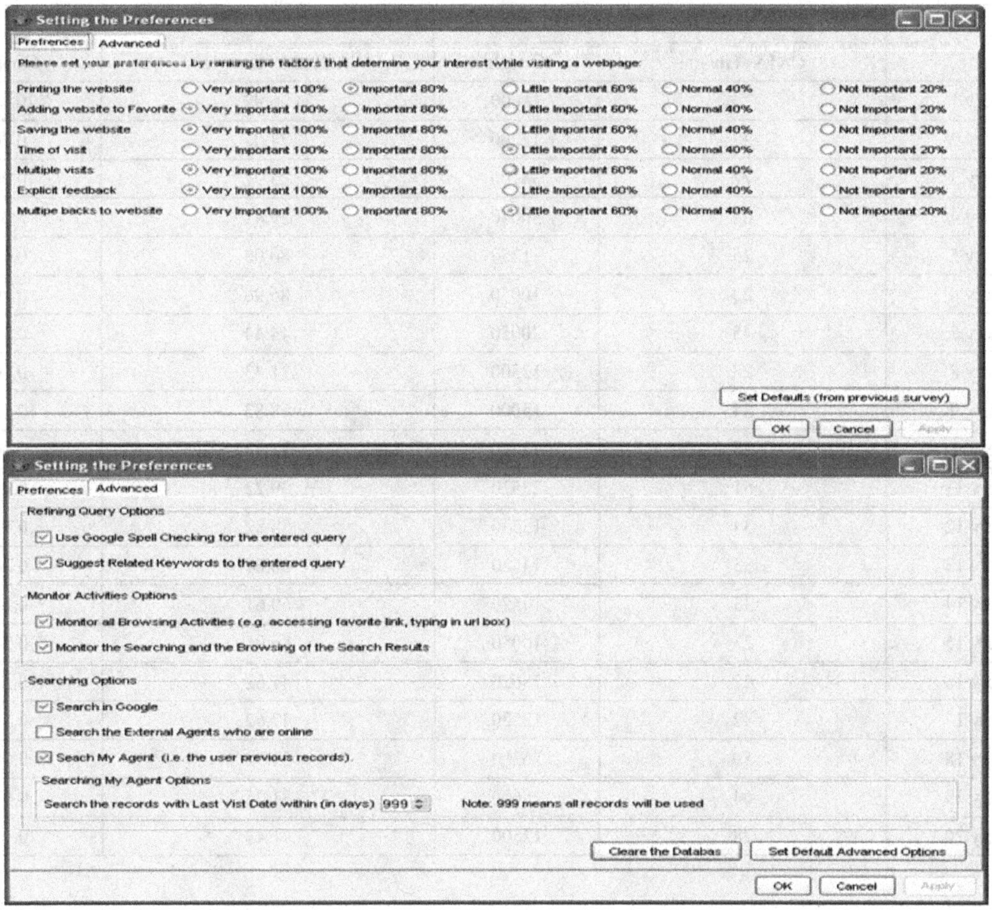

relevant URLs is constant and observe the number of results retrieved by using Google only and the number of results retrieved by using Google + CAIA. Then, we calculate the precision based on the total number of retrieved URLs and assume there are only twenty relevant URLs. Table 8 shows the number of results and the Precision for the 20 queries. The results show that CAIA is improving over trials by decreasing number of results and hence increasing the *Precision* of the retrieved Web services. Table 9 shows the experiment of twenty queries with three trials in CAIA and the improvement is clear.

In the second experiment, we want to measure how much CAIA is being able to adapt the contents of the UP over time. In addition, we want to

measure how good is the correlation between the keywords assigned to the URLs in the UP and the context of the URLs. We use the same formulas as in (Helmy, Al-Nazer, 2007) that define a Fitness value to show the correlation between the weights of the URL's keywords calculated automatically by the CAIA (*T*) and the weights of the URL's keywords calculated by the user (*S*), as follows:

- Weight calculated by the user: $S_{URL} = \sum_{k=1}^{m} b_k . W_k$

Where W_k is the weight of attribute k, and b_k equals to 1 if the user judges the keyword k in the URL, as relevant for the context of the URL, otherwise b_k equals to zero.

Table 8. Number of results and precision for the 20 queries

Query	Number of Results		Precision	
	CAIA+Google	Google	CAIA+Google	Google
Query 1	26	11600	76.92	0.17
Query 2	27	12200	74.07	0.16
Query 3	77	34100	25.97	0.06
Query 4	68	30040	29.41	0.07
Query 5	25	11250	80.00	0.18
Query 6	23	10050	86.96	0.20
Query 7	45	20050	44.44	0.10
Query 8	28	12300	71.43	0.16
Query 9	34	15000	58.82	0.13
Query 10	28	12550	71.43	0.16
Query 11	51	22520	39.22	0.09
Query 12	34	15230	58.82	0.13
Query 13	33	14520	60.61	0.14
Query 14	33	14520	60.61	0.14
Query 15	23	10050	86.96	0.20
Query 16	42	18620	47.62	0.11
Query 17	42	18520	47.62	0.11
Query 18	59	26380	33.90	0.08
Query 19	64	28600	31.25	0.07
Query 20	28	12500	71.43	0.16

- Weight calculated by CAIA: $T_{URL} = \sum_{k=1}^{m} W_k$

Then, we define the Fitness value, which reflects the correlation between the two adaptations for URL_j:

- Fitness value: $F_j = S_j / T_j$

Twenty different queries have been entered. After frequent interactions of retrieval, we checked the correlation of each keyword with the context of the URLs in the UP and calculated S and T values, and then a Fitness value was calculated for the keywords of each URL in the UP. Table 10 shows the Fitness values as they are converging over time to each other. We conclude that CAIA is able to predict and adapt the URL's keywords to reflect well the context of the URLs in the UP over time. It is clear that CAIA needs to be used by the user over time and it then gives better correlation between the URL and the relevant keywords.

CONCLUSION AND FUTURE WORK

CAIA system is intended to personalize the selection of Web services. CAIA is developed to reside in the user's machine not in the Internet to make all private information on user's machine. CAIA learns the user's preferences either explicitly or implicitly from user's browsing behavior. It then stores them along with the Websites' information in a UP. The system is developed in a way that

Table 9. Number of results and precision for three trials

Query	Number of Results			Precision		
	Trail 1	Trail 2	Trail 3	Trail 1	Trail 2	Trail 3
Query 1	11600	302	26	0.17	6.62	76.92
Query 2	12200	329	27	0.16	6.08	74.07
Query 3	34100	2626	77	0.06	0.76	25.97
Query 4	30040	2043	68	0.07	0.98	29.41
Query 5	11250	281	25	0.18	7.12	80.00
Query 6	10050	231	23	0.20	8.66	86.96
Query 7	20050	902	45	0.10	2.22	44.44
Query 8	12300	344	28	0.16	5.81	71.43
Query 9	15000	510	34	0.13	3.92	58.82
Query 10	12550	351	28	0.16	5.70	71.43
Query 11	22520	1149	51	0.09	1.74	39.22
Query 12	15230	518	34	0.13	3.86	58.82
Query 13	14520	479	33	0.14	4.18	60.61
Query 14	14520	479	33	0.14	4.18	60.61
Query 15	10050	231	23	0.20	8.66	86.96
Query 16	18620	782	42	0.11	2.56	47.62
Query 17	18520	778	42	0.11	2.57	47.62
Query 18	26380	1556	59	0.08	1.29	33.90
Query 19	28600	1830	64	0.07	1.09	31.25
Query 20	12500	350	28	0.16	5.71	71.43

it is adaptable. The system learns and adapts the UP from the user's search history and browsing behavior respectively. The system uses UP to find relevant information to the user. The system uses both explicit and implicit feedbacks to capture and adapt user's preferences overtime. The profile is tuning to the user's behaviors and upgrading itself to be more powerful and helpful to the user. The system have some autonomy and the ability to sense and react to its environment, as well as socially communicates and cooperates with other agents in order to accomplish its duties, which are delegated from the user. The collaboration feature in the system guarantees the privacy of the user so it is sharing only the common records of the user. The user can set any Website to be private while s/he is browsing it. The collaboration increases the performance of the agent by improving the communication overhead, instead of communicating to the Internet to get the search results; it can be imported from another agent in the same community. Also, it increases the precision of the search results. Although CAIA provides a great help in searching over the Internet, there are some future improvement areas. *First*, user behaviors' weight could be detected automatically and adopted based on the user's reaction and the frequent user's behaviors. *Second*, CAIA agents could be clustered based on the interests so that the related agents communicate effectively. *Third*, other search engines could be utilized in fining the search process and the results can be filtered and re-ordered based on the UP.

Table 10. Calculated weights by the user and CAIA

URL	S_{URL}	TURL	F_j
URL 1	1.5	2.1	0.71
URL 2	3.5	4.5	0.78
URL 3	2.1	2.6	0.81
URL 4	3.8	4.8	0.79
URL 5	1.9	1.9	1
URL 6	1.8	2.8	0.64
URL 7	2.8	3.8	0.74
URL 8	3	4.5	0.67
URL 9	2.1	2.7	0.78
URL 10	2	2.6	0.77
URL 11	2.8	2.8	1
URL 12	5	6	0.83
URL 13	2.3	2.3	1
URL 14	2.5	2.5	1
URL 15	2.5	2.5	1
URL 16	2.8	2.8	1
URL 17	4.5	4.5	1
URL 18	1.5	1.5	1
URL 19	2.5	2.5	1
URL 20	3.9	3.9	1

ACKNOWLEDGMENT

We would like to thank King Fahd University of Petroleum and Minerals for providing the computing facilities. Special thanks to anonymous reviewers for their insightful comments and feedback. Thanks extended to Mr. David Birkett for his help in proofreading the chapter.

REFERENCES

Al-Nazer, A., & Helmy, T. (2007, November 2-5). A Web Searching Guide: Internet Search Engines & Autonomous Interface Agents Collaboration. In *IEEE/ACM Proceedings of the Joint International Conference on Web Intelligence/Intelligent Agent Technology*, (pp. 424-428). Sillicon Valley, CA.

Eirinaki, M., & Vazirgiannis, M. (2003). Web mining for Web personalization. *ACM Transactions on Internet Technology*, 3, 1–27. doi:10.1145/643477.643478

EZ JCom. (n.d.). *EZ JCom*. Retrieved from http://www.ezjcom.com/

FIPA. (n.d.). *FIPA*. Retrieved from http://jade.tilab.com/papers/JADETutorialIEEE/JADETutorial_FIPA.pdf

Google. (n.d.). *Google Web APIs (beta)*. Retrieved from http://www.google.com/apis/index.html

Helmy, T. (2006). Towards a User-Centric Web Portals Management. *International Journal of Information Technology*, *12*(1), 1–15.

Helmy, T. (2007). Collaborative Multi-Agent-Based E-Commerce Framework. *International Journal of Computers. Systems and Signals*, *8*(1), 3–12.

Helmy, T., Amamiya, S., Mine, T., & Amamiya, M. (2003, October 13-17). A New Approach of the Collaborative User Interface Agents. In *Proceedings of the IEEE/WIC/ACM International Conference on Intelligent Agent Technology* (IAT'03), (pp. 147-153). Halifax, Canada.

JADE. (n.d.). *JADE*. Retrieved from http://jade.tilab.com/

Joachims, T., Freitag, D., & Mitchell, T. (1997). WebWatcher: A tour guide for the World Wide Web. In *Proceedings of the Fifteenth International Joint Conference on Artificial Intelligence*.

Lee, W., & Tsai, T., T. (2003). An interactive agent-based system for concept-based Web search. *Expert Systems with Applications*, 24, 365–363. doi:10.1016/S0957-4174(02)00186-0

Somlo, G., & Howe, A. (2003). Using Web Helper Agent Profiles in Query Generation. In *ACM Proceedings of the Second International Joint Conference on Autonomous Agents and Multiagent Systems*, (pp. 812-818).

Sugiyama, K., Hatano, K., Yoshikawa, M., & Uemura, S. (2004, March 4-6).Adaptive Web Search Based on User's Implicit Preference. In *Proceedings of the 15th Data Engineering Workshop* (DEWS2004).

Tijerino, Y. A., Helmy, T., & Bradshaw, J. M. (2008, December). FAQIH: Framework for Agent-based Query-enabled Integrated Information for Health and Nutrition. In *ACM/IEEE proceedings of the Joint International Conference on Web Intelligence/Intelligent Agent Technology*, (pp. 550-553).

Trajkova, J., & Gauch, S. (2004, April 26-28). Improving Ontology-Based User Profiles. In *Proceedings of RIAO 2004*. University of Avignon, France, (pp. 380-389).

Wintertree Thesaurus. (n.d.). *The Wintertree Thesaurus Engine class library*. Retrieved from http://www.wintertree-software.com/

ENDNOTE

* On leave from the College of Engineering, Department of Computers Engineering and Automatic Control, Tanta University, Egypt.

Section 3
Framework Design

Chapter 8
Mobile Web Services for P2P Computing

Fahad Aijaz
RWTH Aachen University, Germany

ABSTRACT

The Information Technology (IT) and Telecommunication (TelCo) sectors face enormous integration challenges, due to the prominent heterogeneity in existing systems. Service-oriented computing tackles such challenges by providing a fundamental platform that facilitates the convergence of distinct domains based on Web Services (WSs). With the mobility and technological advancements, service-oriented computing has been pushed towards the mobile sector enabling P2P Mobile Web Services (MobWSs) provisioning. In this work, we investigate the interaction, architecture and design characteristics of MobWSs for P2P computing. Here, the two MobWS interaction strategies are presented followed by the architectural discussion, enfolding server and client side components, of a resource-oriented MobWS framework. We follow REST design principles to propose an efficient way of architecting P2P MobWS systems, as an alternative to SOAP, enabling significant payload reduction and performance optimization in mobile servers. The detailed performance evaluation is also presented and compared to SOAP based on real-time measurements. By analyzing performance characteristics, we show that REST is a promising technique to architect P2P MobWS systems for resource-constraint mobile nodes.

INTRODUCTION

The convergence of IT and TelCo face enormous research challenges due the existence of heterogeneity in corresponding systems. Rapid advances in technical and technological aspects of these domains

DOI: 10.4018/978-1-61520-973-6.ch008

intricate the integration requirements while blurring the intersection point. Service-oriented computing is a middle-tier paradigm that facilitates the integration of IT and TelCo domains by providing services with standardized access interfaces. Within the research and industrial sectors, the reference model for Service Oriented Architecture (SOA) is currently the most promising and widely accepted standard for understanding the relationships and integration requirements of dynamic, heterogeneous and distributed entities in service-oriented systems (MacKenzie et al., 2006). From the technology point of view, wide range of competitive SOA implementations exist that help innovate numerous service-oriented business cases and applications.

In recent years, WSs specified by the World Wide Web Consortium (W3C)[1] have evolved as a highly-regarded implementation of SOA for systems' integration. The Internet and mobile networks have started to merge based on WSs spotlighting high-valued consumer and business services, and use cases. The combination of mobile communication systems and WSs is seen to have a high economical potential in terms of WS provisioning from a mobile node, called MobWSs. From research and technological perspective, the process of maturing MobWSs is ongoing; however several challenges must be met to enable a free integration of P2P MobWS systems into IT and TelCo domains.

Though WSs are regarded as an application integration tool due to their interface uniformity, extensibility and neutral behavior towards heterogeneous systems, they tend to introduce more transmission and processing overheads due to extremely long SOAP messages integrating various WS standard specifications. Research efforts have been put towards transitioning from a SOA to the Resource Oriented Architecture (ROA) where WSs exposed as resources are directly accessible using the existing Internet standards. Representational State Transfer (REST) is a style for designing distributed software architectures that are based on resources within the network and can be defined as an implementation of ROA. Fielding (2000) defines REST as "a hybrid style derived from several of the network-based architectural styles and combined with additional constraints that define a uniform connector interface" (p.76). Analogous to the client-server architecture, REST is not a standardized style for architecting networked-software; however

it strongly couples and relies upon the existing Internet standards, such as HTTP and URL. Contrary to the dependency of WSs on SOAP, the messaging in REST is format-independent and strictly relies upon the application requirements, typically being in HTML, XML or JSON document format. Originally, REST was defined for information and media access, but the rapidly growing research and industrial communities have adopted its design principles for WS interactions as well. The representations in REST are defined by the format of information (HTML, XML, JPEG, GIF or JSON etc.) accessed as a resource on the network. As a consequence, the response places the requesting node in some state. Each subsequent resource access transfers the node from one state to another, hence resulting in a ROA.

MobWSs facilitates P2P service provisioning from resource constraint devices. The range of these devices is not limited and can be categorized as consumer-oriented (CO) or process-oriented (PO) mobile nodes. The CO mobile node, such as a smart phone or PDA, provides direct interaction of an end user with the MobWS, whereas in a PO device the services are perceived as embedded or backend processes of some large and highly distributed infrastructure, such as Wireless Sensor Networks (WSNs). The requirements of MobWSs for each type of device are derived from the application context. Limited configuration in terms of processing, battery and storage resources is the shared property of both categories of nodes. Therefore, provisioning MobWSs, with aforesaid restricted degree of technological and resource freedom, to perform P2P computing is a scientific challenge.

The objective of this chapter is to establish a clear understanding of the concept of P2P computing based on MobWSs in terms of their interactions, architectural requirements and messaging frameworks. In the initial phase, two major MobWS interactions strategies are identified and the underlying communication mechanisms are derived based on the operations specified in WSDL standard (Chinnici et al., 2007). The concept of synchronous and asynchronous MobWSs is presented and detailed discussion on their corresponding relationships to the interaction strategies is established. Based on these fundamental principles, requirements for an integrated MobWS framework are presented with a focus on service- and resource-centric access techniques, taking into considerations, the server and client side components. The chapter also presents evaluation and comparison of the influence on the architectural performance of MobWSs framework caused by each access technique. The performance evaluation is conducted based on real-time measurements, which are used to analyze the payload and processing optimizations in prototypical nodes.

BACKGROUND

Extensive efforts put in research and industry for merging IT and mobile TelCo domains at their cross-section point have pioneered the emergence of service-oriented mobile computing era. With the increasing number of mobile devices the mobile software has become a huge business industry providing vast technological and use case driven consumer applications. Requirements for integrating diverse vendor-specific and legacy mobile applications have pushed the adoption of service-oriented computing principles in the mobile domain. Thus, by inheriting the behavioral properties, mobile devices are able to provision and consume MobWSs, consequently enabling the mobile P2P service computing environment.

The global acceptance of MobWSs as a mature platform is still in its infancy. Enabling the true potential of MobWSs in the current highly competitive global market faces several research challenges and requires recommendations for efficient solutions at various technical levels. Riva (2008) presents a detailed study, based on the experience of several research projects, about challenges for developing middleware on smart phones. The

importance of resource management, lightweight communication protocols and asynchronous programming are also highlighted. Srirama (2008) on the other hand develops a Mobile Host platform for provisioning MobWSs. In this work, some use cases of Mobile Host platform are identified and studies towards the technical feasibility of service delivery and management from Mobile Host and are conducted with the focus on Quality-of-Service (QoS), scalability and service discovery. In order to reduce the processing latency within the Mobile Host, the BinXML compression technique is adapted. Gehlen (2007) presents the concept of the first ever Mobile Web Server and comprehensively analyzes the traffic performance characteristics of MobWSs. He further classifies MobWSs into three distinct classes, MobWS Access, MobWS Provisioning and P2P MobWSs, and presents multiple transport protocol bindings for SOAP. Gehlen (2007) addresses the mobility issues in the MobWS domain, and also uses, along with Srirama (2008), the security specification to tackle security and privacy issues. Recently a technical report from Nokia Research Center in Helsinki presented the concept of providing HTTP access to Web Servers running on mobile devices (Wikman & Dosa, 2006). The same group further describes in (Wikman et al, 2006), the technical approach of porting the Apache httpd to the Symbian/S60 mobile platform in order to enable Website hosting and access on mobile phones.

This work is based on the concepts described by Gehlen (2007). Here, the focus is to introduce an efficient architecture of MobWSs by avoiding the overhead related to SOAP. One approach is to opt for REST design principles (Fielding, 2000) by enabling resource-centric access to services. In recent research (Pautasso et al, 2008), REST and SOAP WSs are comprehensively compared taking into consideration variable design and architectural parameters. The paper recommends the use of both based on the requirements of the system. The REST design principles are evaluated to be suitable for tactical and ad-hoc applications integration over the Web. Besides, describing REST services is an issue in focus since several recent years. A Web Application Description Language (WADL) has been specified as a recommended solution by Sun Microsystems (Hadley, 2006). On the other hand, Takase et al, (2008) evaluate the issues of describing REST oriented services by comparing the WADL and WSDL 2.0 (Chinnici et al, 2007). To the best of our knowledge, in this work, the first ever REST architecture for P2P MobWS provisioning is designed and compared to the original work relying on SOAP (Gehlen, 2007). Here, the focus is to architect and optimize the performance of Mobile Web Server by reducing message payloads and decreasing processing latencies which might be useful as we move towards ubiquitous and pervasive environment.

MOBILE WEB SERVICE INTERACTIONS

The interaction of P2P MobWSs does not depend upon the underlying network infrastructure which facilitates service utilization over short- and/or long-ranged communication links. For instance, in a small-scale temporary network infrastructure such as Bluetooth or ZigBee, a mobile user could search for MobWSs provisioned by nearby peers and consume the chosen MobWS over a short-ranged link. For large-scale networks MobWSs may be published by the centralized network elements such as UDDI. In such scenarios, mobile peers may look up the service interface through the WS broker and consume MobWS over a long-ranged communication link, like UMTS in a cellular network. In order to establish a truly transparent relationship between the network infrastructure and MobWS interaction, the mandatory requirement for a service provisioning node is to enable the transport protocol interface that is supported by the underlying network.

At a fundamental level, the MobWS interactions can be classified in two classes. Each class is defined by means of functional properties of a MobWS. Most traditional service-oriented mobile applications will prefer the class of MobWS interaction called Mobile Synchronous Interaction (MSI). Systems conforming to this class perform short-lived operations as a request-response process that instantly delivers the MobWS outcome to the requester. Whereas in more advanced systems, more complex interaction patterns are needed to efficiently qualify the application requirements. Therefore, the second class of interaction, called Mobile Asynchronous Interaction (MAI), defines mechanisms for P2P MobWSs by incorporating polling and callback techniques. In principle, the interaction of MobWSs in a P2P system is derived from the use case requirements. However, each of the aforementioned classes has its own architectural and messaging requirements that support a specialized set of MobWSs. In the following sections, MSI and MAI are discussed in more detail in terms of MobWS.

Mobile Synchronous Interaction (MSI)

The MSI is suitable for systems performing short-lived tasks. Basically, the core mobile access mechanisms in World Wide Web (WWW) and the Internet are based on the MSI type of communication. A standard mobile phone Internet browser can access any lightweight website specially designed for limited configuration devices. In this context, the mobile client navigates to the WWW URL (e.g. http://m.google.com) and fetches the resource which is interpreted by the browser in form of a web page. During the entire process, the mobile client is unable to access any other resource until the response from the service provider has arrived or HTTP timeout occurs. Due to this blocking nature of the WWW, vendors providing services inside the mobile browser (web pages) critically consider techniques to reduce the server-side processing overhead so that a short-lived request-response interaction can be ensured.

Generally, the web pages and WSs are accessible resources hosted in the Internet or a network attached to it. Web pages are strictly coupled with the web browser capable of interpreting content types (e.g. HTML) and provide their services inside the browser environment. The behavior of a single web page may differ within browsers from distinct vendors. However, WSs are independent software components that can be integrated within a mobile application using WS proxies. Most standard mobile WS access mechanisms also rely upon the MSI pattern. For instance, by pressing the "Confirm Order" button in a mobile e-commerce shopping portal, a credit card verification and authorization WS is invoked with all the data necessary to finalize the payment process. During the credit card WS runtime, the mobile client cannot continue its processing until the transaction is completed and the response has arrived, hence remains in a blocked state.

A P2P MobWS provisioning and computing system directly inherits the properties of standard WWW and the Internet. Thus, the MobWSs that are designed to perform short-lived P2P operations strongly integrate MSI as their underlying communication pattern. These MobWSs are termed as Mobile Synchronous Web Services (MSWs). Figure 1 depicts two mobile terminals, MT1 and MT2, provisioning corresponding MSWs. Each

terminal has a mobile application (M1 and M2), that uses a local MobWS proxy to handle the request-response process. The figure illustrates a scenario where M1 of MT1 initiates a request-response process in order to consume the M2-2 service provisioned by MT2. The MobWS proxy of M1 dispatches a request over the underlying network infrastructure and transitions to the blocked state. At some later time depending upon the network delay, the request arrives at M2 through its local proxy. Based on the requested parameters, M2 invokes the M2-2 service and waits for its completion. Since M2-2 is a MSW, the operation it performs is labeled as a short-lived process. Upon the completion of M2-2 service, the outcome is received by M2 and dispatched over the network as a response to M1 via the local MobWS proxy. Subsequent to some network delay, the response from M2 becomes available to M1 after it is received by its local proxy. M1 then transitions from the blocked state to running state which finalizes the request-response process in P2P MSI for MSWs.

MSWs are suitable for use cases demanding immediate response to a request. This is possible by ensuring the completion of service operation within a small time frame. Generally, MSW are widely realized in an RPC-oriented manner; however other techniques may be applied too.

Figure 1. Mobile synchronous web services in P2P system

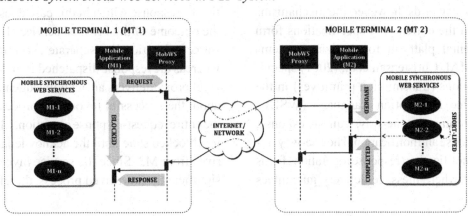

Mobile Asynchronous Interaction (MAI)

Most standard Internet protocols, such as HTTP, are designed with an unspecified presumption of instantaneous feedback. Therefore, opting for MSI to perform complex operations that may last for longer duration, would contribute towards degrading application performance in terms of resource inefficiencies and scalability. Not all WSs based systems require synchronous execution and provide immediate response. Such systems are architected to manage request and response as distinct mutually exclusive transactions, hence cannot rely upon MSI. Providentially, by using the existing Internet protocol standards, a communication technique, called MAI, can be derived to support systems employing WSs performing intricate processing that may take longer time to complete. MAI is not a straight forward technique to realize. One of the requirements of P2P MAI is that the service requester and provider must be capable of supporting same asynchronous MobWS messaging and transport behaviors. Whereas, in an infrastructure where requester and provider consume services through an intermediary network proxy, this requirement is fulfilled by the proxy node where transformation operations are performed to conform to the capabilities of each party, while keeping the proxy node transparent.

The standard bodies in WSs domain have not explicitly specified asynchronous operations within WS standards; however, the mechanisms provided in the current WS specifications form a fundamental platform for realizing systems based on MAI. Christensen et al. (2001) specify four operations (transmission primitives) in the Web Service Description Language (WSDL) specification namely, one-way, request-response, solicit-response and notification. The one-way (request) and notification (response) operations focus on systems where message delivery guarantees are not required. The request and response with these operations are dispatched as two separate datagram transmissions, enabling high level of decoupling between the service consumer and provider. Different from that, request-response and solicit-response operation supports message delivery guarantee by relying upon the standard HTTP. The request-response operation is similar to the MSI pattern where each request is followed by a response, whereas reversing the roles of service consumer and provider in MSI would lead to the solicit-response operation.

MobWSs performing long-lived computations while keeping the client in an unblocked state are called Mobile Asynchronous Web Services (MAWs). In a reliable P2P system of MAWs, MAI is employed as an underlying communication style by incorporating the request-response and solicit-response WSDL operations; however the one-way and notification operations are also possible if delivery guarantees can be compromised. Figure 2 depicts a P2P system based on MAI conforming to the request-response and solicit-response operations. Different from the scenario in Figure 1, the mobile terminals MT1 and MT2 now provision MAWs. The first block of interaction illustrating the request-response operation resembles the scenario of MSI; however a key difference has to be noticed. When the service invocation request from the mobile application M1 arrives at M2, the MAW M2-2 is invoked. Attention has to be paid on the generation of response which in this case does not carry the outcome of the invoked service. The MAWs starts to function in a separate execution thread, whereas the response dispatched from M2 via the local proxy delivers an acknowledgement to M1 about the successful invocation process. During the entire request-response operation, M1 remains in a blocked state until the acknowledgement arrives from M2. Since the service invocation is a significantly short-lived process, therefore it can be modeled using the blocking behavior at the requester. On the other hand, the invoked MAW performs long-lived functions independently and must not be a part of invocation process. Once the acknowledgement from M2 has arrived, M1 transitions from blocked to unblocked state, hence can perform other necessary functions independently.

During the request-response operations, M1 must provide an End Point Reference (EPR) to M2 that can be used to derive the solicit-response operation in a P2P system. The EPR serves as a contact point of M1 that is used by M2 to deliver the service outcome or to notify about alerts and exceptions. The requester during the service invocation process may provide an EPR of a different mobile or fixed terminal, if the responses from M2 are required to be delivered to a different network node. Assuming in the current scenario, the response from M2 is delivered to the requesting node, the lower block in Figure 2 illustrates the solicit-response operation in a MAI. At some later time, the processing of the MAWs M2-2 is completed. The service forwards the outcome to M2 that delivers it through the local proxy to MT1. The local proxy at MT1 receives and forwards the result to M1, which acknowledges M2 by sending a response message. Until the acknowledgement

from M1 has arrived, the corresponding thread of M2 remains in a blocked state.

The request-response operation corresponds to the 'pull' model where the client node initiates the communication with the server in order to perform its desired tasks. This model inherits the properties of a well-known polling interaction and supports decoupled client and server side implementations. On the contrary, solicit-response is a 'push' model where the serving node communicates with the client in order to provide service outcomes or alerts. This operation resembles the callback mechanism and inherently supports decoupled architectures. Both operations rely upon the synchronous flow of information with per-request acknowledgement behavior; however, combining both in a single system of P2P MAWs leads to a reliable MAI. The one-way and notification operations of WSDL support unreliable MAI that can be easily achieved by avoiding the acknowledgements for each transmission primitive in Figure 2.

In principle, the MAI is independent of the underlying network infrastructure. The two network clouds in Figure 2 depict this behavior where MT1 and MT2 communicate over distinct networks based on the request-response and solicit-response operations of WSDL.

Figure 2. Mobile asynchronous web services in P2P system

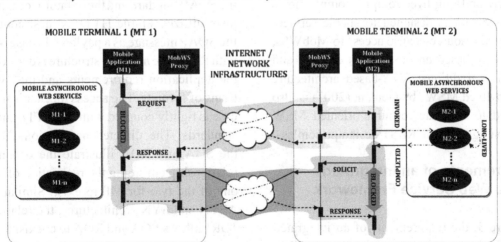

ARCHITECTURES FOR MOBILE P2P WEB SERVICES

The architecture for provisioning MobWSs in a P2P computing scenario can be derived from the standard Internet technologies. At a conceptual level, a P2P system is seen as a highly dynamic subset of a distributed system where each node takes the role of client and server. Unlike the traditional client-server paradigm, a P2P system is not centralized. Since the prime focus of WS technologies was not P2P mobile systems, therefore most existing specifications and standards target traditional enterprise level realization of service-oriented systems with a focus on application or business integration. However, some efforts have been put towards standardizing the minimal set of implementation constraints in mobile P2P systems of limited configuration devices (Driscoll et al, 2009). UPnP[2] on the other hand focuses on systems like home networks by providing a set of protocols for seamless content sharing and communication in an ad-hoc environment over a short-ranged link. Currently, no effort has been put to specify or standardize the systems demanding MobWSs to perform time consuming tasks, especially within a mobile P2P environment.

Within the scope of our research, we have developed a framework for P2P MobWS provisioning environments focusing on performing both short- and long-lived complex computations. The framework is designed to enable service-centric and resource-centric access to MobWSs, respectively based on the notions of SOA and ROA. The traditional SOA-based architecture for short-lived MSWs by Gehlen, (2007) is also extended to facilitate resource-oriented MSW provisioning based on REST design principles.

Requirements of an Integrated Mobile Web Service Framework

In Figure 3, the requirements of an integrated MobWSs framework are depicted as a UML conceptual diagram. The core framework entails two fundamental MobWS architectures, namely Asynchronous (ASYN) and Synchronous (SYN). The multiplicity, $1 - 0...1$, on entailment arcs represents the fact that at least one of the two architectures must be realized in order to obtain a service provisioning environment within a mobile terminal. The directed association between the ASYN and SYN architectures enforces the existence of at least one of the two architectures at a given time. For instance, if a framework does not incorporate ASYN architecture (multiplicity 0), the realization of a SYN architecture (multiplicity 1) becomes mandatory for its existence, and vice versa. The relationship {OR} allows both the architectures to exist simultaneously in a single framework.

The ASYN and SYN architectures must aggregate at least one Messaging Framework (MF) represented by the multiplicity $1-1...*$. The MF is composed of variety of Message Types (MTs) specific to the corresponding aggregating architectures. The composition multiplicity of $1-1...*$ between MF and MTs illustrates the requirement of having at least one existence of MT. The MF on the other hand can be derived from either SOA or ROA or both, which defines the message structures and access requirements of a MobWS. For instance, in case of SOA, the message structure is defined by conforming to the SOAP standard and the default access mechanism utilizes simple HTTP request containing the SOAP message as a payload. In case of ROA with REST, the message structure is derived from the application requirements and may vary in terms of formats. The access mechanism in this case is tightly coupled with the HTTP and URL standards. The directed associations between the SOA and ROA illustrate the dependency relationship enforcing the realization of at least one of the two for MF to exist. Similar to the ASYN and SYN architectures, the relationship {OR} allows SOA and ROA to coexist together in a single system.

Figure 3. Requirements of an integrated mobile web services framework in UML notation

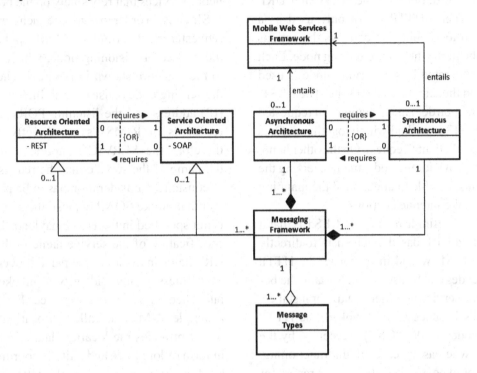

Based on the requirements presented above, an integrated MobWS framework is defined as the one incorporating ASYN and SYN architectures, each supporting SOA and ROA based services provisioning. In this chapter, only the SYN framework architecture is discussed in relation to its corresponding MFs.

Mobile Synchronous Web Services

The MSWs, due to their instantaneous nature, simplify the design process of their underlying architecture. The architecture strongly relies upon the MSI discussed earlier. Gehlen (2007) presents a comprehensive architecture and research findings in the area of SOA based MSWs. Gehlen (2007) uses the SOAP standard to define the MF and presents several MSW access mechanisms over multiple transport protocols. Detailed performance evaluation and theoretical analysis in terms of measurements and analytical models for

SOA based MSWs and their underlying transport protocols are also presented.

In this research, we extend the work done by Gehlen (2007) to support ROA-based MSWs. Here we do not discuss the MSW architecture based on SOA reference model; however we do present its comparison with ROA in terms of message payloads and server processing latencies.

Resource-Oriented Synchronous Messaging Framework

The term ROA cannot be clearly defined due to its tight coupling with the requirements inherited from the application context. In principle, the fundamental REST design principles are used to expose MSWs operations as accessible resources. These services are called "RESTful MSWs (R-MSWs)". The architecture of R-MSWs naturally supports the request-response transmission primitives since it is based on the MSI. The access mechanism of R-MSWs is defined by the HTTP and URL standards. There, HTTP is not only used as a transport protocol, but also conveys the actions that must be performed at the serving node. Each response generated by the serving node is used to transition the client into next state. The REST-based interaction demands a mapping of requested URL with HTTP method which together defines the purpose of clients' request. On the other hand, the service provisioning node, upon receiving the request, must be able to understand the mapping in order to take intended actions.

One of the defining benefits of REST is that it uses standard URL based mechanism to directly access the R-MSW and in response, the HTTP response codes can be used to understand the behavior at the service provider's end. For instance, if R-MSWs is successfully invoked, the HTTP response code of 200 ("OK") is received by the requester, whereas in case of malfunctioning, the code could be in a 3xx, 4xx or 5xx range, for instance 404 ("Not Found") (Richardson & Ruby, 2007). The response codes are used to notify the client about the success or failure during the service invocation or execution process.

URL Structure for Synchronous Access

In the architecture of R-MSWs, the underlying MF demands a clear definition of URL structure that must be used to access the R-MSWs resources. This requirement is met by defining a generic URL structure, as shown in Figure 4, which is shared by every R-MSW. Due to the strict dependency of REST on HTTP, binding to other transport protocols is not recommended since in such case, several design criteria of REST have to be compromised. The R-MSWs are instanta-

neous services that rely solely on the behavior of MSI. Thus, in order to consume such services, the requester must formulate a URL, published by the service provisioning node, which conforms to the structure shown in Figure 4. The URL of the serving node consists of an Internet Protocol (IP) address and the listening PORT. Since the resources of R-MSWs are directly accessed, therefore the SERVICE parameter represents the name of the service that the request intends to consume. Consideration has to be paid on the fact that unlike SOAP request, the service name is not specified in the HTTP payload. The direct specification of the service name in the request URL helps in avoiding the parsing overheads of SOAP message and to identify the invoked service published as a network resource. For instance, a simple R-MSWs, called "LocationService", which provides the location data of a peer host in form of longitude and latitude coordinates can be directly accessed using the URL http://rest.comnets.de:9090/LocationService.

The URL structure alone does not specify the actions that a requester intends to take on the accessed service. Since R-MSW may provide variety of resources, as service operations, therefore it is possible for a peer to access a single service to perform get, update, insert or delete functions. In LocationService example, the service name alone in the URL does not specify the actions intended for that particular request. For this reason, it is required by the requesting peer to establish a mapping between the URL and HTTP method for each request.

Fielding et al (1999) specify several HTTP methods, each with its pre-defined function. The most commonly used among these methods are

Figure 4. URL structure for RESTful mobile synchronous web services

GET, POST, PUT and DELETE. In this work, these four methods are used to establish meaningful mappings with the URL structure for R-MSWs to depict the actions intended at the server side; however, extensions with other HTTP methods are easily possible to meet additional requirements. Considering the same LocationService example, mapping of the service URL to the HTTP methods entirely changes the context of request. For example, if the URL http://rest.comnets.de:9090/LocationService is mapped to the HTTP GET method, the LocationService only provides the geographical coordinates of the host node as a response. In a scenario where the service requester provides its own coordinates to inform about its location, the same URL could be used to access the LocationService, but the mapping to HTTP POST method is established. The POST method is used whenever the requester embeds some data in HTTP payload, in this case the geographical coordinates. Receiving a request with HTTP POST represents an update action and the LocationService modifies its record with the new coordinates from its peer. The PUT method usually focuses on creating new information. In the LocationService scenario, this method can be used to perform an insert operation that creates a new entry in records maintained by the service. For instance, if the requester likes to provide the geographical coordinates of all major tourist spots that he has visited during his journey, the LocationServices is accessed using the same URL mapped to the HTTP PUT method while the list of coordinates is placed in the HTTP payload. The mapping specifies to the service that the request is intended to insert new coordinates in the record instead of update. The same functionality can be achieved with the POST HTTP method; however it solely depends upon the implementation of the application. Similarly, the URL mapping to the DELETE method signifies the removal of a record from the coordinate list that the LocationService is maintaining.

Until now, the LocationService scenario has only considered a case where the service offers one operation of each kind, that is, get, update, insert and delete which are directly mapped to the GET, POST, PUT and DELETE methods of HTTP respectively. Consider a situation where the LocationService offers multiple resources of one kind, such as getX() methods like getElevation, getAddress, getCoordinates etc. In this case, the EPR http://rest.comnets.de:9090/LocationService mapped to HTTP GET does not convey the targeted action of the request. Thus, the URL structure in Figure 4 is extended with an optional parameter for specifying the target RESOURCE. With this extension, the requester can directly specify the target resource in the URL and map to the corresponding HTTP method. For example, in order to fetch the elevation of the service provisioning mobile node, the requester formulates the URL http://rest.comnets.de:9090/LocationService/Elevation and maps it to the HTTP GET method, which clearly indicates the targeted resource; getElevation operation. In order to update, insert or delete the elevation, the same URL is used with its respective mappings to POST, PUT and DELETE methods.

Payload Optimization with REST

In a mobile P2P communication system, the size of message payload significantly influences the performance of mobile applications and networks. Contrary to SOAP based MSWs, the REST approach prominently reduces the message sizes while providing the same functionality. This is particularly beneficial for a mobile P2P service provisioning due to the resource constraints of participating devices. In a MF based on MSI, the freedom to specify distinct types of MTs, in terms of runtime operations, does not exist due to the short-lived nature of MSWs. Thus, in case of R-MSWs, most of the information required to invoke a service is represented by the URL. However, when the URL is mapped to the methods like POST, PUT or DELETE, it may carry a payload necessary for computation by the accessed service. Unlike REST, in a typical SOAP request, the MTs are defined according to the prescribed standard MF (Martin et al, 2007). Naturally, for narrow-band mobile networks, the conformance to the SOAP standard leads to performance degradation due to large payload to be transmitted. In the past, several efforts have been put to reduce the SOAP message size by compression techniques. Werner et al (2008) claim that a SOAP message, in a typical case, causes three times more network traffic compared to conventional techniques such as Java-RMI and CORBA. They further explore several compression strategies and provide a detailed survey and evaluation results of state-of-the-art binary encoding techniques for SOAP. It has been shown that WAP Binary XML (WBXML) is the most effective compressor of SOAP messages. Gehlen (2007) on the other hand, shows an example SOAP message encoding, using WBXML, of the BabelFish translation service. Listing 1 displays the SOAP message having an original un-encoded length of 508 bytes. According to Gehlen (2007), the resulting WBXML encoded SOAP message had a length of 326 bytes and achieved 35% reduction.

Listing 1. The un-encoded SOAP message as shown in Gehlen (2007).

```
<?xml version='1.0' encoding='UTF-8'?>
<SOAP-ENV:Envelope xmlns:xsi="http://
www.w3.org/2001/XMLSchema-instance"
   xmlns:SOAP-ENV="http://schemas.xml-
soap.org/soap/envelope/"
   SOAP-ENV:encodingStyle="http://sche-
mas.xmlsoap.org/soap/encoding/"
     xmlns:xsd="http://www.w3.org/2001/
XMLSchema">
   <SOAP-ENV:Body>
     <ns1:BabelFish xmlns:ns1="urn:xme
thodsBabelFish">
```

```
        <translationmode
xsi:type="xsd:string">
                de_en
        </translationmode>
        <sourcedata
xsi:type="xsd:string">
                Auto
        </sourcedata>
     </ns1:BabelFish>
   </SOAP-ENV:Body>
</SOAP-ENV:Envelope>
```

With the REST-based MSW access, the message payload can be further reduced even without applying the WBXML encoding technique. In case of R-MSWs, the service resource is uniquely identified by the URL from the client. If the same BabelFish translation service is exposed as a directly accessible R-MSW, the message payload can be further reduced by conforming to the URL structure in Figure 4. For instance, if the BabelFish service is provisioned by the mobile host rest.babelfish.com at port 80, then the absolute REST URL to access the service takes the form http://rest.babelfish.com:80/BabelFish. It can be seen that the service is directly identified by the URL; however the input parameters <translationmode> and <sourcedata> must be transmitted as HTTP payload. Due to the existence of data in HTTP payload, the service URL can be mapped to the HTTP POST method. Depending upon the implementation of BabelFish service, the combined effect of the URL-method mapping notifies the service provider about the requested actions. Listing 2 shows the resulting REST message payload with the length of 113 bytes, which is approximately 65% (or ~2.9 times) further reduced compared to the WBXML encoded SOAP message of 326 bytes in (Gehlen, 2007). The reduction is ~78% (~4.5 times) when **compared to the original message in Listing 1.**

Listing 2. The un-encoded REST message of the BabelFish service.

```
<translationmode xsi:type="xsd:string">
de_en
</translationmode>
<sourcedata xsi:type="xsd:string">
Auto
</sourcedata>
```

Further reduction in data volume could be achieved by employing XML encoding techniques such as WBXML or compressing the data using stream compressors, e.g. GZIP (Gailly, 1996), however, the compression and decompression processing overhead in resource-constraint mobile nodes must be considered.

Different from the transmission of input parameters as HTTP payload, it is also possible to directly identify the entire request using a single URL. For example, the BabelFish service could also be accessed using the URL http://rest.babelfish.com:80/BabelFish?translationmode=de_en&sourcedata=Auto. In this case the input requirements are provided as a query string attached to the URL. This URL can be simply mapped to the HTTP GET method as it does not carry any payload. Using this approach, 100% reduction in message payload can be achieved; however this technique is not always recommended due to its limitation of carrying only the string type of data within the query string of the URL. For binary data, the HTTP payload cannot be avoided. From the critical perspective, extending the URL with query string parameters also compromises original design principles of the REST methodology.

REST-Based Architecture for Mobile Terminals

Based on the MSI, Gehlen (2007) originally developed the architecture for MSWs by conforming to the SOA reference model (MacKenzie et al, 2006). He employed the SOAP messaging constructs and designed the corresponding server-side components. Transition from the existing architecture to enable REST based MSW provisioning

requires re-engineering of the server architecture and components. Due to the strict dependency of REST on HTTP, the request listening threads for various other protocols are not required; however, the HTTP protocol listener must be modified to differentiate between REST and SOAP requests.

Synchronous Server Components
The architecture proposed by Gehlen (2007) uses SOAP-RPC mechanism to consume SOAP interfaced MSWs. Thus, any SOAP request has to conform to a modified version of the URL structure discussed earlier (see Figure 4). The main difference is created by replacing the SERVICE parameter in the URL structure with "soaprpc", whereas the RESOURCE parameter is completely omitted. The soaprpc parameter is specific to the SOAP architecture and is required to identify a SOAP RPC call. On the other hand, every SOAP call must carry a SOAP envelope in HTTP payload, therefore the POST HTTP method is specified in the protocol headers. Contrary to SOAP requests, accessing MSWs over the REST interface tightly conforms to the URL structure presented in Figure 4. Therefore, for any REST request, the parameter soaprpc is not required which eases the request-type identification process by relying upon the structure of the received URL. Based on these requirements, the HTTP protocol listener component is modified to identify the target architecture of the request by checking the existence of soaprpc parameter in the received URL. The absence of soaprpc implies a REST request. The process of request handling at the listener level is shared by both architectures (SOAP and REST) and is neutral towards any class of MobWSs; MSW or MAW. In the current implementation, MobWSs can be consumed over a variety of protocols (Gehlen, 2007); however, here we restrict our focus on HTTP only.

Figure 5 illustrates the invocation process of R-MSW in the architecture of a mobile terminal. The flow of information and control transitions between different server components of REST ar-

Figure 5. R-MSW invocation process in a mobile server terminal

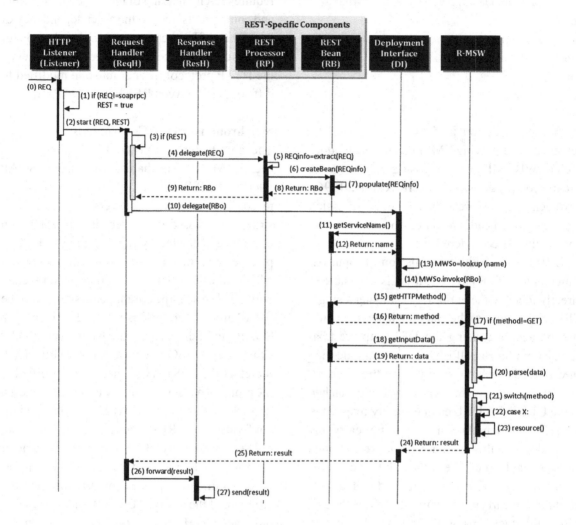

chitecture is shown. Upon arrival of client's request REQ, the HTTP Listener component (Listener) identifies the request-type based on the soaprpc parameter, as explained before. Assuming the request for R-MSW, the Listener initiates a thread called Request Handler (ReqH) by providing REQ and request-type identification flag, REST in this case. The ReqH is a parent server component responsible for managing incoming requests, in accordance to their requirements, which delegates REQ and initializes other server components on demand. The upgraded version of the ReqH is a shared server component among SYN and ASYN architectures for handling either of the REST or

SOAP requests. Since the REQ targets the R-MSW, the ReqH simply delegates the control flow to the REST Processor (RP) after checking the REST flag. The RP is a generic and major server component specially designed, as an extension to the original architecture, for MobWSs based on REST design principles. The responsibility of RP is to extract all the information embedded within the REST REQ and create a read-only bean namely, REST Bean (RB). The RB is a de-serialized version of the REQ that is understandable by all the server components involved in the invocation process. Before the RB is created, the RP has to perform a variety of operations such as, parsing the URL and understanding its structure, obtaining the HTTP Method, extracting the input data from HTTP payload and check for URL faults. Assuming a no-fault scenario, the RP creates a coarse-grained RB that populates all the extracted information in its properties. The read-only nature of RB facilitates in strictly conforming to the REQ, by preventing any server component or service to accidently modify the original information. The REST Bean object (RBo) of RB is returned to the ReqH by RP once it is created. Since the information delivered by the client in the REQ is now encapsulated within the RBo, therefore its reference can be passed around as a single object across other server components instead of multiple individual objects. Upon receiving the RBo from the RP, the ReqH delegates the control flow, along with the RBo, to the Deployment Interface (DI) component which is responsible for lookup and invocation of the requested MobWS. Here, the DI in (Gehlen, 2007) is extended to support R-MWSs in SYN and ASYN (also includes SOAP interface) architectures. The DI uses the RBo to obtain the requested service name from RB. Since in DI, a list of available services along with their corresponding instances is maintained as a key-value mapping, therefore the requested service name facilitates the lookup of the targeted MobWS object (MWSo); in this case the R-MSW. The MWSo is then used to invoke the R-MSW and RBo is provided as an argument.

A single R-MSW may offer multiple service methods as its exposed resources. Therefore at this phase, the service invocation by using the MWSo does not imply the call to the intended service method in the REQ. Thus, the R-MSW is responsible for evaluating the mapping between HTTP method and URL in order to identify the targeted service method from the client. Consequently, the R-MSW obtains the HTTP method from the RB through the received RBo. Upon receiving the method, the service may obtain the target resource using RBo, if desired. Obtaining the target resource is only necessary if the R-MSW

offers multiple methods of the same kind, e.g. many getX() methods. For services offering only one method of each kind, the mapped HTTP method can be used directly for target invocation. Since providing multiple or single kinds of methods is specific to service requirements, therefore for keeping the discussion generic, the call to obtain target the resource from the RB is not shown in the figure. In the next step, the R-MSW must check if the client has provided some input data that should be used by the target resource. Since the URL mapping to the HTTP GET method implies no payload in the REQ, therefore the service only requests the input data from RB (using RBo) if and only if the HTTP method other than GET is mapped. In case the payload exists, the service parses the input data and subsequently the target resource method is invoked which is directly identified by the HTTP method mapping (illustrated as "case X"). Consequently, the target R-MSW resource, upon completion, dispatches the result to the parent server component ReqH through the DI. The ReqH forwards the result to Response Handler (ResH) component which sends the result to the client using the same HTTP connection stream.

Synchronous Client Components

Synchronous client components are responsible for enabling remote access to MSWs. The functionality of each client is derived from the Web Service Description (WSD) published by the service provider. In case of REST, the client strictly couples with the HTTP Transport (Transport) component in order to enable access to R-MSW. Due to the requirements of REST design principles, a client must be able to formulate the URL structure, as in Figure 4, and its mapping to relevant HTTP method based on the targeted service resource. The payload in a REST request has its own significance. Unlike SOAP, read-only R-MSWs may be invoked without incorporating any payload in HTTP request. In such scenario, the invocation requirements are directly identified by the URL at the end of service provider. For conforming to

REST invocation process, a mobile client provides three basic utility tools classified as URL Creator (UC), Method Map (MM) and Payload Creator (PC). Each of these tools is incorporated within a mobile client terminal, specifically for consuming R-MSW.

Figure 6 illustrates a request construction process within a mobile client terminal for consuming R-MSW. The R-MSW client, in the first phase, creates a REST URL by using the UC. The UC is a simple tool that uses the SERVICE and RESOURCE parameters to formulate a URL that conforms to Figure 4. The IP and PORT of service provider is obtained from the WSD. Once created, a UC object (UCo) is returned to the cli-

ent for future use. At this phase, the client must identify the payload requirements of the target R-MSW by analyzing the WSD published by the service provider. For instance, using the WSDL standard (Christensen et al, 2001), the <message> element may define the payload requirements and their types using the nested <part> tag. For more REST compatible description of MSWs, WADL (Marc, 2006) or WSDL 2.0 W3C recommendation (Chinnici et al, 2007) can be employed. During the request construction process, the client must check if the payload is required by the target resource. The PC tool, therefore, is only used to construct the payload on need basis. Here, for explanation, we assume the target resource requires an input

Figure 6. R-MSW request construction process in a mobile client terminal

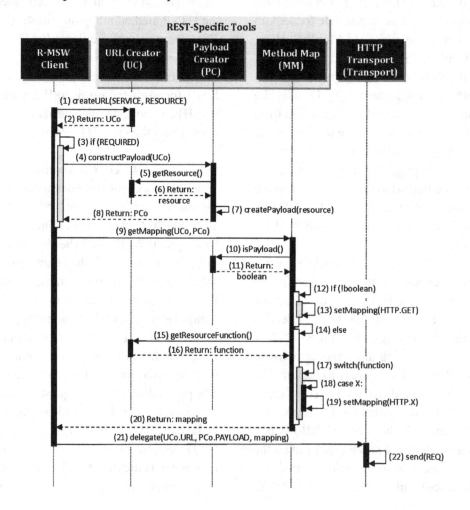

payload to function. After identifying the input data requirements, the PC is used to construct the payload according to the format specified in the WSD. The R-MSW client provides the UCo to PC that is used to fetch the target resource from UC. Once the resource is obtained by the PC, the payload is created, accordingly, and a PC object (PCo) is returned. The R-MSW client uses the UCo and PCo to identify and establish the mapping of URL with the corresponding HTTP method. For this reason, the client invokes the MM tool by providing UCo and PCo as arguments. A read-only R-MSW requiring no input data as HTTP payload is directly identified by the URL. In this case, a direct mapping to HTTP GET method is sufficient to identify the target resource. The MM, after obtaining the UCo and PCo from the R-MSW client, verifies by using PCo if the payload for the target resource has been constructed by the PC. The MM uses the returned Boolean and directly maps the HTTP GET method to the URL in case of no payload. Different from this, the existence of payload implies the mapping possibilities of POST, PUT or DELETE methods. In this case, the UCo is used by MM to obtain the target resource function. The mapping of the HTTP method is a critical process that may entirely change the meaning of a request. Therefore the target resource function is used to specify the mapping. For instance, in the LocationService scenario discussed earlier, the URL to consume the Elevation resource, http://rest.comnets.de:9090/LocationService/Elevation, can be mapped to any of the three HTTP methods to perform update, insert or delete operations. These functional behaviors of the targeted resource are derived from the application context and depend upon implementation by the developer. In R-MSW, it is possible that the same URL is used to access distinct target functions of the same service resource, such as updateElevation(), insertEleva-tion() and deleteElevation(). Here, the Elevation in URL corresponds to the service resource and the mapping to HTTP method identifies its respective function, for e.g. POST for update, PUT for insert

and DELETE for delete. Thus, the information provided to MM by UC must be used to identify the intended functional behavior of the resource for mapping the HTTP method correctly.

After the resource function is obtained, the mapping to HTTP method can be identified which is represented as case X in Figure 6. Consequently, the MM tool returns the identified method mapping to the R-MSW client. The client subsequently delegates the control flow to the Transport component by providing the URL from UC, HTTP payload from PC and the mapping from MM. The Transport component is responsible for dispatching the request REQ to the received URL, after embedding HTTP payload and setting the mapped method in HTTP request headers. The implementation of PC and MM tools is derived from the application requirements; however, the UC provides generic functionality to construct the target URL for accessing P2P R-MWSs.

PERFORMANCE EVALUATION

In software engineering, performance evaluation is a technique to study the real world behavior of applications in order to facilitate design and implementation decisions. For evaluating performance, several criterions must be defined in order to focus on specific aspects of a system. In perspective of functional requirements, the evaluation considers variable sets of parameters, such as data volume, processing delay, load time, memory footprint, to study how fast a system react to events. The performance of functional properties directly influences the end user experience. On the other hand the performance of non-functional requirements of a system is more relevant towards the ease of development and deployment process. Such requirements greatly rely upon the vendor infrastructure and skills of engineering team due to which their evaluation results become difficult to measure.

Within the scope of this work, the performance of functional properties of the MobWS framework comprising both, REST and SOAP architectures, is evaluated by real time measurements. Here, the focus is to evaluate and compare only the SYN architecture of MobWSs in terms of message payloads and processing latencies of the server components. The MobWS framework has been implemented for all mobile terminals compatible with the Java ME platform. The framework is configured to run on a mobile terminal emulator on a Windows Laptop connected to the fast Ethernet and measurements are collected and evaluated for presentation. The client, with a similar configuration, is set up on the same network. The performance of the underlying network infrastructure is out of the scope of this chapter.

Evaluation of Payload Reduction

In the first evaluation experiment, a simple echoString MSW was developed that upon invocation echoed the same string argument to the client as received within the request. The service was deployed on the MobWS framework by enabling both, REST and SOAP access interfaces. Initially, the focus was to measure the size of request message payload requirements for service invocation with each interface. The initial measurements were taken for 20 service invocation requests dispatched by the client in a sequence, first with SOAP and later with the REST interface.

In SOAP invocation, a client is required to generate and parse the SOAP envelope for each request. For this purpose, third party tools, kSOAP and kXML, from an open source project[3] were utilized. Besides constructing the SOAP XML, each request incorporated Custom Data (CD) as a string argument to the echoString service. In the first request, the CD of 5 bytes was imbedded inside the SOAP envelope. For each subsequent request, the data was increased by adding 5 additional bytes. With such sequential increase of CD, the 2nd request imbedded a string of 10 bytes, 3rd of 15 bytes, and 4th of 20 bytes up to the 20th

request imbedding 100 bytes inside the SOAP envelope. Figure 7(A) shows the total payload and CD sizes of the first 20 requests dispatched by the client. It was observed that each input data, as CD, required by the echoString service is significantly smaller in size than the imbedding SOAP XML. The overall SOAP envelope contains a constant amount of 576 bytes of SOAP XML, whereas the imbedded CD ranges from 5 – 100 bytes in 20 requests. The significant difference in ratio between the two constructs of the SOAP envelope increases the processing overhead even for very low input data requirements. During the measurements, it was observed that the percentage of ratio difference decreases as the CD increases. For instance, for echoing 5 bytes of data, the SOAP XML occupies ~99% of the complete 581 bytes SOAP envelope, whereas for 100 bytes of CD in the 20th request, ~85% of the envelope contains SOAP XML. For an equal amount of data and SOAP XML, the occupancy percentage is 50%. Besides the measurement up to 100 bytes of CD, the percentage of ratios' difference for 1 KB and 1 MB of data was calculated to 36% and ~0.05% respectively. Although, the overhead of SOAP XML within the envelope reduces with increasing amount of CD, it cannot be completely avoided.

Different from that, we followed the identical measurement process of 20 requests and increasing data size by using the REST interface. In this case, the requirement at the client side to construct XML can be avoided since the echoString service is directly identified by the URL conforming to the structure in Figure 4. Although the CD in the REST architecture could be imbedded directly in the HTTP payload, 13 bytes of XML meta tags imbedding the data were explicitly created to better represent the payload construct. The measurements obtained by invoking the echoString service with the REST interface showed significant payload reduction, as shown in Figure 7(B), compared to SOAP. The 5 bytes of CD was echoed by sending the total of 18 bytes of the REST pay-

Figure 7. Request message payload and processing latencies in REST and SOAP mobile servers

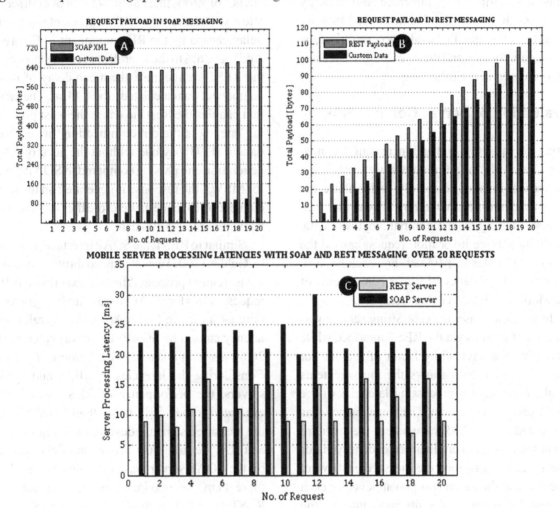

load, achieving ~97% reduction compared to 581 bytes of the SOAP envelope. In case the optional 13 bytes of XML meta tags are removed, ~ 99% of reduction can be achieved. For 100 bytes of CD, ~83% reduction was achieved including the 13 bytes of XML meta tags and ~85% excluding them. Similar to SOAP measurements, the reduction percentage was calculated for 1 KB and 1MB of REST payload including and excluding the 13 bytes of optional tags. The reduction of 36% and ~29% of payload was calculated for 1 KB of CD including and excluding 13 bytes, respectively. For 1 MB of data, a very negligible difference of 0.001% between payload reductions, ~0.054%

and ~0.053%, was observed with and without 13 bytes of meta tags respectively. Increasing the amount of CD slowly decreases the payload reduction percentage; however the REST payload always remains less than the SOAP envelope. Here, only the default SOAP message structure specified in (Gudgin et al, 2007) is compared to REST. Incorporating WS-* specifications within a SOAP envelope may further influence the payload reduction factor.

In Figure 7(C), the influence of message payload on the processing performance of REST and SOAP mobile servers is shown for the 20 request cycle. The measurements show that the payload reduction with REST interface significantly decreases the processing latencies for MSW invocation. More detailed evaluation results of the server components and their processing latencies are discussed in the following.

Evaluation of Server Components

Using the same test-bed and increasing the measurement cycle to 100 requests, the echoString service was invoked repeatedly. In this phase, the CD was again incremented by 5 bytes for each request. Starting from the initial 5 bytes of data, the 100th service invocation request carried the data of 495 bytes in payload. For each request, the processing latency of major components of the Mobile Web Server was measured.

In the first phase, the echoString service was invoked 100 times via the REST interface while increasing the payload by factor of 5 bytes per request. Figure 8(A) shows the measurements results obtained for processing latencies of the REST server architecture. The mean latency was calculated to be 12.35 ms whereas the standard deviation was 3.315 ms. In order to identify major latency causing factors, the measurements were calculated at the server component level for each request. Figure 8(B) presents and compares the processing latencies of major server components in the REST architecture. It is clear from the measurements that significant amount of latency is caused by the ReqH component with the mean of 10.13 ms. Based on the mean server latency in REST architecture, the ReqH consumes ~82% of the overall processing. In an integrated architecture, the latency of ReqH component is not just caused by delegating the request (see Figure 5); rather several sub-operations are performed within the component that is not presented here. Some of these sub-operations include transport protocol identification, recognizing MSW or MAW request, initiating and delegating to architecture specific components, error handling in payload and fault generation. The RP component causes the mean

latency of 5.6 ms that implies 45% of overall server latency. The latency of RP component covers the delay caused by the RB component in Figure 5. Adding ~36% to the overall processing latency of the REST architecture, the mean delay of ResH component was calculated to be 4.44 ms. The factor that enables the ResH to cause the least processing latency is the direct imbedding of response data in HTTP payload without the need of XML generation and parsing compared to SOAP. Since for MSWs, the response is generated on the same connection as request, therefore the URL creation latencies are also avoided.

Similar to REST, the SOAP interface proposed by Gehlen (2007) was evaluated through the same measurement process. After the execution of 100 request cycles for SOAP based echoString invocation, as shown in Figure 8(C), the overall mean latency caused by SOAP server was calculate to 26.64 ms with a standard deviation of 6.47 ms. Considering the latencies of REST and SOAP servers, the performance of REST server was evaluated to be ~55% faster than SOAP. Using the measured standard deviations in Figure 8(A) and (C), the minimum processing delay caused by the SOAP server was calculated to be ~22% more than the maximum processing delay of REST server. The ReqH component of SOAP architecture alone, caused the mean latency of 12.41 ms which is ~18% higher than the corresponding ReqH component in REST, and ~0.5% more than the overall mean processing latency of the REST server. The ResH component in SOAP server showed a significant difference from the same component in REST by measuring the mean latency of 11.95 ms leading to ~63% of reduced performance. It can be observed that the RP component, due to REST specific functionality, does not exist in the measurement results obtained for SOAP architecture.

The overall performance of the REST server architecture showed promising results in comparison to SOAP. The measurements reflect an overall performance behavior by evaluation of

Figure 8. Mean latencies of REST and SOAP mobile servers and their components over 100 requests

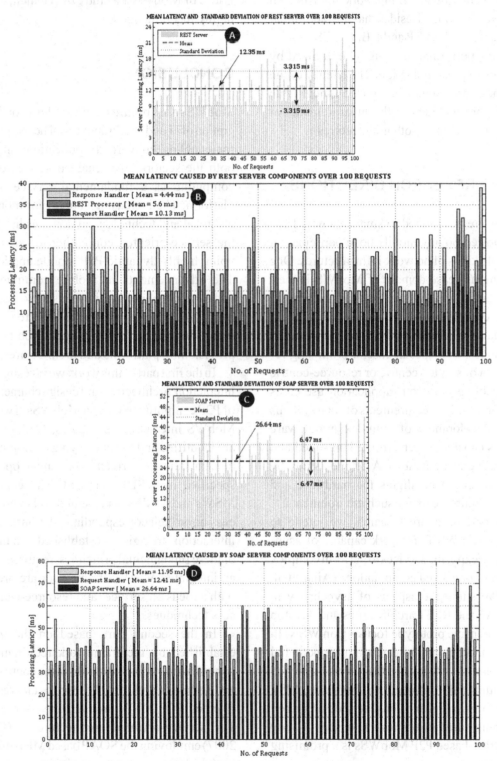

an integrated MobWS framework focusing on MSW provisioning. Besides having additional components, such as RP and RB, in REST architecture, the performance is highly optimized by significant payload reduction. The latency of the DI component presented in Figure 5 is negligible and therefore included in the measurements of ReqH components of both architectures.

FUTURE RESEARCH DIRECTIONS

MobWSs are not limited to smart phones. They can be hosted on any mobile node participating in multiple kinds of network infrastructures. One interesting use case domain of MobWS is their deployment in wireless networks to perform in-network computational processes (Aijaz et al, 2009). Having the WSN with spatially distributed sensor nodes, as a special case, a promising research area of service-centric or resource-centric WSN enabling numerous application use cases can be derived. The requirements of such systems demand development of complex middleware platforms capable of performing long-lived and collaborative computations. A detailed study by Stankovic (2008) highlights the hardware and software requirements for such environments.

As a part of future research, we intend to present a MobWS framework capable of asynchronously exposing services to perform complex in-network long-lived computations (Aijaz et al, 2008). We study the aspects of asynchrony in both SOAP and REST architectures and develop a comprehensive prototype focusing on WSN. In future technology and research, a huge potential can be seen in integrating the service-oriented WSN with the IP Multimedia Subsystem (IMS), in order to gain higher valued services. Further, establishing a framework for a to ensure privacy and contract-based P2P MobWSs is a promising area of research.

In order to obtain valuable insight about the mobility management and traffic performance issues of MobWSs, a study of (Gehlen, 2007) is highly recommended.

CONCLUSION

MobWSs are a promising technology for the integration of IT and TelCo domains. The requirements for enabling converged applications involving both the sectors have enabled service-oriented computing as a fundamental service delivery platform. The increasing support for mobility in technical and technological domains has pushed the service-oriented computing towards developing highly dynamic P2P mobile applications. The advancements in mobile communication and device technology, in terms of software and hardware, have revolutionized the focus of research and industry to investigate mobile service provisioning platforms and architectures.

In the first part of this work, we investigated the interaction, architecture and design characteristics of P2P computing based on MobWSs. Two major MobWS interactions strategies, MSI and MAI, are identified and the underlying communication mechanisms are derived based on the operations specified in WSDL standard. The concept of MSWs and MAWs is presented and detailed discussion on their corresponding relationships to the interaction strategies is established. On the basis of these fundamental principles, requirements for an integrated MobWS framework are presented with a focus on service- and resource-centric access techniques.

In the second part, based on the grounds established by the framework requirements, a comprehensive discussion about the controversies and issues for architecting service- and resource-oriented P2P MSW architectures is presented. The service-oriented architecture in (Gehlen, 2007) employing the SOAP based MF is critically analyzed. Consequently, an alternative resource-oriented MSW architecture is proposed based on REST design principles that avoid the overheads of SOAP oriented MF in terms of message payloads and processing latencies. The requirements of resource-oriented MF are presented and URL structure for synchronous access to MobWSs is defined. The URL structure facilitates uniquely identifying the target resource while optimizing the processing latencies and message payload in REST server architecture. It has been shown that the payload reduction with REST is significantly more than the WBXML-encoded SOAP envelope. In order to provide extensive insight for designing REST based P2P MSWs, a detailed discussion of specific synchronous server and client side architectural components is presented. The exhaustive insight about the functioning of each component is discussed in relation to the REST design principles and the generic URL structure.

The third part evaluates the performance of the MobWS framework, in terms of message payload and processing optimization, achieved with REST architecture for MSWs. The performance evaluation is conducted by obtaining real-time measurements and comparing with the original SOAP based architecture in (Gehlen, 2007). The initial part of evaluation focuses on payload size requirements in SOAP and REST architectures based on 20 request cycles carrying the data ranging from 5 – 100 bytes. It has been observed that transmitting a small amount of data in a SOAP envelope produces significant payload overhead compared to REST. The payload reduction of ~99% and ~85% was achieved, compared to SOAP, by transmitting the respective data of 5 bytes and 100 bytes over the REST architecture. It was observed that by increasing the amount of data in the SOAP envelope, the overhead of SOAP XML can be reduced, however, the reduction achieved with REST is always much higher.

The evaluation of server components in terms of processing latencies is presented. The results show that the REST server, due to reduced message payload, performs ~55% faster than the original SOAP server (Gehlen, 2007). More detailed evaluations showed that the single ReqH component of SOAP architecture caused the mean latency of 12.41 ms which is ~0.5% more than the overall mean processing latency of the REST server. Furthermore, the minimum processing delay caused by the SOAP server was calculated to be ~22% more than the maximum processing delay of REST server. It was shown that besides of having additional components, such as RP and RB in REST architecture, the performance is highly optimized by significant payload reduction compared to SOAP.

The overall performance of REST architecture showed promising results. With the experience gained during the development and research process, we learned that the REST based P2P MSWs framework eases the development and deployment process due to the technical simplicity and optimized performance. Although SOAP offers a wide range of globally accepted WS standard specifications, it produces significant overhead, especially for mobile terminals due to large message sizes and XML manipulation requirements. With the resource-centric nature and coupling of REST with basic Internet standards, HTTP and URL, it has a potential to overcome the controversies and issues existing for SOAP.

ACKNOWLEDGMENT

This work has been jointly supported by the Department of Communication Networks (ComNets) and the UMIC Research Centre of RWTH Aachen University. The author specially appreciates the support of Prof. Dr.-Ing. Bernhard Walke and the ComNets team members throughout the preparation of this chapter.

REFERENCES

Aijaz, F., Adeli, S. M., & Walke, B. (2009). *A Service-Oriented Approach for In-Network Computations in Wireless Networks.* In *Proceedings of the Sixth IEEE and IFIP International Conference on wireless and Optical communications Networks* (WOCN2009), Cairo, Egypt.

Aijaz, F., Hameed, B., & Walke, B. (2008). *Asynchronous Mobile Web Services: Concept and Architecture.* In *Proceedings of 2008 IEEE 8th International Conference on Computer and Information Technology*, (p. 6), Sydney, Australia.

Chinnici, R., Moreau, J., Ryman, A., & Weerawarana, S. (2007). *Web Services Description Language (WSDL) Version 2.0 Part 1: Core Language*. W3C Recommendation 26 June 2007. Retrieved on March 30, 2009 from http://www.w3.org/TR/wsdl20/

Christensen, E., Curbera, F., Meredith, G., & Weerawarana, S. (2001). *Web Services Description Language (WSDL) 1.1*. W3C Note 15 March 2001. Retrieved March 10, 2009, from http://www.w3.org/TR/wsdl

Driscoll, D., Mensch, A., Nixon, T., & Regnier, A. (2009). *Devices Profile for Web Services Version 1.1*. OASIS Working Draft 05. Retrieved March 16, 2009, from http://www.oasis-open.org/committees/documents.php?wg_abbrev=ws-dd

Fielding, R. (2000). *Architectural Styles and the Design of Network-based Software Architectures* (Doctoral dissertation). University of California, Irvine

Fielding, R., Gettys, J., Mogul, J., Frystyk, H., Masinter, L., Leach, P., & Berners-Lee, T. (1999). *Hypertext Transfer Protocol - HTTP/1.1*. Standards Track, Network Working Group. The Internet Society. Retrieved March 17, 2009, from http://www.w3.org/Protocols/rfc2616/rfc2616.html

Gailly, J.-L. (1996). *Gzip documentation*. Internet. Retrieved March 18, 2009 from ftp://prep.ai.mit.edu/pub/gnu/

Gehlen, G. (2007). *Mobile Web Services - Concepts, Prototype, and Traffic Performance Analysis* (Ph. D. Dissertation). RWTH Aachen University, Germany.

Gudgin, M., Hadley, M., Mendelsohn, N., Moreau, J., Nielsen, H. F., Karmarkar, A., & Lafon, Y. (2007). *SOAP Version 1.2 Part 1: Messaging Framework*. W3C Recommendation. Retrieved on March 17, 2009, from http://www.w3.org/TR/soap12-part1/

Hadley, M. J. (2006). *Web Application Description Language* (WADL), (Technical Report). Santa Clara, CA: Sun Microsystems, Inc. Retrieved on April 3, 2009, from http://research.sun.com/techrep/2006/smli_tr-2006-153.pdf

MacKenzie, C. M., Laskey, K., McCabe, F., Brown, P. F., & Metz, R. (2006). *Reference Model for Service Oriented Architecture 1.0*. OASIS Standard. Retrieved March 3, 2009, from http://docs.oasis-open.org/soa-rm/v1.0/soa-rm.html

Pautasso, C., Zimmermann, O., & Leymann, F. (2008). *Restful web services vs. "big" web services: making the right architectural decision*. In *Proceeding of the 17th international conference on World Wide Web*. New York: ACM

Richardson, L., & Ruby, S. (2007). RESTful Web Services. Sebastopol, CA: O'Reilly Media, Inc.

Riva, O., & Kangasharju, J. (2008). *Challenges and Lessons in Developing Middleware on Smart Phones*. Los Alamitos, CA: IEEE Computer Society Press.

Srirama, S. N. (2008). *Mobile Hosts in Enterprise Service Integration* (Ph. D. Dissertation). RWTH Aachen University, Germany. Retrieved on April 3, 2009, from http://darwin.bth.rwth-aachen.de/opus/volltexte/2008/2567/

Stankovic, J. A. (2008). *Wireless Sensor Networks*. IEEE Computer Magazine.

Takase, T., Makino, S., Kawanaka, S., Ueno, K., Ferris, C., & Ryman, A. (2008). *Definition languages for RESTful Web services: WADL vs. WSDL 2.0*. White paper. Tokyo Research Laboratory, IBM Research. Retrieved on April 3, 2009, from http://www.ibm.com/developerworks/library/specification/ws-wadlwsdl/index.html

Werner, C., Buschman, C., & Fischer, S. (2008). *Efficient Encodings for Web Service Messages*. Hershey, PA: IGI Global.

Wikman, J., & Dosa, F. (2006). *Providing HTTP Access to Web Servers Running on Mobile Phones* (Technical Report). Helsinki, Finland: Nokia Research Center. Retrieved on April 3, 2009, from http://research.nokia.com/files/NRC-TR-2006-005.pdf

Wikman, J., Dosa, F., & Tarkiainen, M. (2006). *Personal Website on a Mobile Phone*. (Technical Report). Helsinki, Finland: Nokia Research Center. Retrieved on April 3, 2009, from http://research.nokia.com/tr/NRC-TR-2006-004.pdf

ENDNOTES

[1] http://www.w3c.org
[2] http://www.upnp.org
[3] http://www.enhydra.org/

Chapter 9
Peer–to–Peer Platforms for High–Quality Web Services:
The Case for Load–Balanced Clustered Peer–to–Peer Systems

Ying Qiao
University of Ottawa, Canada

Shah Asaduzzaman
University of Ottawa, Canada

Gregor V. Bochmann
University of Ottawa, Canada

ABSTRACT

This chapter presents a clustered peer-to-peer system as a resource organization structure for web-service hosting platforms. Where service quality, such as response time and service availability, are provided with assurance. The peer-to-peer organization allows integration of autonomous resources into a single platform in a scalable manner. In clustered peer-to-peer systems, nodes are organized into clusters based on some proximity metric, and a distributed hash table overlay is created among the clusters. This organization enables lightweight techniques for load balancing among different clusters, which is found to be essential for providing response time guarantees. Service availability is provided by replicating a service instance in multiple nodes in a cluster. A decentralized load balancing technique called diffusive load balancing is presented in the context of clustered peer-to-peer systems and evaluated for effectiveness and performance.

INTRODUCTION

Web services are autonomous software systems that can be advertised, discovered and accessed through exchanging messages over the Internet using a set

of standard protocols (e.g. SOAP, WSDL, UDDI). The standard protocols bring the interoperability among these autonomous software systems and allow creation of more complex and powerful applications through web service composition. This naturally allows distributed computation through execution of different components of an application

DOI: 10.4018/978-1-61520-973-6.ch009

hosted at autonomous Internet hosts. Computing resources, such as data, storage and CPU processing power of the hosts are thus shared by different users across the Internet.

When web services technology makes it easy to have distributed computing among computers and applications with different platforms, architectures, and programming languages, the role of distributed computing has expanded from assisting daily routines inside an enterprise to participating in the interactions among enterprises. However, the challenge to realize web service applications in a large scale still remains.

As web services are provided by software executed in computers on the Internet, situations like overloaded or failed servers or congested networks can largely affect the quality of web services, where clients could experience unexpected delay and jitter on accessing web services. Consequently, the quality of a web service application can hardly be guaranteed with the unequal performance of its services. This directly challenges the further development of web service applications.

This situation becomes more and more severe with the large deployment of web service applications; it requires a scalable and efficient execution platform to provide high quality services. This chapter discusses the usability of a clustered peer-to-peer system with explicit load-balancing schemes as a platform for hosting web services. Web services hosted on server-pool based *hosting platforms* or data centers often suffer from overloaded servers and congested networks due to the static scale of the platform, which seriously degrades the perceived performance of the services. Highly scalable and adaptable peer-to-peer computing platforms may be desirable in these scenarios. The capability of peer-to-peer systems to efficiently organize large number of Internet-connected computers without any centralized controller makes it a good candidate as a platform for web services. Although there have been several works proposing the use of peer-to-peer techniques for web services discovery (Verma, 2005; Schmidt,

2004), attempts to exploit the scalability of peer-to-peer computing platforms for quality assured hosting of web services are limited.

Peer-to-peer computing platforms are characterized by a huge collection of autonomous and inconsistent resources. A characteristic behavior of the resources in a peer-to-peer system is their intermittent arrival and departure, which is called *churn*. Explicit techniques are necessary to provide reliable and homogeneous services abstracting this behavior. Studies show that organizing these autonomous resources in clusters improves the reliability and the robustness of the platform (Locher, 2006). *Clustered peer-to-peer systems* such as eQuus improves the robustness of the system against churn by organizing the resources in clusters and replicating the resource-states within a cluster; applications built over these systems could have a more deterministic performance, e.g., CliqueStream (Asaduzzaman, 2008) for delivering life video streams over eQuus.

For the heterogeneity of the autonomous resources and the uneven distribution of service requests, some explicit load balancing mechanism is required to smooth out the performance inequalities towards some assured level of quality. A *load balancing* system can arrange resources according to the state of computing nodes and requests, so that the overall performance of the system can be improved. After using load balancing techniques, different web services are expected to have consistent performance characteristics across the platform.

Here we propose a hosting platform for web services using a load-balanced clustered peer-to-peer system. The platform performs load balancing at two levels: intra-cluster, i.e., loads among nodes in a given cluster are balanced, and inter-cluster, i.e., loads among different clusters are balanced. Intra-cluster load balancing is achieved through commonly used techniques such as request routing, and the inter-cluster load balancing is achieved through migration of resources between different clusters. Organization of the physical resources in a clustered peer-to-peer overlay network facilitates such resource migration. A decentralized protocol, namely, *diffusive load balancing* is proposed for low overhead and effective balancing of load through resource migrations between clusters (Qiao, 2009)

The chapter discusses the peer-to-peer hosting platform for web services from two perspectives: the feasibility and advantage of adopting a clustered P2P system as a platform for web service applications, and the effectiveness of the load balancing scheme used for inter-cluster load balancing. The feasibility is discussed in view of supporting quality of service with a clustered P2P system, focusing on service availability and response time as the two primary quality metrics. The effectiveness of the proposed diffusive load balancing scheme in achieving performance objectives is discussed based on simulation results.

WEB SERVICES AND QOS

The deployment of Web Services and their use in a Service-Oriented Architecture (SOA) has many challenges. One of these challenges is the provision of certain levels of *quality of service (QoS)*. Before going into discussion of how a clustered peer-to-peer platform achieves QoS for web services, it is useful to characterize QoS in the context of web services. It is also useful to discuss the commonly used techniques for QoS provisioning in existing server-pool based *hosting platforms*.

QoS Parameters and SLA

Different kinds of qualities can be considered in this context. The most important qualities are probably (a) response time (or latency), (b) availability and (c) cost. For each of these qualities different kinds of guarantees may be given. For the response time, for instance, one may refer to an average response time, possibly with additional

information about percentiles. For the availability, one would typically indicate how small the probability is that, at any given time, the service would not be available. And for the cost, one has to distinguish different schemes, such as freely available (with or without subscription), pay by use, or pay by subscription.

The QoS of a given Web service is often documented in a so-called *service-level agreement (SLA)*. The service provider organization may for instance publish this information as a statement about the service level that is intended to be provided to the public. In other situations, a SLA may be part of a contractual agreement between the service provider and a user organization, where the SLA describes the level of response time and availability that the provider promises, probably in return for some specified costs. The SLA information is also useful for Web Service directories which provide information about available Web Services through interactive search or automatic queries. When a Web Service registers in such a directory, it may provide its SLA information; then the results of a search for a particular service function would provide a list of service instances with their QoS parameters. It would then be easy to find the service instance with the fastest response time, or the lowest cost. We note, however, that other factors may also be important for the selection of a service provider, such as quality of the information provided by the service, the reputation of the service provider, or the established business relationship that already exists.

As engineering tools for dealing with QoS, one needs means for determining the actual QoS provided and for managing the service system to assure that the intended QoS parameters are attained. Monitoring tools can be used to measure the actual QoS provided. Such tools could be used by the user and the service provider to check whether the SLA is satisfied. System management tools must be used by the service provider to manage the server hardware and software in order to optimize its performance and to assure the intended QoS parameters. This is particularly challenging in the case of services for which the demand is difficult to forecast. For certain applications, the load of service requests for various users may fluctuate over the period of a day or over weeks, and in other situations suddenly change due to some external situations. In these circumstances, the service provider should be able to adjust the hardware/software configuration providing the service in order to adapt quickly to the changing requirements.

QoS Provisioning Techniques

Basic approaches for obtaining high-performance, high-availability server configurations are well known. The configuration of a "*server pool*" consists of many identical or heterogeneous servers that provide the same service together with an entry point that distributes the incoming service requests to the different servers. Assuming that the hardware has been purchased previously or is available fast enough, it is relatively easy to introduce additional servers into the pool when the load gradually increases with time. By changing the number of servers in the pool, the average response time can be adjusted. The service availability largely increases because the failure of a single server has no impact on the availability of the service, as long as the other servers can take over the load.

In this *server pool* configuration, the entry point has the task of distributing the incoming service requests such that the load is balanced among all servers in the pool. We call this approach "load balancing through request routing". In the case of identical servers, a simple round-robin algorithm may be adequate; however, for heterogeneous servers more sophisticated approaches may be preferable. For the traditional Web servers providing HTML pages, the problem of load balancing is described in (Bochmann, 2003).

In the *server pool* configuration considered above, there is essentially a single service that must be provided to a very large user community. The situation is different when a large number of different services are to be provided to a large user community; we call this situation *multi-service provisioning*. In this case it is not feasible that each server holds the software and data for all these services. Instead, it is usually assumed that the different services are distributed over the set of available servers in such a way that the load of the different servers would be approximately balanced. This situation is considered, for instance, in (Reich, 2008; Mondejar, 2006). In this situation, one also needs some directory function which locates the server that provides the service requested by a user, which in the simplest case may be the Directory Name Service (DNS). For load balancing between the different servers, it is usually proposed that in the case of an overloaded server, one of the services provided by this server should be moved to another server that is less loaded. We call this approach "load balancing through service migration". In large server systems, the question how to find a server with little load is not straightforward, as discussed in Section C.5.

For providing high availability in the case of *multi-service provisioning*, one may also duplicate each service over two or more servers. In the case that some of the services have a very large load of requests, it is also conceivable to use service duplication for balancing the load, like in the case of server pools. This may lead to a configuration of a set of "clustered servers", where the services are distributed over the clusters and each cluster of servers is responsible for a certain set of services. The minimum size of a cluster is then determined by the availability requirements of the supported services and the actual size of the cluster may be much bigger if the load of the supported services requires a large number of servers.

For managing the response time in the case of *multi-service provisioning* with clustered servers, one needs load balancing at two levels. Within each cluster, the "load balancing through request routing" approach may be used, as in server pools. For the balancing of the load among the different clusters, two approaches are feasible. One possibility is the "load balancing through *service migration*", as described above. Another possibility, called "load balancing through *resource migration*" consists of moving a server from an under-utilized cluster to an over-loaded cluster. This approach is further discussed in Section C.5.4.

PEER-TO-PEER SYSTEMS AND THEIR VARIANTS

Peer-to-Peer Systems

A *Peer-to-Peer (P2P) system* is a form of distributed computing system with autonomous computer nodes located at distributed locations and connected to the Internet. The computers, called *peers* in P2P jargon, are usually end-user personal computers, but sometimes computing servers from service providers. The characteristic feature of a *P2P system* is its decentralized nature of management responsibilities. Computers or peers in a P2P system provide services to each other. There is no distinguished difference concerning the responsibilities of these peers. A peer can take the role of both the client and the server of a distributed system in the sense of Client/Server architecture. Originally, creation of peer-to-peer systems was motivated by the application of decentralized file sharing. Gradually, as the versatility of the peer-to-peer organization of computers was more deeply perceived, applications of peer-to-peer system have included group communication, multimedia streaming, large scale data storage, and sharing of computational resources.

A P2P system can be decomposed into a layered architecture with a P2P application layer on the top of an overlay network layer. These two layers work on top of the IP network layer of Internet that provides the end-to-end physical connectivity. In this sense, this is a three layer system, where the overlay routing functionality at the middle is often term as *middleware*. At the P2P application layer, each peer will perform functions specified by the application, i.e. displaying file directory for a file storage application, or playing movie for a multimedia application. The *overlay network* layer provides a network connecting all peers and a searching mechanism for the application layer to locate objects among peers. It maintains a virtual network topology using physical connectivity of the Internet. Being able to routing lookup messages in this overlay network, P2P systems dynamically search and locate objects without centralized directory services. The ability of peer-to-peer systems to self-organize a large number of computers and to locate objects among these computers across the Internet without any central authority are useful properties for service hosting platform. The popularity of peer-to-peer applications such as Skype, PPLive, and eDunkey, indicates that its scalability, economy of cost corresponding to its large scale, and its capability of providing services on a highly dynamic network are favored by end-users. However, one big challenge that a peer-to-peer system faces is to effectively guarantee the reliability and performance of the services it provides.

Structured and Unstructured P2P Systems

Peer-to-peer systems are broadly classified into *structured and unstructured peer-to-peer systems*. In the structured systems, the peers choose the interconnection neighborhood following a certain pattern which can later be used to facilitate efficient routing of messages such as those for object storage and lookup. In unstructured peer-to-peer systems, peer interconnection does not follow any pattern and thus lacks the efficiency of search in a predefined pattern. Unstructured systems, however, avoid the overhead of maintaining a predefined structure in the interconnection. A structured P2P system in effect, implements a *distributed hash table (DHT)* in its substrate, in which each peer has a unique identifier. Data objects are placed deterministically at the peers with identifiers corresponding to the data object's unique key. The interconnection topology of a particular pattern is maintained, such that a request for a particular object can be routed to its location solely based on local knowledge at each peer. There are well studied variants of such structured peer-to-peer systems, such as Pastry (Rowstron, 2001), Chord (Stoica, 2001), Kademlia (Maymounkov, 2002), CAN (Ratnasamy, 2001) and Viceroy (Malkhi, 2002), which mainly vary in their interconnection patterns. A popular and well studied example of unstructured peer-to-peer system is Gnutella (Oram, 2000). A survey of different peer-to-peer systems can be found in (Bochmann, 2007).

Clustered Peer-to-Peer Systems

In some recently proposed structured peer-to-peer systems, while creating the interconnection topology with a particular pattern, peers organize themselves into groups or clusters. Such clustering actually provides an in-built *membership management* service in addition to the routing service provided by the overlay structure. This in-built membership management can be exploited for on-demand provisioning of resources in a service hosting platform.

In the *clustered peer-to-peer system* eQuus (Locher, 2006), peers that are close-by, based on some proximity metric, are grouped in a single cluster. The proximity metric needs to be such that peers can be placed in a low-dimensional Cartesian space based on their distances. For example network latency, geographic distance, capacity in terms of different resources like CPU and memory, or the type of the service the peer provides, can

be used as the proximity metric. Peers in a single cluster are assigned a single identifier and the clusters are organized in a distributed hash table like interconnection. Thus, all peers in a single cluster share the same cluster-level neighborhood table. Also all the peers in the same cluster know each other. This allows any peer in a cluster to fail or depart without much consequence to the rest of the system. Such built-in membership management by organizing the peers in clusters allows easy service replication and request routing in a service hosting platform where a single cluster is designated for a single type of service. Later, we show in Section C.5 that balancing of load can be performed in a decentralized manner by moving resources among the clusters to adapt to the varying load on different types of services. This is the principle called "load balancing through *resource migration*" in Section C.2.2.

CLUSTERED PEER-TO-PEER SYSTEM FOR HIGH QUALITY SERVICE HOSTING

Clusters of computers or *server pools* are being used for hosting web services for several years. A large number of commodity computers with storage and processing power are aggregated in a data center and interconnected with a high-speed local area network. A wide variety of web services provided by many different providers may be hosted in a single data center platform. Usually, allocation of these server resources to different services are controlled by centralized task schedulers or master controllers. Here we discuss how the resources of a hosting platform can be managed in a decentralized way using the features of a peer-to-peer system organization.

Clustering or aggregating resources in a single unit are done in various forms. In tightly coupled clustered systems, such as super-computers, multiple CPUs, memories, and storages are combined

Figure 1. A clustered peer-to-peer system organizes the nodes in a number of clusters. Nodes in a single cluster may be chosen based on any proximity criterion and may come from different geographic origins

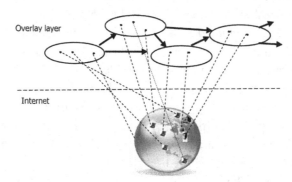

in one unit with high-speed interconnections in a fault-tolerant architecture to provide high reliability and performance for mission-critical applications such as scientific computing, air traffic control or financial forecasting. However, the high cost of building and managing these special purpose systems limit their usage in a small scope. For this reason, *loosely coupled clustered systems*, like pools of commodity computers interconnected in local-area networks, have gained popularity as platforms for general-purpose web service hosting.

For the correctness and liveness of the computations in the loosely-coupled clustered systems, studies have shown several uses of membership management protocols. A *membership management* protocol organizes all the nodes in the system in a number of groups, and for each group provides a correct list of group members to each member of the group. First of all, having a *membership service* allows disseminating the failure status of individual nodes easily among the members of the group. This helps all the nodes to easily find a live node to instantiate a service. Secondly, when replication of data objects is necessary for reliability purpose, it is useful to replicate the objects among the correct members of a group. Having a managed group helps to easily update the replicas with consistency. Third, having a managed group membership helps allocation of

necessary resources among different services. It is usually natural to assign different services to resource-clusters. Having the aggregate status of the clusters helps adaptive re-allocation of the resources as necessary. This also helps prioritizing resources among different classes of services simply by allocating necessary resources to corresponding clusters. Fourthly, the built-in membership management helps to construct an efficient inter-group load balancing mechanism.

Peer-to-peer systems, as discussed in Section C.3.2, provide a key-based message routing service in a large collection of widely distributed computers. A key advantage of peer-to-peer systems is that this routing function and the maintenance of the routing tables in peers are performed in a completely decentralized manner. Such decentralized key-based routing service is used in many computing platforms for discovery of resources. *Clustered peer-to-peer systems* provide an additional service of *membership management* besides the usual key-based routing service. That is why we argue that clustered peer-to-peer systems are more suitable for a multi-service hosting platform, being better equipped for fault-detection, status dissemination, replica consistency management, resource prioritization and load balancing. In comparison, the other non-clustered peer-to-peer systems leave these additional mechanisms to be dealt with by individual applications. For example, in Pastry or Chord, when used as a platform for a distributed file system, consistency among replicas of an object is maintained by the file system application itself, by maintaining and probing the locations of the replicas.

Having a modular *membership management* also makes a clustered peer-to-peer system more scalable because it can avoid redundant implementation of membership management techniques needed for the different purposes. Also, by allowing better and easier implementation of prioritization in resource allocation among different types or groups of services, and system-wide balancing of load by re-assigning resources among different clusters, a hosting platform based on clustered peer-to-peer systems yields better availability and response time characteristics for the supported services.

LOAD BALANCING TECHNIQUES

Load balancing techniques can be applied to any system with multiple computing nodes, for instance, multi-processor, parallel, or distributed computing systems. These multiple computing nodes are organized as clusters. On one side, a load balancing scheme determines when and where to move the load; on the other side, the architecture of a node organization in a load balancing scheme determines how nodes communicate for the purpose of load balancing. In Section C.2.3, we introduced three different approaches of load balancing—request routing, service migration and resource migration in the context of improving service availability and response time in multi-service hosting platforms. Here we discuss the design and evaluation of a diffusive load balancing protocol for the clustered peer-to-peer systems using resource migration, after a brief review of load balancing techniques commonly applied in other distributed computing platforms.

Load Balancing in Distributed Systems

A distributed system moves workload from heavily loaded nodes to lightly loaded nodes according to a predefined load balancing scheme to improve its overall performance (Casavant, 1988). A *load balancing* scheme is a combination of policies that define when and where to initiate a *load migration*, how to monitor and collect the system-wide load information and how to select which workload to move and where (Leinberger, 2000; Cardellini, 2003). The schemes can be broadly classified into two categories, static and adaptive. *Static schemes* works with a predefined set of policy parameters decided based on the average load of the system (Wang, 1984), while *adaptive schemes* or *dynamic schemes* need to monitor the system status and defines the policy parameters based on the observed status (Kunz, 1991). Architecturally, these load balancing schemes may be implemented in a centralized or in a decentralized manner. In a decentralized scheme, all nodes can locally decide to start transferring a load either into it or out from it. Different decentralized schemes vary primarily in terms of how status of the system is aggregated and disseminated. Each node may periodically broadcast its state, or the advertisement can be limited to the times when the node moves from one discrete state to anther (e.g. becoming available from busy) (Livny, 1982). Instead of broadcasting the state, the node that is willing to trigger some load balancing action may probe a selected subset of other nodes for their status. This probing can be sender initiated (Zhou, 1988) as well as receiver initiated (Livny, 1982).

Load Balancing in Peer-to-Peer Systems

Load balancing techniques in peer-to-peer systems, in general, face challenges due to the characteristics of these systems. First of all, the sheer size of a peer-to-peer system indicates that a load balancing technique applied to it must be scalable. Second, all nodes of a peer-to-peer system are not replicas of each other and requests cannot be routed to and executed in any of the nodes. Alternatively, P2P systems place or re-place shared objects optimally among nodes, and overlay routing tables would redirect requests for these shared objects to the right nodes; as a result, the load of the P2P system can be balanced.

In all the peer-to-peer systems, an implicit load distribution is achieved through random placement of the nodes in the overlay structure through random assignment of node identifiers. However, they lack the capability to adjust the placement of the objects, or reroute the requests, based on changing load in different parts of the system. Some explicit and adaptive load balancing techniques are applied in many systems. Combined with techniques of dynamic load balancing, *object placement and node placement* are two types of load balancing techniques used in P2P systems.

In *object placement* techniques, objects are placed at lightly loaded nodes either when they are inserted into the system (Byers, 2003) or through dynamic load balancing. In the latter case, objects can be stored in virtual servers and moved from nodes to nodes. (Rao, 2003; Godfrey, 2004; Surana, 2006) adopted a distributed directory approach similar to a load balancing scheme with partitioned group architecture. Each node reports its node status to a directory, and load is balanced in each directory. In order to globally balance the system, a node registers to one of the directories of the system; after it stays there for some duration, it will leave the directory and register in another one in turn. (Zhu, 2005) proposed a *k-ary* tree architecture for load balancing, where the inner nodes and the root of the tree aggregate load statuses of their sub-trees, and the root disperses the average load status of the system to all nodes down the tree. Accordingly, each node can dynamically identify its relative load situation. In this kind of hierarchical architecture, load can be balanced from the leaves to the root according to

the aggregated load information at inner nodes.

Using the principle of load balancing through *resource migration*, nodes can be placed or re-placed to locations with heavy load. For example, the Mercury load balancing mechanism moves nodes from lightly loaded data ranges to heavily loaded ranges (Bharambe, 2004). Nodes are connected into a ring, and each node periodically samples the ring with a random walk, which selects nodes from the routing tables as next hops. Using an estimation based on sampling, a node is able to detect a lightly loaded range, and request a node from there to move to its neighborhood if it is overloaded.

(Ganesan, 2004) proposed a load balancing mechanism that combines both object placement and node placement in a P2P system. Nodes are connected through a linear chain, and each node balances its load with its two consecutive neighbours. If a node has already balanced its load with its neighbours and it is still overloaded, it will select a lightly loaded node in the system to hand over some of its load. Before this migration, the lightly loaded node will shed all of its current loads to its own neighbors. The load balancing operations occur when a data object is inserted or deleted, and nodes are connected through an extra skip list according to their load information on top of the linear chain; this requires frequent updates of the skip list when the load situation changes.

One common aspect in the *dynamic load balancing* techniques for P2P systems is that they can achieve global load balancing through local balancing procedures. Local balancing means that balancing occurs among nodes in a certain scope, e.g., the two immediate neighborhoods of a node in a linked list, or some subset of nodes in the system, e.g., some nodes randomly selected. Each decision component that runs a load balancing procedure has a scope within which it searches targets: overloaded nodes or under-loaded nodes (senders and receivers) for possible load transfers. The scopes of different decision components may overlap; if this overlapping leads to global connectivity among all local scopes, the system has the property that it will be balanced when all local scopes are balanced.

Some load balancing techniques for P2P systems build extra connections between the nodes on top of the overlay network structure. For instance, a *k-ary* tree requires *(n-1)* connections for aggregating and disseminating load statuses, and a skip list uses a total of $(3n-2-\log_2 n)$ connections for ordering nodes according to their load statuses. These connections are maintained during the life time of the load balancing procedure. When the overlay network experiences churn, these connections are highly dynamic as well.

We propose a diffusive load balancing scheme for structured clustered P2P system using a DHT, where each cluster works as a decision component running a procedure to locally balance the loads among its neighboring clusters. The load balancing among the nodes of a given cluster is assumed to be performed by some other intra-cluster balancing mechanism. With both inter-cluster and intra-cluster load balancing, the system achieves a global balance. All the messages, including load reports from neighbors and the dissemination of load transfer decisions, are transmitted through existing inter-node connections. Load transfers between clusters are realized through moving a node from an under-loaded cluster to an overloaded cluster.

Diffusive Load Balancing

In *diffusive load balancing*, a heavily loaded component sheds portion of its load to any of less loaded components in its "local domain". A diffusive load balancing policy is a policy having three aspects (Corradi, 1999): each component individually performs load balancing; load balancing is achieved locally in the domain of a component; each local domain partially overlaps with other local domains, and, all components of the system must be covered by domains. From these aspects,

we can see that diffusive load balancing policies are simple, where messages for collecting statuses and load migration are only transferred in a local domain; also, they are efficient on achieving global balancing with a small amount of message overheads.

Diffusive load balancing policies can be classified according to two aspects: decision making and *load migration*. While making a decision, the component evaluates its local state through collecting load statuses from other components in its domain; with a sender-initiated policy, after evaluating itself as overloaded, it initiates a load migration to a receiver in its local domain; with a receiver-initiated policy, the component will initiate a load migration if it is under-loaded. Also, a component could decide on senders and receivers in its domain and initiate load migrations among them (termed as a directory-initiated policy). Each component is only allowed to participate in one load migration action at a time, either sending or receiving, which prevents it from receiving or shedding loads multiple times at the same time.

Diffusive Load Balancing for Clustered Peer-to-Peer System

The load balancing in a *clustered P2P system* has two levels: intra-cluster, i.e., loads among nodes in a given cluster are balanced, and inter-cluster, i.e., loads among different clusters are balanced. As research has already intensively studied intra-cluster load balancing, we propose to apply *diffusive load balancing* in the system at the inter-cluster level based on the assumption that intra-cluster load balancing has already been implemented inside each cluster.

We adopt *resource migrations* instead of service migration for load balancing. Resource migration is performed by re-allocating resources from one service to the other, which means re-assignment of computing nodes in a loosely coupled networked computing platform. For peer-to-peer systems, node migration involves reconfiguring the neighborhood table of the concerned nodes, which is very simple compared to moving the service across long-distance network. This also helps avoiding the overhead of maintaining data consistency among a large number of nodes, which could appear in service migration.

Choice of the Load Index: Available Capacity

A dynamic load balancing scheme identifies the system status according to a *load index* for each node. A load index should correctly reflect the amount of load at a node, and from this index, the performance of a node could be evaluated. CPU queue length is generally preferred as a load index (Ferrari, 1986; Zhou 1988; Kunz, 1991) because it has a strong correlation with the mean response time of tasks at the node. Other load indexes include utilization, request-response time and available capacity.

We adopt the average of the available capacities of the nodes in a cluster as the load index for the cluster. Using available capacity to indicate the load of a resource in load balancing has been proposed in (Zhu, 1998) and (Raman, 2003). Using a M/M/1 queuing model, it can be shown that the average response time at a node is the inverse of the available capacity of the node; this means that, when two nodes have the same available capacity, even if they have different maximum capacities, their mean response times, for given requests, will be the same (Qiao, 2009). Under the assumption that the load among the nodes in each cluster have been balanced by using some intra-cluster load balancing procedure, and the load among different clusters has been balanced by the here described procedure, all nodes in the system will have an available capacity close to the overall mean. Hence, the mean response times of all nodes are close to an average value.

Inter-Cluster Diffusive Load Balancing Algorithm

Using the average available capacity as load index, each cluster iteratively runs a *diffusive load balancing* procedure which identifies the state of its own as well of its overlay neighbors, and makes decisions concerning possible load migrations with these neighbors. We use the traditional meaning of sender and receiver here: a sender is a cluster that transfers its load out, and a receiver cluster transfers load in. Because node migration is used here instead of service migration, nodes are in fact transferred from the load-receiver cluster to the load-sender cluster.

We describe in the following the diffusive load balancing (LB) procedure in terms of four phases:

- *LB triggering*: the execution of LB is triggered by a timeout event after a predefined amount of time from the last LB execution, or a state change event when the cluster becomes either receiver or sender.
- *Load determination*: First, the cluster determines its own load status as well as the load status of its neighborhood through sending probing messages to its neighbors, and waits for responses from them; a probed cluster responds with its load index.
- *Decision:* Dynamic thresholds are used to determine whether a cluster is considered overloaded or under-loaded. First, the load average is calculated for all the clusters in the neighborhood. Then the upper and lower load thresholds are calculated by the formula: threshold = average_neighborhood_index * (1 +/- bound). The bound is given in percentage of the average load. A cluster is a candidate receiver (sender) of load if its load index is larger (smaller) than the upper (lower) threshold. The purpose of the decision procedure is to identify one

Figure 2. The state diagram of the load balancing procedure

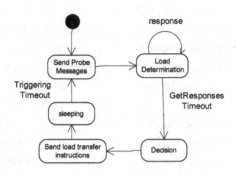

or several receiver-sender pairs and send a load transfer request to the receiver of each pair, including as parameters the ID of the selected sender (which is the target for the node migration) and the amount of load it requires to reach the load average (called required capacity). The details of the decision procedures depends on the *Location* policy:

- *Directory-initiated:* the cluster identifies one or several receiver-sender pairs, as appropriate.
- *Sender-initiated:* if the cluster is a sender, then it tries to identify a corresponding receiver in its neighborhood.
- *Receiver-initiated:* If the cluster is a receiver, then it tries to identify a corresponding sender in its neighborhood.
- *Load transfer:* Note that nodes are moved from a load-receiver cluster to a load-sender cluster to bring the balance. After a receiver cluster receives an instruction of node migration, it will select a node from its own, delete it from its membership list, and let it join the sender cluster. It is important that the node migration should not cause the state of these clusters to be changed to the opposite, e.g., an under-loaded cluster becomes overloaded, or, an overloaded cluster becomes under-loaded. A receiver can only transfer out the portion which is over the load average, and

we call it transferable capacity; in order to avoid this situation, the transferred portion should be close to the smaller one of the required capacity and the transferable capacity.

The required capacity for an overloaded cluster to reach the average load status of the neighborhood is the difference between the current *load index* of the cluster to the average load index of the neighborhood multiplied by the number of nodes in the cluster. As our algorithm only moves a single node at a time, the required capacity of that cluster could be calculated as:

```
required_capacity = average_neigh-
bourhood_index * (current_size + 1)
- current_index * current_size
```

The Inter-Cluster Diffusive Load Balancing Procedure

A procedure is designed to realize the above algorithm. The state diagram of the procedure is shown in Figure 2, where each state corresponds to a phase of the algorithm.

Each cluster selects a leader among its nodes; this nodes acts as coordinator for the load balancing procedure. As in diffusive load balancing, a cluster would participate in the neighborhoods of several other clusters. When the coordinator of a cluster fails before finishing a round, the round will be discarded. Another node will be selected as a coordinator and will start a new round. Those coordinators also take responsibility for monitoring the load status of their own cluster and respond to the probing messages and load transferring instructions from other clusters.

As the load balancing procedures coordinated by different clusters are not synchronized, the load balancing protocol uses asynchronous messaging. When a coordinator is in the "Load Determination" state, it waits for responses from the probed clusters. Since the existing inter-cluster connections of the clustered P2P system are used to transfer the messages for load balancing, the health of the connections can be monitored by the functions in the P2P overlay, and the time for transferring messages can be estimated.

However, a cluster can participate only in one node migration at a time. If the cluster is participating in a node migration, the coordinator will refuse any additional request for node migrations.

Evaluation of Diffusive Load Balancing

In order to evaluate the effectiveness and performance of the diffusive load balancing in the context of *clustered peer-to-peer systems*, we performed several simulation studies. We compared the effectiveness and performance of three different location policies – directory initiated (DI), receiver initiated (RI) and sender initiated (SI), as introduced before. We also compared them with an idealized scheme, called central directory (CD), where a single directory collects status information of all clusters in the system and makes inter-cluster load balancing decisions using the same kind of decision criteria as the other schemes.

Simulation Setup

We have implemented the load balancing procedure with the three different location policies in a simulation of a clustered DHT overlay network (a modified version of eQuus). eQuus is a structured P2P overlay which was proposed to improve the reliability and robustness of a DHT overlay networks. In eQuus, the nodes are organized into clusters according to a proximity metrics, and the clusters are connected using a DHT mechanism: each cluster is identified by a unique ID, and the DHT routing tables are constructed based on these IDs. The system has inter-cluster connections similar to Pastry using prefix matching in its routing algorithm; therefore the number of steps in a lookup procedure is bound by $O(logN)$, where N is the number of clusters. There are no super nodes; each entry in a routing table contains up to k nodes belonging to the same cluster; a node can select a node from these k neighbors to forward a lookup message.

In addition to the operations in regular DHT systems, an eQuus system manages the size of its clusters by keeping their sizes in a fixed range by performing splitting and merging operations of clusters; correspondingly, the system is able to adjust the routing tables. Within an eQuus, the size of a cluster may change through churn (nodes leaving or joining the system). Only when the size of a cluster violates the given size limits, are the cluster splitting or merging operations invoked. Therefore, the number of messages for updating the routing tables is reduced, as compared to P2P systems without clustering.

For our simulation, we constructed a *clustered peer-to-peer system* consisting of 10,000 nodes of equal capacity. In our simulation, the proximity criterion for cluster formation of eQuus is relaxed: a node may join any cluster, so that, the system could allow the node migrations between any pair of clusters. The average size of a cluster was 8 (varying between 4 and 16). We evaluated inter-cluster load balancing only and it is assumed that the load among nodes inside a cluster are balanced by some other mechanism. The simulation starts from an initial state where each cluster is assigned a workload that widely varies among clusters. The *bound* parameter that defines whether a cluster is overloaded or under-loaded is set to +/-20%. The simulated load balancing algorithm keeps moving nodes between different clusters in rounds and the simulation stops when there is no node migration in the last round.

When a cluster is probed during a node migration, the coordinator returns a *load index* which corresponds to the expected load situation after the node migration; the coordinator is able to estimate this value based on the last recorded load index and the capacity lost or gained from the node migration. However, the coordinator would discard another load transfer request before it finishes the current one. For this reason, the delay of node migrations is not considered in our simulation.

Effectiveness of the Different Load Balancing Schemes

To evaluate the effectiveness of different schemes we measured the variation of loads among different clusters at the end of the simulation (standard deviation and *delta* = maximum - average). The capacity of the nodes is assumed to be homogeneous across the system with each node being capable of executing a maximum of 10 units of load. At the initial state, each cluster is assigned a random workload uniformly distributed between 0 and the maximum capacity of the cluster. The histogram of the initial workload across different clusters is shown in Figure-3a.

Except for the receiver-initiated scheme, the three other schemes balance the load tightly around the average load of the clusters. The directory-initiated scheme reaches a load distribution, where the *load index* has a high maximum near the mean; with the sender-initiated and the

receiver-initiated schemes the load index of the clusters is more spread between the lower and upper thresholds. In the receiver-initiated scheme, there are still some overloaded clusters remaining when the simulation stops. This is because a cluster makes a decision on node migration only when it identifies itself as a receiver; in the case that a cluster is not a receiver, node migrations will not occur in its local domain, even when there are overloaded clusters in the domain. The load distributions after load balancing for all the schemes are shown in Figure 3(b-e).

Performance of the Load Balancing Algorithm

To evaluate the performance, we measured how many rounds each variant of the load balancing scheme would take to converge. We also measured the number of *node migrations* that occurred in each case (Table 1). The simulation setup is the same as the one used for evaluating a homogenous system. We observe that the central directory scheme reaches the balanced state with the smallest number of node migrations. Compared with other schemes, the directory-initiated scheme spends less rounds but has more node migrations for balancing, which indicates that its fast convergence is based on more load balancing decisions and node migrations. The receiver-initiated scheme has slowest convergence with the most number of rounds.

To visualize how the system gradually progresses towards a balanced load through execution of the algorithm with different policies, we display in Figure 4 how different measures change with the progression of balancing rounds. During each round, each cluster has the opportunity of executing a load balancing procedure once. Figure-4(a) shows that most of the node migration occurs during the first round in all schemes. The directory-initiated scheme makes 99% of its node migrations during the first round; while the sender-initiated and the receiver-initiated schemes

Figure 3. Distribution of load in different clusters: (a) before balancing, (b) through (e) after balancing

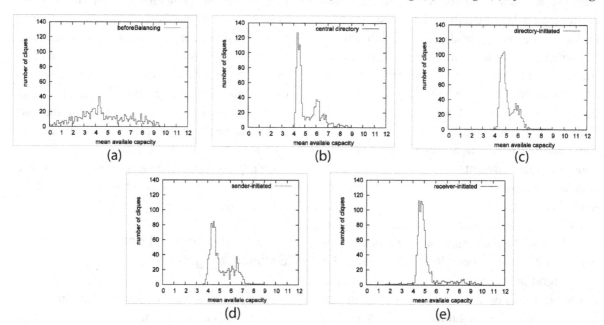

Table 1. Comparison of load balancing results

	CD	DI	SI	RI
Std. dev.	1.033	0.709	0.915	1.098
Delta. (%)	19.63	19.28	25.14	62.3
rounds	4.3	1.1	3.1	4.9
Node mv.	1680	1942	1695	2013
splits	180	219	200	210
merges	81	126	123	81

only move about 90%. This faster node migration corresponds to the faster convergence of the directory–initiated scheme as shown in Figure 4(b).

Load Balancing with Heterogeneous Node Capacities

To exploit the fact that node capacities are heterogeneous in a peer-to-peer system, we modified the *Selection* policies of the load balancing schemes as follows. When a scheme selects a node for migration, it considers the capacity required for the load-sender cluster to reach the mean load index,

and picks from the load-receiver cluster a node with an available capacity closest to the requirement. We call this *capacity-based node selection*.

In our simulation, we assigned node capacities from the range [100, 5000] with a Pareto distribution with shape parameter set to 2, and scale parameter set to 100. The other parameter remains the same. Table 2 summarizes the measured performance results for the four different location policies, with the capacity-based node selection policy and random node selection policy. We observe that the relative differences among the location policies observed in the homogeneous system remain

Figure 4. Progress of load balancing

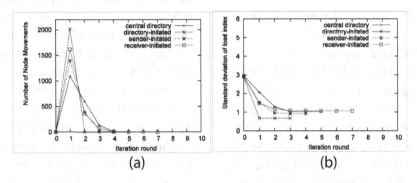

Table 2. Comparison of load balancing results with random and capacity-based policy

	random		Capacity	
	CD	DI	CD	DI
Std. dev.	5.98	4.5	5.5	4.37
Delta. (%)	19.45	20.56	19.92	19.5
rounds	4.8	1.6	4.4	1.6
Node mv.	1722	2011	1204	1645
split	182	213	128	181
merge	90	119	28.4	83

CD: central directory, DI: directory-initiated

present in the heterogeneous system. The number of node migrations is reduced when capacity consideration is applied, compared to random node selection. For instance, in the directory-initiated scheme, the migrations are reduced by almost 20%. This indicates that selecting a node with its maximum capacity matching the smaller one of the required capacity and the transferable capacity is better than random selection.

CONCLUSION

Server clusters have been already adopted as a reliable and high-performance hosting platform for websites and web-service based applications. Their centralized resource-management structure, however, does not allow resource sharing among autonomous resource providers. In this chapter,

we give arguments for a web service hosting platform with clustered peer-to-peer organization of resource nodes. This platform is able to host multiple web services from several providers targeted for a large user-base through sharing of autonomous resources. It provides quality assurance for services in terms of service availability and response time. In other words, it inherits the characters of reliability and performance from server cluster systems and the scalability from peer-to-peer systems.

For providing assurance of service quality in terms of response time and service availability, it is necessary to distribute and balance the workload over different resources. In the clustered peer-to-peer organization, different services may be assigned to the resources of different clusters. The clustered organization allows load balancing to be performed relatively easily by exchanging the node-positions in the cluster structure. Thus, necessary resources can be allocated to an overloaded cluster to balance the load.

Assuming that load among different nodes inside a cluster are balanced using some known technique, we proposed a diffusive load balancing algorithm to conduct the inter-cluster load balancing by moving resources between clusters. As the available capacities of clusters are equalized in this way, the response times provided by the different clusters for the different services approach an overall mean value. The load balancing algorithm works in decentralized manner based on the local knowledge of the load of the clusters in the neighbourhood within the peer-to-peer overlay.

Through simulation study, we measured the effectiveness and performance of the load balancing algorithm for three different decision schemes, namely, directory-initiated, sender-initiated and receiver-initiated. The directory-initiated scheme converges faster and results in a smaller variance of load among the clusters, compared to the other two schemes. However, it results in a larger number of node-migrations. In general, the fast convergence of the loads of clusters around the mean value, demonstrates the effectiveness of the diffusive load balancing algorithm for the clustered peer-to-peer service hosting platform.

However, several problems regarding this platform remain to be solved. In our discussion we explained the technique to balance the load equally among clusters. This would result in a single level of quality for all services. However, different services may require different response times, and different users may ask for the same service with different response times. The question of how different classes of services with different levels of quality could be provided in the proposed platform, needs further investigation.

The QoS of web services is often described by multi-dimensional attributes. In addition to availability and performance, which we discussed here, reputation, price, locality, and other aspects need to be considered as well. It is possible to create different quality profiles for different classes of services based on different value-ranges of these attributes. Cluster of resources may be created to support each of these classes. However, how to maintain the quality profile of each of these clusters, remains a problem to be solved.

There are also some implementation hurdles that need to be resolved. For example, when resources are moved between clusters, services may need to be migrated between nodes inside a cluster. Techniques are needed for encapsulating a stateful service in service containers to facilitate live migrations.

In summary, with a proper implementation, the clustered P2P organization is an efficient way to manage resources in a large-scale web service hosting platform, with assurance for various attributes of service quality.

REFERENCES

Asaduzzaman, S., Qiao, Y., & Bochmann, G. (2008). CliqueStream: An Efficient and Fault-resilient Live Streaming Network on a Clustered Peer-to-peer Overlay. In *Proceeding of 8th International Conference on Peer-to-Peer Computing,* Aachen, Germany.

Bharambe, A. R., Agrawal, M., & Seshan, S. (2004). Mercury: supporting scalable multi-attribute range queries. In *Proceedings of the 2004 Conference on Applications, Technologies, Architectures, and Protocols For Computer Communication,* (SIGCOMM '04). New York: ACM.

Bochmann, G., & Jourdan, G. V. (2007, June). An overview of content distribution and content access in peer-to-peer systems (invited paper). In *Proceedings of NOTERE Conference,* Marrakesh (Maroco).

Bochmann, G., Wong, J. W., Lau, T. C., Bourne, D., Evans, D., & Kerhervé, B. (2003, July). Scalability of Web-based electronic commerce systems. *IEEE Communications Magazine, 41*(7), 110–115. doi:10.1109/MCOM.2003.1215647

Byers, J., & Considine, J. & Mitzenmacher. M. (2003, February). Simple Load Balancing for Distributed Hash Tables. In *Proceedings of the 2nd International Workshop on Peer-to-Peer Systems (IPTPS '03).*

Cardellini, V., Colajanni, M., & Yu, P. S. (2003). Request redirection algorithms for distributed web systems. *IEEE Transactions on Parallel and Distributed Systems, 14*(4), 355–368. doi:10.1109/TPDS.2003.1195408

Casavant, T. L., & Kuhl, J. G. (1988, February). A taxonomy of scheduling in general-purpose distributed computing systems. *IEEE Transactions on Software Engineering, 14*(2), 141–154. doi:10.1109/32.4634

Corradi, A., Leonardi, L., & Zambonelli, F. (1999, January-March). Diffusive Load-Balancing Policies for Dynamic Applications. *IEEE Concurrency, 7*(1), 22–31. doi:10.1109/4434.749133

Ferrari, D., & Zhou, S. (1986). A load index for dynamic load balancing. In *Proceedings of 1986 ACM Fall Joint Computer Conference*, (pp.684-690). Los Alamitos, CA: IEEE Computer Society Press.

Ganesan, P., Mayank, B., & Garcia-Molina, H. (2004). Online Balancing of Range-Partitioned Data with Applications to Peer-to-Peer Systems. In *Proceedings of VLDB, 2004.*

Godfrey, B., Lakshminarayanan, K., Surana, S., Karp, R., & Stoica, I. (2004, March 7-11). Load balancing in dynamic structured P2P systems. *INFOCOM 2004. Twenty-third Annual Joint Conference of the IEEE Computer and Communications Societies, 4*(4), 2253-2262.

Kunz, T. (1991, July). The Influence of Different Workload Descriptions on a Heuristic Load Balancing Scheme. *IEEE Transactions on Software Engineering, 17*(7), 725–730. doi:10.1109/32.83908

Leinberger, W., Karypis, G., Kumar, V., & Biswas, R. (2000). Load balancing across near-homogeneous multi-resource servers. In *Proceeding of the 9th Heterogeneous Computing Workshop, 200o*, (HCW 2000), (pp.60-71).

Livny, M., & Melman, M. (1982). Load balancing in homogeneous broadcast distributed systems. In *Proceedings of the Computer Network Performance Symposium*. New York: ACM.

Locher, T., Schmid, S., & Wattenhofer, R. (2006). eQuus: A Provably Robust and Locality-Aware Peer-to-Peer System. *Sixth IEEE International Conference on Peer-to-Peer Computing (P2P '06).*

Malkhi, D., Naor, M., & Ratajczak, D. (2002, July 21-24). Viceroy: a scalable and dynamic emulation of the butterfly. In *Proceedings of the Twenty-First Annual Symposium on Principles of Distributed Computing*, (PODC '02), (pp. 183-192). Monterey, CA.

Maymounkov, P., & Mazières, D. (2002, March 7-8). Kademlia: A Peer-to-Peer Information System Based on the XOR Metric. In P. Druschel, M. F. Kaashoek and A. I. Rowstron (Eds.), *Proceedings of the Revised Papers from the First international Workshop on Peer-To-Peer Systems,* (Lecture Notes In Computer Science). London: Springer.

Mondejar, R., Garcia, P., Pairot, C., & Gomez Skarmeta, A. F. (2006, June 26-28). Enabling Wide-Area Service Oriented Architecture through the p2pWeb Model. In *Proceedings of the 15th IEEE international Workshops on Enabling Technologies: infrastructure For Collaborative Enterprises*, (WETICE). Washington, DC: IEEE Computer Society.

Oram, A. (2000). *Gnutella and Freenet Represent True Technological Innovation*. Whitepaper.

Qiao, Y., & Bochmann, G. (2009). Applying a diffusive load balancing in a clustered P2P system. In *Proceedings of the 9ᵗʰ International Conference on New Technologies of Distributed Systems*, (NOTERE), Montreal, Canada, ISBN:978-2-9809407-1-2.

Raman, B., & Katz, R. H. (2003, March 30-April 3). Load balancing and stability issues in algorithms for service composition. *INFOCOM 2003. Twenty-Second Annual Joint Conference of the IEEE Computer and Communications Societies. IEEE, 2*(2), 1477-1487.

Rao, A., Lakshminarayanan, K., Surana, S., Karp, R., & Stoica, I. (2003). Load Balancing in Structured P2P Systems. In *Proceeding of 2nd International Workshop on Peer-to-Peer Systems (IPTPS '03)*.

Ratnasamy, S., Francis, P., Handley, M., Karp, R., & Shenker, S. (2001). A scalable content-addressable network. In *Proceedings of the 2001 Conference on Applications, Technologies, Architectures, and Protocols For Computer Communications*. (SIGCOMM '01), (pp. 161-172). New York: ACM.

Reich, C., Bubendorfer, K., & Buyya, R. (2008, May 19-22). An Autonomic Peer-to-Peer Architecture for Hosting Stateful Web Services. In *Proceedings of the 2008 Eighth IEEE international Symposium on Cluster Computing and the Grid* (CCGRID), (pp. 250-257). Washington, DC: IEEE Computer Society.

Rowstron, A., & Druschel, P. (2001). Pastry: Scalable, distributed object location and routing for large-scale peer-to-peer systems. In *Proceedings of Middleware*, (LNCS 2218), (pp. 329-350).

Schmidt, C., & Parashar, M. (2004, June). A Peer-to-Peer Approach to Web Service Discovery. *World Wide Web (Bussum), 7*(2), 211–229. doi:10.1023/B:WWWJ.0000017210.55153.3d

Stoica, I., Morris, R., Karger, D., Kaashoek, M. F., & Balakrishnan, H. (2001). Chord: A scalable peer-to-peer lookup service for internet applications. In *Proceedings of the 2001 Conference on Applications, Technologies, Architectures, and Protocols for Computer Communications*, (pp. 149-160), (SIGCOMM '01). New York: ACM.

Surana, S., Godfrey, B., Lakshminarayanan, K., Karp, R., & Stoica, I. (2006, March). Load balancing in dynamic structured peer-to-peer systems. *P2P Computing Systems. Performance Evaluation, 63*(3), 217–240. doi:10.1016/j.peva.2005.01.003

Verma, K., Sivashanmugam, K., Sheth, A., Patil, A., Oundhakar, S., & Miller, J. (2005, January). METEOR-S WSDI: A Scalable P2P Infrastructure of Registries for Semantic Publication and Discovery of Web Services. *Information Technology and Management, 6*(1), 17–39. doi:10.1007/s10799-004-7773-4

Wang, Y. T., & Morris, R. J. T. (1985, March). Load Sharing in Distributed Systems. *IEEE Transactions on Computers, C-34*(3), 204–217. doi:10.1109/TC.1985.1676564

Zeng, L., Benatallah, B., & Ngu, H. H., A., Dumas, M., Kalagnanam, J., & Chang, H. (2004, May). QoS-Aware Middleware for Web Services Composition. *IEEE Transactions on Software Engineering, 30*(5), 311–327. doi:10.1109/TSE.2004.11

Zhou, S. (1988, September). A Trace-Driven Simulation Study of Dynamic Load Balancing. *IEEE Transactions on Software Engineering, 14*(9), 1327–1341. doi:10.1109/32.6176

Zhu, H., Yang, T., Zheng, Q., Watson, D., Ibarra, O. H., & Smith, T. (1998, July 28-31). Adaptive Load Sharing for Clustered Digital Library Servers. In *Proceedings of the 7th IEEE international Symposium on High Performance Distributed Computing.*

Zhu, Y., & Hu, Y. (2005, April). Efficient, proximity-aware load balancing for DHT-based P2P systems. *IEEE Transactions on Parallel and Distributed Systems, 16*(4), 349–361. doi:10.1109/TPDS.2005.46

Chapter 10
Distributed Libraries Management for Remote Compilation and Execution on Grid Platforms with JaDiMa

Jesús De Oliveira
Universidad Simón Bolívar, Venezuela

Yudith Cardinale
Universidad Simón Bolívar, Venezuela

Eduardo Blanco
Universidad Simón Bolívar, Venezuela

Carlos Figueira
Universidad Simón Bolívar, Venezuela

ABSTRACT

In distributed environments (e.g. grid platform) it is common to find pieces of reusable code distributed among multiple sites. The possibilities of compilation and execution with remote libraries have a great potential to facilitate the integration of pieces of software developed among different organizations. This chapter describes JaDiMa (Java Distributed Machine), a collaborative framework to construct Java applications on grid platforms. JaDiMa automatically manages library repositories to allow users to compile and execute applications which use distributed libraries, without keeping these libraries locally. JaDiMa services are implemented as Web Services following the SOA approach; library repositories are modeled as a JXTA P2P network; and semantic annotations of libraries assist developers on the tasks of discovering libraries. We describe an implementation of JaDiMa as part of SUMA/G, a Globus-based grid environment. We show experiences and an empirical evaluation of JaDiMa execution and compilation processes for an application which uses remote libraries for managing graph and network data.

DOI: 10.4018/978-1-61520-973-6.ch010

INTRODUCTION

Grid platforms increase the capabilities of environments in which multiple users, geographically distant, may share data, pieces of software, computation resources, and even specialized devices (Berman, Fox, & Hey, 2003; Abbas, 2004). In this direction, it is very common that programmers use several library components developed by third parties to achieve the global goal required by an application. Following the principle of reusability, it is much more efficient for developers to delegate specific functionalities to already available software, extensively proven and developed exclusively for such functions, and concentrate themselves on the resolution of their specific problem. Code reuse is a very good way to increase developer productivity and application maintainability.

However, when pieces of reusable code are distributed (e.g. on a grid platform), developers have to find and obtain the suitable libraries, then reference them in their applications such that the compilation process can be accomplished. In addition, end users must have the same libraries in order to be able to execute the application. In general, these applications are distributed along with libraries which they depend on. Hence, the reused pieces of software must remain local to the compilation and execution environment. In a distributed environment, this approach presents serious disadvantages: i) waste of disk space, when a library is used by several applications, or when only a small portion of this library is used; ii) difficulty in handling and updating versions of the library, by leaving in the hands of the developers and end users, the responsibility of updating its local versions with newer ones; and iii) in the case of development of scientific applications for grids, libraries are only required for local compilation, since the application is not going to be executed locally but in some of the remote execution nodes of the grid platform. Downloading the libraries locally only for compilation represents a waste of space and time for developers.

The idea of exploiting resources belonging to different companies and research institutes to solve problems in science and commerce domains is promoting new business models for service providers that lease computing utilities (Vassiliadis et al., 2004). This requires an integration of market-based economic theories in distributed resource management systems to create a trusted and profit environment for competitive customer (Menascé & Casalicchio, 2004). The possibilities of compilation with remote libraries and remote execution have a great potential to facilitate the integration of applications and pieces of software (libraries) developed among different organizations.

A Service-Oriented Architecture (SOA) (Erl, 2005) is essentially a collection of loosely coupled services that inter-operate according to a formal specification, independent of the platform and the programming language used to implement each service. SOA relies on a set of policies, practices, and frameworks by means of which it ensures that right services are provided and consumed, enhancing services inter-connectivity. Flexible SOA connections between services, as well as software components that deliver simple data among other services or that coordinate simple activities, are seen as services which can be combined with other services to achieve specific goals. Thus, SOA provides a scalable and robust framework to integrate heterogeneous software agents and enhance reliability of isolated software components.

Motivated by these considerations, we focused on developing a Java-based framework, called JaDiMa (*Java Distributed Machine*, http://www.sourceforge.net/projects/jadima), a collaborative platform to construct high performance Java applications on grid platforms. JaDiMa is a system that automatically manages remote library repositories used in a Java application. JaDiMa allows users to compile and execute Java applications using those distributed libraries, without the need of keeping them in the developer and user hosts. It leverages on the advantages of portability, modularity, object oriented model, and flexibility of Java, while incorporating well known approaches to implement its functionalities and techniques of communication and security (i.e., Web Services, SOA, SOAP protocol, JXTA and X.509 certificates). We have incorporated JaDiMa as part of SUMA/G (Cardinale & Hernández, 2005), a Globus-based middleware specifically targeted at executing Java bytecode on Globus grids. All JaDiMa services are implemented as Web Services following the SOA approach. Library repositories are modeled as a P2P networking model, using JXTA protocol to provide peer discovery mechanism with the ability to bypass NAT schemes and firewalls.

In grid platforms, when pieces of reusable software are considered to develop an application, the number of possible useful components can be large. If programmers have to select the suitable ones for their specific problem, it becomes unlikely for them to consider all available alternatives. Thus, it is crucial to provide mechanisms that assist developers on selecting the most relevant components (Z. Chen & Qian, 2005). This strategy results in a better suited solution being found faster.

The Semantic Web assumes a service oriented model based on Web Services or Grid Services as the basic element or communication technology. Agents are considered as producers, consumers and intermediate services. Currently there are some proposals that consider the use of Semantic Web technologies inside the grid infrastructure (Kollia, Kafetzoglou, Grammatikou, & S.Papavassiliou, 2008; Tao et al., 2003; L. Chen et al., 2005; Majithia, Walker, & W.A.Gray, 2004; L. Chen et al., 2003; Zhang, Zong, Ding, & Liu, 2005). In this growing infrastructure all resources are semantically described by creating a decentralized system with a large variety of resources (Goble & Roure, 2002; Roure & Hendler, 2004; Pahl, 2004). Software libraries are one of these types of resources.

In the field of service discovery and selection, several approaches have been proposed (Bansal & Vidal, 2003; Paolucci, Kawamura, Payne, & Sycara, 2002; Bachelechner, Siorpaes, Lausen, & Fensel., 2006). Some of these approaches use semantic annotation of services by different formalisms. OWL-S (Martin et al., 2004) is one of such formalism which describes services using different structures: Service Profile and Service Model. The former is associated with domain ontologies specifying service functionalities in terms of inputs, outputs, preconditions, and effects. The latter represents restrictions and control structures that are used to define a service. Following this idea, we propose to incorporate semantic descriptions for libraries stored on JaDiMa repositories. Using these annotations, JaDiMa is able to assist developers on the tasks of discovering and selecting libraries that might facilitate the process of building and maintaining their applications. The semantic annotations of the remote libraries are based on domain ontologies written using OWL (Bechhofer et al., 2004).

We show experiences of executing an application that uses libraries for managing graph and network data, on several scenarios both with SUMA/G and JaDiMa. We empirically evaluate JaDiMa performance of compilation and execution processes.

JADIMA ARCHITECTURE

JaDiMa is a collaborative platform to construct high performance Java applications on grid platforms, that automatically manages remote libraries used in a Java application. It is a simple and efficient distributed environment upon which applications and data are easily shared and highly portable among heterogeneous platforms and multiple users, therefore motivating the reusability and sharing of libraries by inexperienced and advanced programmers. JaDiMa allows users to compile and execute Java applications that use distributed libraries, without the need of keeping those remote libraries in the developer and user hosts.

Compilation is based on small representations of the remote libraries on which Java applications depend. These library representations are referred to as *stubs* and replace the actual libraries in the compilation process. *Stubs* are automatically generated by JaDiMa. At run time, the actual remote library classes (i.e. the real bytecode) are downloaded on demand from pre-defined library repositories, as they are required by the application. The use of a convention for version numbering allows for the automatic updating of libraries at run time. The design of JaDiMa is oriented to satisfy the following goals:

- **Easy to install, configure and use.** JaDiMa avoids difficult installation steps or extensive configuration procedures, hence users do not require in-deep technical knowledge for its installation and use.
- **Flexibility, adaptability and modularity.** By designing the framework into layers and defining general interfaces in all JaDiMa components, JaDiMa allows for integration of different well known communication, security and data access mechanisms.
- **Platform independence.** JaDiMa is fully implemented in Java. Since the Java language and libraries are platform-independent, JaDiMa can be installed, without recompiling, on any platform that has a Java runtime environment.
- **Transparency and non-intrusive operation.** Neither the applications nor the libraries have to be modified to benefit from the functionalities of JaDiMa.
- **High performance and scalability.** In order to avoid the overhead introduced by JaDiMa functionalities on applications' performance, JaDiMa provides mechanisms for class caching and prefetching, thus reducing the impact of class transfer during execution.
- **Security.** The code and data exchange between clients and libraries repositories

must be secure. JaDiMa guarantees that all downloaded code comes from reliable repositories, and that every client that downloads a library is authorized to do so. In addition, library access control was implemented to provide privacy among different user groups, required on corporate environments. To enforce security during execution, the applications run in a *sandbox*, preventing them from stealing or damaging local data.
- **Accessibility.** Users can access a large range of libraries without worrying about their physical location.

JaDiMa Agents

JaDiMa design and implementation can be roughly separated into four components: Repository Agent, Publishing Agent, Compilation Agent, and Execution Agent. Each component corresponds, respectively, to libraries administration, libraries publication, compilation and execution of applications that require the published libraries. Figure 1 presents the general scheme of JaDiMa architecture.

Library Repository Agent

The library Repository Agent is in charge of managing the remote libraries that will be used in compilation and execution processes defined in JaDiMa. For each published library, the Repository will maintain four different though related data sets:

1. The actual class implementation provided by the *publishing user*, which will be used in the execution phase.
2. The *stubs*, which will be used only during the compilation process.
3. The library documentation (*API*).
4. The library semantic annotations using OWL.

Figure 1. JaDiMa architecture

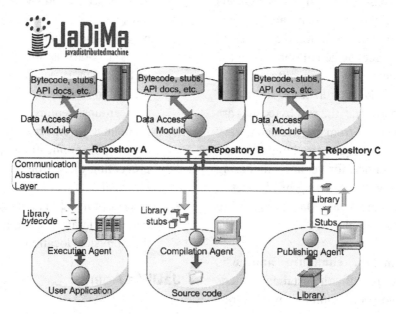

The Repository Agent includes three layers to separate the library recovery operations from the actual storage access. The Data Access Abstraction Layer (DAAL) defines abstract operations for library administration tasks, independent of the storage media (i.e., operations for publishing, querying, downloading, etc.). A specific Data Access Module implements the abstract operations defined on the DAAL, upon the third element, the Actual Storage Media, which could be a RDBMS (e.g., DB2, PostgreSQL, MySQL, Oracle, etc.), a filesystem, or XML files (See Figure 2).

Publishing Agent

The library publishing process in JaDiMa consists of three phases:

1. Automatic generation of *stubs*. A *stub* is automatically generated for each class of the library. First, a class *skeleton* is created; a *skeleton* is a *.java* source file which only contains the definition of all method signatures of the original class. Figure 3

example illustrates a *skeleton*. Second, the generated *skeletons* are compiled using the JaDiMa Compilation Agent, in order to resolve possible dependencies that the library may have with other previously published libraries. From the *skeletons* compilation the *stubs* (.class files) are generated. Each *stub* is marked with a flag, which identifies itself as a *stub*, along with a version number supplied by the publishing user. The version number is based on a three-digit scheme (Our version number scheme is based on the package version numbering system proposed by Sun Microsystems (Sun Microsystems, 2002)): <major>.<minor>.<revision>, in which:

○   **major**: represents changes in external functionalities and in method signatures.

○   **minor**: refers to minor functionality changes, with no changes in method signatures.

○   **revision**: there are no changes in functionality or method signatures, corresponds to corrections on previous

Figure 2. JaDiMa layers

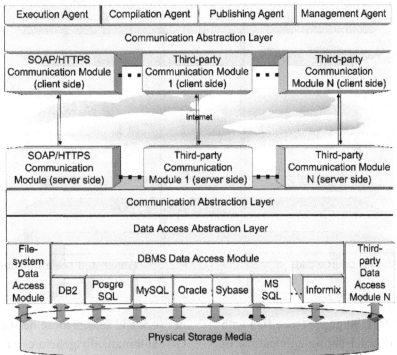

library distributions. *Stubs* generation process uses bytecode analysis techniques to identify method signatures and attributes, thus the original library source code is not required.

2. Generation of semantic annotations. JaDiMa GUI assists the publishing user in the task of describing the library capabilities in terms of a domain ontology.

3. Packaging and transmission of *stubs*, semantic annotations, documentation and real library bytecode from the publishing node to the Repository.

Example 1 shows the publishing process.

Example 1. *Suppose that an user wants to publish a fairly well known mathematics and statistics Java*

library called Apache Commons Math, version 1.2.0. For that purpose, he can use the command jdm-publish in the following form:

```
jdm_publish -b commons-math-1.2.0.jar
-v 1.2.0 -r my-repository -n commons-
math
    -j commons-math-1.2.0.zip -s com-
mons-math-semantic-description.owl
```

The user must possess a *jar* file commons-math-1.2.0.jar, which contains the original library bytecode (specified with the -b option); a *zip* file commons-math-1.2.0-doc.zip, which contains the library *JavaDoc* API documentation (specified with the -j option); and an OWL file commons-math-semantic-description.owl, containing the semantic description of the library functionality

Figure 3. JaDiMa skeleton generation process

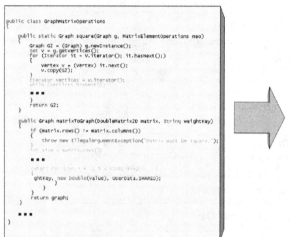

Original class source code

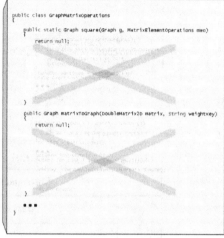

Generated skeleton source code

expressed on the OWL language (specified with the -s option, section 4.1 shows an example of such a description).

This command will start the *stubs* generation process for each class contained on the supplied *jar* file, marking each one with version number 1.2.0 (see option -v in the command jdm-publish). The generated stubs, the JavaDoc documentation, the semantic description, and the original jar file will then be packaged and sent to the my-repository Repository (-r option), using the contact information supplied on a configuration file.

Compilation Agent

The Compilation Agent is in charge of obtaining application dependency information provided by the developer, and making requests to the Repositories P2P network in order to obtain the adequate library *stubs* according to the aforementioned version numbering scheme. Through the JaDiMa GUI, the programmer can query information about the published libraries on the Repositories P2P

network and selects those he/she needs; then the GUI automatically generates a *metadata file* that describes the application dependencies.

During the compilation process, it is not required to download the published classes (original library bytecode). Since the *stubs* mimic the original classes method signatures and attributes, the compilation process succeeds even without the presence of actual libraries bytecode.

Example 2 shows the compilation process.

Example 2. *Suppose now that a different user wants to compile an application which requires the previously published Apache Commons Math library, version 1.2.0. For that purpose, he can use the command jdmc in the following form:*

```
jdmc -s my-application/src -d my-ap-
plication/bin -g:none
```

The user must possess the application source code in a my-application/src directory (specified with the -d option), following the standard Java package path conventions. In this directory, a jdm-build.xml file exists, generated through JaDiMa GUI, stating that the application depends upon a library called commons-math, version 1.2.0. Also, the class files output will be placed on a local filesystem directory my-application/bin (specified with the -d option). Additionally, as the user does not desire debugging information on the generated class files, the javac standard -g:none option is used.

This command will contact the Repository P2P network in order to locate and download the *stubs* for the commons-math library, version 1.2, as described in the jdm-build.xml dependencies specification file. Upon download, the *stubs* will be unpacked on a temporary directory and the standard javac compilation utility will be invoked, including in the source path the directory my-application/src, and adding to the classpath the unpacked *stubs* temporary directory. Also, standard javac flags, such as -g:none in this example, are passed to the javac compilation utility. Since each *stub* contains the same method signatures and attributes of the original library bytecode, compilation will be successful. The application's compiled class files will be placed on my-application/bin directory, along with the downloaded *stubs* class files. In order to distribute this application, the developer can just pack the generated class files directory into a standard *jar* file my-application.jar.

Note that the *stub* class files scattered among the application class files can be later identified as being JaDiMa *stubs*, due to the special flag placed on each one during the publishing phase.

Additionally, notice that the developer does not need to search and download the required libraries, nor worry about how to package them in order to distribute her application. Through the JaDiMa GUI, he can search for available libraries using semantic annotations, query API documentation and select the library that satisfies best her application needs.

Execution Agent

The Execution Agent is in charge of setting up the environment in which an application can be transparently executed. When an execution is requested, the user has a JaDiMa compiled application that contains a set of *stubs* for each remote library used. The application is executed on a Java virtual machine using a custom *ClassLoader*, the jdmClassLoader, which is responsible for analyzing each class file loaded during the application execution, in order to identify JaDiMa *stubs* and download the appropriate original class file from the JaDiMa Repositories P2P network. Hence, the Execution Agent allows for normal execution of the application. Note that this scheme ensures that only the subset of classes within the library actually used by the application are downloaded to the execution platform. By using our proposed version numbering (Cardinale, Blanco, & De Oliveira, 2006b), it is possible to obtain improved library versions that do not affect the execution.

Example 3 shows the execution process.

Example 3. *Suppose now that another user wants to execute the previously compiled JaDiMa application called my-application. For that purpose, he can use the command jdm in the following form:*

```
jdm -p my-application.jar -m ve.usb.
my-application.MyApplication argu-
ment1 argument2
```

Here, the user possesses a my-application.jar *jar* file (specified with the -p option), and an application main class called ve.usb.my-application. MyApplication (specified with the -m option). Additionally, the user wants to pass two parameters (argument1 and argument2) as command-line arguments.

This command will start the standard Java virtual machine but using our custom jdmClassLoader. As the virtual machine starts loading the class files contained on the my-application.jar *jar* file through the jdmClassLoader, each JaDiMa *stub* will be identified, and the associated real bytecode will be downloaded from the JaDiMa Repositories P2P network, effectively substituting the *stubs* class definitions with the real class definitions at run time. For this purpose, the jdmClassLoader examines each loaded class file, looking for the special flag placed during the *stubs* generation process. If a *stub* class is being loaded, the jdmClassLoader extracts the version number from this flag, and requests the real bytecode to the Repository P2P network. Figure 4 shows a graphical scheme of the execution process.

Notice that according to our version numbering scheme, different revision numbers of a library are guaranteed to contain no changes on method signatures or semantic behavior In this sense, even though the application was compiled using stubs for version 1.2.0 of the commons-math library, the application could be successfully executed with the latest version of the 1.2 series (i.e. 1.2.1, 1.2.2, etc). Unless the user specifies the contrary, the default behavior of the jdmClassLoader is to download the latest revision number of each *stub*, allowing the user to benefit for newer and improved releases of the libraries transparently, without breaking the application functionality.

Class Prefetching and Caching

JaDiMa implements a simple prefetching strategy in order to reduce the impact on execution time of remote class loading. Recall that pure Java model consists of loading classes on-demand, one by one. JaDiMa tries to have some of the remote classes loaded before they are instantiated, such that application's idle time waiting for class transfers is diminished.

The prefetching strategy consists on grouping remote classes according to its invocation time: whenever a remote class of a group (called *cluster*) is instantiated for the first time, all members of the group are requested and loaded from their respective remote Repository, including the instantiated class itself. Clusters are computed and adjusted at execution time.

Class Clustering

Classes are grouped according to *temporal proximity*. Temporal proximity computation is based on the *effective time* (defined below) when each remote class is instantiated for the first time (*first execution* time).

The effective time (*ETime*) of a class is the time, measured from the application's start time,

Figure 4. JaDiMa execution model

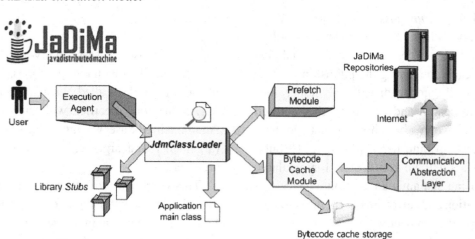

of its *first use* reference, ignoring the time spent transferring previously instantiated remote classes. Starting with the first remote class instantiated (i.e., the main class) at execution time, the algorithm creates the clusters. Let's call C_{Gx} the first class of a cluster G_x, and $ETime(C_{Gx})$ its effective time. Every successively instantiated remote class C_i not yet added to a cluster and such that

$$(ETime(C_i) - ETime(C_{Gx})) < \varepsilon$$

is added to cluster G_x. Clustering depends on ε, the *Prefetch window size* parameter. The first remote class (not yet in a cluster) whose *ETime* is more than ε from *$ETime(C_{Gx})$* becomes the first class of a new cluster; the procedure iterates until all classes are grouped into clusters. Figure 5 depicts class clustering.

The Execution Agent manages the persistence of the downloaded classes in a local cache. This means that after execution, remotely loaded classes remain in the Execution Agent. In this way, it is possible to reduce communication delay and overhead in future executions. The implementation of cache policies are considered using a *plug-in* scheme that reinforces JaDiMa adaptability. A Java interface with generic access methods to the cache is defined, which can be used to implement different class replacement policies. The default policy offered is "Last Recently Used" (LRU).

First execution time for all remote classes instantiated are registered and saved by the jdmClassLoader during execution as an *execution profile*. The next time the application is executed, the most recent *execution profile* is used to improve the class clustering creation.

Whenever a remote class is instantiated, the following steps are executed (see Figure 4):

1. jdmClassLoader asks the *Prefetch Module* to compute the requested class cluster using the *Prefetch window size* specified for this execution
2. the list of cluster members is then passed to the *Bytecode Cache Module*, which checks the classes locally available (in memory or cache) for this cluster
3. classes that are not locally available are requested remotely by JaDiMa *Communication Abstraction Layer* (CAL) module.

The CAL module handles remote classes requests using two concurrent threads: one for the class instantiated by the application, and another for its cluster companions. Thus, whenever the instantiated class is loaded, the application can

Figure 5. JaDiMa class clustering

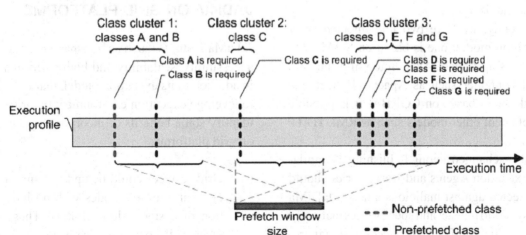

resume execution, while other prefetched classes are transferred. Thus, JaDiMa enables overlapping of class transfers with computation.

The prefetching of a class is triggered by the first instantiation of any member of the cluster it belongs to. If the application is sequential (only one thread), the execution will stall until the instantiated class is transferred. Other members of the same cluster will proceed immediately, if the prefetching is completed before their *first use*. If the application is multi-threaded, a better overlapping of execution and class transfer might be expected.

Communication and Security Schemes

Communication among JaDiMa components is based on *plug-ins*, which allow for implementation of any communication mechanism. The Communication Abstraction Layer (see Figure 1) is a well defined interface providing a communication model abstraction regardless its underlying implementation. Different modules attached to this interface are in charge of carrying out effective communication among Publishing, Compilation, Execution Agents and Repositories for data exchange. In this sense, implementing a new communication scheme consists on developing a module implementing the Communication Abstraction Layer using the desired communication mechanism.

Currently, we have two implemented communication model: one is based on SOAP with HTTPS using Apache Axis on top of a standard servlet container such as Apache Tomcat; the second one is based on CORBA. It is possible to implement other models such as RMI, HTTP or sockets.

Data exchanged among Publishing, Compilation, Execution Agents and Repositories should be protected against malicious attacks. JaDiMa allows users to register and specify roles that every user is entitled of. Each user needs a digital cre-

dential for authentication. Users must authenticate before accessing the Repository. The authentication is made by the communication module. Regarding authorization, roles currently considered by JaDiMa are: i) publishing role, which enables publishing, consulting, and accessing libraries; ii) administration role, in order to perform administration tasks on Repositories; iii) libraries and versions access role, for access control to different library groups. Once the authentication is successful, Repositories receive with each request the effective user role for authorization purposes.

Authentication relies on the *servlet container* by using mutual authentication based on X.509 certificates. The user security information could be managed by using a relational database, plain files, or LDAP directories. On the other hand, authorization is performed once the user is mapped to a security role by the *servlet container*, during the authentication phase. At the Repository level, access to data and operations are granted upon the security role of the requesting user, thus decoupling user management information from the authorization mechanism.

Based on the use of X.509 certificates, it is possible to integrate JaDiMa security model with Globus Security Infrastructure (GSI) (Butler et al., 2000) in order to include all JaDiMa components into Globus-based grids security space.

JADIMA ON GRID PLATFORMS

JaDiMa features (such as transparency, security, accessibility, scalability and high performance), in addition to its execution model, makes it ideal to leverage execution environment on grids. We identify some benefits of incorporating JaDiMa on grid platforms:

- Grid services could be updated simultaneously in multiple nodes with no intervention of system administrators. These services will be automatically updated with newer and fixed versions of used packages, by using the JaDiMa version numbering scheme which guarantees version compatibility.

- Grid users share software easily, supported by centralized administration of libraries. By providing access to Repositories, JaDiMa is virtually distributing every published library to each execution node on the grid.

- Grid users save time, bandwidth, and disk space. They may develop their applications locally to latter execute them on the grid. The use of library *stubs* makes possible for users to relay on JaDiMa mechanisms for library administration. Hence programmers may download just the needed *stubs* for the compilation process. When requesting the execution on a grid node, these *stubs* will travel as part of the application to the selected Execution Agent where they will be substituted for more recent and compatible library versions. This brings a substantial benefit to the platform in general, assuming that Repositories are close to the Execution Agents or interconnected through high speed networks.

We have integrated JaDiMa on a grid platform called SUMA/G (*Scientific Ubiquitous Metacomputing Architecture/Globus*). SUMA/G is a grid middleware that transparently executes Java bytecode on remote machines. The basics of executing Java programs in SUMA/G are simple. Users can start the execution of programs either through a shell running on the client machine or through the SUMA/G portal. SUMA/G extends the Java execution model to grid platforms; in particular, classes and data are dynamically loaded.

SUMA/G security and resource management and access are based on Globus components (The Globus Alliance, 2006). In SUMA/G, Java classes and files are loaded on demand from sev-

eral sources: the user's machines, user controlled external servers, and machines belonging to the grid. This means that it is not necessary neither previous installation of the user's Java code on the execution node nor packing all classes for submission. Instead, only the reference to the main class is submitted; all Java class files, as well as data files, are loaded, supported by prefetching and buffering mechanisms., thus reducing communication overheads (Cardinale, De Oliveira, & Figueira, 2006).

The integration of JaDiMa on SUMA/G extends its execution model by adding a new class source: JaDiMa Repositories. Additionally, JaDiMa adds a compilation functionality to SUMA/G (Cardinale, Blanco, & De Oliveira, 2006a). In order to integrate JaDiMa to SUMA/G, it was necessary to:

- Adapt the security scheme of JaDiMa to GSI. SUMA/G users have a X.509 certificates from which a certificate proxy is generated on each execution. As the proxy is a "reduced version" of original X.509 certificate, it is totally compatible with JaDiMa security scheme, which is based on those certificates. Hence, no modification was necessary to achieve this requirement. JaDiMa receives a X.509 certificate or a certificate proxy and does not distinguish one from the other.

- Incorporate the jdmClassLoader functionality to the sumagClassLoader. To achieve this requirement it was necessary to modify the sumagClassLoader in order to add *stubs* management, allowing *stubs* identification and actual libraries queries from the Repositories P2P network.

Figure 6 shows the SUMA/G extended execution model. According to SUMA/G traditional execution model, sumagClassLoader gets classes from the Client (in case of Execute service), or from a designated Proxy (in case of Submit service), or from remote accounts specified by users. With JaDiMa, some classes can be obtained from the Repositories P2P network. The elements denoted with pentagons represent additions to the original mechanism:

a.   On the client side there are library *stubs* which the application depends on. These *stubs* are transferred to the SUMA/G Execution Node as they are referenced, exactly as it happens with application classes.
b.   sumagClassLoader verifies each class loaded to determine if it is a *stub*.
c.   In case that a *stub* is loaded, sumagClass-Loader requests the actual class to the Repository P2P network.

With this approach, all the benefits of JaDiMa functionalities, such as class loading mechanisms, distributed bytecode and security are incorporated to grid execution nodes. Additionally, SUMA/G advanced users (who develop their own applications) have access to all the published libraries in the Repositories P2P network, allowing them to include these in their applications, and benefit from its automatic management.

LIBRARY AND REPOSITORIES DISCOVERY

Due to the potentially large number of libraries and Repositories, mechanisms that allow users to discover pieces of software need to be incorporated in order to facilitate the task of application development in collaborative environments. On the other hand, in order to provide a dynamic network community for library and bytecode sharing, thus empowering collaborative work, a P2P Repositories discovery mechanism could provide high benefits.

Library Discovery Based on Semantic Annotation

JaDiMa incorporates the possibility for describing libraries kept in the Repositories P2P network using domain ontologies. Thus, annotation of libraries capabilities are specified with ontologies written using OWL. We illustrate the use of semantic annotations in JaDiMa with the following example:

Example 4. *Consider a library Dblp that provides access to information stored in a site that manages information about research publications, such as The DBLP Computer Science Bibliography (*http://dblp.mpi-inf.mpg.de/dblp-mirror/index. php*). A publishing user would use JaDiMa GUI to describe Dblp library in terms of the concepts associated with the data it manages. For this, an ontology that defines terms used in the domain of publication, such as eBiquity (UMBC eBiquity, 2008), needs to be provided.*

This ontology defines the concepts used in the domain of publications: the concept that refers generically to a publication is modeled as OWL classes. Some of its specialization are also defined as OWL subclass: Article, Book, InCollection, Proceedings, etc. The Publication class can be defined in terms of the following attributes: Author, Institution, Year, Conference.

JaDiMa defines an ontology to specify the relation between the domain ontology concepts that defines the library capabilities and those that describe the library itself. This basic ontology comprises the following OWL classes: Library, Publisher, DomainOntology.

Using this ontology, the Dblp library could be annotated in the following terms:

```
<DomainOntology name="$eBiquity$">
    <Location
        url="http://ebiquity.
umbc.edu/ontology/publication.owl"/>
    <IncludesConcept
```

Figure 6. SUMA/G execution model extended with JaDiMa

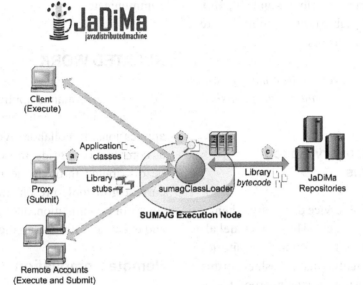

```
ref="#Publication">
        <IncludesConcept
ref="#Proceedings">
        <IncludesConcept
ref="#Bookpublication">
        <IncludesConcept
ref="#Article">
</DomainOntology>
<Publisher name="$\#John Doe$">
        <Publishes library="$\#Dblp$"
version="1.2.3">
        <Publishes library="$\#Dblp$"
version="2.1.1">
<Publisher>
<Library name="$Dblp$" ver-
sion="$1.2.3$">
        <DescribedOver
ontology="$eBiquity$">

<Concept="$\#Publication$">
            <Concept="$\#Book$">
        </DescribedOver>
</Library>
<Library name="$Dblp$" ver-
sion="$2.1.1$">
```

```
            <DescribedOver
ontology="$\#eBiquity$">

<Concept="$\#Publication$">

<Concept="$\#Book$">

<Concept="$\#Proceedings$">
        </DescribedOver>
<Library>
```

These annotations allow developers to submit the following query:

"Libraries that access information related to publications in conferences"

Note the library Dblp is specified as having two different implementations. For this query, JaDiMa can suggest the user that the most suitable library is Dblp version 2.1.1.

JaDiMa current implementation defines these annotations at a library level. Future implementations will allow for the description of methods within the libraries, in such a way that information about the methods capabilities can be annotated in terms of their parameters (inputs and outputs). This extension will enable users to submit more complex and specific queries:

"The methods that may return the names of conferences to which a certain author has published works".

Repository Discovery Based on P2P Protocols

JaDiMa defines a P2P service discovery scheme, based on the JXTA protocol. This P2P model allows JaDiMa Agents to find remote Repositories on the network, in a highly dynamic fashion. In this sense, JaDiMa Repository Agent incorporates an additional component, called the JxtaAdvServer. This component will be responsible for joining the JXTA P2P network, and periodically publishing *advertisements* of the libraries and versions contained on this specific Repository.

When a JaDiMa Agent is initiated in order to perform any repository-related operation, a DiscoveryClient is instantiated, which also joins the P2P network momentarily for capturing every possible published *advertisement*. These captured meta-data elements are locally stored; they include the contact information of each Repository peer, and the libraries, versions and bytecode that each of them offers to the network. We call these first operations the *discovery phase*. Hereinafter, every Repository related operation on the *Communication Abstraction Layer* can be performed by contacting only those Repositories known to hold the required data element (library, version or bytecode). This second group of operations is defined as the *search phase*.

A JXTA-standard Rendezvous or Relay server needs to be instantiated in the case that peers, which require to see each other, are located on separated subnets, private subnets or firewall protected subnets. This service will take care of NAT and firewall traversal operations required

to allow each JxtaAdvServer to transparently communicate.

RELATED WORK

For high performance applications, re-usability offers a benefit to construct component-based applications. In collaborative frameworks, such as computational grids, those components could be distributed through the platform. However, current grid tools present many limitations on supporting compilation, distribution, deployment, and execution of these applications.

Remote Compilation Support

The construction of large scale grid applications represents a challenge to users and developers because of the inherent difficulty of maintaining library versions and deploying corrected applications over large scale heterogeneous grids. In spite of this, user-oriented application deployment tasks have remained unsupported in grid middleware. This lack of support is strongly detrimental to aspects associated with sharing, usability, evolution, uptake and continual development of the grid, and especially of its applications (Goscinski & Abramson, 2004a).

Apache Maven (Apache Software Foundation, 2009) and Krysalis Centipede (Krysalis Community Project, 2004) extend the functionalities of common compilation tools (i.e., ant and make) to allow distributed management of libraries at compilation time. Similar to JaDiMa, both projects provide automatic download jar files from remote Web repositories. This is done following the instructions of package dependencies specified in a configuration file. These tools maintain copies of all packages in the local development environment, while JaDiMa downloads only *stubs* of referred class to the local host. In JaDiMa, web repositories are not mandatory because it supports the specification of several communication protocols that allows for use of libraries located on distributed sites.

The JaDiMa GUI assists users on building the XML configuration files that represent the dependency of the libraries needed by an application.

Apache Maven and Krysalis Centipede can replace the packages for new versions during the compilation only if this is specified on the dependency file. Based on our proposed versioning specification, jdmClassLoader can load new library versions at runtime without alteration of that execution flow. Security in Apache Maven and Krysalis Centipede is managed at the communication protocol level, i.e., access control is defined in terms of repositories. In contrast, JaDiMa allows fine-grain access control by assigning access permissions to packages or libraries instead of repositories.

DistAnt (Goscinski & Abramson, 2004b, 2005) and GridAnt (Amin et al., 2004) specifically address the problem of assisting users deploy their applications on grid resources. They extend ant utility with support for grid specific tasks, which users can employ to define application deployment workflow for their applications. The tasks that can be used are mainly related to the following: compilation, authentication, resource location, code and data packaging, transport and unpacking/installation. These tools can be combined with Apache Maven to leverage the compilation activities. They operate at a higher level than JaDiMa; however, they are oriented to isolated application deployment, instead of the compilation and execution support for distributed applications provided by JaDiMa. Similar to JaDiMa, GridAnt uses X.509 certificates for user authentication, authorization and delegation. GridAnt proposed architecture introduces a runtime environment that offers a globally accessible communication model (Amin et al., 2004). GridAnt assists grid users in orchestrating a set of grid activities and expressing complex dependencies between them in XML. JaDiMa defines an schema that facili-

tates the deployment of corrected version in grid resources.

Remote Execution Support

There are several projects oriented to remote execution of Java programs on grid platforms. Some examples are Addistant (Tatsubori, Sasaki, Chiba, & Itano, 2001), Unicorn (Ong, Lim, Lee, & Yeo, 2002), Javelin++ (Neary, Brydon, Kmiec, Rollins, & Cappello, 1999), JNLP (Zukowski, 2002), Bayanihan (Sarmenta & Hirano, 1999), HORB (Satoshi, 1997), and ADAJ (Felea, Olejnik, & Toursel, 2004).

Addistant is a system which enables distributed execution of software originally developed to be executed on a single JVM, in a way that some objects are executed on a remote host, i.e., it provides functional distribution of a monolithic application on multiple JVM and invocation is done transparently using remote calls. The Addistant execution model is opposite to JaDiMa model because it allows the execution on a single platform (sequential or parallel) of applications with distributed components. JaDiMa does not modify the original execution model of applications because the definition of stubs and the replacement mechanisms is managed by the jdmClassLoader. Developers using Addistant must specify (in a *policy file*) the host where instances of each class are allocated and how remote references are implemented. According to that specification, Addistant automatically transforms the bytecode at load time by generating proxy classes, which take charge of remote references at run-time. Libraries in JaDiMa can be deployed in several repositories, JaDiMa allows for libraries to be downloaded from any of these sites. JaDiMa uses *stubs* at compilation time and the substitution for actual classes is transparently done at run-time.

Unicorn defines an architecture using Java to harness the vast processing power on the Internet for distributed computing applications. Users can either make use of the suite of applications provided by the systems or upload their own applications to the server together with the data to be processed. These tasks are distributed (maybe in parallel) to idle hosts logged on to the corresponding servers. Most of these projects involve the need of using specific programing models and run-time environments for distributing and invoking remote Java classes. JaDiMa runs unmodified Java applications. None of those projects support compilation activities; hence, they could benefit from JaDiMa compilation power.

Javelin++ is a solution to provide execution facilities for distributed application. It defines a Java-based global computing infrastructure that facilitates development of parallel applications. The communication at component level is done thought RMI. The use of Java facilitates the P2P communication schema, thus, allowing the generation of arbitrary graph configurations.

JNLP (Java Network Launching Protocol), is a project that is quite similar to JaDiMa with regard to the execution model. JNLP uses mechanisms related with a ClassLoader to load classes that compose an application from a web server during execution. However, it is not transparent in many aspects: i) applications must be programmed with particular specifications of JNLP specific packages; ii) the developer must specify a metadata file with the application properties and the modules required by the application; iii) in case any of the modules changes, this file must be manually updated; and iv) JNLP requires installing a plug-in in the browser to recognize the metadata file and begin the application module partial download. This is the only project considering class prefetching, but the task of deciding the set of class that are to be loaded together is left to the programmer. In contrast, JaDiMa makes class prefetching transparently and the defined prefetching mechanism ensures efficient use of network bandwidth, on the server side as well as on the client and repositories side.

Bayanihan intends to create a super computer offering a framework that allows programmers to design and develop their applications (Sarmenta, 1998). This approach addresses the problem of collaborative environment and application support. It offers an API for programmers that encapsulates remote communication details. It addresses the performance issue by providing communication over HORB (Satoshi, 1997). HORB is an ORB that sacrifices language interoperability to facilitates optimized implementation over a Java platform; thus, there is no need for users to define signatures using IDL language. HORB intention is to facilitate the access of remote objects in a seamless way, i.e., the users can focus on application functionalities and not on communication mechanisms.

ADAJ is a Java distributed environment that intends to facilitate the execution of applications on a cluster of computers. ADAJ offers both a programming and execution environment, relying on the concept of distributed collections, grouping fragmented objects, and on asynchronous calls. It provides an API so that the programmer can easily develop parallel applications. ADAJ focuses on two objectives: a) easing the programmer's work by hiding issues related to the parallelism management; and b) supporting dynamic and automatic, or semi-automatic, deployment of applications in heterogeneous computing environments. ADAJ presents limitation on multi-user execution environments while JaDiMa delegates the ability of managing user access to grid platforms. ADAJ allows users to seamlessly create global objects and to access them transparently, just like the local ones, while JaDiMa intends to facilitates the versioning of libraries and the deployment on grid platforms.

P2P Protocols Support

P2P networks, protocols and architectures emerged in the recent years as a flexible and highly dynamic alternative to the traditional, static and centralized client-server communication model. All kinds of P2P-based applications, ranging from file and content sharing networks to distributed computation of large scale scientific problems with a divide-and-conquer strategy, have enabled collaborative work and new execution and communication models for a new trend in applications development.

The most notable community effort on providing standardized and implementation independent P2P protocols, is JXTA (Juxtaposition) (Brookshier, Govoni, Krishnan, & Soto, 2002; Community, 2001), an open source project supported by Sun Microsystems. JXTA allows application developers to leverage peer discovery, query and communication, including NAT and firewall traversal techniques through an API which hides these implementation specific details allowing them to focus on applications functionality. Several applications have been implemented with JXTA as the communication and discovery services provider, including flexible content-sharing solutions such as WiredReach (http://www.wiredreach.com/) and collaborative applications such as Collanos Workspace (http://www.collanos.com/). JaDiMa uses JXTA protocols to implement the network of libraries Repositories.

Library Discovery Support

On platforms where the pieces of reusable code are distributed (e.g. grid platform), developers have to find and obtain the suitable libraries that can help them to on their specific problem. However, if the number of the possible useful components is large, it becomes unlikely that all available alternatives can be considered. Thus, it is crucial to provide mechanisms that assist developers to select the most suitable components (Z. Chen & Qian, 2005).

There exist approaches that enable the characterization of software components (Mielnik, Bouthors, Laurire, & Lang, 2004; Mili, Mili, & Mittermeir, 1997). However, they incorporate

mechanisms based on traditional keyword matching techniques which are inefficient, as the meaning of what is being searched is not considered. For instance, keyword matching has a tendency to return unrelated results.

Keyword-based search languages as well as category browsing such as Google, provide a significantly higher number of WSDL (Web Service Description Language) files for a given keyword-based user request (Bachelechner et al., 2006). However, Google is not well suited for Web Service discovery because services are selected in terms of how "good" are them for a given set of keywords, and they are ranked by using link-based metrics that do not necessarily reflect the satisfaction grade of the solutions with respect to the user functional and non-functional requirements.

SemaCS, Semantic Component Selection (Sjachyn & Beus-Dukic, 2006), is a generic method of component identification and classification. It addresses the problem of component selection. It defines a generic taxonomy to annotate the component and analyzes these descriptions in order to allow the adequate selection of components. SemaCS addresses the issues of accuracy using this generic taxonomy. However, the problem of selecting appropriated software libraries requires using specific and common domain knowledge among users of distributed or collaborative platforms.

The area of service discovery addresses the problem of finding a set of services that can perform a specific task or produce specific information. The majority of resource discovery approaches expresses the user requirements in terms of the nature of transformation of the information. These approaches usually rely their computations on reasoning engines that, according to the service semantic descriptions, can select the resources that best fit the requirements.

Algorithms for matching and discovery services range from keyword-based search engines, to ontology-based frameworks for semantically heterogeneous Web Services discovery.

Matchmaking algorithms proposed in (Paolucci et al., 2002) make use of information published in the Service Profile to identify the resources that satisfy a set of functional constraints. A Service Profile specifies the service functionality in terms of inputs, outputs, preconditions, and effects. Inputs and outputs refer to OWL classes describing the types of the instances to be sent to the service and the type of the expected answer (Bansal & Vidal, 2003).

JaDiMa incorporates semantic annotations to describe the libraries published in its Repositories. This will aid developers to interpret component descriptions and to make queries in order to locate libraries that might be useful to solve their specific problem. JaDiMa defines a basic ontology that allows for publishing users to annotate libraries. Library concepts defined in this ontology can also be used by users to specify the characteristics of the software they are looking for.

EXPERIMENTAL RESULTS

In this Section we illustrate JaDiMa functionalities and empirically evaluate JaDiMa performance of compilation and execution processes in several scenarios.

Experiences Using JaDiMa

In order to illustrate concepts handled by JaDiMa and to demonstrate its functionality, we carried out tests with real applications (open source code) with different dependency levels among the used libraries. We refer to the experience with TIE (Siefkes, 2003) (*Trainable Information Extractor*) and JUNG (O'Madadhain, Fisher, Nelson, & Krefeldt, 2003) (*Java Universal Network/Graph*). TIE is a trainable software for information extraction and text classification. JUNG is an open-source software library that provides a language for the modeling, analysis, and visualization of graph and network data.

Dependencies of the libraries used by these two applications are shown in Table 1.

The tests were carried out in a scenario where JaDiMa components were distributed on nodes in three different domains with different environments and platforms. Laboratory resources of Universidad Simón Bolivar (USB) and external resources from this university were used. These resources had the following characteristics:

- Pentium III, 800 MHz with 256 MB of RAM, 10 GB in Disk, in Computation Laboratory (LDC) of USB.
- Dual Pentium III, 800 MHz with 512 MB of RAM, 10 GB in Disk, in the Parallel and Distributed Systems Laboratory (PDS) in the USB
- AMD Athlon XP, 3.1 GHz, with 1 GB of RAM, 80 GB in Disk, and dual Dell of 800 MHz, 512 MB of RAM, 7 GB in Disk, in external nodes to the USB (BSC Consultores C.A.).

All nodes are connected to Internet through links of 256 Kbps in average. The tests carried out in this scenario were the following:

- A LDC Repository, with Apache Tomcat 5.0.16 on Fedora Core 3, with a RDBMS Data Access Module using the MySQL database located in another node of the same domain.
- One Repository in a node of BSC Consultores C.A. (BSC Repository), executing JBOSS Application Server 4.0.0 on RedHat Linux 9, with a RDBMS Data Access Module using a Microsoft SQLServer 2000 database located in another node of the same domain. The operating system of these nodes is Microsoft Windows 2000 Server.
- One Repository in PDS Laboratory (PDS Repository), with Apache Tomcat 5.5.9

Table 1. Library dependencies

Application name	Used Libraries	Description
TIE	Commons-beanutils commons-collections commons-configuration commons-discovery commons-lang commons-logging commons-math commons-pool dom4j jtidy JUnit minorThird velocity BeanShell MontyLingua CRF COLT Gauss-Newton and Conjugate-Gradient optimization JCommon	http://jakarta.apache.org/commons/beanutils/ http://jakarta.apache.org/commons/collections/ http://jakarta.apache.org/commons/configuration/ http://jakarta.apache.org/commons/discovery/ http://jakarta.apache.org/commons/lang/ http://jakarta.apache.org/commons/logging/ http://jakarta.apache.org/commons/math/ http://jakarta.apache.org/commons/pool/ http://www.dom4j.org/ http://jtidy.sourceforge.net/ http://www.junit.org/ http://minorthird.sourceforge.net/ http://jakarta.apache.org/velocity/ http://www.beanshell.org/ http://web.media.mit.edu/hugo/montylingua/ http://crf.sourceforge.net http://cern.ch/hoschek/colt/ http://billharlan.com/pub/code/inv/indexh.html http://www.jfree.org/jcommon
MinorThird	JFreeChart Junit JWF LBFS Libsvm Log4J Trove	http://www.jfree.org/jfreechart/index.html http://www.junit.org http://sourceforge.net/projects/jwf/ http://crf.sourceforge.net/ http://www.csie.ntu.edu.tw/cjlin/libsvm/ http://jakarta.apache.org/log4j/docs/ http://trove4j.sourceforge.net/javadocs/
JUNG	COLT commons-collections JUnit	http://cern.ch/hoschek/colt/ http://jakarta.apache.org/commons/collections/ http://www.junit.org

on Scientific Linux CERN 3, with a Data Access Module through NFS.

- Publication, compilation and execution nodes in PDS Laboratory, with Scientific Linux CERN 3.
- Publication, compilation and execution nodes in LDC with Fedora Core 3.
- One execution node in a portable device connected to a domainless net with Microsoft Windows 2000 Professional.

In all nodes, we used Java Virtual Machine 1.5.0. The test strategy is as follows:

1. Publication of libraries used by the applications (specified in column 2 of Table 1, except for minorThird). Different versions

of these libraries were randomly published among the three Repositories, from different publication nodes. The publication process implies the generation of the respective *stubs*, documentation, and semantic annotations, along with transferring the data (*stubs*, documentation, OWL description file, and the libraries themselves) from the publication node to the specified Repositories. All this process can be done with a simple instruction as the following:

```
jdm_publish -b./commons-discovery.jar
-v 1.6.0 -n commons-discovery
        -r BSC_REPOSITORY -j
commons-discovery-javadocs.zip
```

```
        -s commons-discovery-se-
mantic-description.owl
```

The configuration file has the contact information (for instance, name and url) to at least one Repository in order to be able to contact the Repository P2P network. This file can be automatically generated with the help of the JaDiMa GUI, as well as the OWL file containing the library semantic description.

2. Compilation of the minorThird library in a PDS compilation node. Using the GUI, the different libraries are selected, published on the different Repositories from which minorThird depends on and the dependencies file is generated. To compile the following command is used:

```
jdmc -s /home/yudith/minorThird/
src -d /home/yudith/minorThird/build
-Xlint:none
```

In this phase, the respective *stubs* are downloaded to the compilation node. It is necessary that the configuration file with contact information of, at least, one Repository is located in the compilation nodes. In this way, the Compilation Agent is able to connect to the Repositories P2P network to solve dependencies.

3. Publication of the minorThird compiled version on LDC Repository. The process is similar to that explained in step 1.
4. Compilation of the TIE application in a compilation node of LDC. The process is similar to that explained in step 2.
5. TIE "demo" execution, in an external execution node, is done through the command:

```
jdm -p /home/yudith/tie/build -m
de.fu_berlin.ties.Main
class-train-outdir=.
-classifier=Winnow../*.dsv
```

The Execution Agent first downloads the *stubs* that are not present in the local cache (*stubs* may not be present in the execution node because compilation was executed in another node or because the *stubs* were replaced in the cache); then, the jdmClassLoader is instantiated to load the *main class*. As long as the other classes are being referenced, the jdmClassLoader is in charge of downloading the real classes, taking into consideration the version number that is specified in the respective *stub*.

6. JUNG application is compiled in a LDC compilation node. In this case the Compilation Agent is only connected with the Repositories where the COLT, commons-collection, and JUnit libraries were published.
7. JUNG "demo" is executed from the same node on which it was compiled.

The successful realization of these tests shows the functionality of JaDiMa and illustrates how easy it is to be used.

Performance Evaluation

We first show the performance of the execution process on several scenarios with JaDiMa and SUMA/G, in terms of total execution time and class loading time. We report on the gain obtained by using the JaDiMa prefetching capabilities. Secondly, we evaluate the impact of the P2P protocol to discover libraries during the compilation process.

For the first experiment, we executed a JUNG-based application on a distributed platform: SUMA/G core components running on a double processor 1.8 GHz, 1GB; an Execution Agent running on a dedicated cluster of PC's, double processor 800 MHz, 512 MB, 100 Mbps Ethernet; a JaDiMa Repository on MySQL back-end on a 1.5MHz, 750 MB; a JaDiMa Repository on SQLServer back-end on a double processor 600MHz, 1GB, 100 Mbps Ethernet; and a SUMA/G Client running on a 2.2GHz, 1GB, 768Kbps network connection.

We tested 3 scenarios in order to get performance information: i) the execution takes place using SUMA/G original execution model, i.e. without JaDiMa support, all classes are transfered from Client to the Execution Agent; ii) the libraries used by the application are published at JaDiMa Repositories close to SUMA/G deployment site; and iii) as in ii, but with JaDiMa facilities activated, i.e. class prefetching and caching. In all of them, the client and the execution node were in different networks. Table 2 shows total execution time, class loading time, and time proportion spent loading classes, for each scenario. We took the average of ten runs.

The results show that with the third scenario the total execution time is reduced in 20% with respect the first scenario. The second scenario shows the worst performance because it is necessary to transfer stubs from the Client to the Execution Agent, and then actual classes from Repositories.

For the second experiment, we have compiled JUNG library employing JaDiMa Compilation Agent with and without the P2P JXTA repository discovery protocol, in order to measure the performance impact of the protocol on the library and *stubs* searching processes performed during compilation phase. For this test, we performed ten runs of compilation using four Repositories with a MySQL storage back-end: the first one not containing any of the three required libraries to compile JUNG, and the other three containing only one of the required libraries. The client machine where the Compilation Agent was run and each Repository machine were PCs Intel Pentium 4 CPU 3.391Mhz, 1GB RAM interconnected through an isolated LAN of 100Mbps Ethernet. On each run, we measured the time employed to determine the known Repositories on the network (*discovery phase*), and the time employed to contact the known Repositories to obtain the corresponding *stubs* required for compilation (*search phase*). The results are shown on Table 3.

These results show that even though JXTA spends considerably more execution time during the initialization phase (due to the Repository discovering activities on the peers group), the time required to identify which Repository holds a specific library stub required for compilation represents approximately only a 25% of the time required when not using JXTA discovery protocol. As on the JXTA version the Compilation Agent knows exactly which Repositories hold which libraries *stubs*, during the *search phase* it does not need to probe every Repository on the network, as it is done on the standard, non-JXTA version, on which the Compilation Agent iterates sequentially over a list of known Repositories, probing each one for the required libraries *stubs*.

On the other hand, the JXTA protocol, used as a discovery mechanism, has the advantage that newly instantiated Repositories and its contents become automatically known to every Compilation and Execution Agent on the P2P network group, without requiring the user to manually add the URL contact string to configuration files.

Table 2. Total execution and class load time for each scenario

Scenario	Class Loading	Class Loading	Total Execution	Total Execution	Proportion	Proportion
	Time	σ	Time	σ	Time	σ
SUMA/G	12.40 s	6.73	30.70 s	9.26	38%	0.08
SUMA/G + JaDiMa	18.79 s	3.52	35.80 s	5.18	52%	0.03
SUMA/G + JaDiMa + facilities	9.97 s	1.58	26.90 s	3.98	37%	0.03

Table 3. Average execution time spent on repository discovery and stubs search phases for each test scenario

Scenario	Average execution time	Average execution time
	Discovery phase	Search phase
Standard discovery and search mechanisms	36.4 msec	1893.9 msec
JXTA discovery and search mechanisms	6713.9 msec	482.5 msec

FUTURE RESEARCH DIRECTIONS

Plans for future work include:

- exploring alternatives of *stubs* management on SUMA/G to eliminate *stub* transfer from the *client* to the *execution node*; this will reduce the communication overhead during the execution;
- improving the *discovery* and *search phases* during the compilation time by implementing a query mechanism to identify dynamically which Repositories hold the required *stubs* during the *search phase*; this will reduce the *discovery phase* overhead without affecting the *search phase* performance;
- incorporating semantic descriptions per method, besides the annotation per library to improve library discovery through a fine-grain match;
- conducting experiments with other kinds of applications (e.g., different combination of libraries distribution).

CONCLUSION

JaDiMa extends the Java Virtual Machine potential to a computational grid environment. As a consequence, developers and users are provided with a simple and efficient collaborative platform, which allows them to easily share software resources and motivate code reusability.

JaDiMa takes care of automatic management of remote libraries used by a Java application.

The compilation and execution mechanisms implemented enable easy sharing and porting of applications and data on heterogeneous platforms by multiple users.

The modular and layered design of JaDiMa provides for easy incorporation of well known communication, data access, and security mechanisms. All JaDiMa services are implemented as Web Services following the SOA approach. Library repositories are modeled as a P2P networking model. JaDiMa is able to assist developers on the tasks of discovering and selecting libraries that facilitates the process of building and maintaining their applications.

The results of our exploration show a clear positive vision of the feasibility and practicality of distributed compilation and execution environments with automated management of remote libraries. We have shown a feasible integration of JaDiMa to SUMA/G platform, leveraging on the advantages of both systems.

Our experimental results show the benefits of the functionalities of JaDiMa in grid environments.

REFERENCES

Abbas, A. (2004). *Grid Computing: A Practical Guide to Technology and Applications*. Brookline, MA: Charles River Media.

Amin, K., von Laszewski, G., Hategan, M., Zaluzec, N. J., Hampton, S., & Rossi, A. (2004). *Gridant: A client-controllable grid work.ow system*. Presented at the Hawaii International Conference on System Sciences, 7, 70210c.

Apache Software Foundation. (2009). *Apache Maven Project*. Retrieved from http://maven.apache.org/

Bachelechner, D., Siorpaes, K., Lausen, H., & Fensel, D. (2006). Web Service Discovery - A Reality Check. In *Proceedings of Demos and Posters of the 3rd European Semantic Web Conference.*

Bansal, S., & Vidal, J. M. (2003). Matchmaking of Web Services-Based on the DAMLS Service Model. In *Proceedings of the II Internat. Joint Conf. on Autonomous Agents and Multiagent Systems* (pp. 926–927).

Bechhofer, S., Harmelen, F., van, Hendler, J., Horrocks, I., McGuinness, D. L., Patel-Schneider, P. F., et al. (2004). *OWL Web Ontology Language* (W3C Working Draft). W3C. (OWL Web Ontology Language)

Berman, F., Fox, G., & Hey, A. (Eds.). (2003). *Grid Computing: Making the Global Infrastructure a Reality*. New York: Wiley.

Brookshier, D., Govoni, D., Krishnan, N., & Soto, J. C. (2002). JXTA: Java P2P programming (1st ed.). Ontario, Canada: Sams.

Butler, R., Welch, V., Engert, D., Foster, I., Tuecke, S., & Volmer, J. (2000, Dec). A national-scale authentication infrastructure. *Computer, 33*(12), 60–66. doi:10.1109/2.889094

Cardinale, Y., Blanco, E., & De Oliveira, J. (2006a). JaDiMa: Java applications distributed management on grid platforms. In Proceedings of Hpcc (p. 905-914).

Cardinale, Y., Blanco, E., & De Oliveira, J. (2006b). JADIMA: Virtual Machine Architecture for building JAVA Applications on Grid Platforms. *Clei Electronic Journal, 9*(2), 1-14. Retrieved from http://www.clei.cl/cleiej/volume.php

Cardinale, Y., De Oliveira, J., & Figueira, C. (2006). Remote class prefetching: Improving performance of java applications on grid platforms. In Proceedings of Ispa (p. 594-606). Sorrento, Italy.

Cardinale, Y., & Hernández, E. (2005). *Parallel Checkpointing on a Grid-enabled Java Platform. LNCS, 3470(EGC2005)*. Berlin, Germany: Springer.

Chen, L., Shadbolt, N., Goble, C., Tao, F., Puleston, C., & Cox, S. (2005). Semantics assisted problem solving on the semantic grid. *Journal of Computational Intelligence, special issue, 21*(2).

Chen, L., Shadbolt, N. R., Goble, C. A., Tao, F., Cox, S. J., Puleston, C., et al. (2003). Towards a Knowledge-based Approach to Semantic Service Composition. In *Proceedings of the 2nd International Semantic Web Conference* (ISWC), (Vol. 2870/2003, pp. 319-334).

Chen, Z., & Qian, N. (2005). Research of a semantic-based approach to improve software component reuse. In Proceedings of Skg (p. 93). Beijing, China.

Community, J. (2001). *JXTA community projects*. Retrieved from https://jxta.dev.java.net/

Erl, T. (2005). *Service-oriented architecture: Concepts, technology, and design*. Upper Saddle River, NJ: Prentice Hall PTR.

Felea, V., Olejnik, R., & Toursel, B. (2004). ADAJ: a Java Distributed Environment for Easy Programming Design and Efficient Execution. *Schedae Informaticae, 13*, 9–36.

Goble, C., & Roure, D. D. (2002). The grid: an application of the semantic web. *SIGMOD Record, 31*(4), 65–70. doi:10.1145/637411.637422

Goscinski, W., & Abramson, D. (2004a). *Distributed ant: A system to support application deployment in the grid*. Washington, DC: IEEE Computer Society.

Goscinski, W., & Abramson, D. (2004b). Distributed ant: A system to support application deployment in the grid. In *Proceedings of Grid '04: The 5th ieee/acm international workshop on grid computing* (pp. 436–443). Washington, DC: IEEE Computer Society.

Goscinski, W., & Abramson, D. (2005). Application deployment over heterogeneous grids using distributed ant. In *Proceedings of E-science '05: The first international conference on e-science and grid computing* (pp. 361–368). Washington, DC: IEEE Computer Society.

Kollia, D., Kafetzoglou, S., Grammatikou, M., & Papavassiliou, S. (2008, April). *Discovery of resources in a distributed grid environment based on specific service level agreements* (SLAS). Ischia, Italy.

Krysalis Community Project. (2004). *Krysalis centipede*. Retrieved from http://krysalis.org/centipede/

Majithia, S., Walker, D. W., & Gray, W. A. (2004). Automated Composition of Semantic Grid Services. In *Proceedings of AHM*.

Martin, D., Burstein, M., Hobbs, J., Lassila, O., Mcdermott, D., Mcilraith, S., et al. (2004). OWL-S: Semantic Markup for Web Services. *W3C Submission*.

Menascé, D. A., & Casalicchio, E. (2004). Quality of Service Aspects and Metrics in Grid Computing. In *Proceedings of CMG'04 International Conference* (p. 521-532).

Mielnik, J.-C., Bouthors, V., Laurire, S., & Lang, B. (2004). Using ecots portal for sharing information about software products on the internet and in corporate intranets. In Kazman, R., & Port, D. (Eds.), *ICCBSS* (*Vol. 2959*, p. 1). New York: Springer.

Mili, R., Mili, A., & Mittermeir, R. T. (1997). Storing and retrieving software components: A refinement based system. *IEEE Transactions on Software Engineering, 23*(7), 445–460. doi:10.1109/32.605762

Neary, M. O., Brydon, S. P., Kmiec, P., Rollins, S., & Cappello, P. (1999). Javelin++: Scalability issues in global computing. In *Proceedings of the acm 1999 conference on java grande* (p. 171-180).

O'Madadhain, J., Fisher, D., Nelson, T., & Krefeldt, J. (2003). *JUNG: Java Universal Network/Graph Framework*. Retrieved from http://jung.sourceforge.net/index.html

Ong, T. M., Lim, T. M., Lee, B. S., & Yeo, C. K. (2002). Unicorn: voluntary computing over Internet. *ACM SIGOPS Operating Systems Review, 36*(2), 36–51. doi:10.1145/509526.509532

Pahl, C. (2004). An Ontology-Based Framework for Semantic Grid Service Composition. *Grid Services Engineering and Management, 3270*, 63–77.

Paolucci, M., Kawamura, T., Payne, T. R., & Sycara, K. P. (2002). Semantic matching of web services capabilities. In *Proceedings of the International semantic web conference* (p. 333-347).

Roure, D. D., & Hendler, J. A. (2004). E-science: The grid and the semantic web. *IEEE Intelligent Systems, 19*(1), 65–71. doi:10.1109/MIS.2004.1265888

Sarmenta, L. F. G. (1998). Bayanihan: Web-based volunteer computing using java. In *Proceedings of the second international conference on world-wide computing and its applications* (pp. 444–461).

Sarmenta, L. F. G., & Hirano, S. (1999). Bayanihan: building and studying web-based volunteer computing systems using java. *Future Generation Computer Systems, 15*(5- 6), 675-686.

Satoshi, H. (1997). Horb: Distributed execution of java programs. In *Proceedings of Wwca '97: The international conference on worldwide computing and its applications* (pp. 29–42). London, UK: Springer-Verlag.

Siefkes, C. (2003). *TIE: Trainable Information Extractor*. Retrieved from http://www.inf.fu-berlin. de/inst/ag-db/software/tie/index.html

Sjachyn, M., & Beus-Dukic, L. (2006). *Semantic Component Selection SemaCS*. Presented at the International Conference on Commercial-off-the-Shelf (COTS)-Based Software Systems, 83-89.

Sun Microsystems. (2002). *Package version identification*. Retrieved from http://java.sun. com/j2se/1.5.0/docs/guide/versioning/index.html

Tao, F., Cox, S., Chen, L., Shadbolt, N., Xu, F., Puleston, C., et al. (2003). Towards the Semantic Grid: Enriching Content for Management and Reuse. In *Proceedings of Delivering e-Science, UK e-Science All-hand Conference*.

Tatsubori, M., Sasaki, T., Chiba, S., & Itano, K. (2001). A bytecode translator for distributed execution of "legacy" java software. In *Proceedings of Ecoop '01: the 15th european conference on object-oriented programming* (pp. 236–255). London: Springer-Verlag.

The Globus Alliance. (2006). *The Globus Toolkit*. Retrieved from http://www.globus.org/

UMBC eBiquity. (2008). *eBiquity Publication Ontology*. Retrieved from http://ebiquity.umbc. edu/v2.1/ontology/publication.owl

Vassiliadis, B., Giotopoulos, K., Votis, K., Sioutas, S., Bogonikolos, N., & Likothanassis, S. (2004). Application Service Provision through the Grid: Business models and Architectures. In *Proceedings of ITCC '04: The International Conference on Information Technology: Coding and Computing* (ITCC'04) (Vol. 2).

Zhang, S., Zong, Y., Ding, Z., & Liu, J. (2005). Workflow-oriented grid service composition and scheduling. In *Proceedings of Itcc '05: the international conference on information technology: Coding and computing* (ITCC'05), (Volume II, pp. 214–219). Washington, DC: IEEE Computer Society.

Zukowski, J. (2002). *Deploying Software with JNLP and Java Web Start*. Retrieved from http:// java.sun.com/developer/technicalArticles/Programming/jnlp/

Chapter 11
A Self–Organized Structured Overlay Network for Video Streaming

Khaled Ragab
King Faisal University, Saudi Arabia

ABSTRACT

Peer-to-Peer (P2P) file downloading and streaming applications have recently attracted a large number of users on the Internet. Currently, several P2P video streaming systems have been deployed to reduce the cost at server. They are classified into two categories live and on-demand streaming systems. The live streaming systems disseminate live video contents to all peers in real time. On the other hand, the on-demand video (VoD) streaming system enables peers to enjoy the flexibility of watching video. It realizes the goal of watch whatever you want, whenever you want. The current P2P-VoD systems cannot realize such goals efficiently. This chapter proposes a self-organized structured overlay network of peers to realize that goal and improve performance. Each peer is able to cache some video minutes associated with the current media being played. The proposed overlay network is organized into clusters. Each cluster contains peers with overlapped buffer windows where their playing points are located between lower and upper play point limits. When a peer in the cluster moves its play point within the limits, for example by performing a seek operation, it then can rapidly discover and fetch the required blocks for the playback buffer from peers in the same cluster. Clusters improve both discovery and fetch overheads. However, it needs cluster management overhead.

INTRODUCTION

The video streaming applications have recently fascinated a large number of users over the Internet. According to *AccuStream iMedia Research*, the number of video streams served increased *52%* in *2008*, and reaches 34 billion viewers. In addition, over the last ten years audiences have accessed *142.7* billions of pieces of video (Accustream 2009). According to *comScore*, in July around *91* million viewers watched five billion online video on

DOI: 10.4018/978-1-61520-973-6.ch011

YouTube. Americans watched *558* million hours of online during that month (comScore 2009).

The most familiar solution for streaming video over the Internet is the client-server service model such as *YouTube.* This model uses variants of technologies such as Content *Delivery Network (CDN)* to push video content from server to its clients through delivery servers. These servers are placed strategically at the network edges. A CDN replicates content from the origin server to cache servers, scattered over the globe, in order to deliver content to end-users in a reliable and timely manner from nearby optimal surrogates (Mukaddim Pathan and Rajkumar Buyya 2008). Scalability is the major challenge for server based video streaming solutions as follows. Despite the fact that *Google* has its impressive *CDN,* on *23* November *2008,* it relied on a third party *Akamai,* to stream a *YouTube* live concert to *700,000* concurrent viewers. *Akamai* technologies evolved out of an MIT research effort aimed at solving the flash crowd problem. Even with today's low bandwidth Internet video of 400 kbps, the *YouTube* live concert needed more than 280Gbps server and network bandwidth. *Akamai,* the largest commercial *CDN* service provider reports a peak aggregate capacity of 200Gbps with its tens of thousands of servers (Akamai 2007). Actually, the *Google* and *Akamai CDN* infrastructures are not necessary to handle live video stream effectively. Instead Peer-to-peer *(P2P)* video streaming systems can handle it effectively and far cheaper because peers are serving most of the video to others. P2P file downloading and streaming applications have recently attracted a large number of users on the Internet. The main difference between P2P file sharing and P2P streaming applications is the instant time when content is used. In P2P file sharing, content is completely transferred before files are opened. In contrast to P2P streaming where content is decoded, played immediately and later (probably) is discarded. Currently, several P2P video streaming systems have been deployed to reduce server cost. They are

classified into two categories: *live* and *on-demand* streaming systems. The live streaming systems disseminate live video contents to all peers in real time. On the other hand, the on-demand video *(VoD)* streaming system enables peers to enjoy the flexibility of watching. It realizes the goal of watch whatever you want, whenever you want. The current P2P-VoD systems cannot realize such goals and provide poor performance. For example, if a peer requests a video server to download one hour MPEG1 video (i.e. 540MB) using modem 28.8Kbps, 10Mbps then it has to wait 42 hours, 7.2 minutes to watch the video.

Enormous television networks, news sites, and video sharing sites such as *YouTube* and *Google Video* provide *VoD.* Most of the VoD being delivered today is short-length, low bit-rate clips. For example, *YouTube* videos today are typically less than 10 minutes in length and have a bit rate under 200 kbps. In the near future, we expect a high demand for higher bit rate (potentially DVD quality) and longer videos (including full length movies) streamed over the Internet. P2P-VoD is a new challenge for the P2P technology. Moreover, P2P-VoD has less synchrony in the peers sharing video content compared to streaming live video content. Consequently it is more difficult to reduce load at server while maintaining the streaming performance. Thus, to reduce load at video server this chapter presumes that each peer contributes a small storage for replicating video content. In addition, the video server divides the video data into segments. Each segment maintains video data of five minutes video.

This chapter reviews the state-of-the-art of peer-to-peer technologies for video streaming, and presents taxonomy of various solutions that have been developed. Moreover, this chapter proposes a careful and efficient design to replicate and discover video content. It proposes a self-organized structured overlay network of peers that organizes peers into clusters. Each cluster contains peers with close playing points and overlapped buffer windows. Each peer identifies its neighbors based on relative to their playing positions and its own playing position.

The remainder of this paper is organized as follows. Section 2 presents taxonomy of video streaming systems. Section 3 surveys the emerged approaches to construct video streaming P2P overlay network. Section 4 discusses the proposed video overlay network, the step by step construction scheme, the discover to exchange algorithm to realize video on-demand and the video broadcasting process to realize live streaming. Section 5 presents how the video overlay network can be made fault tolerant. Section 6 draws the conclusion of this chapter.

TAXONOMY OF VIDEO STREAMING

There are two alternatives shown in Figure 1 to disseminate video streams in the Internet which are underlying network layer-based and application layer based. The underlying layer-based video streaming has been implemented at the IP layer and are known as IP multicast model. It is the most efficient solution to the communication needs of multicast groups with a large number of members (S. Deering., 1988). However, the deployment of IP multicast remains limited because of technical and non-technical barriers (S.

Deering, 1991). First, IP multicast requires control support from underlying network devices, such as IP routers that must maintain per-group state. It is clear that this not only violates the stateless architectural principle, but also introduces high complexity and severe scaling constraints at the underlying network layer (B. Zhang and Hussein T. Mouftah, 2003). Second, it requires substantial infrastructure modifications, and complex modifications to IP routers' software. Finally, some of the issues associated with IP multicast, e.g. end-to-end reliability, flow and congestion control schemes, etc offer significant challenges for which no clear solutions have been proposed so far.

The second alternative for disseminating video streams has been implemented in the application layer. It moved the multicast functionality away from routers towards end systems (P. Francis, 1999; S. Q. Zhuang Et. al. 2001; Y. H. Chu, Et al., 2000; Y. Chawathe., 2000; D. Pendarakis, 2001). These approaches employed unicast IP service in multicasting. They implemented group membership, multicast routing, and packet duplication at end systems. Moving multicast functionality to end systems, instead of routers, engages performance penalties such as physical link stress. The physical link stress represents the number of replicated packets per physical link because of the overlay edge may traverse the same physical link.

Figure 1. Video streaming taxonomy

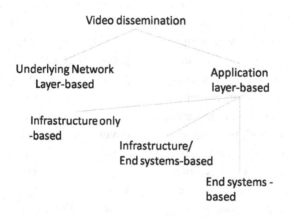

The application layer-based includes three approaches *infrastructure only-based, infrastructure/end systems-based* and *end systems-based*.

In *infrastructure only-based*, an organization uses *CDN* to deploy proxies at strategic locations on the Internet. These proxies broadcast packets to the nearby end systems using unicast. There are two approaches to build CDNs: overlay and network approaches (I. Lazar, and W. Terrill, 2001). The infrastructure only-based pursues the overlay approach. In the *overlay* approach, application-specific servers and caches at several places in the network handle the distribution of the video streams. Other than providing the basic network connectivity and guaranteed QoS for specific request/traffic, the core network components such as routers and switches play no active role in content delivery. Most of the commercial *CDN* providers such as *Akamai, AppStream*, and *Limelight* Networks follow the overlay approach for *CDN* organization. The infrastructure only-based approach is performance-effective but is also very expensive.

The *infrastructure/end systems-based* is an approach to video streaming that combines aspects of infrastructure only-based and peer-to-peer video streaming. Like infrastructure only-based video streaming, the infrastructure/end systems-based seeks to complement rather than replace the traditional client-server framework. Specifically, it considers the problem that arises when the server is overwhelmed by the volume of requests from its clients. For instance, a news site may be overwhelmed because of a large "flash crowd" caused by an event of widespread interest, such as a sports event and/or political event such as the US president *Barack Obama*'s speech from Egypt to all Muslim nations. Most of the famous systems that follow the infrastructure/end systems-based approach are *CoopNet* (V. N. Padmanabhan, Et. al., 2002) and *Hybrid video streaming scheme* (Yufeng Shan, Shivkumar Kalyanaraman, 2003; PROP Lei Guo Songqing Et. al., 2004), etc. The

infrastructure/end systems-based approach is cost-effective but not scalable due to limited storage and bandwidths of centralized broadcast servers that use unicast for the last hop to peers.

The *end systems-based* video streaming systems push the system's functionalities such as administration, maintenance and system operations (streaming) to end-systems (peers). They are referred as a peer-to-peer multicast, overlay multicast, or application-level multicast in the literature. They need to build a self-organized overlay networks that efficiently disseminate video streams. The P2P overlay networks are classified into three different approaches: *tree-first* (e.g. *ALMI* (D. Pendarakis, 2001), *Yoid* (P. Francis, 1999), *mesh-first* (e.g. *Narada* (Y. H. Chu, Et al., 2000), *Scattercast* (Y. Chawathe., 2000)) and *implicit* (e.g. *CAN* (S. Ratnasamy, Et al. 2001), *Community Overlay Network CON* (K. Ragab, K. Mori, 2004), (K. Ragab 2004) approaches. Unfortunately, although these overlay solutions alleviate some of the problems associated with IP multicast, they are often limited in their capabilities. For example, Endsystem Multicast constructs overlays entirely out of unicast connections between end-systems, and hence can scale to only small and medium sized groups. This chapter proposes a novel overlay network that can scale to large sized groups.

P2P VIDEO STREAMING ISSUES

This section discusses the P2P video streaming issues that must be addressed. The P2P video streaming systems require organizing peers into special and efficient overlay networks. These overlay networks should address the requirements to disseminate/share video streams to large scale (thousands of peers) while satisfying the real time and quality of service QoS constraints. Thus to construct and maintain an efficient overlay network, it is required to follow the following criteria:

1. The overlay network must be scalable to disseminate/share video to thousands of peers with reasonable overhead.
2. It should be efficient in disseminating video with high bandwidth and low latencies.
3. The overlay network should be resilience and robust to the dynamic changes such as join, leave, or fail. Moreover, it should be adapt itself to improve the system's performance.
4. The overlay network should be self-organized through applying distributed algorithms to build itself without help of central network administration.
5. Since the video streaming system relies on peers contributing heterogeneous bandwidth, it is required to achieve proper bandwidth sharing among incoming (and outgoing) connections to (from) individual peers. Thus, peers can receive different qualities of video based on their capabilities. To accommodate the bandwidth heterogeneity among peers a *Multiple Description Coding (MDC)* is used. In *MDC*, a stream is encoded into multiple sub-streams called *description*. Each description can be independently encoded.
6. The overlay network should satisfy the locality awareness requirement to improve the high level routing and information exchange in the application layer. This chapter fulfills this requirement by organizing the overlay network into clusters.

It is clear that, the overlay construction and maintenance techniques are very critical and need to be investigated in details as follows. The following section assesses the emerged proposals for p2p video streaming overlay networks.

VIDEO STREAMING P2P OVERLAY NETWORKS

This section surveys the emerged approaches to construct overlay networks. In particular, the approaches can be classified into three categories, namely *mesh-based*, tree-based and data-driven.

In the *mesh-based* approach, peers form a randomly connected overlay, or a *mesh*. Each peer maintains a set of neighbor nodes. Certain number of neighbor nodes are categorized as parents (*i.e.*, incoming degree) and others serve child peers (*i.e.*, outgoing degree). When a peer arrives it contacts a bootstrapping node to receive a set of peers that can potentially serve as parents. The bootstrapping node maintains the outgoing degree of all participating peers. Then, it selects a random subset of peers that can provide slots for new child peers in response to an incoming request for parents. The mesh-based approach facilitates content delivery in either bidirectional or unidirectional fashion. It employs a content delivery that effectively utilizes the outgoing bandwidth of participating peers as the group size grows. This content delivery couples push content reporting with pull content requesting. Individual peers periodically report their newly available packets to their child peers and request specific packets from individual parent peers. A parent peer periodically receives an ordered list of requested packets from each child peer, and delivers the packets in the requested order. For utilizing the available bandwidth effectively, it is required to implement a *packet scheduling algorithm* that determines the number of requested packets from parents.

PRIME, (Nazanin Magharei and Amir H. Rasti, 2007) is one of the mesh-based P2P streaming for live content that effectively incorporates swarming content delivery. It constructs an overlay network of participating peers form a *randomly* connected and *directed* mesh. Each participating peer in the overlay has multiple parents and multiple child peers. All connections in the overlay are congestion controlled using either Rate Adaption Protocol (*RAP*) or TCP Friendly Rate Control *(TFRC)* and are always initiated by the corresponding child peer. Each peer tries to maintain a sufficient number of parents that can collectively fill its incoming access link bandwidth. When a peer needs one (or more) new parent(s), it contacts a bootstrapping node to learn about a random subset of other participating peers in the system and then request those peers to serve as its parent. Such a mesh-based overlay is easy to maintain and is very resilient to churn. Thus, PRIME derived proper peer connectivity to minimize bandwidth bottleneck as well as an efficient pattern of delivery for live content over a random mesh to minimize content bottleneck.

In the *tree-based* approach, an overlay construction mechanism organizes participating peers into multiple trees. Each peer determines a proper number of trees to join based on its access link bandwidth. To minimize the effect of churn and effectively utilize available resources in the system, participating peers are organized into multiple *diverse* trees. Nodes in the tree have well defined relationships, for example, "*Parent-child*" relationships in trees. Toward this end, each peer is placed as an *internal* node in only one tree, and as an *external* (or leaf) node in other trees. Then, each description of MDC encoded content is delivered through a specific tree. The content delivery employs push mechanism where internal nodes in each tree simply forward any received packets for the corresponding description to all of their child nodes. Further, the tree structure must be maintained, as nodes leave and join the group. In addition, if a node crashes or otherwise stops performing effectively, all of its offspring in the tree will stop receiving packets, and the tree must be repaired. The failure of nodes that are higher in the tree may interrupt delivery of data to a large number of peers, and result in poor transient performance. Truly, a majority of nodes are leaves in the tree structure, and their outgoing bandwidth is not being utilized. The authors in (M. Castro, Et. al., 2003; V. N. Padmanabhan, Et. al., 2002) proposed central construction tree algorithms that constructed multiple balanced, stable and short trees. Finally, when constructing tree-based structures, loop avoidance is an impor-

tant issue that must be addressed. Therefore, the main component of the tree-based P2P streaming approach is the tree construction algorithm. This approach has a number of drawbacks as follows. Firstly, it does not utilize the outgoing bandwidth of a large fraction of nodes that are leaves in the tree. Secondly, the received bandwidth is limited by the minimum bandwidth on the path to the source and any loss in the upper level of the tree reduces bandwidth available to nodes lower in the tree. Finally, it has poor resilience to churn (a node departure results in the data stream being lost at all its descendants until the tree is fixed). Multiple tree-based approaches (M. Castro, Et. al., 2003) aim at solving the first two problems, but do not solve the third one as they require more tree structures to be maintained. Motivated by these drawbacks, recent research has focused on constructing and maintaining the overlay topology in mesh-based. (Richard John Lobb, Ana Paula Couto da Silva, Emilio Leonardi, Marco Mellia, and Michela Meo. 2009) proposed an algorithm that optimized the topology to better exploit large bandwidth peers, so that they are automatically moved close to the source. This improves the chunk delivery delay so that all peers benefit, not just the high bandwidth ones. A key property of the proposed scheme is its ability to indirectly estimate the upload bandwidth of peers without explicitly knowing or measuring it.

In contrast to the tree-based approach, the overlay network designs in the *data-driven* approach do not construct and maintain an explicit structure for delivering video streams (X. Zhang, J. Liu, B. Li and T.-S. P. Yum, 2005). The streaming overlay is designed in the data-driven approach, where a node always forwards data to others that are expecting the data, with no prescribed roles like father/child, and down-streaming /up-streaming, etc. In other words, it uses the availability of the video segments to guide the segments flow. Moreover, it needs a scheduling algorithm that struggles to schedule the segments that must be downloaded from various peers to meet the playback deadlines.

The data-driven approach employs gossip algorithms (P. Eugster, R. Guerraoui, A.-M. Kermarrec, and L. Massoulie, 2004) as sample approaches to disseminate video segments without explicitly maintaining a structure. In gossip algorithm, a peer sends a newly generated message to a set of randomly selected peers; these peers in turn send same message to other peers until the message is spread to all peers. The random choices of gossip targets achieve resilience to random failures and enable decentralized operations. Clearly, gossip is not appropriate for video streaming because its random push may cause significant redundancy with the high-bandwidth video. Cool-Streaming (X. Zhang, J. Liu, B. Li and T.-S. P. Yum, 2005) adopts pull-based technique to avoid redundancy, as peer pulls segments from other peers only if it does not already hold it. For that reason, each peer maintains a set of peers (partners), and periodically exchange segments availability information with the partners. Cool-Streaming overlay is robust to failures as any segment may be available at multiple partners.

Gossip protocols incur an extra factor of *log n* overhead as compared to tree based overlay networks because the number of transmitted messages is *O(n log n)* in the former as compared to *O(n)* in the latter. The tradeoff is between higher robustness (gossip protocols) and lower message overhead (tree based protocols).

PROPOSED VIDEO OVERLAY NETWORK

This section describes the proposed *Video Overlay Network* (*VON*) architecture, *VON* node architecture and construction algorithm. In this chapter, video server contains some modules that enable it to split and decode video contents as follows. First, *Video splitter* that works with the help of the content decoder to convert the video contents into series of timeslots (atomic playable parts of the video). The timeslot encapsulates the video data

contents of one second. Second, *Video content decoder* is a part of the codec[1] that knows how to split the video file into independent playable series of timeslots. Each *VON* node retains a buffer window (*BW*) that contains at most B_W timeslots. For example, *Windows media player* can buffer one minute of video contents before playing. Each *VON* node maintains a buffer that can store a *segment* of video data. The *segment* encapsulates the MPEG1 video contents of five minutes (i.e. 45MB) at most. The availability of the video timeslots in the buffer of a *VON* node can be represented by a buffer chart (*BC*) that represents the availability of the timeslots in its buffer. Periodically, each *VON* node exchanges request messages with its neighbors and then schedules which video timeslots are to be fetched from which node as shown in the discover to exchange algorithm in the following sections. Thus, each *VON* node can discover the other nodes that are maintaining the next minute video contents, download and buffer it during the playing of the preceding minute. The proposed overlay network organizes the *VON* nodes into Video Segments Clusters (*VS-cluster*) based on the clustering parameters that are defined as follows.

Definition 1 (<α, β, μ>-Clustering): *Given a graph G = (V, E, <α, β, μ>), where vertex v∈V, edge e∈E. The 3-tuble <α,β, μ> is an integer and called the clustering parameters. It clusters the graph G into connected sub-graphs called Video Segment Clusters (VS-Cluster). The physical distance between any two end-nodes in each VS-Cluster is less than or equal β physical hops. The distance between playing points of any two vertices in the VS-Cluster is less than α (segmentation parameter). The number of logical hops between any vertices in VS-Cluster is bounded by μ.*

Definition 2 (VS-Cluster): *The VS-cluster is defined by a subset of nodes which are mutually playing same video and the differences between their playing points are less than α.*

Definition 3: *The size, |VS| of a VS-Cluster VS is the number of nodes in VS.*

The 3-tiers architecture of *VON* is shown in Figure 2 and will be explained as follows. It is composed of multiple VS-Clusters VS_k; $k=1,...,\omega$ in level 1. Each VS_k has a *supervisor* node called s_k. For pair of peers $i,j \in VS_k$ the distance between their playing point positions is $|Pos_i - Pos_j| \leq \alpha$ where Pos_i and Pos_j is the playing position of peer i and peer j respectively as shown in Figure 2. The *distance* between two vertices i and j, $d(i, j)$, is the number of logical hops of a shortest path between i and j. Its maximum value over all pair of vertices, $D_\tau^{(k)}$ = *max* $\{d(i, j); \forall i, j \in VS_k\}$, is the *diameter* of the VS-Cluster VS_k at instance of time τ. Where $D_\tau^{(k)}$ is less than or equal the upper bound diameter μ. In case of the number of peers watching the same segment is large, the *VS-cluster* will be organized into multiple of *VS-clusters* based on β, and μ. For example, Figure 2 shows two *VS-Clusters* associated with each video segment S1 and S2. Level 2 contains Supervisor-Clusters *S-Clusters*. Each S-Cluster contains the supervisor nodes of the *VS-Clusters* that shared the same video segment. The supervisor nodes elect a node to be a *super-supervisor*. The number of the *VS-Clusters* in level one is denoted by ω. In level 3 a cluster that contains all super-supervisor nodes is constructed and called Super-Supervisors-Cluster *SS-Cluster* as shown in Figure 2.

VON Node Architecture

Each *VON* node has a unique identifier. Such as its IP address and maintains a membership list containing the list of identifiers of its neighbors. We adopt pull-based technique to avoid redundancy, as *VON* node pulls video timeslots from other nodes only if it does not already hold it. For that reason, each *VON* node maintains a set of nodes (partners), and periodically exchange video timeslots availability information with the partners. Figure 3 demonstrates the *VON* node architecture. It has three main modules: (1) *Membership module*, which helps the *VON* node to maintain a list of neighbors in its *VS-Cluster*. It will be called when new nodes join, others leave; (2) *Discover module*, which enables a *VON* node to discover other nodes that cache the required video timeslots to play. It has dual functions: send and receive video timeslots requests; (3) *Scheduler module*, which schedules the transmission of video timeslots. Each *VON* node can be either receiver, supplier, or both depending dynamically on this video timeslots availability.

This chapter proposes three algorithms as follows. First, the *VON* step-step construction scheme that organizes the overlay network into clusters. Second, the discover-to-exchange algorithm that

Figure 2. Video overlay network architecture

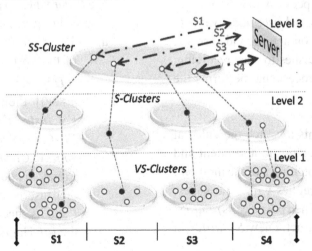

Figure 3. VON architecture

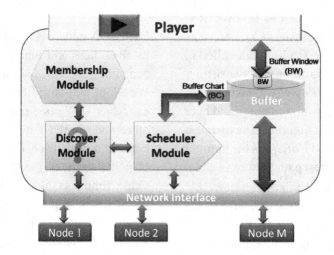

supports the video on-demand. Finally, the video streaming algorithm that supports the live video streaming.

VON Step by Step Construction Scheme

This section broaches the step by step self-construction algorithm for *VON*. A video broadcasting system typically has a single dedicated video source, which is assumed not to fail. The address of the source is known in advance, serving as a rendezvous for new end-users to join the video streaming session. The video server maintains the list of super-supervisor peers, which are located in *SS-Cluster*. When an end-user node wants to watch certain video, it contacts the video server with the position ρ it wishes to start receiving. It calls *Join_VON(ρ)* process that performs the following steps.

1. If new peer *X* wants to watch the video at certain position belongs to a segment and no other peer is watching it at the moment, the video server replies with " no super-supervisor peer". Then peer *X* calls *join(SS-Cluster)* and construct a new *S-Cluster* in

level 2 as shown in Figure 4. It also constructs a new *VS-Cluster*, *VS₇* as shown in Figure 4. Finally, the video server starts to broadcast the contents of the video segment S_5 to node *X*. The number of supervisor peers in *S-Clusters*, ω increases by one. For example, in figure *4* the node *X* becomes a supervisor peer of the new *VS-Cluster VS₇*. This new *VS-Cluster* is denoted by $VS_{\omega+1}$

2. Otherwise new node *Y* wants to watch the video at certain position ρ belongs to a segment and there is some peers watching the same segment, then the video server finds a super-supervisor peer *say, H* of the *S-Cluster* where ρ position held in its video segment (e.g. S_4) as shown in Figure 4.

a. The peer *H* is also the supervisor of the *VS-Cluster VS₅*. It checks if [$\left(\left(D_{\tau}^{(j)}+1\right)\leq\mu\right)$ and *(d(Y, tⱼ)* ≤*r;* δ*=2r)*] then node *H* calls *Join_VSCluster(VSⱼ)* process to join the *VS-Cluster VSⱼ* (e.g. *j=5*). The *Join_VSCluster(VSⱼ)* process chooses χ random nodes $m_l \in VS_j$;*(l=1,...,χ)*and then inserts node *X* between each node l_i and its successor node $(m_l \rightarrow n_s^{(i)})$ in the *i-th* Hamilton Cycle *(HC)* similar to our previous work in (K. Ragab, et. al. 2004).

b. Otherwise, if $[d(Y, t_j) > r$ or $\left(\left(D_\tau^{(j)} + 1 \right) > \mu \right)]$, the supervisor node H broadcasts a join request message in the *S-Cluster* and then waits *time-out* σ period for a reply from any supervisor peer in the *S-Cluster*. There are two cases:

1. No response is received within the time-out interval σ, then node Y creates its own new *VS-Cluster* and becomes a supervisor peer. The number of supervisor peer (*S-Clusters*) ω increases by one. For example, node Y becomes a supervisor peer of the new *VS-Cluster VS_8*.

2. If H receives multiple of replies then it selects the t_s with the smallest distance to X where $d(Y, t_s) \leq r$, $\left(\left(D_\tau^{(s)} + 1 \right) \leq \mu \right)$ and the minimum $|VS_s|_\tau$. Then node Y calls *Join_VSCluster(VS_s)* process to join the *VS-Cluster VS_s*. For example, node Y joins VS_6 as shown in Figure 4.

Discover-to-Exchange Algorithm

Each *VON* node needs to carry out the following *discover-to-exchange (D2E)* algorithm to discover the other *VON* nodes that buffered the following video minute to play. This section illustrates the D2E algorithms as follows:

1. Periodically, the scheduler module at *VON* node (e.g. *X*) finds out what the next video timeslots (minute) to play and emits signal to the discover module to discover the others *VON* nodes in its *VS-Cluster* that hold the required video timeslots.

2. The discover module at *X* creates a request message as shown in Figure 5. It contains IP of node X and movie identifier (*MID*), index of the current minute (*ICM*) and index of the requested minute (*IRM*).

3. As soon as, the discover module acquires the neighbors list of node *X* from the membership module, it sends out the request message to the *X* neighbors.

4. The discover module at each *VON* node (e.g. *Y*) received the request message. To avoid duplication it autonomously monitors the received request message to forward only

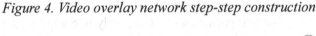

Figure 4. Video overlay network step-step construction

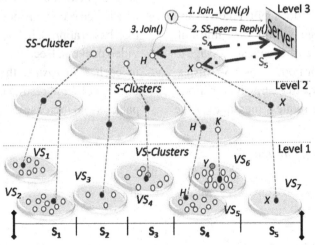

one copy of the duplicated received ones as follows:

a. If *VON* node *Y* does not receive such request message before it forwards it to its schedule module.

b. Otherwise, *Y* omits the received request message.

5. Then, the schedule module at *Y* checks if the index of the required video timeslots with certain movie ID is located in its buffer chart (*BC*) or not. There are two cases as follows:

a. If the required video timeslots is maintained at *VON* node *Y*, then the schedule module coordinates with the discover module to forward its IP to the requester node (*X*).

b. Otherwise, the discover module at *Y* obtains its neighbor list and then forwards the request message to its neighbor *VON* nodes within its *VS-Cluster*.

6. The discover module at the requester *VON* node *X* waits for a *time-out* to receive reply message(s) containing the IP address of the *VON* node(s) that maintain the required video minute. In fact there are two cases as follows:

a. *VON* node *X* collects the received reply and selects the most closest node to download the required video minute. Then, it downloads the required video minute.

b. Otherwise, *X* does not receive any reply message within the time-out, then it forwards the request message to the supervisor node of its *VS-Cluster*. Accordingly, the supervisor node forwards the request message to the

super-supervisor node in *SS-Cluster*. Then, the super-supervisor node downloads the required video minute from the video server and forwards it to the supervisor node that consequently forwards it to the *VON* node *X*. turn

Video Broadcast Process

The video server broadcasts video segments to the super-supervisor peers in *SS-Cluster*, who in turn broadcast to the other peers in *VON* as follows:

1. The membership module at each super-supervisor node determines its neighbors in *S-Cluster*. Then, it forwards the neighbors list to the scheduler modules at peer *H* that broadcasts the video packet *p* to this neighbors list in *S-Cluster*, who in turn broadcast *p* to all their neighbors, except the neighbor form which it was received.

2. When a supervisor peer receives the packet *p*, then it broadcasts this packet to its neighbors in the *VS-Cluster*.

3. This application level-multicast process goes on till the message packet *p* reaches all nodes in *VON*.

In this process, the schedule module of each node/supervisor autonomously monitors the received packets to forward only one copy of the duplicated received ones. It can use data-driven or tree-based approaches to schedules and broadcasts video packets. Because of the existence of cycles in each *VS-Cluster*, the dissemination process floods *VON* and results in many duplicated video packets that increase the network traffic. This dis-

Figure 5. Request message format

IP	MID	ICM	IRM

semination process shows insignificant impacts on network traffic if the disseminated data size is small. On the other hand, video dissemination shows significant impacts on network traffic when disseminating video packets on *VON* because each *VS-Cluster* includes cycles. Thus, it is required to build a *Minimum Spanning Tree* (*MST*) over each *VS-Cluster* to avoid the duplicated packets and reduce the network traffic. *MST* is a well-known combinatorial problem with a rich history (R.L. Graham, Pavol Hell, (1985) and is one of the most widely studied distributed problems for its theoretical and practical implications. Building MST for *VS-Cluster* is out the scope of this chapter and it needs further investigations.

VON FAULT-TOLERANCE

a. *VON Node Leave*: When *VON* node X decides to leave the *VS-Cluster*, it notifies its neighbors and then creates an edge between its successor and predecessor *VON* nodes in each clockwise *i-th HC* as follows.

right_neighbor$^{(i)}$ = X-> $n_p^{(i)}$;

left_neighbor$^{(i)}$ = X-> $n_s^{(i)}$;

right_neighbor$^{(i)}$-> $n_s^{(i)}$ = left_neighbor$^{(i)}$;

left_neighbor$^{(i)}$-> $n_p^{(i)}$ = right_neighbor$^{(i)}$;

Obviously, the leave process requires only local changes in the network with $O(\chi)$ messages (K. Ragab, Et. al. 2004).

b. *VON Node Failure*: It is also required to consider the difficult case of *VON* node failure. For fault-tolerance, we assume that each *VON* node knows the predecessor of its predecessor node and the successor of its successor node in each cycle. The node failure is detected locally as follows. The neighboring nodes of the failed node X, periodically exchange keep-alive mes-

sages with node X. If node X is unresponsive for a period γ, it is presumed that it was failed. Thus, each neighbor node sets

right_neighbor$^{(i)}$-> $n_s^{(i)}$ =

right_neighbor$^{(i)}$-> $n_s^{(i)}$-> $n_s^{(i)}$

left_neighbor$^{(i)}$-> $n_p^{(i)}$ =

left_neighbor$^{(i)}$-> $n_p^{(i)}$-> $n_p^{(i)}$

for each *i-th HC*. This fault-tolerance process connects two *VON* nodes around the failed node in the same cycle and sets the predecessor and successor nodes to its predecessor and successor. It maintains the *HC*. This technique scales well: fault detection is done by exchanging messages among small number of *VON* nodes, and recovery from faults is local; only a small number of nodes (2χ) are involved. In addition, this technique maintains the *VS-Cluster* composed of disjoint HC. If a Hamilton path connects every two nodes of G then G is *Hamilton-connected* (J. A. Bondy and U.S. R. Murty, 1976). Thus, the network is (connected) non partition-able; to guarantee this, we constructed *HC* with ($|VS_s|_\tau \geq 5$). For example if we construct the *VS-Cluster* as 4-regular, 4-connected graph, then it should have two edges-disjoint HC (Tutte W.T., 1956).

c. *supervisor node Leave*: When a supervisor node wants to leave. It selects one of its neighbors in *S-Cluster* randomly to act instead of it after it leaves.

d. *supervisor node Failure*: Periodically, the neighbors of the supervisor node s_j exchange keep-alive messages with s_j to detect its failure. When s_j fails then one from its neighbors becomes a supervisor node. Then this new supervisor node sends join request to the *S-Cluster*. In addition, in the *S-Cluster*, the neighbors of the failed s_j detect its fail and then remove their links to s_j and wait for new supervisor node to join instead. A small number of nodes (3χ) are involved in the supervisor node fault tolerant process.

The details discussion and evaluation of the proposed fault-tolerance are out the scope of this paper. For more details please refer to (K. Ragab, Et. al. 2004).

CONCLUSION

This chapter presents an overview of the video streaming applications and introduces taxonomy of video streaming systems. Moreover, it presents a novel overlay network construction technique. This technique organizes the overlay network into 3-tier architecture of clusters. It clusters the *VON* into *VS-Clusters* based on three parameters (*number of physical links, logical diameter, and sharing video segment*). Implementing and maintaining these parameters improves the performance of video on-demand and video dissemination. Currently, we are studying these parameters carefully through real developments and simulations.

REFERENCES

Akamai (2007). *Akamai Technologies Inc.* Retrieved from www.akamai.com

Bondy, J. A., & Murty, U. S. R. (1976). *Graph Theory with Applications*. New York: Macmilliam Press Ltd.

Castro, M., et al. (2003). SplitStream: High-bandwidth multicast in cooperative environments. In *Proceedings of ACM SOSP '03*. New York.

Chawathe, Y. (2000). *Scattercast: An Architecture for Internet Broadcast Distribution as an Infrastructure Service*. (Ph.D Thesis). Univ. of California, Berkeley.

Chu, Y. H., et al. (2000). A case for end system multicast. In *Proceedings of ACM Sigmetrics*.

ComScore. (2009). *ComScore measuring the digital world*. Retrieved from http://www.comscore.com

Deering, D. (1988) Multicast Routing in Internetworks and Extended LANs. In *Proceedings of the ACM SIGCOMM*.

Deering, S. (1991). *Multicasting routing in a datagram internetwork* (Ph.D. dissertation). Stanford University, California.

Eugster, P., Guerraoui, R., Kermarrec, A. M., & Massoulie, L. (2004). From epidemics to distributed computing, IEEE Computer. *Accustream iMedia Research Homepage*. Retrieved 2009, from http://www.accustreamsearch.com

Francis, P. (1999). *YOID: Extending the Multicast Architecture*. White paper. Retrieved from http://www.aciri.org/yoid

Google video. (n.d.). *Google video*. Retrieved from http://http://video.google.com/

Lazar, I., & Terrill, W. (2001). Exploring Content Delivery Networking. *IT Professional*, *3*(4), 47–49. doi:10.1109/6294.946620

Lobb, R. J., Couto da Silva, A. P., Leonardi, E., Mellia, M., & Meo, M. (2009). *Adaptive overlay topology for mesh-based P2P-TV systems*. Retrieved from http://www.informatik.uni-trier.de/~ley/db/conf/nossdav/nossdav2009.html#LobbSLMM09

Magharei, N., & Rasti, A. H. (2007). Prime: Peer-to-peer receiver-driven mesh-based streaming. In *Proceedings of IEEE INFOCOM*.

Padmanabhan, V. N. (2002). *Distributing Streaming Media Content Using Cooperative Networking*. Miami Beach, FL: ACM NOSSDAV.

Pathan, M., & Buyya, R. (2008). *A Taxonomy of CDNs", Content Delivery Networks*. Berlin, Germany: Springer-Verlag.

Pendarakis, D. (2001). ALMI: an application level multicast infrastructure. In *Proceedings of the 3rd Symposium on USITS.*

Ragab, K. (2004). *Autonomous Decentralized Community Communication Technology for Assuring Information Dissemination,* (Ph.D. Thesis). Tokyo Institute of Technology.

Ragab, K. (2004). Autonomous Decentralized Community Communication for Information Dissemination. *IEEE Internet Computing Magazine, 8*(3), 29–36. doi:10.1109/MIC.2004.1297271

Ragab, K., & Mori, K. (2004). ACIS-Hierarchy: Enhancing Community Communication Delay for Large-Scale Information Systems. *IEICE Trans. on Communication, E87-B*, N(7)

Ratnasamy, S., et al. (2001). A Scalable Content- Addressable Network. In *Proceedings of SIGCOMM'01.* California, USA.

Shan, Y., & Kalyanaraman, S. (2003). *Hybrid Video "Downloading/Streaming Over Peer-to-Peer Networks.* In *Proceedings of the Int. Conf. on Multimedia and Expo* (ICME), (pp. 665–668). Baltimore, MD.

Songqing, L. G., et al. (2004). PROP: a Scalable and Reliable P2P Assisted Proxy Streaming System. In *Proceedings of the Int. Conf. on Distributed Computing Systems* (ICDCS'04).

Tutte, W. T. (1956). A Theorem on Planner graphs. *Transactions of the American Mathematical Society, 82*, 99–116. doi:10.2307/1992980

Youtube. (n.d.). *Youtube.* Retrieved from http://www.youtube.com/

Zhang, B., & Hussein, T. M. (2003). Forwarding state scalability for multicast provisioning in IP networks. In IEEE Communications Magazine, 46–51.

Zhang, X., Liu, J., Li, B., & Yum, T.-S. P. (2005). DONet/CoolStreaming: A data-driven overlay network for live media streaming. In *Proceedings of INFOCOM'05.* Miami, FL.

Zhuang, S. Q., et al. (2001). Bayeux: An architecture for scalable and fault-tolerant wide-area data dissemination. In *Proceedings of NOSSDAV'01.* New York.

ENDNOTE

[1] A codec is a computer program capable of encoding and/or decoding a digital data stream. The word *codec* is a portmanteau of 'compressor-decompressor' or, more accurately, 'coder-decoder'.

Section 4
Web Service Applications

Chapter 12
Web Services for Quality of Service Based Charging

Evelina Pencheva
Technical University of Sofia, Bulgaria

Ivaylo Atanasov
Technical University of Sofia, Bulgaria

ABSTRACT

Parlay X is a set of Web Service interfaces. These interfaces are designed to provide open access to telecommunication network functions in order to hide underlying network technology, and its control protocol complexity, from application developers. The Parlay X "intelligence" is concentrated in a node called Parlay X Gateway which converts interfaces methods in protocol messages and vice versa. An inherent constraint on any implementation requires the Parlay X Gateway to govern the interface to the underlying network i.e., to provide a single point of contact at which vertical signaling is received from the network. This chapter presents a study on alternatives for Parlay X Web Service deployment in Internet Protocol based multimedia networks (IMS). The focus is set on Parlay X Web Services for application-driven quality of service (QoS) management and charging control. It is presented as an analysis of the interfaces. Particularly the discussion is about their applicability to Policy and Charging Control architecture in IMS. Going further, the Web Service interfaces are mapped onto network protocols that they affect, namely Session Initiation Protocol (SIP) and Diameter. On that base an improvement is suggested concerning Parlay X interfaces for QoS management without violating the specified interface functionality. The usage of Web Services is exemplified with an application for charging control based on the provided QoS.

INTRODUCTION

The main motivation behind the definition of Internet Protocol Multimedia Subsystem (IMS) is to support provisioning of all kinds of multimedia services with session control for both mobile and fixed terminals. One of the main features of IMS is the secured open access to network functions through application programming interfaces (APIs) (Poikselka, et al., 2006). The service architecture

DOI: 10.4018/978-1-61520-973-6.ch012

defined for open access to functions in IMS is Parlay / Open Service Access (OSA). The Parlay/OSA APIs allow for 3rd party applications access to network functions such as call control, data session control, mobility, user interaction, charging etc. The network functionality offered to applications is defined as service capability features supported by Service Capability Servers (SCS).

The Parlay/OSA APIs expose telecommunication functions in a neutral way for both the network technology and the programming language aspects (Hanrahan, 2008). Having common programmability paradigm for mobile, fixed, and managed packet networks, the APIs provide a medium level of abstraction of the network capabilities. The APIs are an abstraction from different specific protocol stacks, but the abstraction level of Parlay/OSA APIs is not oriented to what we call traditional group of web developers and this could affect usability. In order to make the accessibility of the network capabilities available to a much wider audience Parlay X provides a set of high level interfaces that are oriented towards the skills of the web developers.

The Parlay X is the name standing for a set of interfaces allowing access to Parlay/OSA APIs via Web Services. In addition to being Web Services interfaces, the Parlay X interfaces are much simplified presentation of Parlay/OSA APIs (Chen, et. al., 2006). A typical Parlay X Web Services deployment model allows publication of Parlay X Web Services through a registry, making those Web Services available for discovery. The applications can use Web Services' access methods to interact with the Parlay X Gateway, where the Web Service interfaces are implemented.

There exist different deployment scenarios for Parlay X Web Services (Grønbæk, 2006). One possible scenario addresses solutions where the Parlay X functionality is an add-on to the Parlay/OSA functionality. Thus, the Parlay X Gateway is connected to OSA SCS through a Parlay/OSA interface, forming a kind of interface wrapping. The lower-level mapping between Parlay/OSA APIs and network protocols is defined in 3GPP TR 29.998 standards. Another scenario for Parlay X deployment addresses hybrid solutions which combine Web Services interfaces and network protocols. The Parlay X Gateway attaches to the network through an interface defined by the corresponding network element. These interfaces (i.e. element defined interface) are not in the scope of Parlay/OSA standardization. No direct mapping is defined between Parlay X and network control protocols.

The chapter presents a study on the functions of Parlay X Gateway which communicates with IMS network elements. The focus is set at one hand on IMS functions for policy and charging control and at the other hand on Parlay X Web Services for application-driven QoS management and payment control. The later means that any deployment of Parlay X applications requires translation between Parlay X interfaces and network protocols. Therefore such a mapping of Parlay X APIs onto IMS protocols is examined. First in the chapter comes a brief presentation of the IMS Policy and Charging Control (PCC) architecture. The PCC architecture encompasses two main functions: flow based charging, including charging control and online credit control, and policy control e.g. gating control, QoS control, QoS signaling, etc. The functionalities of "Application-driven QoS" and "Payment" Web Services are analyzed and the IMS signaling flows in which results the invocation of Web service operations are discussed. An enhancement of the "Application-driven QoS" Web Service is suggested without violating the standardized functionality of the Web Service. An approach is described as combination of these Web Services in order to create a Parlay X Application for online payment that takes into account the QoS provided to the end user.

BACKGROUND

Policy and Charging Control Architecture

The layered approach is widely adopted and applied in the design of IMS architecture in order to provide access independence and to separate the common multimedia session management functions from the way applications are implemented. The IMS consists of three separate planes: User plane, Control plane and Application plane (Poikselka, et al., 2006).

The User plane is composed of traffic carrying network elements like switches, routers, media gateways and access elements at the borders of the core network. The Policy and Charging Enforcement Function (PCEF) encompasses service data flow detection, policy enforcement and flow based charging functionality as specified in (3GPP TS 23.203, 2008). This PCEF is located at the media gateway. The media gateway is also responsible for user traffic handling, triggering the Control plane session management, QoS handling, and service data flow measurement as well as online and offline charging interactions.

The Control plane contains functions for session management and IP policy control.

The IP policy control encompasses mechanisms for authorization and control of bearer traffic intended for IMS media. The IP policy control is based on Diameter protocol which in turn is defined in (Calhoun et al., 2003). As to (3GPP TS 23.203, 2008) the Policy and Charging Rule Function (PCRF) encompasses IP policy control decision and flow based charging control functionality. It is responsible for finding routes in the network that meet requirements for given level of QoS. The PCRF provides network control regarding the service data flow detection, gating, QoS and flow based charging (except credit management) towards the PCEF via Diameter based interface as specified in (ETSI TS 183 017, 2008).

The session control, including management of dynamic inclusion/exclusion of elements in a session, relies on SIP signaling in conjunction with Session Description Protocol (SDP) as to (3GPP TS 24.229, 2008). The Call Session Control Functions (CSCFs) are common for a number of services and in addition to session control they manage the negotiation of QoS parameters for multimedia sessions. The Proxy-CSCF (P-CSCF) is the first point of contact for the user terminal in the IMS. It is responsible for the security of SIP signaling between the user and the IMS, and for the SIP compression. The P-CSCF communicates with the PCRF to allocate resources for media flows via Diameter based interface. The Serving-CSCF (S-SCFC) performs session control and registration of user terminals. The Home Subscriber Server (HSS) is a register that stores the user profiles. The HSS supports Diameter protocol.

The Application plane contains applications that extend network services by using call control, messaging, user interaction, user location and flexible charging. The Application Server (AS) delivers value-added services. If the S-CSCF determines that the AS must be involved into session, it delegates the session control to that AS. The interface between the S-CSCF and the AS is based on SIP. The Parlay X Gateway is a special type of AS that provides Parlay X interfaces for open access to network functions such as QoS management and charging control.

IMS supports both online and offline charging models as specified in (3GPP TS 32.260, 2008).

The Online Charging System (OCS) is responsible for the process in which the real time charging information can affect the service rendered and, therefore, directly interacts with session/service control. The IMS online charging capable entities send charging information to Online Charging Function (OCF) via Diameter based interface (3GPP TS 32.299, 2008). The OCF performs besides both event- and session-based charging, also credit control. The S-CSCF interacts with the OCF via IMS Gateway function (IMS-GWF).

The offline charging system supports the traditional charging model in which the charging information is collected over a particular period and, at the end of the period, it posts a bill to the customer's account. The IMS offline charging capable entities collect charging information and send it to the Charging Data Function (CDF) via Diameter. The CDF constructs the Call Detail Records (CDRs) and sends them to the billing system via Charging Gateway.

IMS functions that are involved in PCC and their interconnections are shown in Figure 1.

Open Access to Quality of Service Management

The necessity of open access to QoS management is substantiated in (Katchabaw, 2005). The (Elkotob, 2008) presents a protocol-based approach to resource management that supports QoS provisioning, where the collected information about the network is provided to external applications in a structurally standardized format. The (Vidal, 2006) suggests a solution in which the QoS management functions are delegated to a node monitoring the signaling interchange by the user equipment and the network. Open access to connectivity management functions is defined in the framework of Parlay/OSA "Connectivity Manager" API (3GPP TS 29.198-10, 2008). The Parlay/OSA "Connectivity Manager" provides configuration and control over the attributes of IP connectivity within and between IP domains. The "Connectivity Manager" interfaces may be used by an enterprise operator subscribed for Virtual Private Network (VPN) service that is already in a relationship with a VPN provider (network operator) to set up a provisioned QoS. The VPN provider may offer to the enterprise operator available templates with QoS parameters for different services, e.g. video conferencing, audio streaming,

Figure 1. IMS entities involved in policy and charging control

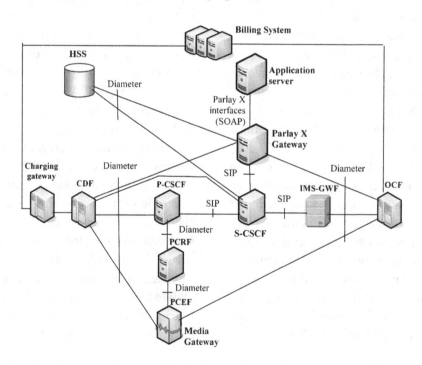

etc. The Parlay/OSA "Connectivity Manager" is more of operation support nature than real time control. In (Pencheva & Atanasov, 2009) an approach is presented to definition of Parlay/OSA compliant interfaces for resource management.

The "Application Driven QoS" Parlay X Web Service is defined in (3GPP 29.199-17, 2008). The Web Service allows applications to change dynamically the QoS available on end user connections. Configurable service attributes are upstream/downstream bandwidth rates, and other QoS features which are explicitly specified by the service provider. Changes in QoS may be applied either for a defined period of time, or each time a user connects to the network. The "Application-driven QoS" Web Service enables applications to register with the service for notifications about network events that affect QoS temporary configured on the end user connection. On such event occurrence the service notifies the applications.

The deployment of "Application-driven QoS" Web Service in IMS requires implementation of Parlay X Gateway which "talks" SIP and Diameter protocols on the network side. When the Application requests change of the default QoS features, an update of user profile data in the HSS takes place and consequently data in the CSCFs and PCRF are updated. To affect an ongoing connection the Application requests temporary QoS feature to be applied. In this case the Parlay X Gateway in a role of Back-to-Back User Agent initiates SIP requests to the parties involved in the session to update the session QoS parameters and the CSCFs report the session modification to the PCRF which in turn authorizes the QoS resources and enforces policy decisions. If the Application is subscribed for specific QoS event types on user connections, the PCRF reports the event when it occurs in the network.

Open Access to Charging Control

The open access to charging control allows external applications to charge for the usage of the applications. The charged user can be the same user as the one used the application. It is also possible that another user has to be charged. Applications can debit or credit amounts and/or units towards a user, create and extend the lifetime of a reservation and get information about the rest of the reservation. The (Bormann, et al., 2006) presents convergent online rating charging and billing mechanism for content-aware mobile service offered by 3rd party Service Provider. The open access to charging control is defined in the framework of Parlay/OSA Charging API specified in (3GPP TS 29.198-12, 2008). The "Charging" API allows both online and offline charging. Similarly to the other OSA interfaces the "Charging" API relies on a large, rich set of data types, that must be well understood by application programmers. It is very rich in methods that operate at a level of abstraction which hides network details but requires detailed control of calls, messaging and database operations.

The Parlay X "Payment" Web Service is defined in (3GPP 29.199-6, 2009). The Web Service supports both pre-paid and post-paid payments. It supports charging of both volume and currency amounts, a conversion function and a settlement function in case of a financially resolved dispute. The Application's requests to charge the user result in Diameter dialogs between the Parlay X Gateway and the CDF. The CDF receives charging information and constructs detailed call records. In case of online charging the Application performs credit control before usage of IMS service/resources. Two different models are supported: direct debiting and unit reservation. The direct debiting model is appropriate when the Application knows that it could deliver the requested service to the user itself. The unit reservation model is suitable when the Application is unable to determine beforehand whether the service could be delivered or when the required number of resources is not known prior the use of specific service (e.g. duration of video call). The Application's requests for online charging control start Diameter dialogues between the Parlay X Gateway and the OCF. The OCF is responsible for interacting in real time with the user's account and for controlling or monitoring the charges related to service usage.

In the next section we present different signaling scenarios concerning the deployment of the Parlay X Web Services in IMS.

PARLAY X WEB SERVICES FOR POLICY AND CHARGING CONTROL

"Application-Driven Quality of Service" Web Service Deployment in IMS

The "Application-driven QoS" Parlay X Web service provides three interfaces, namely ApplicationQoS, ApplicationQoSNotificationManager and ApplicationQoSNotification.

The ApplicationQoS interface allows dynamic changes of QoS available on an end user connection. Changes in QoS features driven by Parlay X Applications result in authorization, modification or release of QoS resources as a part of PCC. The interface provides operations for permanent change in class of service provided over the end user connections in case of rapidly provisioning re-grade. The user data stored in HSS has to be updated when changing the default QoS parameters. The user profile in the CSCFs and the PCRF also need to be updated in order to maintain a consistence view for the related subscription profile and to make resulting PCC decisions. The ApplicationQoS interface provides operations for dynamic control on temporary QoS parameters in the network which will be active for a specified period of time. By using the operations of the interfaces it is possible to modify or release temporary QoS parameters currently set as active on user connections.

The Application can change the default QoS available on the end user's connection using applyQoSFeature operation. Then Parlay X Gateway

opens a Diameter session with the HSS in order to update the user profile and issues Profile-Update-Request (PUR) Diameter command. The HSS stores the updated user profile and answers with Profile-Update-Answer (PUA). To update data in the S-CSCF the HSS initiates a Push-Profile-Request (PPR) Diameter command. The S-CSCF acknowledges the PPR command by Push-Profile-Answer (PPA) command, which indicates the result of the operation. If requested by the PCRF, the HSS notifies the PCRF for the changed profile by opening another Diameter session to push immediately the changes by using Diameter PPR and PRA commands also.

To monitor the temporary changed QoS features on a specific user connection, the Application can register its interest in receiving notifications of specific QoS event types related to the end user. The ApplicationQoSNotificationManager interface is used by the Application to manage its registration for notifications. The interface operations allow the Application to subscribe for receiving notifications of specific QoS event types in the context of specific user and to stop receiving notifications by canceling existing subscription. The ApplicationQoSNotification provides operations for notifying the Application about the impact of certain events on QoS interface features that were active on the end user connection when these events occurred. Having active subscription PCEF opens a Diameter session for reporting QoS events with the PCRF. When a particular QoS event occurs, the PCRF delivers a report and thus the Application is notified. The subscription for and notification of QoS events in the network is performed by means of SIP signaling. The PCEF reports events related to QoS resources to PCRF, which in turn sends the reports to the Application via the CSCF and Parlay X Gateway.

The SIP protocol supports a generic mechanism for subscription to and notification of events. Being an AS the Parlay X Gateway uses the mechanism to manage its registrations to Dialog Event Package. This event package is for INVITE-initiated dialog usages where dialogs refer to the SIP relationship established between two SIP peers (Rosenberg, 2005).

When the Application requests monitoring for QoS events, the Parlay X Gateway opens a SUBSCRIBE dialog with the S-CSCF. The Event header field of the SUBSCRIBE method contains the dialog identifiers, and a notification is generated every time there is a change in the state of any matching dialog for the user identified in the SUBSCRIBE method. The requested QoS information may be transferred in the SUBSCRIBE method body and defines a filter to be applied to the subscription. The Parlay X Gateway sends a SUBSCRIBE method setting the Expires header field set to 0 in order to terminate the subscription. When a QoS event occurs in the network the PCEF opens a Diameter session with P-CSCF/PCRF to report the event. Consequently the P-CSCF sends a NOTIFY message to report the event occurrence to the S-CSCF. Finally, the S-CSCF forwards the message to the Parlay X Gateway which has to notify the Application about the event.

Figure 2 illustrates the way in which the Application affects an ongoing media session. In this scenario the Parlay X Gateway is in a role of Back-to-Back User Agent. When the Application requests to apply a new temporary QoS feature on an existing connection or to modify an active QoS available on the user connection, the Parlay X Gateway sends re-INVITE requests to the parties involved in the session. The requested QoS parameters are described in the SDP media description information. On receiving the re-INVITE request the CSCF communicates with the PCRF to authorize the QoS resources. The P-CSCF sends the relevant SDP information to the PCRF together with the indication of the originator. For this purpose Diameter commands are utilized. The PCRF notes and authorizes the IP flow of the chosen media components by mapping from SDP parameters to authorized QoS parameters.

The signaling message flow is as follows:

1. The Application requests a temporary QoS to be set up on the end user connection.
2. The Diameter agent in the Parlay X Gateway requests user data update in the HSS by sending Profile-Update-Request (PUR).
3. The temporary QoS feature is stored in the user profile.
4. The HSS initiates immediate change of the user data in the CSCF by sending Push-Profile-Request (PPR).
5. The CSCF stores the updated user data.
6. The CSCF acknowledges the PPR by Push-Profile-Answer (PPA), which indicates the result of the operation.
7. If requested by the PCRF, the HSS notifies the PCRF on the changed profile.
8. The PCRF stores the updated profile and makes resulting PCC decisions. The PCRF provides all new PCC decisions to the PCEF (not shown in the figure).
9. The PCRF responds to the HSS.
10. The HSS responds with Profile-Update-Answer (PUA).
11. After the user profile has been changed, the ongoing connection has to be affected. The SIP agent in the Parlay X Gateway initiates new INVITE requests to the CSCFs of parties involved in session. The SDP session description reflects the requested changes in the QoS parameters.
12. The P-CSCF receives the SDP parameters defined by the Application within the SDP offer and identifies the relevant changes in the SDP.
13. The P-CSCF forwards the SDP offer in SIP signaling.
14. The P-CSCF gets the negotiated SDP parameters from the terminating side through SIP signaling interaction. The P-CSCF identifies the relevant changes in the SDP

Figure 2. Parlay X application changes temporary QoS parameters on an existing user connection

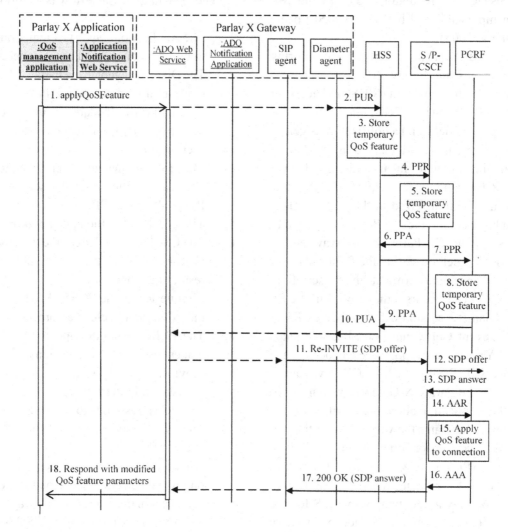

and sends a Diameter AA-Request for an existing Diameter session including the derived updated service information.

15. The P-CSCF interacts with the PCEF to enforce the PCC rules. The PCRF sends a Diameter Re-Auth-Request (RAR) to the PCEF to open/close the "gate" by updating the PCC rules. The PCEF opens the "gate" and enable the use of the authorized resources. The PCEF sends a Diameter Re-Auth-Answer (RAA) back to the PCRF.

16. The PCRF stores the received updated session information and answers with a Diameter AA-Answer.

17. The P-CSCF forwards the SDP answer in SIP signaling.

18. The result of the requested temporary change is reported to the Application.

In case of temporary change of QoS parameters in the user profile, when the duration elapses, the HSS initiates new Diameter sessions with the CSCFs and the PCRF in order to remove the updates and to recover the original information in the user data. After that the Application is notified by the Parlay X Gateway that the temporary QoS feature that was active on end user connection has been released.

Figure 3 shows the way in which the Application manages registrations for notifications about temporary changed QoS features. The signaling flow for this scenario is as follows:

1. The Application registers its interest in receiving notifications of specific QoS event types related to a specific end user.
2. The Parlay X in a role of Application Server subscribes for receiving QoS event types with the CSCFs.
3. The P-CSCF opens a new Diameter session with the PCRF and uses AA-Request (AAR) command to subscribe for reporting the QoS events.

4. The PCRF performs session binding and identifies corresponding PCC rules related to IMS signaling. The PCRF confirms the subscription to QoS events and replies with a Diameter AA-Answer (AAA) back to the P-CSCF. If the PCRF had not previously subscribed to the requested QoS events from the PCEF for the affected PCC rules, then the PCRF sends Diameter Re-Auth-Request (RAR) to the PCEF in order to do so now. The PCEF confirms the subscription to QoS events and replies with Diameter Re-Auth-Answer (RAA) back to the PCRF. This interaction between PCRF and PCEF is not shown in the figure.
5. The P-CSCF acknowledges the subscription.
6. The Application is informed about successful registration for QoS event notifications.
7. A specific QoS event related to the temporary active QoS parameters (for example release of bearer) occurs in the network.

Figure 3. Parlay X application subscribes for QoS event types, receives notifications and terminates the subscription

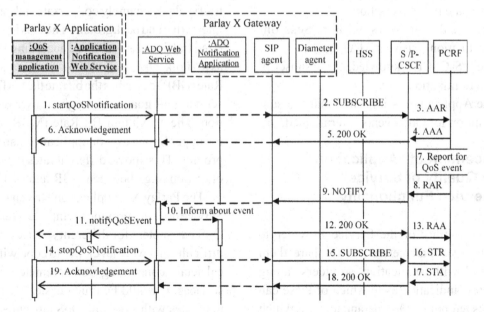

8. The PCEF sends Diameter Credit-Control-Request (CCR) indicating the event. The PCRF identifies the affected IP flow and acknowledges the event by sending a Diameter Credit-Control-Answer (CCA). The PCRF indicates the event by sending a Diameter RAR to the P-CSCF.

9. The P/S-CSCF sends a SIP NOTIFY message to report the event.

10. The event is forwarded to the Application-driven QoS Notification Application.

11. The Application is notified.

12. The SIP agent in the Parlay X Gateway acknowledges the notification.

13. The P-CSCF responds by sending Diameter RAA to the PCRF.

14. The Application may cancel the subscription to QoS event notifications. When the Application decides to terminate the notifications it invokes stopQoSNotification operation.

15. The SIP agent in the Parlay X Gateway sends a SUBSCIBE message with Expire header field equal to 0.

16. The P-CSCF uses a Session-Termination-Request (STR) command to the PCRF to terminate the subscription.

17. The PCRF answers with a Session-Termination-Answer (STA).

18. The P/S-CSCF acknowledges the subscription termination.

19. The Application is informed that the subscription for QoS events is terminated.

Enhancement of "Application-Driven Quality of Service" Web Service Functionality

It is responsibility of the Service Provider to define the QoS parameters and to share them beforehand with application providers, along with a clear indication as to which of these can be used as temporary QoS parameters and which can be used to set a default QoS on an end user

connection. XML schema data type definitions for "Application-driven QoS" describe among the others a structure with configurable properties related to the QoS. The QoSFeatureProperties structure contains elements Duration, UpStreamSpeedRate and DownStreamSpeedRate. It is possible to define additional configurable properties related to the QoS parameters specified by the Service Provider. These additional QoS parameters may be specific for the underlying network. The detailed description of the QoS parameters can be found in (3GPP TS 23.107, 2008).

From the PCC point of view, the QoS parameters that present interesting values include the following:

- Traffic class
- Guaranteed bit rate for uplink
- Guaranteed bit rate for downlink
- Maximum bit rate for uplink
- Maximum bit rate for downlink

The Traffic class describes the type of application for which the bearer service is optimized. For example, in Universal Mobile Telecommunication Service (UMTS) network there are four different traffic classes namely conversational, streaming, interactive and background. The maximum authorized traffic class is derived according to Table 1, as to (Poikselka, et al., 2006). The Guaranteed Bit Rate (GBR) describes the bit rate the UMTS bearer service will guarantee to given user or application. The Maximum Bit Rate (MBR) describes the upper limit a user or application can accept or provide. This allows different rates to be used for operation (e.g., between GBR and MBR).

The Parlay X "Application Driven QoS" Web Service does not provide a template interface with QoS parameters for different services. It may be difficult for a web developer to cope with technical details concerning QoS parameters of various services. It would be much easier to have filled templates with available QoS attributes oriented to specific multimedia services.

Table 1. UMTS traffic classes per media type

Media type	Traffic class
Bidirectional audio or video	Conversational
Unidirectional audio or video	Streaming
Application	Conversational
Data	Interactive
Control	Interactive
Others	Background

A possible enhancement of the Parlay X "Application Driven QoS" interfaces might specify different configurations of values for the requested QoS parameters in set of templates. Following the Parlay/OSA "Connectivity Manager" approach two new interfaces – QoS template interface and QoS menu interface might be defined. The QoS menu interface will provide a list of filled templates, each of which specifies the QoS parameters that are offered by the Service Provider. The template interface is used to specify the value of service parameters that are offered by the Service Provider, and can be selected by the client, in this case this is the web developer, for service configuration. Each QoS service offered (e.g. Interactive) is specified in a separate template.

The Service Provider may offer a set of templates e.g. for video call, audio conferencing, video streaming etc. Using the templates the client specifies the QoS parameters for user connections. The access to the available QoS templates might be through the QoSMenu interface which holds the QoS menu offered by the Service Provider. The

QoSMenu interfaces support operations used to get reference to give specific template and to get a list of templates, each of which specifies QoS parameters. The QoSTemplate interface provides "get" operation to discover QoS details and to browse the available QoS parameter values or limits within which the parameter value can vary. Each service template parameter is tagged by the Service Provider to indicate the value which cannot or can be modified for the template, and the value that is not applicable to this template. The interface operations are summarized in Table 2.

"Payment" Web Service Deployment in IMS

The "Payment" Web Service provides two interfaces for offline charging and two interfaces for online charging.

The AmountCharging interface provides charging operations by currency amount, while the VolumeCharging interface provides charging operations by volume. These interfaces can be used for post-paid charging. Both session- and event-based charging are supported. A chargeable trigger could be session initiation, session modification, session termination request, i.e. session-based or it could be based on any SIP transaction – e.g. MESSAGE, PUBLISH, SUBSCRIBE requests i.e. event-based charging. After receiving non-session related request (for example, PUBLISH) the P-CSCF collects necessary information from the request and constructs an Accounting-Request

Table 2. Interface operations for access to templates with predefined QoS parameters

Interface	Operation	Operation description
QoSTemplate	getTemplateDescription	Used to get the template type e.g. Conversational, Streaming, Interactive or Background and the description of the QoS parameters stored in this template type.
QoSMenu	getTemplate	Used to get an interfaces reference to a specific template that contains all the QoS parameters for this template (e.g. Conversational).
QoSMenu	getTemplateList	Used to get a list of templates, each of which specifies QoS parameters, such as Conversational or Streaming.

(ACR) Diameter command to indicate event-based charging. As a result of ACR the CDF knows to apply event-based charging, generates appropriate CDR and transfers it to the P-CSCF. In case of multimedia session, three ACR requests are sent: upon session initiation, upon session modification and upon session release. The ACR request at the moment of session initiation prompts the CDF to open a CDR, the ACR request at session modification triggers change of charging information, and the last ACR request at the session termination forces creation of a single CDR including total session time.

The ReserveAmountCharging and ReserveVolumeCharging are interfaces that provide operations to manage reservation charging by currency and volume amount respectively. These interfaces are used for online charging. The online charging performs credit control before any usage of IMS services/resources. In direct debiting, the CSCF contacts the OCF and asks permission to grant the usage of services/resources. In the unit reservation model the OCF receives a credit control request from the CSCF, determines the tariff and price, reserves a suitable amount of money and returns the corresponding number of resources to the CSCF. When resources granted to the user have been consumed, or the service has been successfully delivered, or terminated, the CSCF informs the OCF of the number of resources consumed. Finally, the OCF deducts the used amount from the user's account. Figure 4 illustrates both charging schemes.

The leftmost part of Figure 4 shows an example of event-based offline charging. The "Payment" interfaces are always used in the context of delivered Web Service e.g. "Multimedia Messaging". When the Application using "Multimedia Messaging" and "Payment" Web Service is notified that the message has been delivered, which is not shown in the figure, it opens a Diameter session which forces sending charging information to the CDF. The rightmost part of the Figure 4 shows the Application control over the volume-based online

charging. The Application may use for example "Audio call" and "Payment" to apply volume based online charging control on a multimedia call. On call initiation, for brevity not show in the figure, the Application requests charging reservation by volume, say for 5 minutes. A Diameter credit control session is opened to reserve the amount for specified units used for measuring the volume. If the call continues more than 5 minutes, the Application reserves additional amount for units which results in a new Diameter credit control session. On session termination, the Application requests to charge the reservation and to return the amount left in a reservation to the account.

In next section an approach is presented which aims to combine the "Application Driven QoS" and "Payment" Web services in order to provide QoS based charging control. The usage of the proposed enhancement of the "Application Driven QoS" Web Service is exemplified.

PARLAY X WEB SERVICES FOR QUALITY OF SERVICE BASED CHARGING

The Parlay X Web Service can be used to create an application for charging based on the provided QoS. The "Application Driven QoS" interfaces are used to apply the requested QoS parameters on the ongoing connection or to the subsequent connections when the end user next comes online. The "Application Driven QoS" interfaces are also used to register the Application's interest in receiving notifications of specific QoS event types and to receive reports on QoS event occurrence. The "Payment" interfaces are used for online or offline charging control which can depend on the provision of the requested QoS.

An example of such application could be a multimedia service. The "QoS-based charging" Application will charge the user on base of the provided QoS for an interactive game. An end user of a WiMAX service is playing an interactive game

Figure 4. Parlay X Application provides charging control: event-based offline charging on the left and volume-based online charging on the right

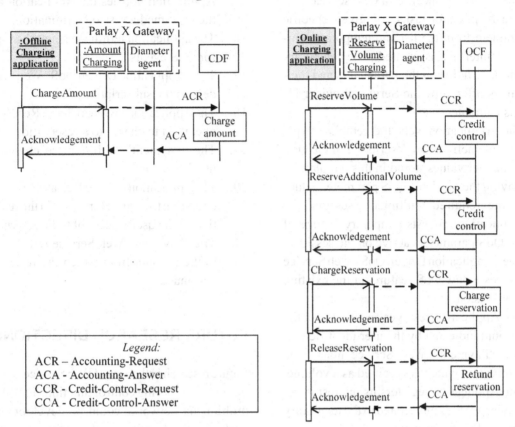

with a friend. During the game the user decides to make a video call while gaming to comment details on the game. The current service offering, e.g. 1 Mbps, does not allow simultaneous usage of video call and gaming and hence the user requires a temporary bit rate upgrade for the duration of the call, say to 2 Mbps. The "QoS-based charging" application requests from the "Application-driven QoS" Web service the list of filled templates with the QoS attributes offered by the Service Provider. After choosing an appropriate template the Application formulates the necessary QoS and then makes a request to the "Application-driven QoS" Web Service to apply new QoS feature to the end user connection, specifying the higher bit rate and the duration for which the temporary QoS feature should be applied. Assuming that the network can

provide the requested bit rate, the end user's rate is increased to the requested rate for the specified duration. The Application reserves the appropriate amount with the operator to ensure that the user can fulfill his payment obligation using the "Payment" Web Service. During the call while the user is gaming, the QoS provided goes down and this event is reported to the Application. The Application reduces the amount from the existing reservation and the rest of funds are returned. Once the game finishes and the call terminates the end user is charged to the reservation and the user service resumes to the original QoS. The sequence diagram for the above scenario shown in Figure 5 describes the following Web Service interactions:

1. The Application gets the list of templates, each of which specifies a QoS service.
2. The Application asks for given specific template from the list and temporary template interface is created. The temporary interface holds all the parameters and their values offered by the Service Provider for this template.
3. The Application gets the template type, e.g. Interactive, and description of the QoS parameter values stored in this template.
4. Having the available QoS parameter values of the required multimedia session, the Application requests temporary change of the QoS parameters active on the session.
5. The "Application Driven QoS" Web Service applies a new QoS feature on the existing user session.
6. The Application reserves an amount on the account indicated by the user identifier.
7. The "Payment" Web Service makes the reservation which is specified as a volume.
8. The Application registers its interest in receiving QoS events related to the temporary changed QoS parameters.
9. The "Application Driven QoS" Web Service stores the reservation.
10. When a particular QoS event occurs in the network, the "Application Driven QoS" Web Service generates a notification to inform the Application.
11. The "Application Driven QoS Notification" Application notifies the Application about the impact that this event had on the temporary QoS parameters of the user session.
12. The Application reduces the volume to the existing reservation.
13. The "Payment" Web Service subtracted the identified volume from the reservation.
14. When the user terminates the session (the game is over and the video call is finished), the "Application Driven QoS" Web Service generates notification to the Application.
15. The "Application Driven QoS Notification" Application notifies the Application about the multimedia session termination.
16. The application terminates the subscription for QoS events.
17. The "Application Driven QoS" Web Service deletes the subscription.
18. The Application invokes ChargeReservation operation to charge to a reservation.
19. The "Payment" Web Service charges the user's account.
20. The Application invokes ReleaseReservation operation to request funds left in the reservation to the user's account to be returned.
21. The "Payment" Web Service returns funds to the account from which the reservation was made.

FUTURE RESEARCH DIRECTIONS

Future research in the area of Web Service access to policy and charging control functions in IP-based multimedia networks could be development of Parlay X Web Service interfaces for connectivity management in Virtual Private Networks (VPN). As stated above, the Parlay/OSA "Connectivity Manager" API is defined to establish QoS parameters for an enterprise network traffic travelling through a provider network. Assuming that the underlying packet network can be configured as a VPN, the Connectivity Manager interfaces provide methods that allow management applications to configure inter-site virtual connections. Due to the complexity and low level of abstraction provided by Parlay/OSA interfaces, the "Connectivity Manager" interfaces might be difficult for use for web developers. Following the simplification approach to definition of Parlay X Web Services, a simpler API for VPN configuring is to be defined.

The Parlay X Web Services is a technology which is going to evolve further. There are contradictory arguments and trends in the process of its evolution. If we consider the estimation

Figure 5. Parlay X Application for charging control based on provided QoS

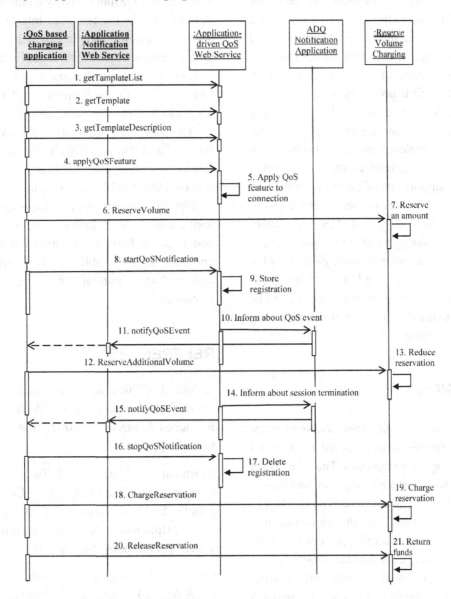

of the developers community support versus the expression complexity of given technology it is obvious that the rule "the simpler, the better" is in full force. The above statement is depicted without claim to be accurate in (Hanrahan, 2008) and roughly says that developers with protocol expertise worldwide are about 10^4, those who are capable to program using CORBA and Parlay/OSA APIs are about 2.5×10^5, while the Web Service developers are over 10^6.

Summarizing the different versions of Parlay X Web Services specifications leads us to observation that at one hand the interface expressiveness increases and at the other hand the overall number of interfaces increases also. Extensions and enhancements to the Parlay X interfaces provide more flexibility in the process of application creation but augment the complexity. The increased number of Parlay X interfaces aims to multiply the Parlay/OSA API functionality for more customer-oriented Web services. For example, while the Parlay X 2.2 version supports just 14 interfaces, currently there are 22 interfaces in version 3.0 of Parlay X. It is necessary to find the compromise between the number of customized Parlay X interfaces and their expressiveness.

The price that has to be paid for keeping the open interfaces easy-for-use for application developers is the implementation of the Parlay X Gateway. The existing implementations of Parlay X Gateways support sets of interfaces reflecting the network capabilities proved over the years. However, the more advanced IMS-based functions, like QoS management, will require certain amount of time in order to push on the Parlay X Gateway extension. In addition to interface-protocol mapping, more "intelligence" has to be embedded into the Parlay X Gateway concerning service orchestration.

CONCLUSION

The chapter presents the open access concept to advanced functions in IP-based multimedia networks through Web Services. The focus is set on Parlay X Web Services for policy and charging control. The "Application-driven Quality of Service" and "Payment" interfaces are examined and their functionalities are mapped onto network protocols. Any changes in the default QoS parameters result in updates of the user profile, while the temporary changes in QoS require updates in session control functional entities also. Both types of change lead to Diameter sessions. To affect the quality of service on ongoing connection and to notify the application for quality of service events that have been occurred, SIP transactions are initiated.

An improvement of "Application-driven Quality of Service" Web service is suggested without violating the existing Web service functionality. Configuration quality of service parameters for different services might be specified in templates.

The Web service functionality is enhanced by two new interfaces: the template interface provides access to specific template which contains the QoS parameters and their values from which the client may choose to request a new QoS feature to be applied; the QoS menu interface provides access to the list of existing templates.

The usage of "Application-driven Quality of Service" and "Payment" Web services is exemplified by combining their functions in an application that provides QoS-based charging.

Opening the network interfaces for third party application control provides opportunities for convergence between information technology applications and public network services and thus leading to more effective usage of network resources.

REFERENCES

Aitken, J. (2005). *Role of Parlay/Parlay X in Service Enablement for the Next Generation*. Retrieved January 15, 2009, from http://www.parlay.org

Bormann, F., Flake, S., & Tacken, J. (2006). Convergent Online Charging for Context-aware Mobile Services. Retrieved February 2, 2009, from http://www.loms-itea.org/publications/ConvergentOnlineCharging.pdf

Calhoun, P., Loughney, J., Guttman, E., Zorn, G., & Arkko J. (2003). RFC 3588 Diameter Base Protocol.

Chen, R., Su, E., Shen, V., & Wang, Y. (2006). *Introduction to IP Multimedia Subsystem (IMS), Part 1: SOA Parlay X Web services, The Next Generation Network architecture for Telecom industry*. Retrieved January 15 from http://www.ibm.com/developerworks/webservices/library/ws-soa-ipmultisub1/

Elkotob, M. (2008). *Autonomic Resource Management in IEEE 800.11 Open Access networks.* Retrieved February 2, 2009, from http://epubl.ltu. se/1402-1757/ 2008/38/LTU-LIC-0838-SE.pdf

ETSI TS 183 017 v2.3.1 (2008). Resource and Admission Control: DIAMETER protocol for session based policy set-up information exchange between the Application Function (AF) and the Service Policy Decision Function (SPDF); Protocol specification

3GPP TS 23.107 v8.0.0 (2008). *Quality of Service (QoS) Concept and Architecture.* Valbonne, France: 3GPP

3GPP TS 23.203 v8.4.0. (2008). *Policy and Charging Control architecture.* Valbonne, France: 3GPP

3GPP TS 24.229 v8.6.0. (2008). *(IP Multimedia Call Control Protocol based on Session Initiation Protocol (SIP) and Session Description Protocol (SDP).* Valbonne, France: 3GPP

3GPP TS 29.198-10 v8.0.0, (2008). *Open Service Access (OSA); Application Programming Interface (API); Part 10: Connectivity Manager Service Capability Feature (SCF).* Valbonne, France: 3GPP

3GPP TS 29.198-12 v8.0.0, (2008). *Open Service Access (OSA); Application Programming Interface (API); Part 12: Charging Service Capability Feature (SCF).* Valbonne, France: 3GPP

3GPP TS 29.199-17 v8.0.0. (2008). *Open Service Access (OSA); Parlay X Web Services; Part 17: Application-driven Quality of Service (QoS).* Valbonne, France: 3GPP

3GPP TS 29.199-6 v8.0.0. (2009). *Open Service Access (OSA); Parlay X Web Services; Part 6: Payment.* Valbonne, France: 3GPP

3GPP TS 32.260, v8.6.0 (2008). *Charging Management; IP Multimedia Subsystem (IMS) charging.* Valbonne, France: 3GPP

3GPP TS 32.299 v8.5.0 (2008). *Charging Management; Diameter Charging Applications 3.* Valbonne, France: 3GPP

Grønbæk, I. (2006). *NGN, IMS and service control – collected, Information, R&I Research Note.* Retrieved March 23, 2007 from http://www. telenor.com/ri/pub/not06/n_31_06.pdf

Hakala, H., Mattila, L., Koskinen, J., Stura, M., & Loughney, J. (2005). *RFC 4006 Diameter Credit Control Application.* Freemont, CA: IETF.

Hanrahan, H. (2008). *Network Convergence, Services, Applications, Transport and Operations Support, University of the Witwatersrand, Johannesburg, South Arica.* New York: Wiley.

Katchabaw, M., Lutfiyya, H., & Bauer, M. (2005). Usage based service differentiation for end-to-end quality of service management. *Computer Communications, 28*(18), 2146–2159. doi:10.1016/j. comcom.2004.07.041

Maes, S., & Stretch, R. (2004). *Policy Enforcement, Parlay X, Parlay and OMA.* Retrieved January 16, 2009, from http://www.parlay.org/en/ docs/may2004mm/Technical_Discussion/Parlay_ Evolution.pdf

MultiService Forum. (2004). *Implementation Agreement of Parlay X API for GMI.* Retrieved March 10, 2007 from http://www.msforum. org/techinfo/approved/MSF-IA-PARLAY.004-FINAL.pdf

Pencheva, E., & Atanasov, I. (2009). Open Access to Resource Management (Tech. Report on Project DO 02-135/2008). Research on Cross Layer Optimization of Telecommunication Resource Allocation, Bulgarian Ministry of Education and Science), Technical University of Sofia, Bulgaria

Poikselka, M., Mayer, G., Khartabil, H., & Niemi, A. (2006). *The IMS Multimedia Concepts and Services* (2nd ed.). Nokia, Finland: Wiley.

Rosenberg, J., Schulzrinne, H., & Mahy, R. (2005, May). *RFC 4235 An INVITE-Initiated Dialog Event Package for the Session Initiation Protocol* (SIP). Freemont, CA: IETF.

Santoni, D., & Katchabaw, M. (2007). Resource Matching in a Peer-to-Peer Computational Framework. In *Proceedings of the International Conference on Internet Computing,* (pp. 89-95). Las Vegas, NV.

Vannucci, D., & Hanrahan, H. (2007). *Extended Call Control Telecom Web Service.* Retrieved February 2, 2009, from http://www.ee.wits.ac.za/comms/Telecomms%20output/output/2007/Paper% 20114%20-%20Vannucci.pdf

Vidal, I., Garcıa, J., Valera, F., Soto, I., & Azcorra, A. (2006). *Adaptive Quality of Service Management for Next Generation Residential Gateways.* Retrieved February 10, 2009, from http://www. it.uc3m.es/ividal/articulos/MMNS2006_JaimeGarcia_20517.pdf

Compilation of References

3GPP TS 23.107 v8.0.0 (2008). *Quality of Service (QoS) Concept and Architecture.* Valbonne, France: 3GPP

3GPP TS 23.203 v8.4.0. (2008). *Policy and Charging Control architecture.* Valbonne, France: 3GPP

3GPP TS 24.229 v8.6.0. (2008). *(IP Multimedia Call Control Protocol based on Session Initiation Protocol (SIP) and Session Description Protocol (SDP).* Valbonne, France: 3GPP

3GPP TS 29.198-10 v8.0.0, (2008). *Open Service Access (OSA); Application Programming Interface (API); Part 10: Connectivity Manager Service Capability Feature (SCF).* Valbonne, France: 3GPP

3GPP TS 29.198-12 v8.0.0, (2008). *Open Service Access (OSA); Application Programming Interface (API); Part 12: Charging Service Capability Feature (SCF).* Valbonne, France: 3GPP

3GPP TS 29.199-17 v8.0.0. (2008). *Open Service Access (OSA); Parlay X Web Services; Part 17: Application-driven Quality of Service (QoS).* Valbonne, France: 3GPP

3GPP TS 29.199-6 v8.0.0. (2009). *Open Service Access (OSA); Parlay X Web Services; Part 6: Payment.* Valbonne, France: 3GPP

3GPP TS 32.260, v8.6.0 (2008). *Charging Management; IP Multimedia Subsystem (IMS) charging.* Valbonne, France: 3GPP

3GPP TS 32.299 v8.5.0 (2008). *Charging Management; Diameter Charging Applications 3.* Valbonne, France: 3GPP

Abbas, A. (2004). *Grid Computing: A Practical Guide to Technology and Applications.* Brookline, MA: Charles River Media.

Abowd, G. D., Dey, A. K., Brown, P. J., Davies, N., Smith, M., & Steggles, P. (1999). Towards a better understanding of context and context-awareness. In *Proceedings of the 1st international symposium on handheld and ubiquitous computing* (p. 304-307). Karlsruhe, Germany.

Abraham, A. (2001). Neuro-fuzzy systems: state-of-the-art modeling techniques, connectionist models of neurons, learning processes, and artificial intelligence. In Jose, M., & Alberto, P. (Eds.), *Lecture Notes in Computer Science* (Vol. 2084, pp. 269–276). Springer.

Adelstein, F., Gupta, S. K. S., Richard, G. S., III, & Schwiebert, L. (2005). Fundamentals of mobile and pervasive computing. In Chapman, S. S. (Ed.), 1st edition Communication Engineering. New York: McGraw-Hill Press.

Agentcities Task Force. (2003, November). *Integrating Web Services into Agentcities.* Agentcities Web Services Working Group.

Aggarwal, G. (2008). Theory research at Google. *ACM SIGACT News, 39*(2), 10–28. doi:10.1145/1388240.1388242

Aijaz, F., Adeli, S. M., & Walke, B. (2009). *A Service-Oriented Approach for In-Network Computations in Wireless Networks.* In *Proceedings of the Sixth IEEE and IFIP International Conference on wireless and Optical communications Networks* (WOCN2009), Cairo, Egypt.

Aijaz, F., Hameed, B., & Walke, B. (2008). *Asynchronous Mobile Web Services: Concept and Architecture.* In *Proceedings of 2008 IEEE 8th International Conference on Computer and Information Technology,* (p. 6), Sydney, Australia.

Aitken, J. (2005). *Role of Parlay/Parlay X in Service Enablement for the Next Generation.* Retrieved January 15, 2009, from http://www.parlay.org

Akamai (2007). *Akamai Technologies Inc.* Retrieved from www.akamai.com

Al-Nazer, A., & Helmy, T. (2007, November 2-5). A Web Searching Guide: Internet Search Engines & Autonomous Interface Agents Collaboration. In *IEEE/ACM Proceedings of the Joint International Conference on Web Intelligence/Intelligent Agent Technology,* (pp. 424-428). Sillicon Valley, CA.

Amin, K., von Laszewski, G., Hategan, M., Zaluzec, N. J., Hampton, S., & Rossi, A. (2004). *Gridant: A client-controllable grid work.ow system.* Presented at the Hawaii International Conference on System Sciences, 7, 70210c.

Apache Software Foundation. (2009). *Apache Maven Project.* Retrieved from http://maven.apache.org/

Ardon, S. (2003). MARCH: A distributed content adaptation architecture. *International Journal of Communication Systems, 16,* 97–115. doi:10.1002/dac.582

Asaduzzaman, S., Qiao, Y., & Bochmann, G. (2008). CliqueStream: An Efficient and Fault-resilient Live Streaming Network on a Clustered Peer-to-peer Overlay. In *Proceeding of 8th International Conference on Peer-to-Peer Computing,* Aachen, Germany.

Atkinson, M., Roure, D. D., Dunlop, A., Fox, G., Henderson, P., & Hey, T. (2005). Web Service Grids: An Evolutionary Approach. *Concurrency and Computation, 17*(2-4), 377–380. doi:10.1002/cpe.936

Axis2. (2006). *Axis2 SOAP Stack Implementation.* Retrieved from http://ws.apache.org/axis2

Bachelechner, D., Siorpaes, K., Lausen, H., & Fensel, D. (2006). Web Service Discovery - A Reality Check. In *Proceedings of Demos and Posters of the 3rd European Semantic Web Conference.*

Baldauf, M., Dustdar, S., & Rosenberg, F. (2006). A survey on context-aware systems. *International Journal of Ad Hoc and Ubiquitous Computing.*

Bansal, S., & Vidal, J. M. (2003). Matchmaking of Web Services-Based on the DAMLS Service Model. In *Proceedings of the II Internat. Joint Conf. on Autonomous Agents and Multiagent Systems* (pp. 926–927).

Barber, D. (2007). Machine Learning: A Probabilistic Approach, pg.107, 2007.

Bardram, J. E. (2005). The Java Context Awareness Framework (JCAF) A service infrastructure and programming framework for context-aware applications. In Pervasive Computing (p. 98-115). Springer.

Batagelj, V., & Brandes, U. (2005). Efficient generation of large random networks. *Physical Review, 71*(036113).

Bechhofer, S., Harmelen, F., van, Hendler, J., Horrocks, I., McGuinness, D. L., Patel-Schneider, P. F., et al. (2004). *OWL Web Ontology Language* (W3C Working Draft). W3C. (OWL Web Ontology Language)

Bellifemine, F., Caire, G., Poggi, A., & Rimassa, G. (2008). JADE: a Software Framework for Developing Multi-Agent Applications. Lessons Learned. *Information and Software Technology, 50,* 10–21. doi:10.1016/j.infsof.2007.10.008

Bellifemine, F., Poggi, A., & Rimassa, G. (1999). JADE - A FIPA-compliant agent framework. In Practical Applications of Intelligent Agents. *Applied Artificial Intelligence, 11*(5), 3–4.

Bellifemine, F., Poggi, A., & Rimassa, G. (2001). Developing multi agent systems with a FIPA-compliant agent framework. *Software, Practice & Experience, 31,* 103–128. doi:10.1002/1097-024X(200102)31:2<103::AID-SPE358>3.0.CO;2-O

Bergenti, F., Poggi, A., Burg, B., & Caire, G. (2001). Deploying FIPA-Compliant Systems on Handheld Devices. *IEEE Internet Computing, 5*(4), 20–25. doi:10.1109/4236.939446

Berhe, G., Brunie, L., & Pierson, J.-M. (2004). Modeling service-based multimedia content adaptation in pervasive computing. In *Proceedings of the 1st Conference on Computing Frontiers* (pp. 60-69). New York: ACM Press.

Berhe, G., Brunie, L., & Pierson, J.-M. (2005). Content adaptation in distributed multimedia systems. *Journal of Digital Information Management: Special Issue on Distributed Data Management, 3*(2), 96–100.

Berman, F., Fox, G., & Hey, A. (Eds.). (2003). *Grid Computing: Making the Global Infrastructure a Reality.* New York: Wiley.

Bharambe, A. R., Agrawal, M., & Seshan, S. (2004). Mercury: supporting scalable multi-attribute range queries. In *Proceedings of the 2004 Conference on Applications, Technologies, Architectures, and Protocols For Computer Communication,* (SIGCOMM '04). New York: ACM.

Bishop, M., Cheung, S., Wee, C., Frank, J., Hoagland, J., & Samorodin, S. (1997). The Threat from the Net. *IEEE Spectrum, 34*(8), 56–63. doi:10.1109/6.609475

BlueJade. (2003). *BlueJade software Web site.* Retrieved June 28, 2009, from http://sourceforge.net/projects/bluejade

Bochmann, G., & Jourdan, G. V. (2007, June). An overview of content distribution and content access in peer-to-peer systems (invited paper). In *Proceedings of NOTERE Conference,* Marrakesh (Maroco).

Bochmann, G., Wong, J. W., Lau, T. C., Bourne, D., Evans, D., & Kerhervé, B. (2003, July). Scalability of Web-based electronic commerce systems. *IEEE Communications Magazine, 41*(7), 110–115. doi:10.1109/MCOM.2003.1215647

Bondy, J. A., & Murty, U. S. R. (1976). *Graph Theory with Applications.* New York: Macmilliam Press Ltd.

Boniface, M. J., Phillips, S., & Perez, S.-M. A., & Surridge, M. (2007, September). *Dynamic Service Provisioning using GRIA SLAs.* Paper presented at NFPSLA-SOC '07. Vienna, Austria.

Booth, D., et al. (Eds.). (2004). W3C working group note 11: Web Services architecture. *World Wide Web Consortium.* Retrieved Nov 6, 2008, from http://www.w3.org/TR/ws-arch/#stakeholder

Bormann, F., Flake, S., & Tacken, J. (2006). Convergent Online Charging for Context-aware Mobile Services. Retrieved February 2, 2009, from http://www.loms-itea.org/publications/ ConvergentOnlineCharging.pdf

Bradley, J., Brown, C., Carpenter, B., Chang, V., Crisp, J., Crouch, S., et al. (2006, September). *The OMII Software Distribution.* Paper presented at the All Hands Meeting. Nottingham, UK.

Brock, M., & Goscinki, A. (2008). Publishing dynamic state changes of grid resources through state aware WSDL. In *Proceedings of the 8th IEEE Int. Symposium on Cluster Computing and the Grid.* New York.

Bromuri, S., & Stathis, K. (2008). Situating Cognitive Agents in GOLEM. In Weyns, D., Brueckner, S. A., & Demazeau, Y. (Eds.), *Engineering Environment-Mediated Multi-Agent Systems* (pp. 115–134). Berlin/Heidelberg, Germany: Springer Verlag. doi:10.1007/978-3-540-85029-8_9

Bromuri, S., Urovi, V., Morge, M., Stathis, K., & Toni, F. (2009). A Multi-Agent System for Service Discovery, Selection and Negotiation. In *Proceedings of the 8th International Joint Conference on Autonomous Agents and Multiagent Systems* (AAMAS), (Vol 2., pp. 1395-1396). Budapest, Hungary.

Brookshier, D., Govoni, D., Krishnan, N., & Soto, J. C. (2002). JXTA: Java P2P programming (1st ed.). Ontario, Canada: Sams.

Buford, J., & Burg, B. (2006). Using FIPA Agents with Service-Oriented Peer-to-Peer Middleware. In *Proceedings from the 7th Int. Conf. on Mobile Data Management,* (pp. 81). Nara, Japan.

Burstein, M. H., Bussler, C., Zaremba, M., Finin, T. W., Huhns, M. N., & Paolucci, M. (2005). A Semantic Web Services Architecture. *IEEE Internet Computing, 9*(5), 72–81. doi:10.1109/MIC.2005.96

Butler, R., Welch, V., Engert, D., Foster, I., Tuecke, S., & Volmer, J. (2000, Dec). A national-scale authentication infrastructure. *Computer, 33*(12), 60–66. doi:10.1109/2.889094

Buyya, R., Pathan, M., & Vakali, A. (Eds.). (2008). *Content delivery network*. Berlin, Heidelberg: Springer-Verlag Press. doi:10.1007/978-3-540-77887-5

Byers, J., & Considine, J. & Mitzenmacher. M. (2003, February). Simple Load Balancing for Distributed Hash Tables. In *Proceedings of the 2nd International Workshop on Peer-to-Peer Systems (IPTPS '03)*.

Caire, G., Gotta, D., & Banzi, M. (2008a). WADE: a software platform to develop mission critical applications exploiting agents and workflows. In *Proceedings from the 7th international Joint Conference on Autonomous Agents and Multi Agent Systems: Industrial Track*, (pp. 29-36). Estoril, Portugal.

Caire, G., Quarantotto, E., Porta, M., & Sacchi, G. (2008b). WOLF - An Eclipse Plug-in for WADE. *Proceedings from ACEC: the 6th International Workshop on Agent-based Computing for Enterprise Collaboration*. Rome, Italy. Retrieved June 28, 2009, from http://jade.tilab.com/wade/papers/Wolf_ACEC_2008.pdf

Calhoun, P., Loughney, J., Guttman, E., Zorn, G., & Arkko J. (2003). RFC 3588 Diameter Base Protocol.

Canali, C., Cardellini, V., Colajanni, M., & Lancellotti, R. (2005). Performance comparison of distributed architectures for content adaptation and delivery of Web resources. *In Proceedings of the 25th IEEE International Conference on Distributed Computing Workshops* (pp. 331-337). New York: IEEE Press.

Canali, C., Cardellini, V., Colajanni, M., Lancellotti, R., & Yu, P. S. (2005). A two-level distributed architecture for efficient Web content adaptation and delivery. In *Proceedings of the 2005 Symposium on Applications and the Internet* (pp.132-139). New York: IEEE Press.

Cardellini, V., Colajanni, M., & Yu, P. S. (2003). Request redirection algorithms for distributed web systems. *IEEE Transactions on Parallel and Distributed Systems, 14*(4), 355–368. doi:10.1109/TPDS.2003.1195408

Cardinale, Y., & Hernández, E. (2005). *Parallel Checkpointing on a Grid-enabled Java Platform. LNCS, 3470(EGC2005)*. Berlin, Germany: Springer.

Cardinale, Y., Blanco, E., & De Oliveira, J. (2006a). JaDiMa: Java applications distributed management on grid platforms. In Proceedings of Hpcc (p. 905-914).

Cardinale, Y., Blanco, E., & De Oliveira, J. (2006b). JADIMA: Virtual Machine Architecture for building JAVA Applications on Grid Platforms. *Clei Electronic Journal, 9*(2), 1-14. Retrieved from http://www.clei.cl/cleiej/volume.php

Cardinale, Y., De Oliveira, J., & Figueira, C. (2006). Remote class prefetching: Improving performance of java applications on grid platforms. In Proceedings of Ispa (p. 594-606). Sorrento, Italy.

Cardoso, J., & Sheth, A. (2003). Semantic E-Workflow Composition. *Journal of Intelligent Information Systems, 21*(3), 191–225. doi:10.1023/A:1025542915514

Cardoso, J., Miller, J., Sheth, A., & Arnold, J. (2002). Modeling Quality of Service for Workflows and Web Service Processes. *Journal of Web Semantics*.

Casavant, T. L., & Kuhl, J. G. (1988, February). A taxonomy of scheduling in general-purpose distributed computing systems. *IEEE Transactions on Software Engineering, 14*(2), 141–154. doi:10.1109/32.4634

Castro, M., et al. (2003). SplitStream: High-bandwidth multicast in cooperative environments. In *Proceedings of ACM SOSP '03*. New York.

Chakravarthy, U., Grant, J., & Minker, J. (1990). Logic-based approach to semantic query optimization. *ACM Transactions on Database Systems, 15*(2), 162–207. doi:10.1145/78922.78924

Chatel, P. (2006). WSDL 2.0 to UDDI mapping, SAWSDL to UDDI mapping (Technical note). Neuilly-sur-Seine, Frace: Thales Group.

Chawathe, Y. (2000). *Scattercast: An Architecture for Internet Broadcast Distribution as an Infrastructure Service.* (Ph.D Thesis). Univ. of California, Berkeley.

Chebrolu, S., Abraham, A., & Thomas, J. P. (2005). Feature deduction and ensemble design of intrusion detection systems. *Elsevier Computers & Security, 24*(4), 295–307.

Chen, H., Finin, T., & Joshi, A. (2003). An ontology for context aware pervasive computing environments. *The Knowledge Engineering Review, 18*(3), 197–207. doi:10.1017/S0269888904000025

Chen, L., Shadbolt, N. R., Goble, C. A., Tao, F., Cox, S. J., Puleston, C., et al. (2003). Towards a Knowledge-based Approach to Semantic Service Composition. In *Proceedings of the 2nd International Semantic Web Conference* (ISWC), (Vol. 2870/2003, pp. 319-334).

Chen, L., Shadbolt, N., Goble, C., Tao, F., Puleston, C., & Cox, S. (2005). Semantics assisted problem solving on the semantic grid. *Journal of Computational Intelligence, special issue, 21*(2).

Chen, Q., Hsu, M., Dayal, U., & Griss, M. (2000). Multi-agent cooperation, dynamic workflow and XML for e-commerce automation. In *Proceedings from the 4th international Conference on Autonomous Agents,* (pp. 255-256). Barcelona, Spain.

Chen, R., Su, E., Shen, V., & Wang, Y. (2006). *Introduction to IP Multimedia Subsystem (IMS), Part 1: SOA Parlay X Web services, The Next Generation Network architecture for Telecom industry.* Retrieved January 15 from http://www.ibm.com/developerworks/webservices/library/ws-soa-ipmultisub1/

Chen, Z., & Qian, N. (2005). Research of a semantic-based approach to improve software component reuse. In Proceedings of Skg (p. 93). Beijing, China.

Chinnici, R., Moreau, J., Ryman, A., & Weerawarana, S. (2007). *Web Services Description Language (WSDL) Version 2.0 Part 1: Core Language.* W3C Recommendation 26 June 2007. Retrieved on March 30, 2009 from http://www.w3.org/TR/wsdl20/

Chmiel, K., Gawinecki, M., Kaczmarek, P., Szymczak, M., & Paprzycki, M. (2005). Efficiency of JADE agent platform. *Science Progress, 2,* 159–172.

Christensen, E., Curbera, F., Meredith, G., & Weerawarana, S. (2001). *Web Services Description Language (WSDL) 1.1.* W3C Note 15 March 2001. Retrieved March 10, 2009, from http://www.w3.org/TR/wsdl

Chu, Y. H., et al. (2000). A case for end system multicast. In *Proceedings of ACM Sigmetrics.*

Cisco Systems Inc. (1998). *NetRanger Intrusion Detection System Technical Overview.* Retrieved from David S. (2004). *The ID3 Decision Tree Algorithm.* MONASH UNIVERSITY http://www.csse.monash.edu.au/courseware/cse5230/2004/assets/decisiontreesTute.pdf

Clement, L., Hately, A., von Riegen, C., & Rogers, T. (2004). *UDDI Version 3.0.2. (UDDI Spec Technical Committee Draft).* Billerica, MA: Organization for the Advancement of Structured Information Standard.

Colgrave, J., Januszewski, K., Clement, L., & Rogers, T. (2004). *Using WSDL in a UDDI Registry, Version 2.0.2. (Technical Note).* Billerica, MA: Organization for the Advancement of Structured Information Standards.

Comer, D. E. (2006). *Internetworking with TCP/IP: Principles, protocols and architecture* (5th ed.). Upper Saddle River, NJ: Prentice Hall Press.

Community, J. (2001). *JXTA community projects.* Retrieved from https://jxta.dev.java.net/

Computer and Automation Research Institute. (2005). *WSDL2Agent.* Retrieved from http://sas.ilab.sztaki.hu:8080/wsdl2agent/

ComScore. (2009). *ComScore measuring the digital world.* Retrieved from http://www.comscore.com

Corradi, A., Leonardi, L., & Zambonelli, F. (1999, January-March). Diffusive Load-Balancing Policies for Dynamic Applications. *IEEE Concurrency, 7*(1), 22–31. doi:10.1109/4434.749133

Cup, K. D. D. (1999). *Datasets.* Retrieved from http://www.acm.org/sigs/sigkdd/kddcup/index.php?section=1999&method=data

Curcin, V., Ghanem, M., & Guo, Y. (2009) Analysing scientific workflows with Computational Tree Logic. Journal of Cluster Computing: Special issue on Recent Advances in e-Science.

Curcin, V., Ghanem, M., Guo, Y., Stathis, K., & Toni, F. (2006). Building Next Generation Service-Oriented Architectures using argumentation agents. In *Proceedings of the 3rd International Conference on Grid Services Engineering and Management (GSEM 2006)*. Berlin, Germany: Springer Verlag.

Deering, D. (1988) Multicast Routing in Internetworks and Extended LANs. In *Proceedings of the ACM SIGCOMM.*

Deering, S. (1991). *Multicasting routing in a datagram internetwork* (Ph.D. dissertation). Stanford University, California.

Definition (n.d.). *Universal Description Discovery and Integration.* Retrieved Oct 29, 2008, from http://en.wikipedia.org/wiki/UDDI

Dey, A. K. (2000). *Providing architectural support for building context-aware applications.* (PhD thesis), College of Computing, Georgia Institute of Technology, USA.

Domingue, J., Cabral, L., Hakimpour, F., Sell, D., & Motta, E. (2004). IRS-III: A Platform and Infrastructure for Creating WSMO-based Semantic Web Services. In *Proceedings of the WIW 2004 Workshop on WSMO Implementations.*

Dragoni, N., & Gaspari, M. (2005). An Object Based Algebra for Specifying A Fault Tolerant Software Architecture. *Journal of Logic and Algebraic Programming, 63*(2), 271–297. doi:10.1016/j.jlap.2004.05.006

Dragoni, N., & Gaspari, M. (2006). Crash failure detection in asynchronous agent communication languages. *Autonomous Agents and Multi-Agent Systems, 13*(3), 355–390. doi:10.1007/s10458-006-0006-y

Dragoni, N., Gaspari, M., & Guidi, D. (2006). An Infrastructure to Support Cooperation of Knowledge-Level Agents on the Semantic Grid. *International Journal of Applied Intelligence. Special issue on Agent-Based Grid Computing, 25*(2), 159-180.

Dragoni, N., Gaspari, M., & Guidi, D. (2007). An ACL For Specifying Fault-Tolerant Protocols. *Applied Artificial Intelligence, 21*(4), 361–381. doi:10.1080/08839510701252643

Driscoll, D., Mensch, A., Nixon, T., & Regnier, A. (2009). *Devices Profile for Web Services Version 1.1.* OASIS Working Draft 05. Retrieved March 16, 2009, from http://www.oasis-open.org/committees/documents.php?wg_abbrev=ws-dd

Eibe, F., & Mark, H. (2001). A Simple Approach to Ordinal Classification (Lecture Notes in Computer Science). In *Proceedings of the 12th European Conference on Machine Learning* (Vol. 2167, pp. 145-156).

Eirinaki, M., & Vazirgiannis, M. (2003). Web mining for Web personalization. *ACM Transactions on Internet Technology, 3*, 1–27. doi:10.1145/643477.643478

El-Khatib, K., Bochmann, G., & El-Saddik, A. (2004). A QoS-based framework for distributed content adaptation. In *Proceedings of the 1st International Conference on Quality of Services in Heterogeneous Wired/Wireless Networks* (pp. 308-312). New York: IEEE Press.

Elkotob, M. (2008). *Autonomic Resource Management in IEEE 800.11 Open Access networks.* Retrieved February 2, 2009, from http://epubl.ltu.se/1402-1757/ 2008/38/LTU-LIC-0838-SE.pdf

Elson, J., & Cerpa, A. (2003). Internet content adaptation protocol (ICAP). *Network Working Group.* Retrieved Nov 6, 2008, from http://www.icap-forum.org/documents/specification/rfc3507.txt

Endriss, U., Kakas, A., Lu, W., Bracciali, A., Demetriou, N., & Stathis, K. (2006). Crafting the Mind of a PROSOCS Agent. *Applied Artificial Intelligence, 20*(2-4), 105–131. doi:10.1080/08839510500479496

Erl, T. (2005). *Service-oriented architecture: Concepts, technology, and design.* Upper Saddle River, NJ: Prentice Hall PTR.

ETSI TS 183 017 v2.3.1 (2008). Resource and Admission Control: DIAMETER protocol for session based policy set-up information exchange between the Application Function (AF) and the Service Policy Decision Function (SPDF); Protocol specification

Eugster, P., Guerraoui, R., Kermarrec, A. M., & Massoulie, L. (2004). From epidemics to distributed computing, IEEE Computer. *Accustream iMedia Research Homepage.* Retrieved 2009, from http://www.accustreamsearch.com

EZ JCom. (n.d.). *EZ JCom.* Retrieved from http://www.ezjcom.com/

Farrel, J., & Lausen, H. (2007). *Semantic annotations for WSDL.* W3C Working draft.

Fawaz, Y., Berhe, G., Brunie, L., Scuturici, V.-M., & Coquil, D. (2008). Efficient Execution of Service Composition for Content adaptation in Pervasive Computing. *International Journal of Digital Multimedia Broadcasting, 1-10.*

Felea, V., Olejnik, R., & Toursel, B. (2004). ADAJ: a Java Distributed Environment for Easy Programming Design and Efficient Execution. *Schedae Informaticae, 13*, 9–36.

Feng, L., Wang, W., Zhu, L., & Zhang, Y. (2009). Predicting intrusion goal using dynamic Bayesian network with transfer probability estimation. *Journal of Network and Computer Applications, 32*(3), 721–732. doi:10.1016/j.jnca.2008.06.002

Fensel, D., Bussler, C., Ding, Y., & Omelayenko, B. (2002). The Web Service Modeling Framework WSMF. *Electronic Commerce Research and Applications, 1*(2). doi:10.1016/S1567-4223(02)00015-7

Ferrari, D., & Zhou, S. (1986). A load index for dynamic load balancing. In *Proceedings of 1986 ACM Fall Joint Computer Conference*, (pp. 684-690). Los Alamitos, CA: IEEE Computer Society Press.

Fielding, R. (2000). *Architectural Styles and the Design of Network-based Software Architectures* (Doctoral dissertation). University of California, Irvine

Fielding, R., Gettys, J., Mogul, J., Frystyk, H., Masinter, L., Leach, P., & Berners-Lee, T. (1999). *Hypertext Transfer Protocol - HTTP/1.1.* Standards Track, Network Working Group. The Internet Society. Retrieved March 17, 2009, from http://www.w3.org/Protocols/rfc2616/rfc2616.html

Finin, T., Fritzson, R., McKay, D., & McEntire, R. (1997). KQML as an agent communication language. *Software Agents*, 291-316.

FIPA. (2000). *FIPA Specifications.* Retrieved June 28, 2009, from http://www.fipa.org.

FIPA. (2002). *FIPA SL Content Language Specification.* Retrieved from: http://www.fipa.org/specs/fipa00008/

FIPA. (2003). *Agent Discovery Service Specification.* Retrieved June 28, 2009, from http://www.fipa.org/specs/fipa00095/PC00095.pdf.

FIPA. (2004). *JXTA Discovery Middleware Specification.* Retrieved June 28, 2009, from http://www.fipa.org/specs/fipa00096/PC00096A.pdf

FIPA. (n.d.). *FIPA.* Retrieved from http://jade.tilab.com/papers/JADETutorialIEEE/JADETutorial_FIPA.pdf

FIPA. Foundation for Intelligent Physical Agents. (2002). *FIPA Webpage.* Retrieved from http://www.fipa.org

Foster, I., Kesselman, C., Nick, J., & Tuecke, S. (2002). *The Physiology of the Grid: An Open Grid Services Architecture for Distributed Systems Integration.* Open Grid Service Infrastructure WG, Global Grid Forum.

Francis, P. (1999). *YOID: Extending the Multicast Architecture.* White paper. Retrieved from http://www.aciri.org/yoid

Gaertner, D., & Toni, F. (2007). CaSAPI – A System for Credulous and Sceptical Argumentation. In *Proceedings of the First International Workshop on Argumentation and Nonmonotonic Reasoning.* (p.p. 80-95). Arizona, USA.

Gailly, J.-L. (1996). *Gzip documentation*. Internet. Retrieved March 18, 2009 from ftp://prep.ai.mit.edu/pub/gnu/

Ganesan, P., Mayank, B., & Garcia-Molina, H. (2004). Online Balancing of Range-Partitioned Data with Applications to Peer-to-Peer Systems. In *Proceedings of VLDB, 2004.*

Garvey, T. D., & Lunt, T. F. (1991). *Model based intrusion detection.* In *Proceedings of the 14th national computer security conference* (pp. 372-385).

Gaspari, M. (1998). Concurrency and Knowledge-Level Communication in Agent Languages. *Artificial Intelligence, 105*(1-2), 1–45. doi:10.1016/S0004-3702(98)00080-0

Gehlen, G. (2007). *Mobile Web Services - Concepts, Prototype, and Traffic Performance Analysis* (Ph. D. Dissertation). RWTH Aachen University, Germany.

Genesereth, M. R. (1997). An agent-based framework for interoperability. In Bradshaw, J. M. (Ed.), *Software Agents* (pp. 317–345). Cambridge, MA: MIT Press.

Ghanem, M., Azam, N., Boniface, M., & Ferris, J. (2006). Grid-Enabled Workflows for Industrial Product Design. In *Proceedings of the Second IEEE International Conference on e-Science and Grid Computing (e-Science'06)* (p.p. 96). Amsterdam, The Netherlands.

Ghanem, M., Curcin, V., Wendel, P., & Guo, Y. (2008). Building and Using Analytical Workflows in Discover Net. In Dubitzky, W. (Ed.), *Data Mining Techniques in Grid Computing Environments* (pp. 119–140). London: Wiley-Blackwell. doi:10.1002/9780470699904.ch8

Ghezzi, C., Jazayeri, M., & Mandrioli, D. (1991). *Fundamentals of software engineering.* New York: Prentice-Hall.

Goble, C., & Roure, D. D. (2002). The grid: an application of the semantic web. *SIGMOD Record, 31*(4), 65–70. doi:10.1145/637411.637422

Godfrey, B., Lakshminarayanan, K., Surana, S., Karp, R., & Stoica, I. (2004, March 7-11). Load balancing in dynamic structured P2P systems. *INFOCOM 2004. Twenty-third Annual Joint Conference of the IEEE Computer and Communications Societies, 4*(4), 2253-2262.

Google video. (n.d.). *Google video.* Retrieved from http://http://video.google.com/

Google. (n.d.). *Google Web APIs (beta).* Retrieved from http://www.google.com/apis/index.html

Goscinski, W., & Abramson, D. (2004a). *Distributed ant: A system to support application deployment in the grid.* Washington, DC: IEEE Computer Society.

Goscinski, W., & Abramson, D. (2004b). Distributed ant: A system to support application deployment in the grid. In *Proceedings of Grid '04: The 5th ieee/acm international workshop on grid computing* (pp. 436–443). Washington, DC: IEEE Computer Society.

Goscinski, W., & Abramson, D. (2005). Application deployment over heterogeneous grids using distributed ant. In *Proceedings of E-science '05: The first international conference on e-science and grid computing* (pp. 361–368). Washington, DC: IEEE Computer Society.

Greenwood, D., & Callisti, M. (2004). Engineering Web Service-Agent Integration. In *Proceedings from 2004 IEEE Conference of Systems, Man and Cybernetics,* (pp. 1918-1925). The Hague, Netherlands. Retrieved June 28, 2009, from http://www.whitestein.com/library/WhitesteinTechnologies_Paper_IEEESMC2004.pdf

Greenwood, D., Nagy, J., & Calisti, M. (2005). Semantic Enhancement of a Web Service Integration Gateway. In *Proceedings from SOCABE: the AAMAS 2005 Workshop on Service Oriented Computing and Agent Based Engineering,* Utrecht, Netherlands.

Grønbæk, I. (2006). *NGN, IMS and service control – collected, Information, R&I Research Note.* Retrieved March 23, 2007 from http://www.telenor.com/ri/pub/not06/n_31_06.pdf

Gruber, T. (1993). A Translation Approach to Portable Ontologies. *Knowledge Acquisition*, 5(2), 199–220. doi:10.1006/knac.1993.1008

Gudgin, M., Hadley, M., Mendelsohn, N., Moreau, J., Nielsen, H. F., Karmarkar, A., & Lafon, Y. (2007). *SOAP Version 1.2 Part 1: Messaging Framework*. W3C Recommendation. Retrieved on March 17, 2009, from http://www.w3.org/TR/soap12-part1/

Hadley, M. J. (2006). *Web Application Description Language* (WADL), (Technical Report). Santa Clara, CA: Sun Microsystems, Inc. Retrieved on April 3, 2009, from http://research.sun.com/techrep/2006/smli_tr-2006-153.pdf

Hakala, H., Mattila, L., Koskinen, J., Stura, M., & Loughney, J. (2005). *RFC 4006 Diameter Credit Control Application*. Freemont, CA: IETF.

Hanrahan, H. (2008). *Network Convergence, Services, Applications, Transport and Operations Support, University of the Witwatersrand, Johannesburg, SouthArica*. New York: Wiley.

Hashimi, S. (2001). Service-oriented architecture explained. *O'Reily ONDotnet.com*. Retrieved Nov 6, 2008, from http://www.ondonet.com/pub/a/dotnet/2003/08/18/soa_explained.html

He, J., Gao, T., Hao, W., Yen, I.-L., & Bastani, F. (2007). A flexible content adaptation system using a rule-Based approach. *IEEE Transactions on Knowledge and Data Engineering*, 19(1), 127–140. doi:10.1109/TKDE.2007.250590

Heberlein, T. (1995, February). *Network Security Monitor (NSM) Final Report*. U.C. Davis. Retrieved from http://seclab.cs.ucdavis.edu/papers/NSM-final.pdf

Helmy, T. (2006). Towards a User-Centric Web Portals Management. *International Journal of Information Technology*, 12(1), 1–15.

Helmy, T. (2007). Collaborative Multi-Agent-Based E-Commerce Framework. *International Journal of Computers. Systems and Signals*, 8(1), 3–12.

Helmy, T., Amamiya, S., Mine, T., & Amamiya, M. (2003, October 13-17). A New Approach of the Collaborative User Interface Agents. In *Proceedings of the IEEE/WIC/ACM International Conference on Intelligent Agent Technology* (IAT'03), (pp. 147-153). Halifax, Canada.

Henocque, L., & Kleiner, M. (2007). Composition - combining web services functionality in composite or-chestrations. In Studer, R., Grimm, S., & Abecker, A. (Eds.), *Semantic Web Services - Concepts, Technologies and Applications* (pp. 245–286). Berlin, Germany: Springer.

Hsiao, J.-L., Hung, H.-P., & Chen, M.-S. (2008). Versatile transcoding proxy for Internet content Adaptation. *IEEE Transactions on Multimedia*, 10(4), 646–658. doi:10.1109/TMM.2008.921852

Huang, W., Shi, Y., Zhang, S., & Zhu, Y. (2006). The communication complexity of the hamming distance problem. *Journal of Information Processing Letters*, 99, 149–153. doi:10.1016/j.ipl.2006.01.014

Huhns, M. N., Singh, M. P., Mark, H. M. H., Decker, K. S., Durfee, E. H., & Finin, T. W., Gasser, l., Goradia, H. J., Jennings, N. R., Lakkaraju, K., Nakashima, H., Parunak, K., Rosenschein, J. S., Ruvinsky, A., Sukthankar, G., Swarup, S., Sycara, K. P., Tambe, M., Wagner, T., & Zavala Gutierrez, R. L. (2005). Research Directions for Service-Oriented Multiagent Systems. *IEEE Internet Computing*, 9(6), 65–70. doi:10.1109/MIC.2005.132

Hull, D., Wolstencroft, K., Stevens, R., Goble, C., Pocock, M. R., Li, P., & Oinn, T. (2006). Taverna: A Tool for Building and Running Workflows of Services. *Nucleic Acids Research*, 34(Web Services Issue), W729-W732.

Hull, R., Neaves, P., & Bedford-Roberts, J. (1997). Towards situated computing. In *Proceedings of the First international symposium on wearable computers* (ISWC '97) (p. 146-153).

Indulska, J., & Sutton, P. (2003). *Location management in pervasive systems*. In *Proceedings Workshop on wearable, invisible, context-aware, ambient, pervasive and ubiquitous computing* (Vol. 21, p. 143-152).

JADE Board. (2008). *Jade Web Services Integration Gateway (Wsig) Guide.* Retrieved from http://jade.cselt.it/doc/tutorials/WSIG_Guide.pdf

JADE. (2009). *JADE software Web site.* Retrieved June 28, 2009, from http://jade.tilab.com

JADE. (n.d.). *JADE.* Retrieved from http://jade.tilab.com/

JADE. Java Agent Development Framework. (2001). *Jade webpage.* Retrieved from http://jade.tilab.com

Jayram, T. S., Kumar, R., & Sivakumar, D. (2008). The one way communication complexity of hamming distance. *Journal of Theory and Computing, 4,* 129–135. doi:10.4086/toc.2008.v004a006

Jemili, F., Zaghdoud, M., & Ahmed, M. (2007). *A Framework for an Adaptive Intrusion Detection System using Bayesian Network.* ISI IEEE.

Jesen, F. (2001). *Bayesian Networks and Decision Graphs.* New York, USA: Springer.

Joachims, T., Freitag, D., & Mitchell, T. (1997). WebWatcher: A tour guide for the World Wide Web. In *Proceedings of the Fifteenth International Joint Conference on Artificial Intelligence.*

Jorstad, I., Dustdar, S., & Thanh, D. (2005). A service oriented architecture framework for collaborative services. In *Proceedings of the 14th IEEE Int. Workshops on Enabling Technologies: Infrastructure for Collaborative Enterprise* (121-125). New York: IEEE Press.

JXTA. (2007). *JXTA Web Site.* Retrieved June 28, 2009, from https://jxta.dev.java.net/

Kassoff, M., Petrie, C., Zen, L.-M., & Genesereth, M. (2009). Semantic email addressing. *IEEE Internet Computing, 13*(1), 48–55. doi:10.1109/MIC.2009.20

Katchabaw, M., Lutfiyya, H., & Bauer, M. (2005). Usage based service differentiation for end-to-end quality of service management. *Computer Communications, 28*(18), 2146–2159. doi:10.1016/j.comcom.2004.07.041

Klusch, M., Fries, B., & Sycara, K. P. (2006). Automated semantic web service discovery with OWLS-MX. In *Proceedings from the 5th international Joint Conference on Autonomous Agents and Multi Agent Systems,* (pp. 915-922). Hakodate, Japan.

Kollia, D., Kafetzoglou, S., Grammatikou, M., & Papavassiliou, S. (2008, April). *Discovery of resources in a distributed grid environment based on specific service level agreements* (SLAS). Ischia, Italy.

Korkea-aho, M. (2000). *Context-Aware Application Survey. (Technical Report Tik-110.551).* Finland: Helsinki University of Technology.

Kourtesis, D., & Paraskakis, I. (2008). Combining SAWSDL, OWL-DL and UDDI for Semantically Enhanced Web Service Discovery. In Heidelberg, S. B. (Ed.), *The Semantic Web: Research and Applications* (Vol. 5021). Berlin, Heidelberg: Springer/Verlag. doi:10.1007/978-3-540-68234-9_45

Kourtesis, D., Paraskakis, I., Friesen, A., Gouvas, P., & Bouras, A. (2007). Web Service Discovery In A Semantically Extended Uddi Registry: The Case Of Fusion. In []. Boston]. *Proceedings of Establishing The Foundation Of Collaborative Networks, 243,* 547–554. doi:10.1007/978-0-387-73798-0_59

Krauter, K., Buyya, R., & Maheswaran, M. (2002). A taxonomy and survey of grid resource management systems for distributed computing. *Software, Practice & Experience, 32*(2), 135–164. doi:10.1002/spe.432

Krysalis Community Project. (2004). *Krysalis centipede.* Retrieved from http://krysalis.org/centipede/

Kumar, S., & Spafford, E. H. (1995). Software architecture to support misuse intrusion detection. In *Proceedings of the 18th national information security conference* (pp. 194-204).

Kunz, T. (1991, July). The Influence of Different Workload Descriptions on a Heuristic Load Balancing Scheme. *IEEE Transactions on Software Engineering, 17*(7), 725–730. doi:10.1109/32.83908

Lawrence Livermore National Laboratory. (1998). *Network Intrusion Detector (NID) Overview.* Retrieved from http://ciac.llnl.gov/cstc/nid/intro.html.

Lazar, I., & Terrill, W. (2001). Exploring Content Delivery Networking. *IT Professional, 3*(4), 47–49. doi:10.1109/6294.946620

Lee, W., & Tsai, T., T. (2003). An interactive agent-based system for concept-based Web search. *Expert Systems with Applications, 24,* 365–363. doi:10.1016/S0957-4174(02)00186-0

Lei, Z., & Georganas, N. D. (2001). Context-based media adaptation in pervasive computing. In *Proceedings of IEEE Canadian Conf. on Electrical and Computer* (pp. 913-918). New York: IEEE Press.

Leinberger, W., Karypis, G., Kumar, V., & Biswas, R. (2000). Load balancing across near-homogeneous multi-resource servers. In *Proceeding of the 9th Heterogeneous Computing Workshop, 200o,* (HCW 2000), (pp.60-71).

Liu, S., Küngas, P., & Matskin, M. (2006). Agent-Based Web Service Composition with JADE and JXTA. In *Proceedings from the 2006 International Conference on Semantic Web and Web Services,* (pp. 110-116). Las Vegas, NV.

Livny, M., & Melman, M. (1982). Load balancing in homogeneous broadcast distributed systems. In *Proceedings of the Computer Network Performance Symposium.* New York: ACM.

Lobb, R. J., Couto da Silva, A. P., Leonardi, E., Mellia, M., & Meo, M. (2009). *Adaptive overlay topology for mesh-based P2P-TV systems.* Retrieved from http://www.informatik.uni-trier.de/~ley/db/conf/nossdav/nossdav2009.html#LobbSLMM09

Locher, T., Schmid, S., & Wattenhofer, R. (2006). eQuus: A Provably Robust and Locality-Aware Peer-to-Peer System. *Sixth IEEE International Conference on Peer-to-Peer Computing (P2P'06).*

Ludäscher, B., Altintas, I., Berkley, C., Higgins, D., Jaeger, E., & Jones, M. (2006). Scientific Workflow Management and the Kepler System: Research Articles. In *Concurrency and Computation: Practice & Experience* (pp. 1039–1065). Chichester, UK: John Wiley and Sons Ltd.

Lum, W., & Lau, F. (2002). A context-aware decision engine for content adaptation. *IEEE Pervasive Computing / IEEE Computer Society [and] IEEE Communications Society, 29*(3), 41–49.

Lum, W., & Lau, F. (2003). User-centric content negotiation for effective Adaptation service in mobile computing. *IEEE Transactions on Software Engineering, 29*(12), 1100–1111. doi:10.1109/TSE.2003.1265524

Lunt, T. (1993). Detecting intruders in computer systems. In *Proceedings of the conference on auditing and computer technology.*

Lunt, T., Tamaru, A., Gilham, F., Jagannath, R., Neumann, P., & Javitz, H. (1992). *A real-time intrusion detection expert system (IDES), (Final Technical Report). Computer Science Laboratory.* Menlo Park, CA: SRI International.

Lymberopoulos, L., Bromuri, S., Stathis, K., Kafetzoglou, S., Grammatikou, M., & Papavassiliou, S. (2007). Towards a P2P Discovery Framework for an Argumentative Agent Technology assist GRID. In *Proceedings of CoreGRID Workshop on Grid Programming Model, Grid and P2P Systems Architectures, Grid Systems, Tools, Environments.* Crete, Greece.

MacKenzie, C. M., Laskey, K., McCabe, F., Brown, P. F., & Metz, R. (2006). *Reference Model for Service Oriented Architecture 1.0.* OASIS Standard. Retrieved March 3, 2009, from http://docs.oasis-open.org/soa-rm/v1.0/soa-rm.html

Maes, S., & Stretch, R. (2004). *Policy Enforcement, Parlay X, Parlay and OMA.* Retrieved January 16, 2009, from http://www.parlay.org/en/docs/may2004mm/Technical_Discussion/Parlay_Evolution.pdf

Magharei, N., & Rasti, A. H. (2007). Prime: Peer-to-peer receiver-driven mesh-based streaming. In *Proceedings of IEEE INFOCOM.*

Majithia, S., Walker, D. W., & Gray, W. A. (2004). Automated Composition of Semantic Grid Services. In *Proceedings of AHM*.

Malik, Z., & Bouguettaya, A. (2009). Reputation bootstrapping for trust establishment among Web Services. *IEEE Internet Computing, 13*(1), 40–47. doi:10.1109/MIC.2009.17

Malkhi, D., Naor, M., & Ratajczak, D. (2002, July 21-24). Viceroy: a scalable and dynamic emulation of the butterfly. In *Proceedings of the Twenty-First Annual Symposium on Principles of Distributed Computing*, (PODC '02), (pp. 183-192). Monterey, CA.

Martin, D., Burstein, M., Hobbs, J., Lassila, O., Mcdermott, D., Mcilraith, S., et al. (2004). OWL-S: Semantic Markup for Web Services. *W3C Submission*.

Martinez, E., & Lespérance, Y. (2004). IG-JADE-PKSlib: An Agent-Based Framework for Advanced Web Service Composition and Provisioning. In *Proceedings from the AAMAS 2004 Workshop on Web-services and Agent-based Engineering*, (pp. 2-10). New York.

Maymounkov, P., & Mazières, D. (2002, March 7-8). Kademlia: A Peer-to-Peer Information System Based on the XOR Metric. In P. Druschel, M. F. Kaashoek and A. I. Rowstron (Eds.), *Proceedings of the Revised Papers from the First international Workshop on Peer-To-Peer Systems*, (Lecture Notes In Computer Science). London: Springer.

McCarthy, J. (1993) Notes on Formalizing Context. *IJCAI*, 555-562.

McGuinness et al. (2004). *OWL Web Ontology Language Overview*. W3C Recommendation.

Md Fudzee, M. F., & Abawajy, J. H. (2008). Classification of content adaptation system. In *Proceedings of the 10th International Conference on Information Integration and Web-based Application and Services* (pp. 426-429). New York: ACM Press.

Medjahed, B., Bouguettaya, A., & Elmagarmid, A. K. (2003). Composing Web services on the Semantic Web. *The VLDB – The International Journal on Very Large Databases, 12*(4), 333-351.

Menascé, D. A., & Casalicchio, E. (2004). Quality of Service Aspects and Metrics in Grid Computing. In *Proceedings of CMG'04 International Conference* (p. 521-532).

Mielnik, J.-C., Bouthors, V., Laurire, S., & Lang, B. (2004). Using ecots portal for sharing information about software products on the internet and in corporate intranets. In Kazman, R., & Port, D. (Eds.), *ICCBSS (Vol. 2959*, p. 1). New York: Springer.

Mili, R., Mili, A., & Mittermeir, R. T. (1997). Storing and retrieving software components: A refinement based system. *IEEE Transactions on Software Engineering, 23*(7), 445–460. doi:10.1109/32.605762

Mitra, N., & Lafon, Y. (2007). *SOAP Version 1.2 Part 0: Primer*. W3C Recommendation.

Mohan, R., John, S., & Li, C.-S. (1999). Adapting multimedia Internet content for universal access. *IEEE Transactions on Multimedia, 1*(1), 104–114. doi:10.1109/6046.748175

Mondejar, R., Garcia, P., Pairot, C., & Gomez Skarmeta, A. F. (2006, June 26-28). Enabling Wide-Area Service Oriented Architecture through the p2pWeb Model. In *Proceedings of the 15th IEEE international Workshops on Enabling Technologies: infrastructure For Collaborative Enterprises*, (WETICE). Washington, DC: IEEE Computer Society.

Morge, M., & Mancarella, P. (2007). The Hedgehog and the Fox: An argumentation-based decision support system. In *Proceedings of the Fourth International Workshop on Argumentation in Multi-Agent Systems*, (p.p. 55-68).

Morge, M., McGinnis, J., Bromuri, S., Mancarella, P., & Stathis, K. (2008). An Argumentative Model for Service-Oriented Agents. In *Proceedings of the International Symposium on Architectures for Intelligent Theory-Based Agents, AAAI Spring Symposium Series*. Stanford University, CA.

Mukkamala, S., Sung, A. H., & Abraham, A. (2003). Intrusion detection using ensemble of soft computing paradigms. In *Proceedings of the 3rd international conference on intelligent systems design and applications*, (pp. 239-248).

Mukkamala, S., Sung, A. H., & Abraham, A. (2004). Modeling intrusion detection systems using linear genetic programming approach. *Lecture Notes in Computer Science, 3029*, 633–642.

Mukkamala, S., Sung, A. H., Abraham, A., & Ramos, V. (2004). Intrusion detection systems using adaptive regression splines. In Seruca, I., Filipe, J., Hammoudi, S., Cordeiro, J. (eds.), *Proceedings of the 6th International Conference on Enterprise Information Systems*, (ICEIS'04), (vol. 3, pp. 26-33).

MultiService Forum. (2004). *Implementation Agreement of Parlay X API for GMI*. Retrieved March 10, 2007 from http://www.msforum.org/techinfo/approved/MSF-IA-PARLAY.004-FINAL.pdf

Neary, M. O., Brydon, S. P., Kmiec, P., Rollins, S., & Cappello, P. (1999). Javelin++: Scalability issues in global computing. In *Proceedings of the acm 1999 conference on java grande* (p. 171-180).

Negri, A., Poggi, A., Tomaiuolo, M., & Turci, P. (2006). Dynamic Grid tasks composition and distribution through agents. *Concurrency and Computation, 18*(8), 875–885. doi:10.1002/cpe.982

Newcomer, E. (2002). *Understanding Web Services: XML, WSDL, SOAP and UDDI*. Boston: Addison-Wesley.

Newell, A. (1982). The knowledge level. *Artificial Intelligence, 19*, 87–127. doi:10.1016/0004-3702(82)90012-1

Nguyen, T. X., & Kowalczyk, R. (2007). WS2JADE: Integrating Web service with Jade Agents. In *Service-Oriented Computing: Agents, Semantics, and Engineering* (Vol. 4504, pp. 147–159). Berlin, Heidelberg: Springer. doi:10.1007/978-3-540-72619-7_11

Nguyen, X. T., & Kowalczyk, R. (2005). Enabling Agent-Based Management of Web Services with WS2JADE. In *Proceedings from ISEAT 2005: the 1st International Workshop on Integration of Software Engineering and Agent Technology*, (pp. 407-412). Melbourne, Australia.

Nilsson, N. J. (1998). *Artificial intelligence: a new synthesis*. San Francisco: Morgan Kaufmann.

O'Brien, P., & Nicol, R. (1998). FIPA - Towards a Standard for Software Agents. *BT Technology Journal, 16*, 51–59. doi:10.1023/A:1009621729979

O'Madadhain, J., Fisher, D., Nelson, T., & Krefeldt, J. (2003). *JUNG: Java Universal Network/Graph Framework*. Retrieved from http://jung.sourceforge.net/index.html

Ong, T. M., Lim, T. M., Lee, B. S., & Yeo, C. K. (2002). Unicorn: voluntary computing over Internet. *ACM SIGOPS Operating Systems Review, 36*(2), 36–51. doi:10.1145/509526.509532

Oram, A. (2000). *Gnutella and Freenet Represent True Technological Innovation*. Whitepaper.

Overeinder, B. J., Posthumus, E., & Brazier, F. M. T. (2002). Integrating Peer-to-Peer Networking and Computing in the AgentScape Framework. In *Proceedings from P2P02: the 2nd IEEE Int. Conf. on Peer-to-Peer Computing*, (pp. 96-103). Linköping, Sweden.

OWL-S 1.0 Release. (2004). *OWL-S: Semantic Markup for Web Services*. Retrieved from http://www.w3.org/Submission/OWL-S

Padmanabhan, V. N. (2002). *Distributing Streaming Media Content Using Cooperative Networking*. Miami Beach, FL: ACM NOSSDAV.

Pahl, C. (2004). An Ontology-Based Framework for Semantic Grid Service Composition. *Grid Services Engineering and Management, 3270*, 63–77.

Palathingal, P., & Chandra, S. (2004). Agent Approach for Service Discovery and Utilization. In *Proceedings of the 37th Annual Hawaii International Conference on System Sciences* (HICSS 2004).

Paolucci, M., Kawamura, T., Payne, T. R., & Sycara, K. P. (2002). Semantic matching of web services capabilities. In *Proceedings of the International semantic web conference* (p. 333-347).

Pathan, M., & Buyya, R. (2008). *A Taxonomy of CDNs", Content Delivery Networks*. Berlin, Germany: Springer-Verlag.

Pautasso, C., Zimmermann, O., & Leymann, F. (2008). *Restful web services vs. "big"' web services: making the right architectural decision*. In *Proceeding of the 17th international conference on World Wide Web*. New York: ACM

Peddabachigari, S., Abraham, A., Grosan, C., & Thomas, T. (2007). Modeling intrusion detection system using hybrid intelligent systems. *Journal of Network and Computer Applications, 20*, 114–132. doi:10.1016/j.jnca.2005.06.003

Pencheva, E., & Atanasov, I. (2009). Open Access to Resource Management (Tech. Report on Project DO 02-135/2008). Research on Cross Layer Optimization of Telecommunication Resource Allocation, Bulgarian Ministry of Education and Science), Technical University of Sofia, Bulgaria

Pendarakis, D. (2001). ALMI: an application level multicast infrastructure. In *Proceedings of the 3rd Symposium on USITS*.

Poggi, A. Tomaiuolo, M., & Turci, P. (2007). An Agent-Based Service Oriented Architecture. In *Proceedings of WOA 2007*, (pp. 157-165). Genoa, Italy.

Poggi, A. Tomaiuolo, M., & Vitaglione, G. (2005). A Security Infrastructure for Trust Management in Multi-agent Systems. In. R. Falcone, S. Barber, & M. P. Singh (eds.), Trusting Agents for Trusting Electronic Societies, Theory and Applications in HCI and E-Commerce. Lecture Notes in Computer Science, (Vol. 3577, pp. 162-179). Berlin, Germany: Springer.

Poikselka, M., Mayer, G., Khartabil, H., & Niemi, A. (2006). *The IMS Multimedia Concepts and Services* (2nd ed.). Nokia, Finland: Wiley.

Ponnekanti, S. R., & Fox, A. (2002). SWORD: A developer toolkit for Web service composition. In *Proceedings of the 11th World Wide Web Conference*, Honolulu, HI.

Pountain, D., & Szyperski, C. (1994). Extensible software systems. *Byte Magazine*, 57-62.

Prangl, M., Hellwagner, H., & Szkalicki, T. (2006). Fast adaptation decision taking for cross-modal multimedia content adaptation. In *Proceedings of the International Conference on Multimedia Expo* (pp. 137-140). New York: IEEE Press.

Prangl, M., Szkalicki, T., & Hellwagner, H. (2007). A framework for utility-based multimedia adaptation. *IEEE Transactions on Circuits and Systems for Video Technology, 17*(6), 719–728. doi:10.1109/TCSVT.2007.896650

Profiti, G. (2008). *Integrazione di servizi Web in una piattaforma multi-agente*. (Unpublished Master's thesis). Italy: University of Bologna, Department of Computer Science.

Qiao, Y., & Bochmann, G. (2009). Applying a diffusive load balancing in a clustered P2P system. In *Proceedings of the 9th International Conference on New Technologies of Distributed Systems*, (NOTERE), Montreal, Canada, ISBN:978-2-9809407-1-2.

Quinlan, J. R. (1986). Induction of Decision Trees. *Machine Learning, 1*, 81–106. doi:10.1007/BF00116251

Quinlan, J. R. (1993). *C4.5: Programs for Machine Learning*. San Francisco: Morgan Kaufmann.

Ragab, K. (2004). *Autonomous Decentralized Community Communication Technology for Assuring Information Dissemination*, (Ph.D. Thesis). Tokyo Institute of Technology.

Ragab, K. (2004). Autonomous Decentralized Community Communication for Information Dissemination. *IEEE Internet Computing Magazine, 8*(3), 29–36. doi:10.1109/MIC.2004.1297271

Ragab, K., & Mori, K. (2004). ACIS-Hierarchy: Enhancing Community Communication Delay for Large-Scale Information Systems. *IEICE Trans. on Communication, E87-B*, N(7)

Rajesh, P., Ranjiith, S., Soumya, P. R., Karthik, V., & Datthathreya, S. (2006). Network management system using Web Services and service oriented architecture – A Case Study. In *10th IEEE/IFIP Network Operations and Management Symposium* (pp. 1-4). New York: IEEE Press.

Raman, B., & Katz, R. H. (2003, March 30-April 3). Load balancing and stability issues in algorithms for service composition. *INFOCOM 2003. Twenty-Second Annual Joint Conference of the IEEE Computer and Communications Societies. IEEE, 2*(2), 1477-1487.

Ran, S. (2003). A model for Web Services discovery with QoS. *ACM SIGcom Exchanges, 4*(1), 1–10. doi:10.1145/844357.844360

Rao, A., Lakshminarayanan, K., Surana, S., Karp, R., & Stoica, I. (2003). Load Balancing in Structured P2P Systems. In *Proceeding of 2nd International Workshop on Peer-to-Peer Systems (IPTPS '03).*

Rao, J., & Su, X. (2004). A Survey of Automated Web Service Composition Methods. In *Proceedings of the First International Workshop on Semantic Web Services and Web Process Composition, SWSWPC* 2004. California, USA.

Ratnasamy, S., et al. (2001). A Scalable Content- Addressable Network. In *Proceedings of SIGCOMM'01.* California, USA.

Ratnasamy, S., Francis, P., Handley, M., Karp, R., & Shenker, S. (2001). A scalable content-addressable network. In *Proceedings of the 2001 Conference on Applications, Technologies, Architectures, and Protocols For Computer Communications.* (SIGCOMM '01), (pp. 161-172). New York: ACM.

Reich, C., Bubendorfer, K., & Buyya, R. (2008, May 19-22). An Autonomic Peer-to-Peer Architecture for Hosting Stateful Web Services. In *Proceedings of the 2008 Eighth IEEE international Symposium on Cluster Computing and the Grid* (CCGRID), (pp. 250-257). Washington, DC: IEEE Computer Society.

Richardson, L., & Ruby, S. (2007). RESTful Web Services. Sebastopol, CA: O'Reilly Media, Inc.

Riva, O., & Kangasharju, J. (2008). *Challenges and Lessons in Developing Middleware on Smart Phones.* Los Alamitos, CA: IEEE Computer Society Press.

Roesch, M. (1999). Snort: lightweight intrusion detection for networks. In Proceedings of LISA 99 (USENIX), (pp. 229-238).

Rosenberg, J., Schulzrinne, H., & Mahy, R. (2005, May). *RFC 4235 An INVITE-Initiated Dialog Event Package for the Session Initiation Protocol* (SIP). Freemont, CA: IETF.

Roure, D. D., & Hendler, J. A. (2004). E-science: The grid and the semantic web. *IEEE Intelligent Systems, 19*(1), 65–71. doi:10.1109/MIS.2004.1265888

Rowe, A., Kalaitzopolous, D., Osmond, M., Ghanem, M., & Guo, Y. (2003). The Discovery Net System for High Throughput Bioinformatics. *Bioinformatics (Oxford, England), 19*, 225–231. doi:10.1093/bioinformatics/btg1031

Rowstron, A., & Druschel, P. (2001). Pastry: Scalable, distributed object location and routing for large-scale peer-to-peer systems. In *Proceedings of Middleware,* (LNCS 2218), (pp.329-350).

Salameh, W. A. (2004). Detection of Intrusion Using Neural Networks. *Studies in Informatics and Control, 13*(2).

Salber, D., Dey, A. K., & Abowd, G. D. (1999). Aiding the development of context-enabled applications. In *Proceedings of chi'99* (pp. 434–441). The Context Toolkit.

Sandhya, P., Ajith, A., Crina, G., & Johnson, T. (2007). Modeling intrusion detection system using hybrid intelligent system. *Elsevier Journal of Network and Computer Application, 30*, 114–132.

Santoni, D., & Katchabaw, M. (2007). Resource Matching in a Peer-to-Peer Computational Framework. In *Proceedings of the International Conference on Internet Computing,* (pp. 89-95). Las Vegas, NV.

Sarmenta, L. F. G. (1998). Bayanihan: Web-based volunteer computing using java. In *Proceedings of the second international conference on world-wide computing and its applications* (pp. 444–461).

Sarmenta, L. F. G., & Hirano, S. (1999). Bayanihan: building and studying web-based volunteer computing systems using java. *Future Generation Computer Systems, 15*(5- 6), 675-686.

Satoshi, H. (1997). Horb: Distributed execution of java programs. In *Proceedings of Wwca '97: The international conference on worldwide computing and its applications* (pp. 29–42). London, UK: Springer-Verlag.

Savarimuthu, B. T., Purvis, M., & Fleurke, M. (2004). Monitoring and controlling of a multi-agent based workflow system. In *Proceedings of the 2nd Workshop on Australasian information Security, Data Mining and Web intelligence, and Software Internationalisation*, (pp. 127-132). Dunedin, New Zealand.

Schilit, B., Adams, N., & Want, R. (1994). *Context-aware computing applications*. In *Proceedings of the IEEE workshop on mobile computing systems and applications*. Santa Cruz, CA.

Schmidt, C., & Parashar, M. (2004). A peer-to-peer approach to Web service discovery. *Journal of World Wide Web*, 7(2), 211–229. doi:10.1023/B:WWWJ.0000017210.55153.3d

Shafiq, M. O., Ali, A., Ahmad, H. F., & Suguri, H. (2005). AgentWeb Gateway - a middleware for dynamic integration of Multi Agent System and Web Services Framework. In *Proceedings of the IEEE International Workshops on Enabling Technologies: Infrastructure for Collaborative Enterprise*.

Shafiq, M. O., Ali, A., Ahmad, H. F., & Suguri, H. (2006). AgentWeb Gateway - a middleware for dynamic integration of Multi Agent System and Web Services Framework. In *Proceedings of WETICE 2005: the 14th IEEE International Workshops on Enabling Technologies*, (pp. 267-270). Linköping, Sweden.

Shah, K., Dave, N., Chavan, S., Mukherjee, S., Abraham, A., & Sanyal, S. (2004). Adaptive neuro-fuzzy intrusion detection system. In *Proceedings of the IEEE International Conference on Information Technology: Coding and Computing* (ITCC'04), (vol. 1. pp 70-74).

Shahidi, M., Attou, A., & Aghvami, H. (2008). Content adaptation: requirements and architecture. In *Proceedings of ERPAS: The 10ᵗʰ International Conference on Information Integration and Web-based Application and Services* (pp. 626-429). New York: ACM Press.

Shan, Y., & Kalyanaraman, S. (2003). *Hybrid Video "Downloading/Streaming Over Peer-to-Peer Networks.* In *Proceedings of the Int. Conf. on Multimedia and Expo* (ICME), (pp. 665–668). Baltimore, MD.

Siefkes, C. (2003). *TIE: Trainable Information Extractor.* Retrieved from http://www.inf.fu-berlin.de/inst/ag-db/software/tie/index.html

Singh, M. P., & Huhns, M. N. (1999). Multiagent systems for workflow. *Intelligent Systems in Accounting. Financial Management*, 8(29), 105–117.

Sjachyn, M., & Beus-Dukic, L. (2006). *Semantic Component Selection SemaCS*. Presented at the International Conference on Commercial-off-the-Shelf (COTS)-Based Software Systems, 83-89.

Somlo, G., & Howe, A. (2003). Using Web Helper Agent Profiles in Query Generation. In *ACM Proceedings of the Second International Joint Conference on Autonomous Agents and Multi-agent Systems*, (pp. 812-818).

Songqing, L. G., et al. (2004). PROP: a Scalable and Reliable P2P Assisted Proxy Streaming System. In *Proceedings of the Int. Conf. on Distributed Computing Systems* (ICDCS'04).

Soto, E. L. (2006). Agent Communication Using Web Services, a New FIPA Message Transport Service for JADE. In P. Petta J.P. Müller, M. Klusch, & M. Georgeff (Eds.). Multiagent System Technologies, Lecture Notes in Computer Science, (Vol. 4687, pp. 73-84). Berlin, Germany: Springer.

Springer.Mari, M., Poggi, A., Tomaiuolo, M., & Turci, P. (2008). *Enhancing Multi-Agent Systems with Peer-to-Peer and Service-Oriented Technologies*. (AT2AI-6 Working Notes). From Agent Theory to Agent Implementation Workshop.

Srirama, S. N. (2008). *Mobile Hosts in Enterprise Service Integration* (Ph. D. Dissertation). RWTH Aachen University, Germany. Retrieved on April 3, 2009, from http://darwin.bth.rwth-aachen.de/opus/volltexte/2008/2567/

Stankovic, J. A. (2008). *Wireless Sensor Networks*. IEEE Computer Magazine.

Stoica, I., Morris, R., Karger, D., Kaashoek, M. F., & Balakrishnan, H. (2001). Chord: A scalable peer-to-peer lookup service for internet applications. In *Proceedings of the 2001 Conference on Applications, Technologies, Architectures, and Protocols for Computer Communications*, (pp. 149-160), (SIGCOMM '01). New York: ACM.

Strang, T., & Linnho-Popien, C. (2004). A context modeling survey. In Proceedings of Ubicomp, The 1st international workshop on advanced context modelling, reasoning and management (p. 34-41).

Sugiyama, K., Hatano, K., Yoshikawa, M., & Uemura, S. (2004, March 4-6).Adaptive Web Search Based on User's Implicit Preference. In *Proceedings of the 15th Data Engineering Workshop* (DEWS2004).

Sun Microsystems. (2002). *Package version identification*. Retrieved from http://java.sun.com/j2se/1.5.0/docs/guide/versioning/index.html

Surana, S., Godfrey, B., Lakshminarayanan, K., Karp, R., & Stoica, I. (2006, March). Load balancing in dynamic structured peer-to-peer systems. *P2P Computing Systems. Performance Evaluation, 63*(3), 217–240. doi:10.1016/j.peva.2005.01.003

Surridge, M., Taylor, S., De Roure, D., & Zaluska, E. (2005). Experiences with GRIA – Industrial Applications on a Web Service Grid. In H. Stockinger, R. Buyya & R. Perrett (Eds.), *First International Conference on e-Science and Grid Computing*, (Vol. 1, Issue 1, pp98-105). Melbourne, Australia.

Takase, T., Makino, S., Kawanaka, S., Ueno, K., Ferris, C., & Ryman, A. (2008). *Definition languages for RESTful Web services: WADL vs. WSDL 2.0*. White paper. Tokyo Research Laboratory, IBM Research. Retrieved on April 3, 2009, from http://www.ibm.com/developerworks/library/specification/ws-wadlwsdl/index.html

Talia, D. (2002). The Open Grid Services Architecture: Where the Grid Meets the Web. *IEEE Internet Computing, 6*(6), 67–71. doi:10.1109/MIC.2002.1067739

Tao, F., Cox, S., Chen, L., Shadbolt, N., Xu, F., Puleston, C., et al. (2003). Towards the Semantic Grid: Enriching Content for Management and Reuse. In *Proceedings of Delivering e-Science, UK e-Science All-hand Conference.*

Tatsubori, M., Sasaki, T., Chiba, S., & Itano, K. (2001). A bytecode translator for distributed execution of "legacy" java software. In *Proceedings of Ecoop '01: the 15th european conference on object-oriented programming* (pp. 236–255). London: Springer-Verlag.

Taylor, I., Shields, M., Wang, I., & Harrison, A. (2005). VisualGrid Workflow in Triana. *Journal of Grid Computing, 3*(3-4), 153–169. doi:10.1007/s10723-005-9007-3

The Globus Alliance. (2006). *The Globus Toolkit*. Retrieved from http://www.globus.org/

Tijerino, Y. A., Helmy, T., & Bradshaw, J. M. (2008, December). FAQIH: Framework for Agent-based Query-enabled Integrated Information for Health and Nutrition. In *ACM/IEEE proceedings of the Joint International Conference on Web Intelligence/Intelligent Agent Technology*, (pp. 550-553).

Toni, F., Grammatikou, M., Kafetzoglou, S., Lymberopoulos, L. S., Papavassileiou, S., Gaertner, D., et al. (2008). The ARGUGRID Platform: An Overview. In *Proceedings of the 5th International Workshop on Grid Economics and Business Models. Lecture Notes in Computer Science*, (Vol. 5206, pp. 217-225).

Trajkova, J., & Gauch, S. (2004, April 26-28). Improving Ontology-Based User Profiles. In *Proceedings of RIAO 2004*. University of Avignon, France, (pp. 380-389).

Trappey, C. V., Trappey, A. J. C., Huang, C., & Kud, C. C. (2009). The design of a JADE-based autonomous workflow management system for collaborative SoC design. *Expert Systems with Applications, 36*(2), 2659–2669. doi:10.1016/j.eswa.2008.01.064

Tsai, W. T., Paul, R., Cao, Z., Yu, L., & Saimi, A. (2003). Verification of Web Services using an enhanced UDDI server. In *Object Oriented Real-Time Dependable System* (pp. 131–138). New York: IEEE Press.

Tutte, W. T. (1956). A Theorem on Planner graphs. *Transactions of the American Mathematical Society, 82*, 99–116. doi:10.2307/1992980

UMBC eBiquity. (2008). *eBiquity Publication Ontology.* Retrieved from http://ebiquity.umbc.edu/v2.1/ontology/publication.owl

Urovi, V., Bromuri, S., McGinnis, J., Stathis, K., & Omicini, A. (2008). Automating Workflows Using Dialectical Argumentation. *IADIS International Journal on Computer Science and Information System, 3*(2), 110–125.

Vaibhav, G., Csilla, F., & Marco, V. (2005). PAID: A Probabilistic Agent-Based Intrusion Detection System. *Elsevier Journal of Computers & Security, 24,* 529–545.

Vannucci, D., & Hanrahan, H. (2007). *Extended Call Control Telecom Web Service.* Retrieved February 2, 2009, from http://www.ee.wits.ac.za/comms/Telecomms%20output/output/2007/Paper%20114%20-%20Vannucci.pdf

Vassiliadis, B., Giotopoulos, K., Votis, K., Sioutas, S., Bogonikolos, N., & Likothanassis, S. (2004). Application Service Provision through the Grid: Business models and Architectures. In *Proceedings of ITCC '04: The International Conference on Information Technology: Coding and Computing* (ITCC'04) (Vol. 2).

Verma, K., Sivashanmugam, K., Sheth, A., Patil, A., Oundhakar, S., & Miller, J. (2005, January). METEOR-S WSDI: A Scalable P2P Infrastructure of Registries for Semantic Publication and Discovery of Web Services. *Information Technology and Management, 6*(1), 17–39. doi:10.1007/s10799-004-7773-4

Vidal, I., Garcıa, J., Valera, F., Soto, I., & Azcorra, A. (2006). *Adaptive Quality of Service Management for Next Generation Residential Gateways.* Retrieved February 10, 2009, from http://www.it.uc3m.es/ividal/articulos/MMNS2006_JaimeGarcia_20517.pdf

Vidal, J. M., Buhler, P., & Stahl, C. (2004). Multiagent Systems with Workflows. *IEEE Internet Computing, 8*(1), 76–82. doi:10.1109/MIC.2004.1260707

Virgilio De, R., Torlane, R., & Houben, G.-J. (2007). Rule-based adaptation of Web information systems. *Journal of World Wide Web, 10,* 443–470. doi:10.1007/s11280-007-0020-2

W3C. (n.d.). *Composite Capabilities/Preferance Profile (CC/PP).*

W3C. (n.d.). *OWL - Web Ontology Language.*

Wang, Y. T., & Morris, R. J. T. (1985, March). Load Sharing in Distributed Systems. *IEEE Transactions on Computers, C-34*(3), 204–217. doi:10.1109/TC.1985.1676564

Werner, C., Buschman, C., & Fischer, S. (2008). *Efficient Encodings for Web Service Messages.* Hershey, PA: IGI Global.

Wikman, J., & Dosa, F. (2006). *Providing HTTP Access to Web Servers Running on Mobile Phones* (Technical Report). Helsinki, Finland: Nokia Research Center. Retrieved on April 3, 2009, from http://research.nokia.com/files/NRC-TR-2006-005.pdf

Wikman, J., Dosa, F., & Tarkiainen, M. (2006). *Personal Website on a Mobile Phone.* (Technical Report). Helsinki, Finland: Nokia Research Center. Retrieved on April 3, 2009, from http://research.nokia.com/tr/NRC-TR-2006-004.pdf

Willmott, S., Padget, J., Poggi, A., Díaz de León, J. L., Casasola, E., Latorre, H., & de Los Angeles Junco Rey, M. (2006). The case for open source in information and network technology education: experiences from the EuropeAid@lis technology net project. *International Journal of Continuing Engineering Education and Lifelong Learning, 17*(1), 67–83. doi:10.1504/IJCEELL.2007.013231

Willmott, S., Pujol, J. P., & Cortés, U. (2004). On Exploiting Agent Technology in the Design of Peer-to-Peer Applications. In *Proceedings from the 3rd International Workshop on Agents and Peer-to-Peer Computing,* (pp. 98-107). New York.

Wintertree Thesaurus. (n.d.). *The Wintertree Thesaurus Engine class library.* Retrieved from http://www.wintertree-software.com/

Wong, S. C., Tan, V., Fang, W., Miles, S., & Moreau, L. (2005). Grimoires: grid registry with metadata oriented interface: robustness, efficiency, security. In Cluster Computing and Grid (CCGrid), Cardiff, UK.

WS-BPEL. (2007). Web Services Business Process Execution Language Version 2.0, OASIS. Retrieved March 15, 2009, from http://docs.oasis-open.org/wsbpel/2.0/wsbpel-v2.0.pdf

WSMO Working Group. (2004). *Web Service Modeling Ontology (WSMO)*, Working Draft D2v1.2. Retrieved from: http://www.wsmo.org/TR/d2/v1.2/D2v1-2_20050414.pdf

Xiang, C., & Lim, S. M. (2005). Design of Multi-Level Hybrid Classifier for Intrusion Detection System. In IEEE proceedings of Machine Learning for Signal Processing Workshop (pp. 117-122).

XPDL. (2008). *XPDL support and resources Web site*. Retrieved June 28, 2009, from http://www.wfmc.org/xpdl.html

Yalagandula, P., Sharma, P., Banerjee, S., Basu, S., & Lee, S.-J. (2006). *S3: A scalable sensing service for monitoring large networked systems*. In Proceedings of INM '06: The 2006 sigcomm workshop on internet network management (p. 71-76). Boca Raton, FL: ACM Press.

Yan, J., Yang, Y., Kowalczyk, R., & Nguyen, X. T. (2005). A Service Workflow Management Framework Based on Peer-to-Peer and Agent Technologies. In *Proceedings of the 5th international Conference on Quality Software*, (pp. 373-382). Melbourne, Australia.

Yang, S. J., Zhang, J., Huang, A. F., Tsai, J. J., & Yu, P. S. (2008). A context-driven content adaptation planer for improving mobile Internet accessibility. In *IEEE International Conference on Web Services* (pp. 88-95). New York: IEEE Press.

Yang, S., & Shao, N. (2007). Enhancing pervasive Web accessibility with rule-based adaptation strategy. *Journal of Expert Systems with Applications, 32*, 1154–1167. doi:10.1016/j.eswa.2006.02.008

Youtube. (n.d.). *Youtube*. Retrieved from http://www.youtube.com/

Zegura, E. W., Calvert, K. L., & Bhattacharjee, S. (1996). How to model an internetwork. In Proceedings of IEEE infocom (Vol. 2, p. 594-602). San Francisco.

Zeng, L., Benatallah, B., & Ngu, H. H., A., Dumas, M., Kalagnanam, J., & Chang, H. (2004, May). QoS-Aware Middleware for Web Services Composition. *IEEE Transactions on Software Engineering, 30*(5), 311–327. doi:10.1109/TSE.2004.11

Zhang, B., & Hussein, T. M. (2003). Forwarding state scalability for multicast provisioning in IP networks. In IEEE Communications Magazine, 46–51.

Zhang, D. (2007). Web content adaptation for mobile handheld devices. *Communications of the ACM, 50*(2), 75–79. doi:10.1145/1216016.1216024

Zhang, L.-J., Chao, T., Chang, H., & Chung, J.-Y. (2003). XML-based advanced UDDI search mechanism for B2B integration. *Electronic Commerce Research, 3*(1), 25–42. doi:10.1023/A:1021573226353

Zhang, S., Zong, Y., Ding, Z., & Liu, J. (2005). Workflow-oriented grid service composition and scheduling. In *Proceedings of Itcc '05: the international conference on information technology: Coding and computing (ITCC'05)*, (Volume II, pp. 214–219). Washington, DC: IEEE Computer Society.

Zhang, X., Liu, J., Li, B., & Yum, T.-S. P. (2005). DONet/CoolStreaming: A data-driven overlay network for live media streaming. In *Proceedings of INFOCOM'05*. Miami, FL.

Zhao, Z., Belloum, A., De Laat, C., Adriaans, P., & Hertzberger, B. (2007). Using Jade agent framework to prototype an e-Science workflow bus. In *Proceedings of the 7th IEEE international Symposium on Cluster Computing and the Grid*, (pp. 655-660). Rio de Janeiro, Brazil.

Zhi-Song, P., Song-can, C., Gen-bao, H., & Dao-qiang, Z. (2003). Hybrid Neural Network and C4.5 for Misuse Detection. In *IEEE Proceedings of the second international Conference on Machine Learning and Cybernetics* (pp. 2463-2467).

Zhou, S. (1988, September). A Trace-Driven Simulation Study of Dynamic Load Balancing. *IEEE Transactions on Software Engineering, 14*(9), 1327–1341. doi:10.1109/32.6176

Zhu, F., Mutka, M., & Ni, L. (2005). Service discovery in pervasive environments. *IEEE Pervasive*, *4*(4), 81–90. doi:10.1109/MPRV.2005.87

Zhu, H., Yang, T., Zheng, Q., Watson, D., Ibarra, O. H., & Smith, T. (1998, July 28-31). Adaptive Load Sharing for Clustered Digital Library Servers. In *Proceedings of the 7th IEEE international Symposium on High Performance Distributed Computing*.

Zhu, Y., & Hu, Y. (2005, April). Efficient, proximity-aware load balancing for DHT-based P2P systems. *IEEE Transactions on Parallel and Distributed Systems*, *16*(4), 349–361. doi:10.1109/TPDS.2005.46

Zhuang, S. Q., et al. (2001). Bayeux: An architecture for scalable and fault-tolerant wide-area data dissemination. In *Proceedings of NOSSDAV '01*. New York.

Zhuowei, L., Amitabha, D., & Jianying, Z. (2005). Unifying Signature-Based and Anomaly-Based Intrusion Detection. In *Proceedings of Springer PAKDD LNAI # 3518* (pp. 702–712). USAID.

Zimmermann, R., Winkler, S., & Bodendorf, F. (2006). Supply Chain Event Management with Software Agents. In Kirn, S., Herzog, O., Lockemann, P., & Spaniol, O. (Eds.), *Multiagent Engineering - Theory and Applications in Enterprises* (pp. 157–175). Berlin, Germany: Springer.

Zukowski, J. (2002). *Deploying Software with JNLP and Java Web Start*. Retrieved from http://java.sun.com/developer/technicalArticles/Programming/jnlp/

About the Contributors

K. Ragab is an assistant professor at Department of Computer Science, College of Computer and Information Technology, King Faisal University, Saudi Arabia. Moreover, he is on leave assistant professor of Computer Science at Department of Mathematic, Computer Science division, Ain Shams University. He joined Department of Computer Science, Tokyo University in 2005 as postdoctoral position. He was born in 1968 and received his B.Sc., M.Sc. degrees in Computer Science from Ain Shams University, Cairo, Egypt in 1990, 1999, respectively and Ph.D. degree in Computer Science from Tokyo Institute of Technology in 2004. He has worked in Ain Shams University, Cairo Egypt in 1990-1999 as assistant lecturer. He has worked as research scientist in Computer Science Dept., Technical University of Chemnitz, Germany in 1999-2001. His research interests include autonomous decentralized systems, Peer-to-Peer Systems, video streaming systems, Overlay Networks, Web-services and application-level multicast.

Tarek Helmy is currently with the department of Information and Computer Science, College of Computer Science and Engineering at King Fahd University of Petroleum and Minerals (KFUPM). On leave from the College of Engineering, Department of Computers Engineering and Automatic Control, Tanta University, Egypt. He received his Ph.D. in Intelligent Systems from Kyushu University, Japan, in 2002. His research interests include Operating Systems, Multi-Agent Systems, Personalized Web Services, and Cooperative Intelligent Systems. He has published more than 40 papers in major international journals and conferences in the fields of cooperative intelligent agents, artificial intelligence and operating systems. Dr. Helmy is on the program/organizing committee of various international journals/ conferences in the fields of artificial intelligence, multi-agents, intelligent and distributed systems.

Aboul Ella Hassanien received his B.Sc. with honors in 1986 and M.Sc degree in 1993, both from Ain Shams University, Faculty of Science, Pure Mathematics and Computer Science Department, Cairo, Egypt. On September 1998, he received his doctoral degree from the Department of Computer Science, Graduate School of Science & Engineering, Tokyo Institute of Technology, Japan. Currently, he is an associated Professor at Cairo University, Faculty of Computer and Information, IT Department, Egypt.

* * *

Davide Guidi is Research Associate at the Department of Computing, Imperial College London. He received a Laurea degee in Computer Science from the University of Bologna in 2003 and a Ph.D. in Computer Science from the same university in 2007. After completing his Ph.D. he was Research

Fellow in the Knowledge Media Institute, The Open University, UK. He published a number of research papers in the areas of Distributed Systems, Knowledge Bases and their applications.

Mauro Gaspari is Associate Professor at the Department of Computer Science of the University of Bologna, Italy. He received a Laurea degree in Computer Science from the University of Pisa in 1986. Successively, he was at the Department of Computer Science of the University of Pisa (Italy), at Delphi SpA (Viareggio Italy), and at the Human Cognition Research Laboratory of The Open University (UK).

He has carried out research in Artificial Intelligence and Programming Languages for more than twenty years and has published in a number of areas including: declarative programming languages, agent communication languages, concurrent and distributed programming, environment for artificial intelligence, and applications of artificial intelligence. He is a member of ACM and AAAI.

Giuseppe Profiti was born in Tropea, Italy in 1980. He enrolled at University of Bologna where his main topics of study were distributed systems, software agents and complex adaptive systems. He graduated in Computer Science in 2008 with a thesis titled "Integrazione di servizi Web in una piattaforma multi-agente" ("Web services integration in a multi-agent framework").

Agostino Poggi is full professor of Computer Engineering at the Faculty of Engineering of the University of Parma. He coordinates the Agent and Object Technology Lab and his research focuses on agent and object-oriented technologies and their use to develop distributed and complex systems. He is author of more than a hundred of technical papers in refereed journals and conferences and his scientific contribution has been recognized through the "System Research Foundation Outstanding Scholarly Contribution Award" and the "System Innovation Award". Moreover, he is in the editorial board of the following scientific journals: Software Practice & Experience, International Journal of Hybrid Intelligent Systems, International Journal of Agent-Oriented Software Engineering, International Journal of Multiagent and Grid Systems e International Journal of Software Architecture.

Michele Tomaiuolo is a researcher at the University of Parma, Department of Information Engineering, since the 1st of November, 2008. He obtained a master degree in Information Engineering, on the 24th of April, 2001 at the University of Parma, defending a thesis on the "Definition and realization of tools to manage the security in multi-agent systems", about the introduction of multiuser capabilities, authentication and encryption in JADE, an agent framework developed in Java by the University of Parma in conjunction with Telecom Italia Lab. He obtained a PhD in "Information technologies", at the University of Parma, Department of Information Engineering, on the 31st of March, 2006, defending a thesis on "Models and Tools to Manage Security in Multiagent Systems". His current research activity is focused in particular on security and trust management, but it also deals with multi-agent systems, semantic web, rule-based systems, peer-to-peer networks.

Nabeel Azam is a Solutions Architect at InforSense Ltd. and has contributed to a large number of research projects in the company, including ARGUGRID, SIMDAT, BRIDGE, EVINCI and TOPCOMBI. He is currently enrolled for a PhD degree at the University of Bradford focusing on Grid-based workflow systems and has a BSc in Computing and Information Systems from the same institution.

Vasa Curcin is a Research Associate at Department of Computing, Imperial College London, working as the healthcare theme coordinator at the Social Computing Group, and also closely associated with the Department of Primary Care and Social Medicine. He received his BSc from King's College London, and MSc and PhD from Imperial College London. His main research is in the areas of scientific workflows, having been one of the authors of Discovery Net software, and in particular the application of process algebras and other formal models to analysis of workflows. Another research focus is on the use of workflows as a methodology for in-silico studies on repositories of electronic health records.

Li Guo is a Research Associate at the Social Computing Group, Imperial College, where he is working on peer-to-peer/multi-agent based Grid economic topics. He holds PhD. in Artificial Intelligence from the University of Edinburgh. He has a number of publications in international journals and his research investigates the multi-agent/peer-to-peer based system for large, decentralised and collaboration based applications.

Moustafa Ghanem is a Research Fellow at the Department of Computing, Imperial College London and Director of Research of its spinout company InforSense Ltd. He is also is founder and co-Director of the Centre for Informatics Science at Nile University in Cairo, Egypt. He was the technical project manager of the award winning Discovery Net project at Imperial College and the principal investigator of the ARGUGRID project at InforSense Ltd. His research interests are in large-scale informatics applications and data and text mining technologies. He holds a BSc. in Electronics and Telecommunications Engineering from Cairo University and an Msc and PhD in High Performance Computing from Imperial College London.

Antje Barth received her diploma degree in Computer Science from the "Eberhard-Karls-Universität Tübingen" (Germany) in 2007. In July 2007,she started her professional career at Cisco Systems as Associate Systems Engineer, running through Cisco's 1-year international graduate program in Amsterdam, Netherlands. Since August 2008 she has been working as Internetworking Consultant for Cisco Germany, focusing on Network Management and Datacenter Virtualization technologies.

Michael Kleis received a degree in Mathematics from the University of Saarbrücken, Germany in 1999. He joined Fraunhofer FOKUS in August 2001 and worked in the fields of signaling protocols for multimedia streaming, QoS support for multimedia traffic and error correction techniques. In 2009 he received a Dr. rer. nat. degree in Computer Science from Technical University Munich. His current research activities are in the fields of peer-to-peer and overlay networks with an emphasis on autonomic networking principles and service composition.

Andreas Klenk received his diploma degree in computer science from the Ulm University, Germany, in 2003. He is a research assistant at the University of Tübingen in the area of computer networks and Internet technology. As a Ph.D. candidate he is supervised by Professor Georg Carle from Technische Universität München. He contributes to European research projects in the telecommunication field. His research interests include methods to achieve autonomic behavior through communication, agreement negotiation, and the integration of security into overlay signaling. He published 17 peer reviewed papers on his work in conferences and journals. He is active in the development of the open source project 'pam_xacml' for transparent support of XACML authorization and the 'NAT Tester' with one of the most comprehensive databases of NAT behavior and working NAT Traversal methods in the Internet.

Benoit Radier received the engineering degree from the "Institut Supérieur de l'Electronique et du Numérique" (ISEN), Brest in 2000. Since 2000 he joined France Telecom R&D. He was working on the field of nomadism management between high bandwidth access for fix access and IMS management. Since 2006 his research activities are in the fields of Autonomic Networking, Autonomic Mobility with context awareness and Autonomic Management.

Sanaa Elmoumouhi received her degree as Telecommunications ingenieur from TELECOM LILLE 1 of Villeneuve d'ascq (France) in 2004. She joined France Télécom R&D in October 2004 and worked in the fields of IMS core Network Integration and Services IMS Network Integration. Her current research activities are in the fields of IMS, Peer-to-Peer networks and Autonomic Networking.

Mikaël Salaün is an Engineer in Informatics and telecommunication, a professor assistant and a senior expert in France Telecom. He joined France Télécom R&D Lannion, France, in 1999. He was responsible for security projects against DoS and DDos attacks with active networks. Since 2002, his research activities are in the fields of Autonomic Networking. He is responsible for many projects such as Autonomic Information Networking, Home autonomic Networking and Autonomic IMS.

Georg Carle is professor at the department of computer science at Technische Universität München, holding the chair for Network Architectures and Services. He received an M.Sc. from Brunel University London in 1989, an electrical engineering diploma from Universität Stuttgart in 1992, and a doctoral degree in computer science from Universität Karlsruhe in 1996. In 1997 he worked at Institut EURECOM, Sophia Antipolis, France. From 1997 to 2002 he was with Fraunhofer FOKUS in Berlin. From 2003 to 2008 he was professor at Universität Tübingen, holding the chair for Computer Networks and Internet.

Jemal Abawajy is a faculty member at Deakin University and has published more than 100 articles in refereed journals and conferences as well as a number of technical reports. He is on the editorial board of several international journals and edited several international journals and conference proceedings. He has also been a member of the organizing committee for over 60 international conferences and workshops serving in various capacity including best paper award chair, general co-chair, publication chair, vice-chair and program committee. He is a frequent reviewer for international research Journals, Book series (e.g., Springer), Grants (e.g., Australian Research Council) and external examiner of PhD and Masters Degree (e.g., Leeds University, Monash University, RMIT University, etc.). He is actively involved in funded research in building secure, efficient and reliable infrastructures for large-scale distributed systems. Towards this vision, he is working in several areas including: Pervasive and Networked Systems (Mobile, Wireless Network, Sensor Networks, Grid, Cluster, and P2P), E-Science and E-Business Technologies and Applications, and Performance Analysis and Evaluation.

Mohd Farhan Md Fudzee is a faculty member at Tun Hussein Onn University of Malaysia (UTHM) and Software & Multimedia Centre, UTHM. He has completed diploma in computer science, bachelor science in IT (honours), and Master Science in IT. Currently, he is attached to Deakin University,

Australia, as a post graduate student/researcher. He has completed several research grants, won several medals in innovation competitions, and awarded a teaching and learning award. He has published a book in IT, several papers in reviewed conferences as well as technical reports and contributed to the academic activities as reviewer. He has also been a member of IEEE, ACM, NAUI Scuba Diver, IIWAS and Malaysian Educational Technology Association. My research interest includes Multimedia Computing (Content Adaptation, Performance Analysis) and E-Learning Applications.

Ahmed Al-Nazer graduated from King Fahd University of Petroleum and Minerals (KFUPM) in 2001 with a B.S. degree in computer science with a second honor. His senior project "e-trip portal" was awarded as one of the best university projects in the 2001 annual exhibition. Since 2001, he is working in the IT of the largest oil producer company in the world, Saudi Aramco. It gave him the exposure to real world information technology deployments. While working in the company, he had completed the M.S. degree in Computer Science in January 2006 with thesis title: "Collaborative Autonomous Interface Agent for Personalized Web Search". He is currently pursuing the PhD degree as a part time. His research areas are in personalization, Search Engines technologies, artificial intelligent and software engineering.

Fahad Aijaz received his Bachelors in Computer Science from Mohammad Ali Jinnah University, Karachi in 2002. Later in 2006, he earned his Masters degree in Multimedia and Communication Systems (Media Informatics) from RWTH Aachen University (RWTH). Since then he is serving the Department of Communication Networks (ComNets) of RWTH, where he is working towards his Ph.D. degree. He participated in an international European project "MYCAREVENT", and is also responsible for Mobile Web Services research projects within UMIC Excellence Research Cluster (http://www.umic-aachen. de). Some of his research interests include Mobile Web Services, mobile middleware and applications, ubiquitous computing, asynchrony and synchrony in mobile services, service- and resource-oriented architectures, service-level agreements and service-oriented Wireless Sensor Networks. More information about his work and activities is available at http://www.fahad-aijaz.com.

Gregor V. Bochmann is professor at the School of Information Technology and Engineering at the University of Ottawa since January 1998, after 25 years at the University of Montreal. He is a fellow of the IEEE and ACM and a member of the Royal Society of Canada. He has worked in the areas of programming languages, compiler design, communication protocols, and software engineering and published many papers in these areas. He was also actively involved in the standardization of formal description techniques for communication protocols and services in the 1980ies. He had many research projects in collaboration with industry and, from 1989 to 1997, held the Hewlett-Packard - NSERC - CITI Industrial Research Chair on communication protocols at the University of Montreal. His present work is in the areas of software engineering for distributed systems, peer-to-peer systems, quality of service and security management for Web applications, and control procedures for optical networks.

Shah Asaduzzaman is currently a postdoctoral research fellow at School of Information Technology and Engineering at University of Ottawa, Canada. He obtained his Ph.D. in Computer Science from McGill University, Canada in 2008. Earlier, he obtained his M.Sc. and B.Sc. in Computer Science and Engineering from Bangladesh University of Engineering and Technology, Dhaka, Bangladesh. Shah is active in the general research area of networks and distributed systems for several years and have authored several scientific articles. His research interests include cloud computing platforms, peer-to-peer systems, overlay networks, mobile ad-hoc networks, content sharing networks, privacy and trust, social networks.

Ying Qiao is a Ph.D. candidate at the Electrical and Computer Engineering Department at the University of Ottawa. She is working on her thesis about improving the reliability and performance of a P2P system. Her research interests include distributed computing systems, protocols and algorithms. She received her M.EEng from Carleton University at 2001, and B.Eng from Hefei University of Technology at 1992. She had worked as a software engineer in Information Department of Bank of China, Shanghai, China, from 1992 to 1997, and Nortel Networks, Ottawa, Canada, from 2000 to 2004. She did one year's internship at the Web Services Group at the Bell Labs, Alcatel-Lucent, Ottawa, Canada, in 2005.

Jesus De Oliveira is a research assistant at the Computer Science Department at Simon Bolivar University, Venezuela. He graduated in Computer Engineering in 2005 at Simon Bolivar University, obtaining honorable mention on his undergraduate thesis project. His research interests include grid computing, high performance scientific applications, distributed systems and software engineering. He is an active participant of the international grid computing project EELA-2 helping on the training, dissemination and integration activities of HPC centers between Europe and Latin America, teaching grid computing technologies to over 500 persons in 6 Latin American countries during the current year. His home page is http://www.ldc.usb.ve/~jdeoliveira.

Yudith Cardinale is a Full Professor in Computer Science Department at Universidad Simón Bolívar since 1996. She graduated with honors in Computer Engineering in 1990 at Universidad Centro-Occidental Lisandro Alvarado, Venezuela. She received her M.Sc degree and PhD in Computer Science from the Universidad Simon Bolvar, Venezuela, in 1993 and 2004. Her research interests include parallel processing, distributed object processing, operating systems, high performance on grid platforms, web services composition, including web and grid semantic. She is a member of the Parallel and Distributed Systems Group. She has written a range of publications in areas such as parallel computing, grid computing, parallel checkpointing, collaborative frameworks, and Semantic Web. Her home page is http://www.ldc.usb.ve/~yudith.

Eduardo Blanco is Assistant Professor in Computer Science Department at Universidad Simón Bolívar since 2003. He graduated in Computer Engineering in 1998 at Universidad Simón Bolívar, Venezuela. He received his M.Sc degree Computer Science from the Universidad Simon Bolvar, Venezuela, in 2002 and he is currently finishing his PhD studies at t he same University. His research interests include distributed object processing, operating systems, high performance on grid platforms, web services composition, web service discovery, including web and grid semantic. He is a member of the Parallel and Distributed Systems Group. He has written a range of publications in areas such as grid computing, sequential and parallel profiling for java applications, collaborative frameworks, and Semantic Web. Hisr home page is http://www.ldc.usb.ve/~eduardo.

Carlos Figueira is Professor, Computer Science Department, Universidad Simón Bolívar (USB), Caracas, Venezuela. Born June 8th, 1961. Received PhD in Computer Science, 2003, USB; MSc. in Computer Science, 1994, USB; D.E.A. in Telecommunications and Signal Processing, Université de

Rennes I, France, 1986; Electronic Engineer, USB, 1983. Carlos Figueira has done research on Grid and Metacomputing systems, Performance evaluation tools, and Parallel and Real Time systems. He has 9 publications on international indexed journals, and more than 30 presentations on international scientific conferences. He teaches Parallel Systems, Computer Networks, and Operating and Distributed Systems to undergraduate and graduate students of Computer Science and Engineering at USB since 1990; has been invited research and lecturer at University of Wisconsin-Madison and Universidad Pompeu Fabra (Barcelona, Spain). Carlos Figueira is President of Nacional Center of Information Technology since 2007. He was appointed Sub-secretary of the Ministry of Telecommunications and Informatics of Venezuela, April-May 2009.

Evelina Pencheva received her M.S. degree in mathematics at the University of Sofia, Bulgaria. She obtained her PhD degree in Telecommunications from Technical University of Sofia. Since 1996 she is Associate Professor at Faculty of Telecommunications, Technical University of Sofia. Her academic experience is in teaching courses on telecommunication networks and service technologies. Her interests include next generation mobile applications and middleware platforms. She is a member of Specialized Science Council in Radio Electronics and Communication Technologies, Bulgarian Higher Attestation

Ivaylo Atanasov received his M.S. degree in electronics at the Technical University of Sofia, Bulgaria. He obtained his PhD degree in Telecommunication networks. His current position is Associate Professor at Faculty of Telecommunications, Technical University of Sofia. His academic experience is in teaching courses on object-oriented programming, mobile networks and service creation technologies. His main research focus is in development of open service platforms for next generation networks.

Index